"In an enormously ambitious and significant research programme, Professor Barbier has been reworking economic history from the deep past to the present by including environmental assets in societal accounts. In this book he adds to that account of history by providing quantitative estimates of the place of those assets in a society's wealth. This is work of a very high order and insight."

– Sir Partha Dasgupta, Frank Ramsey Professor
Emeritus of Economics, University of Cambridge, UK

"Ed Barbier has masterfully brought together environmental degradation and wealth inequality into a coherent and practical development strategy. He spells out how pricing nature and targeting inefficient natural resource use can be combined with human capital investment to tackle poverty in developing countries. It is a blueprint for a sustainable future."

– Dieter Helm, author of *Natural Capital – Valuing the Planet*

"In *Nature and Wealth* Ed Barbier traces the origins of today's imbalance between our economies and our environment, graphically illustrating how the economic invisibility of nature has led to a pervasive and enduring misallocation of capital: one that privileges resource extraction for short-term gains, while leaving large segments of society without the skills or jobs they need to create income and sustain livelihoods. Lucidly written and anchored in empirical data, this book makes a timely and compelling contribution to the literature showing why a fundamental realignment of market institutions, policies and prices is needed to create and sustain wealth beyond the ephemeral pursuit of growth – and how this can be achieved."

– Steven Stone, Chief, Economy and Trade Branch,
United Nations Environment Programme

"Edward Barbier's wide-ranging and provocative book lays out the case for how low levels of human capital and the failure to account for the true costs of over-reliance on non-renewable natural resources reinforce each other, leading to unsustainable and non-inclusive patterns of economic growth. The book provides a welcome nudge to expanded collaboration on development and environmental policies."

– Mike Toman, World Bank

"This thoughtful, informative, and very important book explains why countries face a double imbalance – an environmental imbalance from over exploitation of environmental capital and a social imbalance from widening income inequality due to insufficient investments in human capital. The proposed Balanced Wealth Strategy lays the intellectual framework for why, and what needs to be done – the challenge going forward is how to put into practice the needed incentives across advanced, emerging, and developing countries alike."

– Ian Parry, Principal Environmental Fiscal Policy Expert,
International Monetary Fund

"Twenty-five years ago, Edward Barbier, along with a few other leading thinkers, launched the concept of green economy with his seminal work, *Blueprint for a Green Economy*. Once again, Professor Barbier breaks new ground by offering a cogent analysis of why our failure to accurately value, account for, and distribute the benefits of nature has and will continue to lead us down a path of environmental degradation and increasing wealth disparity. His concrete recommendations for what can be done to overcome this imbalance between nature and wealth are lucid, precise, and most importantly, with effort and courage, achievable."

– Benjamin Simmons, Head, Green Growth Knowledge Platform

"Barbier's new book, *Nature and Wealth*, presents an innovative and exciting approach to the twin challenges of our time: inequality and environmental scarcity. The premise is that income and human well-being are underpinned by wealth, defined in its broadest form to include not only the familiar manufactured capital, but also natural capital (all the natural resources and environmental services we depend on) and human capital (the skills and capacities of the work force). He identifies the cause of our current global problems in an imbalance of assets – we are underpricing natural capital, and as a result we are rapidly depleting and degrading it. At the same time we are underinvesting in human capital so that only a relatively small number of people obtain the high-level skills needed to generate high incomes, resulting in growing inequality. The book provides a sweeping historical review of human development over millennia but the innovation is to view this through the lens of wealth and the accumulation of wealth. This provides a fresh perspective on inequality and the role of natural capital in human history. This focus on natural capital makes the book a useful companion to the recent, widely acclaimed work by Thomas Piketty, *Capital in the 21st Century*. Furthermore he doesn't just leave us with an incisive analysis of our current problems but also, in the Balanced Wealth Strategy, he also suggests a way out to restore the right mix of different kinds of wealth needed for a more equitable and sustainable world. The book is written in a passionate manner, without sacrificing economic rigor, that will be enjoyed a wide audience. It is a very useful and engaging exposition for anyone interested in the critical challenges the world faces today."

– Glenn-Marie Lange, Global Partnership for Wealth Accounting and Valuation of Ecosystem Services (WAVES), The World Bank

Nature and Wealth

Overcoming Environmental Scarcity and Inequality

Edward B. Barbier
University of Wyoming, USA

First published 2015 by
PALGRAVE MACMILLAN

Palgrave Macmillan in the UK is an imprint of Macmillan Publishers Limited, registered in England, company number 785998, of Houndmills, Basingstoke, Hampshire RG21 6XS.

Palgrave Macmillan in the US is a division of St Martin's Press LLC, 175 Fifth Avenue, New York, NY 10010.

Palgrave Macmillan is the global academic imprint of the above companies and has companies and representatives throughout the world.

Palgrave® and Macmillan® are registered trademarks in the United States, the United Kingdom, Europe and other countries.

ISBN: 978–1–137–40337–7 hardback
ISBN: 978–1–137–40338–4 paperback

This book is printed on paper suitable for recycling and made from fully managed and sustained forest sources. Logging, pulping and manufacturing processes are expected to conform to the environmental regulations of the country of origin.

A catalogue record for this book is available from the British Library.

Library of Congress Cataloging-in-Publication Data

Barbier, Edward, 1957–
    Nature and wealth : overcoming environmental scarcity and inequality / Edward B. Barbier.
        pages cm
    ISBN 978–1–137–40337–7 (hardback) – ISBN 978–1–137–40338–4 (paperback)
        1. Economic development – Environmental aspects. 2. Environmental economics. 3. Natural resources. 4. Nonrenewable natural resources. 5. Wealth. I. Title.
HC79.E5.B3583 2015
333.7—dc23   2015017600

To Jo, Lara, Becky, James and Charlotte "Live Well, Laugh Much, Love Often"

Contents

List of Figures   viii

List of Tables   x

Preface   xi

Acknowledgments   xiii

Introduction   1

1   The Origins of Economic Wealth   9

2   Natural Capital and Economic Development   31

3   Wealth, Structure and Functioning of Modern Economies   59

4   The Age of Ecological Scarcity   81

5   Structural Imbalance   101

6   The Underpricing of Nature   123

7   Wealth Inequality   142

8   Redressing the Structural Imbalance   165

9   Making the Transition   184

Conclusion   208

Notes   212

Index   263

List of Figures

0.1	Structural imbalance and wealth	6
1.1	National wealth and economic wealth	10
1.2	Economic wealth and human well-being	12
1.3	The emerging world economy, ca. 1200–1300 AD	20
1.4	The world up to 1750	23
1.5	The Atlantic economy triangular trade, 1500–1860 AD	26
2.1	Global energy consumption, 1800–2013	33
2.2	Key timelines of the Industrial Revolution, 1750–1970	34
2.3	Long-run material use in the US economy, 1900–2000	43
2.4	Long-run global land use change, 1700–1990	45
2.5	Long-run global land use change, 1961–2010	47
2.6	Agricultural land share (%) of national wealth for nine major economies, 1680–1980	48
2.7	Contributions (%) to economic wealth by income group, 1990–2010 average	49
2.8	The rate of natural capital depreciation, 1970–2012	51
2.9	Financial asset share (%) of national wealth for six major economies, 1680–1980	53
2.10	Financial asset share (%) of national income for seven major economies, 1960–2010	54
2.11	Adjusting gross national income (GNI) for reproducible and natural capital depreciation	58
3.1	Resource dependency in exports, 1960–2012	61
3.2	Resource dependency and GDP per capita in developing countries, 2000–2012	62
3.3	Resource dependency and adjusted NNI per capita in developing countries, 2000–2012	64
3.4	Resource dependency and adjusted net savings in developing countries, 2000–2012	65
3.5	Resource dependency and poverty in developing countries, 2000–2012	66
3.6	Carbon dioxide emissions by region, 1850–2011	69
3.7	Greenhouse gas emissions per capita and adjusted net savings in major economies, 1990–2011	75

3.8	Adjusting gross national saving (GNS) for changes in reproducible, natural and human capital	80
4.1	National wealth and economic wealth	83
4.2	Ecological scarcity and the economy–environment trade-off	85
4.3	How ecosystems generate economic benefits	87
4.4	Accounting for mangrove capital, Thailand, 1970–2009	96
4.5	Adjusting gross national income (GNI) for reproducible, natural and ecological capital depreciation	100
5.1	The rate of human capital investment, 1970–2012	104
5.2	Human capital investment per person, 1970–2012	105
5.3	Educational attainment, 1950–2010	106
5.4	The structural effects of increasing the price of human to natural capital	112
5.5	An increase in the supply of natural capital	115
5.6	An increase in the supply of human capital	117
5.7	Adjusting national income (NI) for reproducible, human, natural and ecological capital	122
6.1	The vicious cycle of excessive environmental degradation	124
6.2	The underpricing of mangroves and their conversion to shrimp farms, Thailand	131
6.3	The costs of overcoming the institutional inertia to environmental policy change	135
6.4	The political cost of overcoming vested interests	138
7.1	The supply and demand for human capital	145
7.2	The vicious cycle of insufficient human capital accumulation	148
7.3	The global wealth pyramid, 2014	152
7.4	Wealth inequality and increasing financial risks	160
8.1	Key timelines of the second phase of the Industrial Revolution, 1870–2015	167
8.2	Structural imbalance and wealth	169
9.1	Policy strategy for green innovation and structural transformation	186
9.2	Policy strategy for reducing financial risk and increasing human capital accumulation	196

List of Tables

1.1 Ocean empires and natural resource trade, 17th and 18th centuries   25
2.1 Land use trends for selected regions, 1700–1910   38
3.1 Key development indicators by region, 2000–2012   67
3.2 Global greenhouse gas emissions, 1990–2011   71
3.3 Global greenhouse gas intensity, 1990–2011   73
3.4 Global greenhouse gas per capita, 1990–2011   74
4.1 Examples of ecosystem functions and structure producing ecosystem services of salt marsh and mangroves   90
4.2 Global status of key ecosystem goods and services   92
4.3 Main threats to and impacts on freshwater ecosystems   94
6.1 Underpricing of fossil fuels, Group of 20 economies   128
6.2 Institutional inertia barriers to establishing water markets and trading   136
7.1 Trends in wealth inequality across countries, 2000–2014   153
7.2 Increase in wealth of the world's rich, 1987–2013   154
8.1 Green stimulus during the Great Recession, 2008–2009   173
8.2 Environmentally motivated subsidies in selected economies   179
9.1 Induced innovation and public policies for reducing carbon dependency   190
9.2 Potential revenues from a financial activity tax, selected countries   194
9.3 Summary of key structural features of developing economies   197
9.4 Financing mechanisms for funding global ecosystem conservation   205
9.5 Transboundary water availability   206

Preface

When I was eleven, my mother took me on a train journey from Jakarta, the capital of Indonesia, to Surabaya. It was a long train ride from one end of the island of Java to another, and there was much for me to see – cities, villages, paddy fields, mountains, and above all, people. The year was 1968, and Indonesia had emerged from a period of civil unrest, factional violence, political turmoil, and economic stagnation. Poverty was rife, especially in the countryside.

The poorest people lived right next to the train tracks, with barely any land to cultivate, in dirty and often polluted sites, with little or no sanitation, and inhabiting shacks made out of whatever materials were to hand. Often, there were children standing nearby, watching our train as it sped by. I pointed out one small boy to my mother, and asked her why his arms and legs seemed so skinny, yet his belly was protruding and his head unusually large. She explained that the boy was suffering from severe malnutrition, and although he appeared to be the size of a five- or six-year-old, he was probably my age if not older.

For the rest of that train journey, I thought a lot about that boy, and about poverty, malnutrition and opportunities in life. I also wondered why some children, like me, were fortunate to come from relatively wealthy countries and households, whereas many others, such as the boy I had seen, lived in extreme poverty. Destitution, it seemed, went hand-in-hand with marginal land, unhealthy environments and lack of public services and amenities.

Nearly 50 years later, and I still reflect on the relationship between nature and wealth, or more specifically, how we use nature to create wealth and how that wealth is distributed among people. I believe these two lines of enquiry to be inexorably linked. This is especially true in the world today, which is facing two major threats: increasing environmental degradation and a growing gap between rich and poor.

Too often, environmental degradation and wealth inequality are treated as separate problems with distinctly different causes. The purpose of this book is to suggest otherwise. Drawing on historical and contemporary evidence, I argue that these two threats are symptomatic of a growing structural imbalance in all economies. This imbalance has arisen because of the way we currently mismanage and accumulate wealth, and specifically, how nature is used to create wealth and who benefits from this wealth.

Rather than face the rising economic and social costs of increasing natural resource use and ecological scarcity, modern economies have chosen to hide these costs by underpricing nature. And, rather than investing sufficiently in educating and training people to keep pace with technological change that demands more skills, we allow skilled labor to become scarce and thus attract excessive wages. Meanwhile, those with little or no skills face barriers to appropriate training and education.

However, as outlined in this book, there is another way forward for the world economy – a Balanced Wealth Strategy. Ending the persistent underpricing of natural capital and spurring additional human capital accumulation offer the promise of a new era of innovation and structural transformation that both transcends the fossil fuel age and will lead to a boost in long-term productivity worldwide. Implementing the Balanced Wealth Strategy is of course extremely difficult. But unless the world economy makes the transition to a new era of innovation and growth, the current threats of environmental scarcity and inequality will continue to worsen. As suggested in this book, overcoming these threats by redressing the structural imbalance between nature and wealth is the only way to usher in a new era of innovation, sustained growth and inclusive prosperity.

Modern economies have the opportunity to develop successfully and sustainably, as a means to ensuring the well-being of current and future generations. For the sake of the children today and those who will be born in tomorrow's world, we should take that opportunity while we still can.

Edward B. Barbier

Acknowledgments

I am grateful to Taiba Batool for working with me to develop the idea of this book, and for Rachel Sangster and Laura Pacey of Palgrave Macmillan for helping me see it through to publication.

Over the years, I have benefited from interactions with my many colleagues and friends, but especially at the institutions where I pursued much of my work on natural resources and development, such as the International Institute for Environment and Development (IIED), the London Environmental Economics Center of IIED and the Department of Economics of University College London, the Environment Department of the University of York, and the Department of Economics & Finance of the University of Wyoming. I also thank the University of Wyoming for granting me a sabbatical semester so that I could finish this book.

I benefited greatly from the insights, comments and suggestions provided by Joanne Burgess on earlier drafts of this manuscript. This book is much improved as a result. I am especially grateful for her suggesting Balanced Wealth Strategy as the name for the set of policy actions recommended in this book.

Thanks to Diane Bowersock for providing assistance in obtaining reference materials and making enquiries that aided my writing this book. Thanks also to Becky Barbier for finding the final quote by Mahatma Gandhi for the concluding chapter.

Introduction

A parable from Beijing

Beijing, China is one of the largest and fastest growing cities in the world. Its current population is more than 20 million people, and the population is expected to exceed 25 million by 2020 and possibly 50 million by 2050.[1]

Beijing's extraordinary growth has been accompanied by industrial development, greater reliance on coal-fired power plants, increased traffic and congestion, urban sprawl, and as a consequence, notoriously high levels of air pollution. Over a six-year period, from April 2008 to March 2014, there were at least 1,812 days where air quality in Beijing reached unhealthy levels, and only two days where air quality exceeded good levels.[2] Pollution exposure in Beijing and other urban areas in China is linked to cardio-respiratory illnesses and premature deaths, in particular from heart disease, stroke and lung cancer.[3] In January 2015, the city's mayor made global headlines by announcing that, because of its noxious smog, "Beijing is not a livable city".[4]

But there is a great difference in how the rich and poor residents of Beijing are able to cope with its air pollution.

Among the urban population of Beijing and other major cities in China, it is the disadvantaged groups – such as the poor, ethnic minorities and migrants from rural areas – that are the most exposed to sources of air pollution and more susceptible to any resulting health effects.[5] These disadvantaged groups are confined to the most polluted urban neighborhoods, which also suffer from high crime rates, inadequate infrastructure and services, and poor living conditions, from which they commute long distances for work. Moving away from dirty neighborhoods and closer to work is not an option; 48% of all jobs in Beijing are located within three miles of the city center, yet it is only the rich that can afford to live downtown.[6]

In contrast, the rich have many more options for coping with Beijing's air pollution.[7] The rich can afford the cleaner urban neighborhoods, which also have better jobs and high-quality public services, such as good schools and hospitals. The very wealthy can also afford extraordinary measures to protect themselves from air pollution. For example, elite private schools in Beijing are building gigantic, inflatable and air-conditioned domes to protect their students from air pollution hazards as they play sports and attend classes. As one school official explains: "A non-toxic learning environment is perhaps the least parents might expect, when they're paying £20,000-a-year fees."[8] Increasingly, many of Beijing's wealthy send their children overseas to school, simply to protect their health.

Overview

This example of Beijing's air pollution – and the stark contrast between how the rich and poor are able to respond to the problem – illustrates the main theme of this book. The world economy today is facing two major threats:

- increasing environmental degradation, and
- a growing gap between rich and poor.

Drawing on historical and contemporary evidence, this book argues that these two threats are symptomatic of a growing structural imbalance in all economies, which is how *nature* is exploited to create *wealth* and how it is shared among the population. The root of this imbalance is that natural capital is underpriced, and hence overly exploited, whereas human capital is insufficient to meet demand, thus encouraging wealth inequality.

Economists have always maintained that the key measure of an economy's progress is its ability to create wealth. Today, it is widely recognized that the "real wealth" of a nation comprises three distinct assets: manufactured, or *reproducible, capital*, such as roads, buildings, machinery and factories; *human capital*, such as skills, education and health embodies in the workforce; and *natural capital*, including land, forests, fossil fuels and minerals.[9] In addition, natural capital also comprises those ecosystems that through their natural functioning and habitats provide important goods and services to the economy, or *ecological capital*.[10] But the world economy today is squandering, rather than accumulating, key sources of wealth.

Despite rising environmental and ecological costs, the growth and structure of production in modern economies continues to use more resources and energy. Rather than face the rising economic and social costs of increasing natural resource use and ecological scarcity, we hide these costs by underpricing natural capital. As a consequence, we are using up natural resources as fast as ever, and our endowment of ecological capital is declining rapidly.

Over the past 50 years, ecosystems have been modified more rapidly and extensively than in any comparable period in human history, largely to meet rapidly growing demands for food, fresh water, timber, fiber and fuel. The result has been a substantial and largely irreversible loss in biological diversity, ecosystems and the ecological services that they provide. Approximately 15 out of 24 major global ecosystem services have been degraded or used unsustainably, including freshwater, capture fisheries, air and water purification, and the regulation of regional and local climate, natural hazards and pests.[11] Over the next 50 years, the rate of biodiversity loss is also expected to accelerate, leading to the extinction of at least 500 of the 1,192 currently threatened bird species and 565 of the 1,137 mammal species.[12]

Meanwhile, global concern is mounting over the growing gap between rich and poor.[13] The World Economic Forum's *Global Risk Report 2013* highlights severe income disparity as the greatest risk facing the world over the next ten years.[14] This global concern is not surprising. Since the 1980s, in most countries the gap between the rich and poor has grown considerably. Over this period, in the wealthiest nations, the household incomes of the richest 10% grew faster than that of the poorest 10%, so that today the gap between the two income groups is at its highest ratio of 9 to 1.[15] Increases in household income inequality have been largely driven by changes in the distribution of wages and salaries, caused mainly by education and other investments failing to keep up with "skill-biased technological change", which encourages more use of skilled rather than unskilled labor in production.[16]

In both rich and poor countries, it is the households that are poor, unemployed, or from disadvantaged groups (e.g., ethnic or racial minorities) that are increasingly clustered into the urban areas that suffer not only from deteriorating environmental conditions but also have poor schools and health facilities, high crime and inadequate public services. Not surprisingly, these urban locations have become "poverty sinks" of deprivation and worsening environmental quality, as the above example of Beijing illustrates. Developing countries face the additional problem of persistent rural poverty, especially the tendency of the very poor to be concentrated in remote and less favored lands that suffer from low agricultural productivity and degradation.[17] Estimates for 2010 suggest that in developing countries there are around 1.5 billion rural people found on less favored agricultural land, which is over 35% of the rural population.[18]

These two global trends – excessive environmental degradation from overuse of natural resources and the growing wealth gap between rich and poor – point to a systematic structural imbalance in the world economy. The purpose of the following book is to explain how this imbalance has come about, and what can be done to overcome environmental scarcity and inequality to launch the world economy onto a new path of innovation, sustainable growth and economic prosperity.

The second phase malaise

Chapter 1 provides the important context for understanding how the current structural imbalance in the world economy today has arisen. The chapter begins by tracing the historical origins of our present-day concept of wealth and examines how human perceptions of wealth have evolved over previous eras. These changing perceptions are important for understanding our present predicament – which is to "undervalue" the contribution of nature to our economies. This misalignment between our exploitation of *nature* and the creation of economic *wealth*, which is fundamental to the structural imbalances in modern economies, is explored further in subsequent chapters.

For example, as long as agriculture remained the dominant economic activity, land and natural resources were the main sources of economic wealth for both individuals and society. However, the advent of the Industrial Revolution beginning in the mid-18th century changed the structural dependence of an economy on its agricultural land base and available natural resources. Instead, the spread of manufacturing and industrial processes around the world meant that reproducible assets, such as factories, office and government buildings, railroad tracks, public roads, etc., overtook agricultural land as the major form of wealth in advanced economies. In addition, as economies industrialized, they developed the financial institutions and assets required for facilitating large-scale capital investments. Thus, by the 20th century, wealth in the richest economies was no longer closely associated with agricultural land and natural resource endowments. Instead, reproducible capital and financial assets became the most important sources of wealth.[19]

As Chapter 2 explains, the current structure of production in the world economy has been mainly determined by the *second phase* of innovations of the Industrial Revolution. These innovations occurred from 1870 to 1900, and were based largely on electricity and the internal combustion engine, which were in turn made possible by the new hydrocarbons oil and gas, along with coal. Harnessing these technological and economic changes eventually led to the rise of the United States, which became the model for 20th century industrialization. As industrialization spread worldwide, fostered by trade in energy and resources, there was a large boost to global productivity, which lasted until the early 1970s.

This second phase of the Industrial Revolution was also an outcome of the *fossil fuel era*. Since the 1890s, coal, oil and gas have accounted for at least half of global energy consumption. And, despite the rise in renewable energy and nuclear power, fossil fuels still account for 80% of energy use worldwide. In addition, as economies became more energy-intensive during the second phase, they also increased non-renewable material use, such as minerals and ores, construction materials and non-renewable organics, which currently comprise 95% of material consumption.

Chapter 3 explores the consequences of this pattern of natural resource use for current economic progress. As we have seen, in the modern world economy, as countries become richer, less of their wealth comprises natural capital, such as agricultural land, forests, protected areas, minerals and fossil fuels. Paradoxically, however, this does not mean that economic development requires less exploitation of natural resources. To the contrary, as economies grow and become wealthier, they consume more energy – mainly fossil fuels – and more natural resources generally. Thus, to supply this growing demand, the vast majority of low and middle-income countries depend on exporting a large percentage of primary products relative to total merchandise exports. As a consequence, the current pattern and structure of modern global development encourages *carbon-dependent* rich and large emerging market countries, and *resource-dependent* developing countries.

One of the consequences of this pattern of global natural resource use is the overexploitation of ecological capital in the pursuit of economic development, growth and progress, which is explored further in Chapter 4. Over time, as ecological impacts and associated economic losses become apparent, the costs of irreversible ecosystem conversion, overexploitation and the risk of collapse may be significant. But, unfortunately, today's economies continue to exploit natural resources for raw material and energy inputs or use the environment to assimilate pollution and other waste by-products, while ignoring any consequences in terms of increasing ecological impacts and risks. The outcome is one of the most important "hidden costs" of modern economies – *rising ecological scarcity*.

The key message of Chapters 1 through 4 of this book is that, by the 1970s, the world economy was still in the midst of the fossil fuel age, the productivity boost of the second phase of innovations was waning, and the growth and structure of production carried on using more resources and energy. Consequently, starting in the 1970s, a number of economic trends symptomatic of a growing structural imbalance in the world economy began emerging. Chapters 5, 6 and 7 focus on these key trends, and explain how they are related to the misuse of nature and wealth.

Two long-term trends that accompanied the second phase of industrialization have occurred since the early 20th century: skill-biased technological change and increased resource and energy use. Both trends are fundamental to understanding the structural imbalance that has arisen since the 1970s.

Moreover, modern economies are exacerbating this imbalance. Rather than face the rising economic and social costs of increasing natural resource use and ecological scarcity, we hide these costs by underpricing natural capital. And, rather than investing in sufficient human capital to keep pace with skill-biased technological change, we allow skilled labor to become scarce and thus attract excessive wages. It seems that we are prepared to accept the economic and social consequences of excessive environmental degradation and rising wealth inequality.

Figure 0.1 below summarizes the key arguments put forward in Chapter 5 through 7 of this book as to why the way in which modern economies accumulate and use their wealth is leading to structural imbalance. As explained previously, *economic wealth* consists of three main assets: reproducible capital, human capital and natural capital, which also includes ecological capital. Along with financial assets, economic wealth comprises the overall wealth of countries, which is often referred to as *national wealth*. In recent decades, financial capital has become the dominant form of wealth, and more of the income and wealth of the rich is from the financial sector. Moreover, its unchecked expansion has led to greater financial risk and instability, increasing the concentration of wealth and global imbalances. Reproducible capital continues

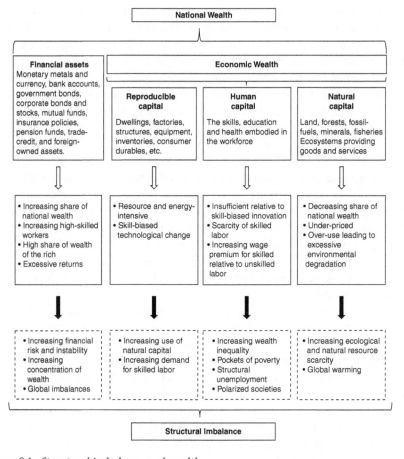

Figure 0.1 Structural imbalance and wealth

to be overly resource and energy-intensive, and is the main conduit for skill-biased technological change. As a result, accumulation of reproducible capital encourages more use of natural capital and rising demand for relatively skilled labor. However, human capital accumulation in modern economies is failing to keep pace with this demand, which has caused the wage gap between highly skilled and less skilled workers to grow. The global implications are increasing wealth inequality, pockets of poverty, structural unemployment, and increased social polarization. Finally, the underpricing of natural capital has led to increasing overuse and excessive environmental degradation. The result is increasing ecological and natural resource scarcity, and the emergence of global environmental problems, such as climate change and concerns over freshwater availability.

In sum, since the 1970s, the world economy has been in a *second phase malaise*. The productivity boost of the second phase of innovations of the Industrial Revolution has diminished, yet we persist with the same pattern and structure of resource and energy-intensive production and growth that were fostered by these innovations. It is not surprising that the outcome of this second phase malaise is that we are facing increasing economic, social and environmental costs of maintaining the same pattern and structure of production. This has led in turn to profound structural imbalances.

Clearly, then, the starting point to address the current structural imbalance in most modern economies today is to tackle these twin problems of excessive environmental degradation and insufficient human capital. As this book demonstrates, most of the current economic ills – whether it is ecological scarcity and climate change, or the growing gap between rich and poor and structural unemployment – can be traced back to these key symptoms of structural imbalance. A policy strategy to end this imbalance must target the fundamental distortion in modern economies, which is the overpricing of human capital and the underpricing of natural capital. The purpose of Chapters 8 and 9 is to outline this Balanced Wealth Strategy.

As explained in these chapters, in addition to ending the second phase malaise of excessive environmental degradation and rising wealth inequality, the Balanced Wealth Strategy needs to be inclusive. This means that it must also be accompanied by policies aimed directly at benefiting the large number of resource-dependent economies and ending the significant pockets of poverty found especially in rural areas worldwide. In addition, the global impacts of environmental degradation are becoming a pressing problem. Most of the impending environmental crises facing the world economy – climate change, ecological scarcity and declining availability of water – are examples of market failures on a global scale. These need to be addressed as well.

Consequently, there are essentially four key elements of the Balanced Wealth Strategy:

- ending the persistent underpricing of natural capital that leads to its overuse in all economies;
- ending insufficient human capital accumulation that contributes to increasing wealth inequality;
- adopting policies targeted at inefficient natural resource use and poverty in developing economies;
- creating markets to address key global environmental impacts.

The Balanced Wealth Strategy is clearly not costless, and will require substantial commitments by all economies. But unless such a strategy is pursued, and the world economy makes the transition to a new era of innovation and growth, the current global threats of environmental scarcity and inequality will continue to worsen.

Thus, Chapter 10 concludes this book by offering two possible visions of the future, one in which the second phase malaise persists and one in which the world economy enters a *third phase* of innovation, sustainable growth and economic prosperity. Making the transition will not be easy, but the consequences for the majority of the world's population of the current pattern of using nature to accumulate wealth could be bleak, if not catastrophic.

1
The Origins of Economic Wealth

Introduction

The purpose of the following chapter is to trace the historical origins of our present-day concept of wealth, by examining how human perceptions of wealth have evolved over previous eras. These changing perceptions are important to understanding our present predicament – which is to "undervalue" the contribution of nature to our economies. This misalignment between our exploitation of *nature* and the creation of *wealth* is fundamental to the structural imbalance in modern economies. In subsequent chapters, we explore the causes and consequences of this imbalance.

If you asked anyone today "what is wealth?" chances are you would get similar answers: precious jewels, bank accounts, mansions, estates, stocks and bonds, personal art collections, private yachts and jets. These material possessions and financial assets are what we recognize in modern society to be the "trappings of wealth".

Yet, for most of our existence, humans would have been puzzled by this modern view of "riches". They would even have had trouble in defining a term like *wealth*. The reason is that it is actually a fairly new social concept; what we consider to be wealth today has evolved through many millennia of human social and economic development.

For hundreds of thousands of years, humans lived as hunter-gatherers and had little interest in accumulating material possessions or land and natural resources. In these societies, mobility and adaptability to nature were the key social traits that guaranteed communal economic survival. Wealth was a meaningless concept for early humans.

Once hunter-gatherers were supplanted by farmers and herders, around 10,000 years ago, *wealth creation* began in earnest. For thousands of years, with agriculture as the dominant economic activity, humans associated affluence with the accumulation of fertile land and possession of abundant natural resources, such as wood, water, building stone, precious stones and gems, and metals. Labor was important, but less so than livestock for food, transport, work and even warfare. In other words, basic natural resource assets – or *natural capital* – were the main sources of economic wealth for both individuals and human societies.

For the past couple of hundred years, and especially since the Industrial Revolution in the mid-18th century, we have come to view wealth a little differently. Today, the close association between natural resources (including land) and wealth accumulation no longer exists. In modern societies, wealth is often referred to as "capital", which is defined as the sum total of non-human assets that can be owned and exchanged on some market.[1]

As depicted in the top part of Figure 1.1, a distinction is usually made between two types of capital. The first is *tangible assets*, which support the production of goods and services in an economy. The second form of capital is *financial assets*, which represent various stores of wealth as well as claims on others in the economy. Together, financial and tangible assets comprise the *national*

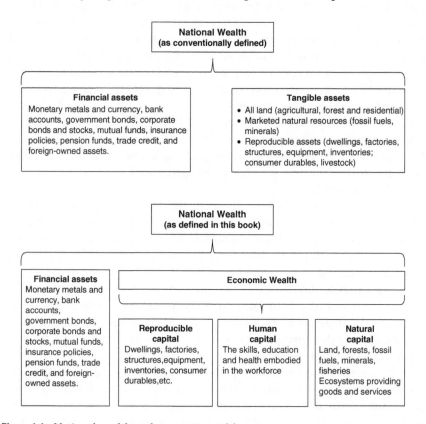

Figure 1.1 National wealth and economic wealth

wealth or *national capital* of an economy, which is the total market value of everything owned by the residents and government of a given country at a given point in time.[2]

Because they can contribute to current or future production, the tangible assets of an economy are conventionally defined as all land (e.g., agricultural, forest and residential) and reproducible capital (e.g., dwellings and real estate; factories, structures, equipment, etc.; inventories; consumer durables; and livestock).[3] However, some economists also include as tangible assets those natural resources of an economy, such as oil, natural gas, coal and other minerals that can also be owned and exchanged on markets.[4] In contrast, financial assets include monetary metals and currency, bank accounts, mutual funds, bonds, stocks, insurance policies, pension funds, mortgages, government bonds, corporate bonds and stocks, trade credit and foreign-owned assets.

In principle, there is an important connection between financial and tangible assets, namely that many investments in land, dwellings and reproducible capital are funded by an enterprise or an individual borrowing, or incurring debt, in order to pay for such investments. Such new debt or borrowing is referred to as acquiring *financial liabilities*. But incurring additional financial liabilities in an economy can only happen if another individual or enterprise is willing to finance this debt, which becomes the latter's financial asset. Thus, the acquisition of new financial assets by all domestic sectors of an economy should be balanced by the sum total of new financial liabilities.[5]

Although the accumulation of financial and tangible assets is important, they may not represent all the capital that is fundamental to the successful working of an economy, both now and into the future. Instead, if we are interested in the *economic wealth* of a nation, we are interested in *all forms of capital that can contribute to the current and future well-being of all those who depend on the economy for their livelihoods.*

In this book, we make the case that the conventional definition of tangible assets is incomplete, because it leaves out several important assets that are essential to current and future economic livelihoods. Instead, as indicated in Figure 1.1, we consider the national wealth of an economy to include financial assets and economic wealth. The latter comprises three distinct assets: manufactured, or *reproducible, capital* (e.g., roads, buildings, machinery, factories, etc.), which we noted above is also an important tangible asset; *human capital*, which are the skills, education and health embodied in the workforce; and *natural capital*, including land, forests, fossil fuels, minerals, fisheries and all other natural resources, regardless of whether or not they are exchanged on markets or owned (see Figure 1.1).[6] In addition, natural capital also consists of those ecosystems that through their natural functioning and habitats provide important goods and services to the economy, or *ecological capital.*[7]

These three forms of capital – reproducible, human and natural – should be considered the real wealth of an economy, because they can either benefit the well-being of humans directly (e.g., a person is better off if she is healthy; people enjoy a cleaner environment and well-functioning ecosystems, etc.), or they benefit humans indirectly through contributing to current or future production (e.g., more machines, raw material and energy inputs, and better skilled workers can increase the output of goods and services that people consume). Because the accumulation and maintenance of reproducible, human and natural capital contribute either directly or indirectly to increasing human well-being, both currently as well in the future, these three forms of capital comprise economic wealth. Figure 1.2 illustrates this fundamental relationship diagrammatically.

Reproducible, human and natural capital either directly support current and future well-being or do so indirectly through contributing to current and future production of goods and services in an economy. Thus, these three assets comprise the economic wealth of a country.

To summarize, in this book we define *national wealth* to consist of *financial assets* and *economic wealth*. The focus of this book is mainly on the three assets that comprise economic wealth – *reproducible, human* and *natural capital* – that support the production of goods and services in an economy. As we shall

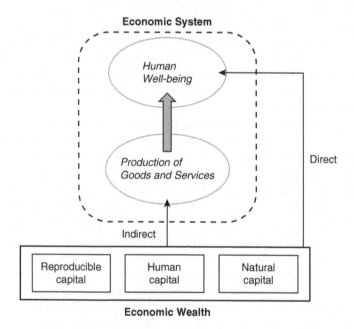

Figure 1.2   Economic wealth and human well-being

see, how economies today accumulate and use these three types of capital affects current and future well-being, as well as the composition of our overall national wealth. For example, while we are busy accumulating financial assets and reproducible capital, depreciation of our natural and ecological capital is proceeding at an alarming rate. We may also be under-investing in human capital. This pattern of wealth accumulation and composition has led to structural imbalances in modern economies that threaten their sustainability.

The creation of wealth

The accumulation of wealth is, in fact, a relatively new social phenomenon. *Homo sapiens* emerged 200,000 to 250,000 years ago, and for around 90% of our existence, we survived by hunting wildlife and gathering wild plants and foods. Early human societies that engaged in such activities had little interest in amassing wealth. Hunter-gatherers had few material possessions, and they were shared or divided equally. Accumulation was simply not a priority for this way of life, for three principal reasons.[8]

First, hunters had to follow their prey and foragers had to gather new sources of wild resources. They lived in small bands and groups, so that they could move quickly across wide stretches of territory. Such highly mobile and small hunter-gatherer societies could not carry around much in the way of material possessions – other than what was essential for catching, collecting or containing food.

Second, mobile and small hunter-gatherer societies were never in one place long enough to own much land or other natural resources. If they did claim territory, land and resources, it was generally through communal ownership and equal use. If one group or individual tried to control the richest land or resources, the others could simply "vote with their feet" and move elsewhere. Humans were scarce, so finding new hunting and foraging grounds was relatively easy. In contrast, natural wealth was everywhere and plentiful, so there was no need to hoard, possess or protect it.

Finally, the tools, clothing and other essential items for survival were relatively easy to make. The knowledge and skills to make such objects were shared and taught, and the raw materials for manufacturing were readily available in the wild. Any special ceremonial or ritual objects were communal property.

The absence of wealth and inequality among hunter-gatherer societies changed with the development of agriculture as the dominant human economic activity. The long period of history that encompasses the demise of hunting-gathering and the rise of agriculture is often called the Agricultural Transition, because it took around 7,000 years to unfold and spread globally. This process may have started in 10,000 BC, with early experimentation in crop planting by sedentary hunter-gatherers in different parts of the world. By

5000 BC much of the global population lived by farming, and by 3000 BC the first agricultural-based "empire states" emerged.[9]

The Agricultural Transition fostered agricultural-based production systems that routinely created food and raw material surpluses, which in turn facilitated urbanization, manufacturing, trade, and of course, the creation and accumulation of wealth. The principle stores of value were land, livestock and material possessions. However, the difference in wealth and status among early farmers is also evident through lavish burials and other ritualistic practices, the type and distribution of ceremonial goods, the size and location of dwellings and storage facilities, and evidence of improving stature and health.[10] And, as such distinctions in wealth and status grew within early farming societies, so did social inequality.

Around 3000 BC, agriculture had become sufficiently advanced that it was able to support complex, urban-based societies in some regions. These societies quickly evolved into the first "ancient civilizations" of Mesopotamia, Ancient Egypt and India, and also the Greek city-states and Roman Empires. From 1200 BC onwards, large cities and empires were also present in China and East Asia.

Although dependent on surrounding agricultural land for food surpluses, the urban centers that controlled these great empires and early civilizations also required a variety of natural resources to sustain their economic wealth and power, and to provide security in times of drought, plague, war and other calamities. Imperial expansion and urban growth required securing new supplies of fertile land, natural resources and raw materials. As described by the historian Herbert Kaufman, obtaining such sources of wealth was essential to the "polities" governing these empires:

> Labor, arable land, water, wood, metals, and minerals (building stone, precious stones, and semi-precious stones) were the major resources of the polities... although draft animals and horses for warfare were also important in some cases. Where these were in plentiful supply, economies prospered, sustaining government activities that assisted and facilitated productivity. The political systems that lasted long, or that displayed great recuperative powers, were usually well-endowed in many of these respects and were therefore able to acquire by trade or intimidation or conquest what nature did not bestow on them.[11]

Not surprisingly, it was these ancient land-based empires that first recognized *wealth creation* as the primary goal of an economy. Wealth and its accumulation were elevated to the highest social status. For example, ancient Greek religion and myths even had a god of wealth, Plutus, who was the subject of a popular Greek comedy written by Aristophanes in 388 BC.

For early agricultural societies and civilizations, the most valuable capital was fertile land, natural resources and raw materials. Precious gems and metals were also accumulated, both as status symbols and as "stores" of value. Essential forms of reproducible capital included dwellings, basic tools and utensils, and livestock, which could be raised for food, provide transport, perform work and be used in warfare. Because labor was a valuable input into production and often scarce, it too became an asset; slavery was common, and slave ownership a sign of affluence.

Early land-based empires also began associating the success of an economy with its ability to create more wealth. One of the first tracts on economics was the *Arthaśāstra*, composed around 300 BC by Kautilya, minister to Chandragupta, the founder of the Maurya Empire of Northern India. Much of this text is devoted to the "science" of *artha*, or "wealth", and it describes the "wealth creation" goal of economic activity in the following way: "agriculture, cattle-rearing and trade...constitute economics" and are "beneficial as they yield grains, cattle, money, forest produce and labour."[12]

The emphasis on accumulating wealth also fostered urbanization.[13] As a result, wealth creation and the concentration of populations in urban centers became self-reinforcing. Urban population growth facilitated the division of labor and specialization in tasks, which made early economies even more efficient in creating wealth. But an important by-product of this process was also increased social stratification and economic inequality.

One initial motivation for urbanization was defense, especially in the case of the rise of the early urban centers from smaller agricultural settlements.[14] However, as the economic success of cities became tied to the division of labor and specialization, urbanization quickly evolved more complex social relationships. For example, an important precondition for the creation of a city was that farmers in surrounding agricultural areas could produce surpluses of food beyond what they required for their own subsistence. This agricultural surplus, in turn, meant that much of the urban-based population did not have to grow its own food. Urban dwellers could then engage in other economic and social activities, such as skilled crafts, manufacturing and trade, defense, policing and other military tasks, religion, science and the arts. Cities also began trading their surplus products with each other, which led urban areas to specialize in producing specific commodities suited to their endowments of land and natural resources.

Such division of labor, specialization and trade led to more efficient production, greater surpluses and even larger urban populations. In early agricultural communities in the Near East, a typical peasant village consisted of 10–50 families, with a total population of around 300 persons at most. In comparison, the first city-state, the Sumerian capital of Uruk in Mesopotamia established around 2800 BC, supported a population of about 80,000. It stretched over

600 hectares, controlled the entire economy and territory of Sumer (ca. 60,000 km²) and dominated a network of smaller Sumerian cities that, together with Uruk, contained 89% of the Mesopotamian population.[15]

The complex division of labor, trade and economic organization of cities created a social hierarchy, which at the top consisted of a ruling class of elites, priests and warriors. Wealth and political power were concentrated in the hands of the elite, who ruled from their urban bases. Since agricultural surpluses and other forms of wealth accumulated in urban centers, social institutions of exchange, such as markets, weights and measures, and money, began to emerge as cities developed. The elites were assisted by an administrative bureaucracy and managerial class that supervised the overall running of government as well as economic and military activities, including the extraction of wealth from surrounding regions through tribute, taxation and slavery. Although much of the state revenue funded professional armies, public buildings, art and religious works, it also financed a new "professional" class, such as architects, engineers, scientists, teachers and doctors, who were generally urban dwellers.

Wealth creation in these early economies also led to technological innovation, which also fostered the accumulation of more wealth, stronger economies and greater military power. For example, in the first cities of Sumer, the full-time artisans specializing in the manufacturing of textiles, metalworking, pottery and other crafts were responsible for important technical innovations in all these skilled crafts, especially improvements in metallurgy that utilized copper. The professional and managerial class invented mathematics and writing, systems of weights and measures, and early scientific and medical procedures. They also developed key agricultural innovations, such as techniques of land drainage and irrigation, which were vital to extending the area of cultivated land and ensuring its high productivity. From 1000 BC to 0 AD, technological innovations and adoption in agriculture, transportation, communication, writing and the military occurred in the wealthiest and most powerful empires of Southwest Asia and China. As ancient civilizations developed in India and southern Europe (e.g., Greek city-states and the Roman Empire), these empires also adopted such key technological innovations.[16]

In sum, the creation of wealth is actually a relatively new economic phenomenon in human history – starting around 10,000 years ago with the development and spread of agriculture across the world. However, accumulating wealth received its main impetus about 5,000 years ago, once early civilizations and land-based empires started emerging. The resulting process of urbanization in these empires led to the concentration of wealth, skills and populations in cities. Division of labor, social specialization and technological innovation made wealth accumulation even more efficient and pervasive. As we shall see next, the wealth creation process of early economies was further boosted through trade.

Trading networks and the accumulation of wealth

Even before domestication of plants and animals occurred, long-distance trading networks were prominent among some hunter-gathering societies, such as the Natufians and other sedentary populations who inhabited the Eastern Mediterranean around 12,000–10,000 BC. For instance, Kauri shells from the Red Sea were traded from settlement to settlement and reached as far as Anatolia (Southern Turkey). Anatolian obsidian passed through the same trade network back into the Eastern Mediterranean. As plant and animal domestication developed, so did these exchange networks, as well as the range of goods traded. Early trade soon included gold, precious gems, furs, feathers, grain, meat, nuts and other valued commodities. It is likely that this fledgling trade network also gradually spread the newly cultivated seed-grains around the Mediterranean, thus facilitating the development of the earliest farming systems in the region.[17]

Early human societies established a connection between trade and wealth. Trade allowed these societies to obtain rare, and thus highly valued and desired, commodities. As economies and urban centers developed, their trade networks became more complex and highly differentiated. Cities and civilizations were dependent, not only on their surrounding agricultural regions that produced large food surpluses for their urban-based populations, but also on securing raw materials from trade with nearby resource-abundant regions.[18]

New cities fostering trade and supplying manufactures and natural resources would spring up along the overland and sea routes connecting major empires. From 3000 BC to 1500 BC, one such major trade network linked two of the first great empires, the Mesopotamian and the Indus Valley Civilizations. Other regions developed similar patterns of trade. At the height of the Ancient Egyptian civilization in the Nile Valley (ca. 3200–1200 BC) the urban centers of Memphis, Thebes and Alexandria became the trading core linked to several natural-resource supplying regions. One region was North Africa, the Middle East and the Aegean, which provided wine, olive oil, silver and bronze; the other was northern Europe and the British Isles, which supplied amber and tin. The new urban centers that flourished in the trading network were the Aegean city-states, which eventually produced the various Greco-Roman Empires that succeeded the Egyptians. By the time of the Roman Empire (ca. 300 BC to 476 AD), Egypt reverted to being an agricultural producer and exporter of wheat in the new imperial trading network dominated by Rome.[19]

Trading networks also developed in Central and South America. During the Classic Maya civilization (200–900 AD) trade occurred across the Central American lowlands, with the great cities such as Tikal serving as the urban core of the trading network. Smaller cities near the water trading routes also sprung up, especially centers in the Yucatán that supplied cacao and cotton. When the Mayan civilization in the south collapsed, for a time Yucatán cities, such as Uxmal, Sayil, Kabah and Labná, took over, but then declined from 1000 AD onwards.[20]

The first great civilization in South America, the Wari city-state empire of the Peruvian Andes (600–1000 AD) traded textiles, stone figurines, ceramic vessels, metal objects and other items across a wide area of Peru and the highlands of the Central Andes in exchange for obsidian, rock salt, copper and ochre. Also in the Andes, near modern-day Bolivia, the city-state of Tiwanaku with 20,000 to 30,000 inhabitants developed its own trading network. Eventually, it extended to exchange with the Wari Empire. The growth of the combined Wari-Tiwanaku trading network stimulated the development of many smaller trading centers throughout the Central Andes, which helped facilitate the extraction of raw materials and their export to Wari and Tiwanaku. When both city-states at the center of this network eventually collapsed around 1000 AD, the new core trading center of Cuzco, located midway along the main trading route between Wari and Tiwanaku, emerged as the new urban center of the Inca Empire.[21]

The ancient civilizations of China were slower to develop trading networks. However, the Qin (or Chin) and Han Dynasties (221 BC to 220 AD) fostered the first intercontinental trading network, the Silk Road, which eventually linked several large empires from the Mediterranean to Asia.[22] The first land-based Silk Road from East Asia to the Mediterranean gradually evolved through trade connections across these empires, probably around 200 BC. By the 1st century AD, the Silk Road trade involved a vast network of sea and land routes linking China, South Asia and Southeast Asia with West Asia and the Roman Empire. Silk was initially the main commodity exported by China and demanded by Rome and other Western cities. Other manufactured and semi-processed products, such as steel, iron, muslin, textiles and ink, soon followed, however. In addition, China and its Southeast Asian trading partners provided ginger, cinnamon and other spices. As sea routes through South Asia and Southeast Asia developed, additional tropical products such as cloves, pepper, pearls, precious stones, cotton, sugar, teakwood, ebony and frankincense and myrrh were included. In exchange for this trade, the Chinese and other Asian empires wanted mainly gold and silver, which the Roman Empire supplied through mines in its conquered territories, such as Gaul, Spain and Britain. In addition, the urban centers in Rome, northern Italy and Gaul produced manufactures, such as pottery, glassware, perfumes, jewelry and textiles, which were exported throughout the Roman Empire in exchange for raw materials, cotton, grain, wool, flax and precious gems.[23]

The early trade networks also established and promoted slavery across the ancient world. Because labor was such a valuable input into production, it became a scarce asset. As a result, slavery was common, and slave ownership denoted affluence and status. This meant that acquiring and trading slaves became a highly profitable activity. For example, across its vast territory, the Roman Empire had an abundance of fertile, unoccupied land, mineral resources, timber forests and other natural resources. To exploit these lands and resources, the Romans increasingly resorted to large-scale plantations and extractive industries that utilized slave labor. The demand for slaves, and for additional resource-abundant territories to develop extractive industries and bring more land into agricultural production, became complementary economic incentives behind the Roman drive for new military conquests that yielded both more territory and war-captive slaves. However, the Roman Empire could not always obtain enough slaves through military victories to meet demand. Soon, the Romans were trading for slaves from their North African and Arabian territories. As utilizing slave labor for extractive resource-based industries and plantations became common throughout the ancient world, the international market for selling human captives into slavery was created.

In sum, the development of trade networks further spurred the wealth accumulation motive of early economies. Trade allowed cities and empires to obtain surpluses of food, raw materials, precious metals, gems and other valued commodities that they could not produce themselves. As economies began trading their surplus products with each other, they had to specialize in producing specific commodities suited to their endowments of land and natural resources. These endowments therefore continued to be the most valuable form of economic wealth, which the growth of trade networks further reinforced.

Emergence of a world economy

So successful was trade in helping nations accumulate wealth, the expansion of trade networks continued across the globe. These networks coalesced into a nascent "world economy" by 1000 AD, and from 1000 to 1500 AD, the upsurge in trade between countries and regions ushered in an unprecedented era of global population and economic growth. By 1500, an international economy was firmly established. [24] Over this 500-year period, world population nearly doubled, and the value of global production per person increased from $436 to $566.[25]

Trade fostered wealth creation because it facilitated access to the most important sources of "wealth" across the world. By 1000 AD, the rapid expansion of international trade was mainly due to the growth and development of three regional economic powers, the Islamic states of North Africa and West Asia, the Delhi sultanates of Northern India and the imperial dynasties of China. During this era, China, India and the Middle East each had a share of world GDP that far exceeded the entire share of Western Europe.[26] In addition, the vast majority of large cities were in China, the Islamic states and India, and the handful of mega-cities of over a million inhabitants were located in China and West Asia.[27] As a result, 1000 to 1500 AD was the era of the "Golden Age of Islam" in North Africa, West Asia and Northern India (ca. 1000–1492) and the Sung (or Song) Dynasty in China (960–1279), as well as its successor Yuan (1260–1368) and Ming Dynasties (1368–1644).[28]

Figure 1.3 characterizes the major regions involved in the emerging world trade system around 1200 to 1300 AD, and indicates how differences in natural resource endowments and ecological conditions influenced the specialization and trade in different natural resource-based products by each region. It was not yet a global economy, as it excluded the American and Australian continents, as well as large parts of sub-Saharan Africa and much of the Pacific. However, the largest economies, which contained most of the world's population, were connected by this extensive trading network.

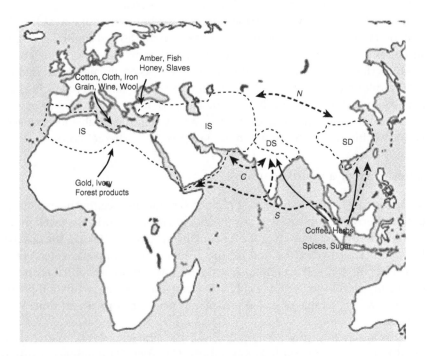

Figure 1.3   The emerging world economy, ca. 1200–1300 AD

Notes: IS = Islamic states of North Africa, Middle East and West Asia (e.g., Abbasids, Almohads, Arabs, Ayyubids, Ghurids, Kwaresmians, Ortoquids, Salgharids, Seljuks and Zengids, ca. 1200 AD); DS = Delhi Sultanates (Mamluk Dynasty, 1206–1290 AD); SD = Sung Dynasty (during Southern Sung, 1127–1279 AD); N = Northern east–west trade route; C = Central east–west trade route; S = Southern east–west trade route

Source: Edward B. Barbier (2011) *Scarcity and Frontiers: How Economies Have Developed Through Natural Resource Exploitation*. Cambridge and New York: Cambridge University Press, figure 4.1.

In the Western Hemisphere, the Islamic states stretching from North Africa, across the Middle East and Southwest Asia all the way to Northern India were at the center of the main trading network. The resource-abundant regions supplying this center with raw materials included Europe, West Africa, Eurasia and Russia. In the Eastern Hemisphere, there were two additional trade networks. The smaller was in South Asia, where the Delhi Sultanates of Northern India were the center of the network, and the rest of South Asia and parts of Southeast Asia the periphery. Further east was the larger trading network dominated by China, which imported raw materials from resource-rich South and Southeast Asia.

Linking these hemispheric trade blocs was a weaker series of east–west trading networks. There were three principal routes, connecting the Mediterranean economy to the Eastern Hemisphere regions. The northern overland route went through the Black Sea region, across Central Asia to China. The central route was a combination of an overland and sea route, through Baghdad via the Persian Gulf into the Indian Ocean and reaching to India. Finally, there was the southern route, which was largely by sea. It went overland from Cairo to the Red Sea, through the Indian Ocean, the Southeast Asian archipelago and finally to the South China Sea. These trade routes were not new; they more or less established the east–west routes of the old Silk Roads trade from 300 BC to 600 AD.

Through the years 1000 to 1500, economies were overwhelmingly agrarian. This meant that the main sources of wealth had not changed since the emergence of agricultural-based empires starting around 3,000 BC. Economic wealth was still principally defined by three most important assets of agricultural societies: fertile land, natural resources and raw materials. Precious gems and metals were status symbols of wealth but were growing in importance as "stores" of value, especially to pay for items of trade. The most important forms of reproducible capital were dwellings, basic tools and utensils, livestock, and labor, especially in the form of slaves.

The large agrarian societies at the "core" of the trading networks of the world economy, such as the Islamic states spanning the Middle East to North India and the successive Chinese dynasties, contained both vast rural areas capable of producing agricultural surpluses as well as urban and industrial centers that processed raw materials or produced simple manufactures such as textiles, porcelain, iron and silk. Although trade was important, the power and wealth of these empires relied mainly on land and resource exploitation within their imperial territories. Trade facilitated this wealth creation process, but it did not supplant internal agricultural development and resource exploitation for economic development. As a consequence, the major imperial economies in China, the Middle East and India had no need to engage in trade as the main means of wealth creation.

In contrast, as a peripheral region in the emerging world economy, Western Europe had little choice but to pursue trade to foster wealth accumulation. The highly diverse and abundant natural environment of Western Europe meant that its nation states benefited from specializing and trading in a wide range of natural resource products. Agricultural land expansion within the region ensured a growing agricultural sector that generated surpluses. In the aftermath of the Black Death, wars and other calamities of the 14th century that decimated populations, Western Europe had even more abundant land relative to scarce labor. As a result, Europeans adopted agricultural innovations and institutions that improved productivity and increased surpluses of food and raw materials. Because populations remained small, these growing surpluses could be exported through maritime trade. The proceeds in turn financed manufacturing expansion and new natural resources to exploit, which ultimately created more diversified economies. Thus a "virtuous circle" of economic growth was created in European states through specialization in bulk trade of natural products, the development of markets and commercial institutions, and dependence on expanding trade revenues.

Competition between rival Western European states and their growing dominance of maritime trade further reinforced their desire to gain control of key regional and global trading networks. The improvements in shipping technology, vessels, navigation, naval weaponry and building materials meant that Western European maritime states could compete for and dominate international sea routes, from the Baltic Sea and Atlantic to the Indian Ocean and the Sea of Japan. By 1500, Western Europe had moved from the periphery to the center of the world economy, and it was poised to pursue its resource-based trade and development strategy on the global stage.

Global frontiers and the rise of the West

Between 1500 and 1900, global economic development was spurred by finding and exploiting new frontiers of land and other natural resources, which is why this period is often referred to as the era of "Global Frontiers".[29]

The world economy also fully emerged during this era. The voyages of Columbus in the 1490s led to an Atlantic trade route connecting Europe and the "New World" colonies in the Americas, whereas Vasco da Gama's journeys during the same decade established a European trade route to the Indian Ocean via the Cape of Good Hope. By 1521, the Pacific Ocean was crossed, and in 1571 the first Asia–Americas trade link was established via the entrepôt port of Manila. Thus, in less than a century, a global trade network was created linking all the major populated continents of the world and exchanging products continuously. Global trade facilitated the growth of many important markets and trading routes for a variety of resource commodities, which in turn were fostered by the discovery and exploitation of new sources of land and natural resources across the world. From 1500 onwards, the expansion of global trade and frontiers was therefore mutually self-reinforcing.

In addition, global migration changed significantly after 1500. Before the 16th century, when people migrated to settle new lands or exploit abundant natural resources, they were restricted to moving to nearby uninhabited areas, such as previously untouched forests, wetlands, grassland and hills, or to adjacent territories and borderlands. As shipping technologies and long-distance sea transport improved and became less costly, from the 16th century onwards migration became more global. For the first time in world history, transoceanic settlement and exploitation of new lands occurred.

The era of global frontier exploitation and population migration from 1500 to the early 20th century also led to the Industrial Revolution and the rise of the West.[30] But the eventual economic dominance of Western Europe took some time to develop. As indicated in Figure 1.4, even up to the dawn of the Industrial Revolution in 1750, Western Europe was just one of five major economic regions of the world, which were similar in terms of economic wealth, capital, land and resource endowments, as well access to overseas markets, trade and territories. In fact, India and China were still the more wealthy and

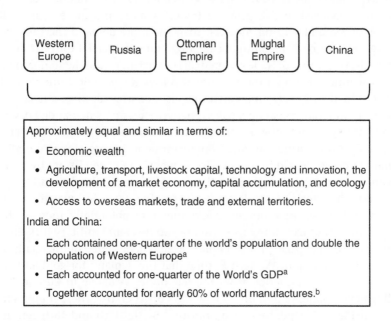

Figure 1.4   The world up to 1750

Notes: [a] Angus Maddison (2003) *The World Economy: Historical Statistics*. Paris: Organization for Economic Cooperation and Development; [b] Paul Bairoch (1982) "International Industrialization Levels from 1705 to 1980", *Journal of European Economic History*, 11: 269–333.

populous economies. Each contained one-quarter of the world's populations and double the population of Western Europe. India and China accounted for about a quarter each of the global economy, and by 1750, were producing nearly 60% of global manufactures.

As discussed previously, although China and India had the economic means to explore, colonize and exploit overseas territories, these large empires chose instead to utilize the abundant land and natural resources that lay within their imperial territories. In contrast, Western Europe pursued trade, colonization and migration as the means to develop global frontiers and thus accumulate vast amounts of wealth. By the 16th century, the European maritime states, Portugal, Spain, England, the Netherlands and France, had the naval power, commercial services and shipping fleets to extend their rivalry and competition for natural resource-based products worldwide. This soon became a competition for *bullionism* – the accumulation of gold and silver reserves either directly through acquiring new mines overseas or indirectly through creating trade surpluses.

By 1500, the key indicator of any state's economic wealth, political influence and military might was its ability to accrue gold, silver and other precious metals. The emergence of the world economy resulted in not only the expansion of international trade in goods and services but also the "monetization" of the economies involved in this growing trade. As more and more commodities were produced and sold on markets, then the more demand increased for a reliable and common "medium of exchange" for commercial transactions.

From the beginning of trade and markets in ancient times, the standard monetary instrument for such transactions was *coinage*, metallic coins minted in predetermined weights from precious metals such as gold, silver and copper.[31] As markets and trade expanded, governments increasingly demanded payment in coins for taxes and other revenues extracted on behalf of the state; and in turn, public expenditures ranging from investments in irrigation to mobilizing military forces were paid in money. Consequently, as expenditures by individuals and governments increased in the economy, so did the demand for gold, silver and other precious metals necessary to coin money. By amassing reserves of gold and silver, an economy could therefore potentially increase these expenditures, thus extending its economic, political and military influence.

After 1500, the pace of economic development and commercialization proceeded so rapidly in Western Europe that the demand for gold and silver soon outstripped production from the few mines available in Europe. Thus, finding new supplies of bullion, or new ways of generating these supplies from lands outside of Europe, became a priority.[32] By the 17th and 18th centuries, a handful of European states had leveraged their dominance of key sea routes into powerful "ocean empires" that controlled the lucrative global trade in key natural resource products (see Table 1.1). This trade and imperial strategy

Table 1.1   Ocean empires and natural resource trade, 17th and 18th centuries

Regions	Main Products	European States
East Indies (Malaysian peninsula; Indonesian archipelago)	Spices, pepper, medicinal herbs, dyestuffs, woods, sugar	Portugal, the Netherlands, France, England
India (Cambay, Malabar and Coromandel coasts; Bengal; Ceylon)	Textiles, metalwork, silk, pepper, spices, indigo, saltpeter	Portugal, the Netherlands, France, England, Denmark
China	porcelain, silk, tea	Portugal, the Netherlands, France, England
Guinea (west coast of Africa from Cape Verde to Cape Lopez)	Slaves, gold, ivory, feathers	Portugal, the Netherlands, France, England, Denmark, Sweden, Spain, Brandenburg States
West Indies (Caribbean islands)	Sugar, tobacco, cotton, rice, dyestuffs	Spain, the Netherlands, France, England, Denmark, Sweden
South America (e.g., Mexico, Guyana and Brazil)	Sugar, silver, tobacco, cotton, rice, dyestuffs	Spain, the Netherlands, Portugal
North America (e.g., Canada and thirteen American colonies)	fish, fur, timber, cotton, tobacco, rice	England, France, Spain, the Netherlands, Russia, Denmark, Sweden

Source: Edward B. Barbier (2011) *Scarcity and Frontiers: How Economies Have Developed Through Natural Resource Exploitation*. Cambridge UK and New York: Cambridge University Press, table 5.3.

allowed the small European maritime states to accumulate the reserves of gold and silver necessary to become global economic and military powers.

The rise of Western European states and their pursuit of economic wealth also had further important implications: the rise of the Atlantic Economy, including the "triangular trade" involving the slave trade with Africa and the expansion of slavery in the Americas, the Industrial Revolution, and the development of novel financial institutions and instruments.

Slavery and wealth

Sub-Saharan Africa had been the source of a growing global slave trade for many centuries. Between 750 and 1500, around 10,000 Africans were enslaved annually, with the cumulative total of slaves over this period reaching 5 to 10 million. This growing demand for African slavery originated largely in the Islamic empires of the Middle East, and the principal source of slaves was mainly from the western and central Sudan regions via overland and coastal routes throughout Africa.[33] The intervention of the Portuguese and other Europeans in the African slave trade not only increased significantly the demand for slaves but also shifted trade routes to the Atlantic coast of West Africa. Between 1500 and 1810 Europeans accounted for around 10 million African slaves, almost all taken from the Atlantic coast and shipped to the New World.[34]

Thus, with the rise of the Western European states and their conquest and exploitation of Global Frontiers, a new "Atlantic economy" emerged to supplant the old Europe–Islamic world–Africa trade in raw materials, manufactures and slaves. From 1500 to 1860, growth in the Atlantic economy was based on a "triangular" pattern of trade (see Figure 1.5).[35]

One "side" of the triangular trade involved the European states importing sugar, cotton, tobacco and other valuable raw materials from their colonies and former colonies in North and South America. The European states, particularly Great Britain, then exported manufactures and processed raw materials (e.g.,

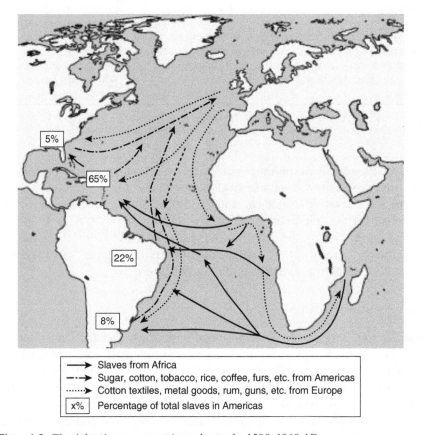

Figure 1.5   The Atlantic economy triangular trade, 1500–1860 AD

Source: Edward B. Barbier (2011) *Scarcity and Frontiers: How Economies Have Developed Through Natural Resource Exploitation*. Cambridge UK and New York: Cambridge University Press, figure 6.1.

cotton textiles, construction materials, metal goods, refined white sugar and rum) back to the Americas.

A second "side" consisted of the European states also exporting manufactures (and gold) to Africa, in exchange for slaves. However, instead of bringing the slaves to Europe they were instead shipped to the plantations in the Americas where they became the principal labor force for the production of the key raw materials exported from the New World. This was the third "side" of the triangular trade.

The Atlantic economy triangular trade continued for centuries, until abolition of the slave trade by European states and the United States by the mid-19th century. The key feature was the "peculiar institution" of slavery, which was essential to the Atlantic economy. Or, as Patrick O'Brien and Stanley Engerman succinctly put it: "The development of an Atlantic Economy is impossible to imagine without slavery and the slave trade."[36]

A major consequence of the stark division of labor of the Atlantic economy is that it led to far-reaching changes in the composition of economic wealth and the process of wealth creation in the three different regions involved in the triangular trade – the Americas, Africa and Europe.

Because in the New World virtually all the key export commodities were produced by slave labor, this form of labor became essential to the appropriation and use of the natural resources of tropical Latin America and the Southern United States. Thus, the key economic assets for these regions consisted of land, natural resources and slaves. Wealth creation and accumulation of these assets were spurred on by production that yielded key export commodities of gold, sugar, coffee, cotton, tobacco and rice demanded by Europe and the rest of the world.

For Africa, the main export commodity was people. In effect, the human capital of Africa was itself exported, with devastating consequences for the region. Given that the most desirable slaves captured or procured were young men and women in prime health and reproductive condition, the slave trade had long-lasting demographic and economic effects. The sheer demographic impact of the slave trade alone was considerable; estimates suggest that the slave trade from 1500 to 1860 accounted for up to one fifth of the African population at the beginning of the era.[37] In addition, the disruptive impacts of continual violence, war and armed raids, on the African societies targeted by the slave trade led to ethnic fragmentation, the ability of households and communities to accumulate surpluses, savings and investments, and reduced the provision of public goods, such as education, health facilities, access to water, and transportation infrastructure, all of which are important for long-term economic development.[38]

In contrast, in Europe and especially Great Britain, the key export commodities were manufactures. As Ron Findlay states, "There is therefore little doubt that British growth in the 18th century was 'export-led' and that, among exports, manufactured goods to the New World and re-export of colonial produce from the New World led the way."[39] Commercial expansion of the Atlantic economy in the 18th and early 19th centuries generated substantial export opportunities for British manufactures. Moreover, the most strategically important industries to Britain – with the exception of coal – were highly dependent on overseas exports. For example, by 1801, cotton textiles were selling 62% of their output overseas, wool textiles 35% and iron 24%.[40] The Atlantic economy triangular trade also contributed to Western European economic growth from 1500 to 1850 indirectly – especially in Great Britain and the Netherlands – by enriching and strengthening commercial interests and "merchant groups" outside of the monarchy, including overseas merchants, slave traders and various colonial planters. As these commercial groups gained in wealth and political influence, they were able to demand and obtain significant institutional reforms and property rights that in turn provided the incentives to undertake investments leading to sustained economic growth.[41]

The human capital of slaves was an important and very large component of the national wealth of slave-owning societies in the New World. Thomas Piketty estimates that the total market value of slaves represented nearly a year and a half of US national income in the late 18th century and the first half of the 19th century, which is roughly equal to the total value of farmland. In the American South, the total value of slaves ranged between two and a half and three years of national income, so that the combined value of farmland and slaves exceeded four years of national income.[42]

The economic development of the United States, and especially New England, also benefited substantially from its participation in the Atlantic triangular trade. The trade was critical to the development of New England's maritime trade and shipping, which in turn laid the foundation for industrial development in the region.[43] Given New England's importance in the industrialization of the US economy in the 19th century as well as to specialization and trade among three key regions in the economy – the industrialized northeast, the cotton-producing south and the food-producing mid-west – the early modern development of New England through its Atlantic commercial relationships was pivotal to the eventual take-off of the modern US economy.[44] In addition, the regional specialization of the US economy after the Civil War accelerated the process of western frontier expansion, which in turn was vital to the emergence of the United States as a successful resource-based economy in the late 19th and early 20th centuries.

However, the advent of the Industrial Revolution beginning in the mid-18th century changed the structural dependence of an economy on its agricultural land base. As Great Britain and other Western economies industrialized throughout the 19th century, they began accumulating the reproducible assets associated with a developing manufacturing capacity, such as factories, stores, office and government buildings, railroad tracks, public roads, sewage installations, energy infrastructure, machinery, vehicles and stock inventories. These reproducible assets soon overtook agricultural land as the major component of the wealth of the advanced economies. In addition, as economies industrialized, they developed the financial institutions and assets required for facilitating large-scale capital investments in industries and modern economies. Thus, by the 20th century, wealth in the richest economies was no longer closely associated with agricultural land and natural resource endowments, and reproducible capital and financial assets became the most important sources of the national wealth of an economy.[45] This is the structure of wealth that all modern economies emulate today.

Conclusion

The role of wealth accumulation, and in fact, what constitutes wealth has evolved over the past 10,000 years. These changes are important for understanding how we view the relationship between nature and wealth today.

The first major development was the rise of agriculture. For thousands of years, with agriculture as the dominant economic activity, humans associated affluence with the accumulation of fertile land and abundant natural resources. In other words, basic natural resource assets – or *natural capital* – were the main sources of economic wealth for both individuals and human societies.

The second major development was the emergence of the world economy, from 1000 to 1500, followed by the rise of Western European economies over the next few centuries through trade, colonization and settlement of global frontiers. National wealth became associated with the accumulation of gold and silver reserves either directly through acquiring new mines overseas or indirectly through creating trade surpluses. Yet, the dominant form of economic wealth remained natural capital – fertile land and natural resources.

The third major development was the rise of the Atlantic Economy triangular trade, which led to a distinct division of labor among participating regions and countries. This in turn changed the composition and accumulation of wealth. Along with natural resources and land, slaves comprised much of the national wealth of slave-owning societies in the New World. But for Great Britain, and later in the rest of Europe and the United States, the triangular trade was a spur for manufacturing exports. Although the development of the Atlantic Economy triangular trade preceded the advent of the Industrial Revolution, both ensured that industrialization was the principal means for economic take-off into sustained wealth creation. What is more, accumulating the reproducible assets associated with a developing manufacturing capacity, such as factories, stores, buildings, machinery and equipment, soon overtook agricultural land and natural resources as the major component of economic wealth of industrializing countries.

In the next chapter, we will explore further how the importance of natural capital as a form of economic wealth has changed, especially since the Industrial Revolution, and what this means for today's economies.

2
Natural Capital and Economic Development

Introduction

The purpose of this chapter is to introduce the concept of natural capital, and to explain in more detail its role in modern economic development.

As we saw in the previous chapter, before the Industrial Revolution, exploiting new sources of land and natural resources was fundamental to successful economic development. Obtaining more natural capital became an important objective of conquering and occupying new lands, monopolizing trade links, and colonizing and populating other regions of the world. However, over the course of the Industrial Revolution and especially over the last century, supplies of strategic raw material, mineral and energy commodities have become cheaply available through global trade. Technological applications to land, fisheries, forests and other natural resource endowments have also become sufficiently productive and routine that the common perception is that human ingenuity and innovations can overcome most, if not all, resource scarcity problems.[1]

In addition, since the Industrial Revolution, the composition of *natural capital* that is valuable for production has broadened to include not just agricultural land, fisheries and forests but also industrially important fossil fuels and minerals.[2] As a result of the transport revolution, however, economies no longer have to accumulate their own sources of natural wealth or to possess an abundant endowment of natural resources. Since World War II, increased trade and globalization has resulted in declining trade barriers and transport costs, fostered global integration of commodity markets, and severed the direct link between natural resource wealth and the development of domestic industrial capacity. Or, as the economic historian Gavin Wright maintains, in today's world economy, "there is no iron law associating natural resource abundance with national industrial strength".[3]

The consequence is that natural capital is essential to modern economic development. Yet, at the same time, a large share of natural capital to total economic wealth is a key indicator of "underdevelopment". For example, in the modern world economy, a low-income country will typically have 41% of its wealth consist of natural capital, a lower-middle-income country 39% and an upper-middle-income country 25%. But, for a high-income economy, natural capital comprises only 12% of its economic wealth.[4]

To understand this shift in the relationship between natural capital and economic development, this chapter first explores how the Industrial Revolution radically changed our conception of economic wealth. We then explore the importance of the rise of finance and the prominence of financial capital in the modern economy. Finally, we discuss the role of natural capital in modern economic development.

Industrial Revolution: redefining wealth

Much has been written about the causes and consequences of the Industrial Revolution. Here, we will focus mainly on how the profound economic structural transformation caused by industrialization changed the composition of capital and thus redefined wealth. This redefinition of wealth has important implications as to how we view nature, and especially natural and ecological capital (see Figure 1.1).

In essence, the Industrial Revolution changed the balance sheet of national wealth in favor of financial capital. Agricultural land also declined in importance compared to manufactured, or reproducible, capital (e.g., roads, buildings, machinery, factories, etc.). In addition, reproducible and human capital became more important sources of economic wealth compared to natural capital. This latter outcome is rather ironic, given that it was the harnessing of a new source of natural capital – fossil fuels – that made the Industrial Revolution possible.[5]

There are several "stylized facts" concerning the Industrial Revolution that are relevant to how it changed economic wealth and capital.

First, as discussed in Chapter 1, up until the mid-18th century, the economic wealth of Western Europe and the other great economic powers in Asia and the Near East was roughly equal. This is reflected not only in the standard indicators of regional economic performance but also in the fact that all economic powers of the time, Western Europe, China, the Ottoman and Mughal Empires and Russia, had access to overseas markets, trade and commerce and indeed monopolized large portions of the world trading economy (see Figure 1.4).

Second, the early modern period up to the 18th century was not an era of continuous economic growth which culminated gradually with industrialization in Western Europe. Instead, industrialization in Europe represented a monumental transformation from an "advanced organic economy" dependent on land and traditional energy sources, such as water, wind, animal and manpower, to a mineral-based economy, capable of achieving unprecedented levels of sustained growth in manufactures and agriculture through exploiting the new and relatively abundant fossil fuel energy resources.[6] Or, as the historian David Landes has succinctly put it, this remarkable transition to an industrialized economy in Europe, starting with Britain in the mid-18th century, amounted to *"buildup* – the accumulation of knowledge and knowhow; and *breakthrough* – reaching and passing thresholds".[7]

Third, an important consequence of the transition to and spread of industrialization was that, by the late 19th century, the world had entered into a new age, the *global fossil fuel era*.[8] The rapid exploitation of these new energy sources by industrializing economies, starting with coal then followed by oil and natural gas, led to two important global energy trends. First, as indicated in Figure 2.1, world energy consumption began growing exponentially, and second, energy consumption by fuel type changed dramatically. Vaclav Smil has shown that biomass sources, i.e., fuelwood, charcoal and crop residues, comprised around 80% of world energy consumption in 1800. However, during the 19th century industrialization in major economies led to the rapid spread

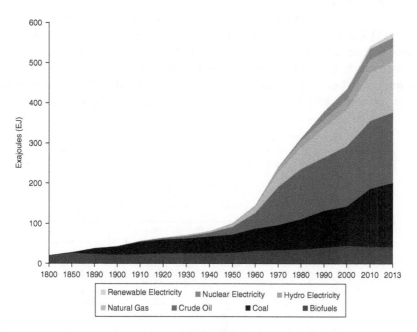

Figure 2.1   Global energy consumption, 1800–2013

Notes: EJ = exajoules, or 10^{18} joules. 1 EJ is approximately 23.885 million metric tonnes of oil equivalent (Mtoe). Renewable electricity is based on gross generation from wind, geothermal, solar, biomass and waste. 2008 biofuels estimate used as proxy for 2010 and 2013.

Source: For 1800–1960, Vaclav Smil (2010) *Energy Transitions: History, Requirements, Prospects*. Santa Barbara, CA: Praeger. For 1970–2013, BP Statistical Review of World Energy June 2014, http://www.bp.com/statisticalreview, except biofuels estimate which is from Smil (2010), *op. cit*.

of coal consumption and the replacement of charcoal for indoor heating and metallurgy by coal, coke and gas. By 1900, fossil fuels had surpassed biomass in global energy consumption. In the early 20th century, gas and oil use, for heating, electricity generation and transportation, began their meteoric rise, with oil supplanting coal as the dominant fuel by the early 1960s.[9]

Innovation and structural change

These stylized facts of the Industrial Revolution reflect that it represented a massive shift in the innovation, productivity and structure of economies. However, these changes did not happen all at once over the past 250 years, but can be discerned by two distinct "phases" of innovations that in turn lead to long-lasting impacts on global economic productivity. Figure 2.2 summarizes these key innovation, productivity and energy timelines of the two phases of the Industrial Revolution. Although many economies benefited from these changes, each phase is also associated with the emergence of a leading world economic power.[10]

For example, the first phase of the Industrial Revolution occurred from 1750–1830, and centered on key inventions during this period, such as the steam engine, cotton spinning, railroads and steamships (see Figure 2.2). Such innovations helped propel Great Britain to global economic and political dominance, and they had lasting economic impacts on all industrializing economies up until 1900. The second phase of the Industrial Revolution centered

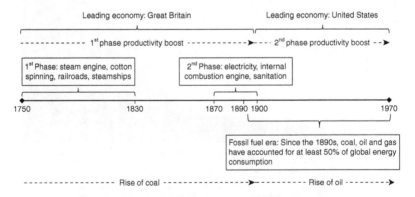

Figure 2.2   Key timelines of the Industrial Revolution, 1750–1970

Note: The first phase of key innovations of the Industrial Revolution occurred from 1750 to 1830, and centered on steam power and coal. They led to the global economic dominance of Great Britain and boosted the productivity of all industrializing nations that followed Britain's example until 1900. The second phase of innovations of the Industrial Revolution were from 1870 to 1900, and were based largely on electricity and the internal combustion engine – made possible by the new hydrocarbons oil and gas, along with coal. These innovations led to the economic rise of the United States, which became the model for 20th century industrialization and boosted global productivity until the 1970s.

on key innovations from 1870–1900, such as electricity, the internal combustion engine, water and sanitation systems, refrigerated transport, and oil and gas refining. These innovations spurred considerable industrial, transport and urban developments that boosted productivity until the 1970s, and led to the economic rise and worldwide dominance of the United States.

As discussed previously, these two phases of the Industrial Revolution also led to the emergence of the global fossil fuel age, which began in the 1890s when coal, oil and natural gas first accounted for more than half of energy consumption worldwide (see Figures 2.1 and 2.2). However, each phase of innovation and its boost to productivity over subsequent decades also fostered a leading energy resource. For example, the industrial and transport innovations of 1750–1830 were based largely on steam power, and led to the rise of coal use. The innovations from 1870–1900 and the expansion of modern industries and transport networks over the next 70 years propelled oil to be the major global fuel, with natural gas also emerging as a significant energy source in more recent decades (see Figure 2.1).

Although not shown in Figure 2.2, there were also a series of pre-1750 innovations that gave Great Britain the know-how and capacity to exploit its cheap and available sources of coal for heat, steam power and blast furnaces. That is, the 1st phase of Industrial Revolution innovations over 1750 to 1830 arose through a long process of continuing and self-sustaining inventions in Western Europe that had started evolving throughout the 18th century, and possibly as far back as the late Middle Ages.[11] This wide-ranging Western lead in technology not only made mining and transporting coal possible but also the industrial processes that allowed its concentrated use in all sectors of the economy – agriculture, manufacturing and transport. Nevertheless, the two phases of innovations beginning in 1750, and the subsequent structural economic transformation over the next 250 years, are the lasting legacy of the Industrial Revolution.

To understand fully the implications of the Industrial Revolution for the role of nature in economic wealth, it is worth highlighting the major structural changes that occurred with each innovation phase. We begin first with the changes from the first phase, which affected natural resource use up to the early 20th century, and then the major impacts on natural resource use from the second phase.

Changes in natural resource use from the 1st phase

British innovations in the late 18th and early 19th centuries were spurred by technical inventions in manufacturing processes, such as spinning and weaving in the cotton textile industry and metallurgy in iron production. But the new global wave of industrialization that spread from Britain to other economies from the mid-19th century onwards benefited from rapidly evolving industrial and transport technologies based on the steam engine. Steam technology enabled mechanization of manufacturing processes, facilitated pumping and mining innovations, and fostered innovations in railroads and steamships. Thus, by the late 19th century, Great Britain, Western Europe and the world's newly emerging industrialized regions had become reliant on a new energy source: coal.[12]

Cheap and more accessible fossil fuel energy also sparked a dramatic fall in the costs of shipping bulk raw material goods across oceans and continents.[13] Since 1500, gradual improvements in transportation technologies and falling freight costs allowed European maritime countries to dominate world trade and monopolize high-valued food, raw material and other precious commodities from client regions and overseas colonies. For example, Ron Findlay and Kevin O'Rourke note that "throughout the sixteenth and early seventeenth centuries, pepper, other spices, and indigo constituted the bulk of Portuguese imports from Asia, while in the eighteenth century imports of tea and coffee became important in both the Dutch and English cases. Indeed, as late as the middle of the eighteenth century a small number of commodities that were clearly non-competing (pepper, tea, coffee, spices, sugar, and tobacco) accounted for 57.6% of European imports from the Americas and Asia." But the decline in freight costs in the second-half of the 19th century not only increased the volume of bulk commodity trade, it also increased the range of agricultural and raw materials shipped globally: "Over the course of the nineteenth century, trans-oceanic trade in bulk commodities such as grains, metals, and textiles became more and more common."[14]

The expansion and development of railways also led to the "opening up" of new lands for agricultural development. For example, length of railways worldwide grew from 8,000 kilometers (km) in the 1840s to in excess of 1 million km by 1914.[15] But the most impressive railway development occurred in regions outside of Europe from the mid-19th century onwards. Although railway lines continued to expand in the United Kingdom and other Western European countries, the growth of lines in the developing regions was much more extensive. Even countries in Africa which had no railways in 1870, such as Ghana, Morocco, South Africa and Tunisia, had developed extensive transport systems by the start of World War I. Major Great Frontier regions, such as Argentina, Australia and the United States, went from only partial coverage of all their territory by railway lines in the mid-19th century to a continent-wide rail network system by 1914.[16]

The world transport and trade boom of the late 19th century therefore translated into a primary product export boom, mainly from periphery regions and colonies to industrialized Western Europe. Almost two-thirds of world exports consisted of primary products. Food accounted for 29% of world exports, agricultural raw materials 21% and minerals 14%.[17]

Transport costs were an important factor why the primary product trade boom was dominated by food and agricultural raw materials. Despite the fall in freight costs, it was still economical to transport only a handful of high-value minerals, such as silver, gold, guano nitrates, tin, copper and diamonds, over long distances. The more important strategic minerals and fossil fuels for industrial production, such as iron ore and coal, were too expensive to ship across oceans. For example, by 1910 it was economically feasible to send coal from Britain to industrializing northern Italy, but the freight cost was over half the price of coal.[18] To transport coal from the United States or Australia to Europe was still prohibitively expensive by World War I. Thus, coal, iron ore and other industrial minerals and fossil fuels remained too costly to trade internationally over long distances or across oceans.[19] As a result, Great Britain and Western Europe imported only negligible amounts of minerals and fossil fuels from the rest of the world.[20]

In comparison, the agricultural and raw material trade boom during the late 19th and early 20th centuries fostered an unprecedented expansion of cropland across many regions of the world. As the economic historian Knick Harley has shown, the classic example of the relationship between international commodity price booms, railroad construction and frontier cropland expansion in the late 19th century was the extension of wheat cultivation across the western United States. Harley demonstrates that high export prices for wheat not only stimulated railroad construction and crop cultivation in the west, but, in turn, settlement by more farmers driven by higher wheat prices and cheaper transportation to extend the "wheat frontier".[21] However, such an expansion was not confined to temperate frontiers but occurred in the many tropical regions as well, given the growing global demand for agricultural and raw material products from all over the world.[22]

Table 2.1 illustrates the land use trends for different world regions from 1700 up until just before World War I.[23] In all regions, cropland expansion from 1700 to 1910 occurred mainly at the expense of forest land as well as savannah and grassland. Although global cropland area increased by over 50% in the 18th century, it nearly doubled in the 19th century. But cropland expansion clearly accelerated from 1870 to 1910, with the majority occurring in those regions with abundant land for conversion to agriculture, such as Australia and New Zealand, Latin America and North America. In contrast, only modest cropland expansion occurred in Europe over this period, because the availability of new land to cultivate was limited. Similarly, by 1870 the three largest and most populous countries in Asia – China, Java (Indonesia) and India – had limited land to expand cultivation further, despite growing population pressures. Instead, cropland expansion took place in smaller tropical Asian countries where land was available, such as Burma (Myanmar), Ceylon (Sri Lanka), Malaya (Malaysia) and Thailand. Cropland expansion in Africa increased

Table 2.1 Land use trends for selected regions, 1700–1910

Region	Vegetation cover	Area (1000 ha)				Percentage change over		
		1700	1800	1870	1910	1700–1800	1800–1870	1870–1910
World	Cropland	407,154	683,513	940,491	1,240,791	67.9%	37.6%	31.9%
	Forest land	5,391,113	5,205,291	5,034,956	4,886,363	-3.4%	-3.3%	-3.0%
	Savannah and grassland	3,218,723	3,151,583	3,088,202	2,961,379	-2.1%	-2.0%	-4.1%
Africa	Cropland	79,325	95,116	100,371	107,655	19.9%	5.5%	7.3%
	Forest land	532,708	528,688	527,494	525,946	-0.8%	-0.2%	-0.3%
	Savannah and grassland	1,124,871	1,114,868	1,111,825	1,107,773	-0.9%	-0.3%	-0.4%
Asia	Cropland	198,537	305,211	410,729	492,099	53.7%	34.6%	19.8%
	Forest land	960,142	890,067	819,198	765,555	-7.3%	-8.0%	-6.5%
	Savannah and grassland	608,425	584,836	565,192	549,753	-3.9%	-3.4%	-2.7%
Australia & New Zealand	Cropland	2,686	3,020	3,352	8,254	12.4%	11.0%	146.2%
	Forest land	36,330	36,304	36,319	35,990	-0.1%	0.0%	-0.9%
	Savannah and grassland	313,552	313,377	313,269	310,402	-0.1%	0.0%	-0.9%
Europe	Cropland	116,133	222,993	305,631	349,926	92.0%	37.1%	14.5%
	Forest land	1,587,316	1,515,357	1,460,761	1,434,790	-4.5%	-3.6%	-1.8%
	Savannah and grassland	271,913	244,210	221,450	204,847	-10.2%	-9.3%	-7.5%
Latin America & Caribbean	Cropland	7,388	15,990	23,778	55,530	116.4%	48.7%	133.5%
	Forest land	1,135,867	1,131,415	1,127,117	1,115,026	-0.4%	-0.4%	-1.1%
	Savannah and grassland	567,414	564,539	562,311	547,817	-0.5%	-0.4%	-2.6%
North America	Cropland	3,021	41,108	96,549	227,117	1260.7%	134.9%	135.2%
	Forest land	1,104,923	1,069,643	1,030,256	975,359	-3.2%	-3.7%	-5.3%
	Savannah and grassland	327,334	324,540	308,942	235,588	-0.9%	-4.8%	-23.7%

Source: N. Ramankutty and Jonathon A. Foley (1999) "Estimating Historical Changes in Global Land Cover: Croplands from 1700 to 1992", Global Biogeochemical Cycles, 13: 997–1027. Data downloaded from Global Land Use Database, Center for Sustainability and the Global Environment (SAGE), Nelson Institute for Environmental Studies, University of Wisconsin, www.sage.wisc.edu

modestly during the Golden Age, but this expansion was limited to a few select regions that had abundant land, such as Egypt, South Africa and the Gold Coast (Ghana).

To summarize, the first phase of innovations during the Industrial Revolution, from 1750 to 1830, had a profound impact on global natural resource use up to the beginning of the 20th century. It was during this period that the global fossil fuel era began, and the predominant energy source was coal. However, minerals and fossil fuels were too costly to transport over long distances or across oceans, and thus domestic sources of these natural resources became the most important sources of natural capital for the growing wealth of industrializing nations. In contrast, the transport and trade boom in food and raw materials ended the importance of agricultural land as a form of economic wealth.

Changes in natural resource use from the 2nd phase

The second phase of innovations of the Industrial Revolution occurred during 1870 to 1900, and included electricity, the internal combustion engine and improved sanitation (see Figure 2.2). These innovations fostered other industrial and transport advances in the 20th century, which had lasting global economic impacts until the 1970s. Throughout this period, the United States was the lead economy, and it became the model for industrial development worldwide that other economies sought to emulate. Thus, to illustrate the key changes in natural resource use from the second phase, we will focus mainly on the structural changes that occurred from 1870 onwards in the United States.

In the late 19th and early 20th centuries, the United States experienced the most extensive territorial and frontier land expansion of any country or region in the world. For example, over 40% of the increased cropland area that occurred outside of Western Europe from 1870 to 1910 took place in the United States.[24] Yet this extraordinarily rapid cropland expansion was not the only remarkable feature of US economic development over this period. In the mid-19th century, the US economy was still predominantly dependent on its land wealth, but by World War I, its national wealth was firmly rooted in its reproducible capital and financial assets.[25] In just over half a century, the United States was transformed from one of several emerging manufacturing nations to the leading global industrial power, surpassing even the United Kingdom.[26]

However, neither cropland expansion nor the development of agriculturally related industries was responsible for the phenomenal rise of the United States as a global industrial power. Instead, the economic ascendency of the US was attributable to exploitation of its vast energy and mineral wealth, which fostered the expansion of its resource-based manufacturing exports, notably from the iron and steel industry, copper manufactures and refined mineral oil.[27] Although for most of the 19th century the United States exploited its comparative advantage in agriculture and exported mainly agricultural goods, such as raw cotton, grains and animal products, by 1890 manufactured goods accounted for 20% of US exports, 35% by 1900, and nearly 50% by 1913.[28] In addition, from 1880 to 1920, the intensity of US manufacturing exports in terms of non-renewable resources grew both absolutely and relative to the resource-intensity of imports.[29]

Several unique factors enabled the US to exploit rapidly its abundant "mineral frontier" for industrialization. First, by virtue of its vast resources, the United States soon became the global leader in mineral and fossil fuel production. Second, with its growing population and industries, it was also one of the world's largest consumer and intermediate goods markets. Third, high international transport costs and tariff barriers made foreign imports of manufactures into the United States prohibitively expensive; in contrast, low-cost domestic transportation meant that US industries could deliver their manufactures cheaply to consumers all over the United States. US industries also had exclusive access to domestically produced natural resource inputs, because high transport costs and distance from Europe discouraged exporting extracted mineral and energy resources from the United States to industrialized Europe. Finally, because US industries were dependent on the vast quantities of resources that were available domestically, investment in basic technologies for extracting and processing natural resources was very profitable.[30] The result of these factors was that the US became a naturally protected free trade area for internal commerce and industrial expansion that benefited from "economic distance" from the rest of the world. By the end of the 19th century, US resource-based manufactures became sufficiently cheap to produce that they could be exported to foreign markets, especially as international shipping costs had fallen significantly. As summarized by the economic historian Douglas Irwin, "resource abundance formed the basis for the US export success around the turn of the century directly, by lowering the prices of key material inputs in a way that turned to the domestic advantage because those materials were not exported, and indirectly, by translating into higher elasticity of final goods supply that enabled US exporters to capture a larger share of the international market."[31]

During the first half of the 20th century, agriculture still remained an important sector in the US economy. Throughout the many economic disruptions from 1910 to 1950 – two world wars, the Dust Bowl and the Great Depression – US agriculture continued to be highly commercialized and productive. By the 1930s, the degree of "commercialization" of US agriculture – the share of marketed to total output – reached 87%, the highest rate in the world, and by the early 1950s, 94% of US agriculture was fully commercialized.[32] Cheap fossil fuel energy made other inputs, notably fertilizer, machines and even irrigation water, inexpensive substitutes for land, draught animals and labor. Falling transportation costs and the expanding road and rail networks facilitated the rapid transport of both farming inputs and outputs around the country. Total factor productivity of agriculture in the United States grew even faster from 1910 to 1938 than it did from 1870 to 1910.[33] As a result, US agriculture value added rose from US$7.7 billion in 1910 to US$32.8 billion by 1950.[34]

However, despite becoming more productive, increasingly energy-intensive and fully commercialized, US agriculture would never regain its economic prominence. Around the turn of the 20th century, agriculture still accounted for about one quarter of US gross domestic product (GDP). But by 1925 its contribution to GDP had halved to 12%, and by 1950, agriculture's share had fallen to 7%.[35] The reason, of course, was that the improvements in agricultural productivity and commercial development were more than matched by the phenomenal resource-based industrialization that was the main dynamic driving force behind the US economy. In turn, rapid industrialization was facilitated by the exponential growth in fossil fuel energy use, largely attributable to three "prime movers" that radically altered productive capacities and industrial energy efficiency in the economy: electricity generation, the internal combustion engine and the development of the petroleum-based chemical industry.

The first three decades of the 20th century saw a remarkable transition in the United States from firm-generated steam power to electrical energy purchased from central power stations. In 1902, just over 2.5 billion kilowatt-hours was generated in central electric power stations, but by 1929 central generating stations produced 91 billion kilowatt-hours. Because electricity generation was for residential, commercial and industrial use, its impact on the productivity of US manufacturing was pervasive.[36] The rapid transition to centrally generated electricity during the first half of the 20th century was made possible by the abundant and cheap fossil fuel supplies in the United States. Centralization of electricity generation and expansion of the grid network led, in turn, to an exponential growth in energy use by US firms and households in less than three decades. In 1910, 25% of factories used electric power, but by 1930, 75% of factories used electricity; similarly, the use of electric lighting by urban households increased from 33% in 1909 to 96% by 1939.[37]

The abundant US supplies of petroleum also led to the development of the internal combustion engine, the automobile and the use of roads. As with electrification, the development of the automobile and a national road network helped transform the entire US economy.[38] From the 1920s onward, the parallel development of the aircraft industry and air transport across the United States spurred further economic integration through increasing the mobility of people, cargo and even the mail. By 1950, total air traffic in the United States reached a billion miles, which for the first time equaled total railroad mileage in the country.[39] The development of the petroleum industry in the United States in the 1920s and 1930s led to the rise of the economically important petro-chemical industry. The latter industry and its products, including plastics, oils and resins, chemical fertilizers and synthetic rubber, would in turn have important linkages to the development of other sectors of the economy, including as we have seen, the development of the automobile and aircraft industries and the transformation of US agriculture.[40]

As the US economy became more energy-intensive during the 20th century, it also increased its use of raw materials, such as industrial minerals, metals, agricultural and wood products, non-renewable organics and crushed stone, sand and gravel. In a modern economy, material and energy use is inexorably linked. For example, the construction and maintenance of paved roads for automobiles and other motorized transport requires more crushed stone, sand and gravel, and the demand for these road-building materials requires additional freight transport. Increased electrification allows improvement in mining and extractive technologies, and the processing of the resulting minerals and ores, as well as the creation of improved alloys, entail more energy use.[41] As a consequence, non-fuel material use in the US economy also increased exponentially throughout the 20th century (see Figure 2.3A). In 1900, on a per-weight basis, the US economy used 161 million tonnes of non-fuel materials; by 1950, this material use had increased to well over 500 million tonnes, and by 2000 nearly 3,500 million tonnes. However, the composition of materials employed in the economy changed considerably over this period (see Figure 2.3B). In 1900, about 41% of total material use came from renewable resources, such as agricultural, fishery, forestry and wildlife products. But by 1950, the share of renewable resources had declined to just 10% of overall material use. Crushed stone, sand and gravel for road building and maintenance accounted for 62% of material use, industrial minerals for 17%, metals 8% and non-renewable organics 4%. In 2000, materials from renewable resources accounted for just 5% of material consumption in the US economy, and non-renewables 95%.[42]

As remarked by Nelson and Wright, "the special US conditions of cheap resources, high wage rates, and large markets, could be understood to induce the high labor productivity, large-scale, capital-intensive production methods that became known as characteristically American."[43] This pattern of material and energy use in the US became the model for global industrialization development after World War II. In the post-war era, all modern economies worldwide became entirely dependent on fossil fuel energy use and non-renewable material use. However, there was an important difference between the source of non-renewable resource use before and after the war. As we noted previously, before World War II, international transportation costs for minerals and fossil fuels were extremely expensive, and thus countries with abundant domestic sources of these natural resources – most notably the US – had a

A Material use

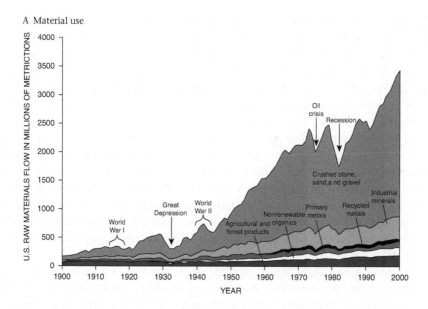

B Renewable vs. non-renewable material use

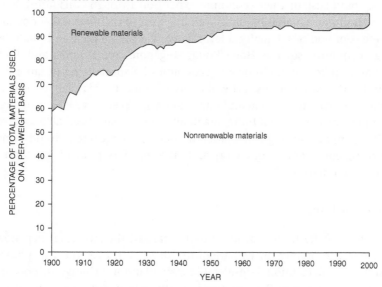

Figure 2.3 Long-run material use in the US economy, 1900–2000

Source: Grecia Matos and Lorie A. Wagner (1998) "Consumption of Materials in the United States, 1900–1995", *Annual Review of Energy and the Environment*, 23: 107–122; and Lorie A. Wagner (2002) *Materials in the Economy – Material Flows, Scarcity, and the Environment*. US Geological Survey Circular 1221, US Department of the Interior, US Geological Survey, Denver, CO.

"geographic" comparative advantage in resource-based industrialization. In contrast, by 1950, falling world transport rates meant that all natural resources, including fossil fuels, ores and metals became fully tradable on global markets. Countries were no longer limited by their natural resource endowments; instead, world trade in all types of raw material, energy and mineral commodities allowed any economy to industrialize through supplementing its own domestic supplies of these commodities.

As lower transport costs and trade barriers in the post-war era fostered the global integration of commodity markets, the direct link between natural resource wealth and the development of domestic industrial capacity was severed. As summarized by Gavin Wright, "the unification of world commodity markets (through transportation cost reductions and elimination of trade barriers) has largely cut the link between domestic resources and domestic industries...To a degree, natural resources have become commodities rather than part of the 'factor endowment' of individual countries."[44]

In addition, the globalization of commodity markets and trade has allowed all economies to have better and cheaper access to natural resources than reliance on just their own endowments would allow. The result is that high-income economies, such as the United States, Western Europe, Japan and others, could sustain their economic expansion through consuming energy, mineral and raw material products well in excess of their natural endowments of these commodities. Equally, a few relatively resource-poor and small developing economies, such as Hong Kong, Singapore, South Korea and Taiwan, could also emerge as high-income economies by specializing in labor-intensive industrialization for export while relying almost exclusively on imported natural resource inputs, food and raw materials.[45] Even large emerging market economies, such as China, India, Brazil and Russia, have been able to develop rapidly by supplementing exploitation of their own large resource endowments with rising consumption of energy and other primary products purchased in international markets.[46]

Decline of land

The advent of the Industrial Revolution changed the structural dependence of a modern economy on its agricultural base. Yet, over the two phases of the Industrial Revolution, considerable global land use change still occurred. As indicated in Figure 2.4, for the past three hundred years, global forest and woodland area has declined by about 10 million km^2 as cropland area has expanded dramatically.[47] Since 1950, the pace of global land conversion has shown little signs of abating. However, underlying these global trends are significant differences in land use changes in developed and developing countries.

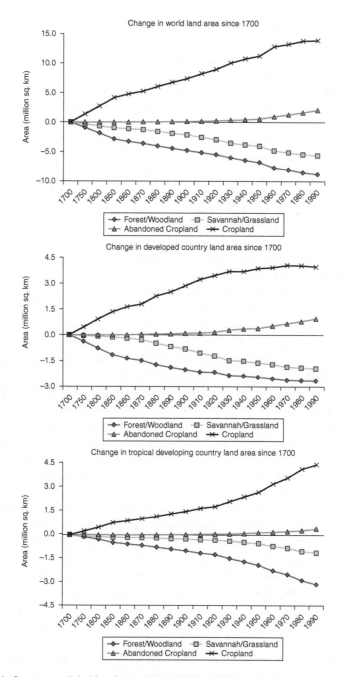

Figure 2.4 Long-run global land use change, 1700–1990

Source: N. Ramankutty and Jonathon A. Foley (1999) "Estimating historical changes in global land cover: Croplands from 1700 to 1992", *Global Biogeochemical Cycles*, 13: 997–1027. Data downloaded from Global Land Use Database, Center for Sustainability and the Global Environment (SAGE), Nelson Institute for Environmental Studies, University of Wisconsin, www.sage.wisc.edu

For example, as indicated in Figure 2.4, for most of Western Europe, North America and the Pacific developed countries (e.g., Australia, Japan and New Zealand), starting in the early 20th century, cropland area slowed its growth, and eventually stabilized and then declined slightly by the late 20th century. Throughout the 20th century, abandoned cropland increased and then rose quickly in the latter decades. As a result, the decline of forest and woodland has halted in developed countries in aggregate, and since 1990, total forest area has increased.[48] Not only has primary forest area recovered but the growth in plantations has also been strong.

In recent years, there have been signs of forest recovery in some low and middle-income nations, notably Bangladesh, China, Costa Rica, Dominican Republic, India, Morocco and Vietnam.[49] But on the whole, the long-run land use change for tropical developing countries is a continuing and rapid decline in forest area (see Figures 2.4 and 2.5). Over the past 50 years, agricultural land area in the tropics has still been expanding, and consequently, forest area declining (see Figure 2.5). More problematic for the major developing regions of Africa, Asia and Latin America is that the demand for new land required for future crop production growth shows little sign of abating in the near future. Feeding a growing world population is expected to require an additional 3 to 5 million hectares (ha) of new cropland each year from now until 2030, which could contribute to additional clearing of 150 to 300 million ha in total area of natural forests.[50]

Thus, most developing economies, especially those in tropical regions, are continuing a long-run trend of converting primary forest to agriculture. In contrast, in developed countries, forest land has been increasing and agricultural land declining. It is either being abandoned, reverted to forest or replanted with timber stands and tree crops, or converted for urban and residential use. The wealth of the richest countries of the world no longer depends on accumulating agricultural land.

This transition in land use is a direct consequence of the Industrial Revolution, which ensured that, as an economy industrialized and modernized, agricultural land became less vital as a source of national wealth. For example, as shown in Figure 2.6, the share of agricultural land in national wealth has declined dramatically since the late 17th century for Great Britain, the United States, Japan and six other major Western European economies. Prior to industrialization, agricultural land accounted for 35–50% of national wealth in these economies. However, with industrialization, they began accumulating the reproducible assets associated with a developing manufacturing capacity, such as factories, office and government buildings, railroad tracks, public roads, sewage installations, energy infrastructure, machinery, vehicles and stock inventories. These reproducible assets soon overtook agricultural land as the major component of the national wealth of the advanced economies. In addition, as economies

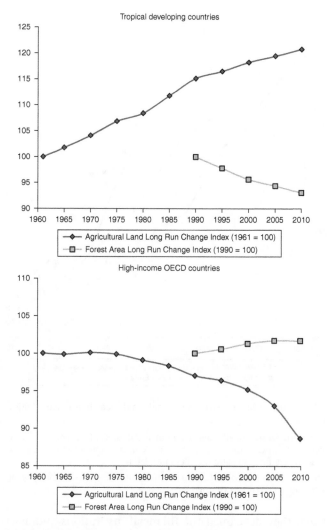

Figure 2.5 — Long-run global land use change, 1961–2010 (charts: "Tropical developing countries" and "High-income OECD countries" showing Agricultural Land Long Run Change Index (1961 = 100) and Forest Area Long Run Change Index (1990 = 100))

Figure 2.5   Long-run global land use change, 1961–2010

Notes: Agricultural land refers to the share of land area that is arable, under permanent crops, and under permanent pastures. Forest area is land under natural or planted stands of trees of at least 5 meters in situ, whether productive or not, and excludes tree stands in agricultural production systems, urban parks and gardens; Tropical developing countries are low- and middle-income economies in which 2013 Gross National Income (GNI) per capita was $12,745 or less, from the East Asia and Pacific, Latin America and Caribbean, South Asia and Sub-Saharan Africa regions. High-income OECD countries are members of the Organization for Economic Cooperation and Development (OECD) in which 2013 GNI per capita was $12,746 or more.

Source: World Bank, World Development Indicators, available from http://databank.worldbank.org/data

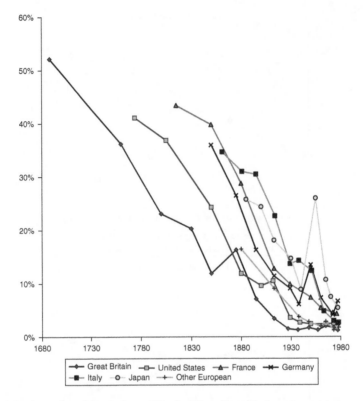

Figure 2.6   Agricultural land share (%) of national wealth for nine major economies, 1680–1980

Note: National wealth consists of all tangible and financial assets of an economy (see Chapter 1, and especially Figure 1.1). Other European countries are Denmark, Norway and Switzerland. For Norway and Switzerland, agricultural land also includes forest land.

Source: Raymond W. Goldsmith (1985) *Comparative National Balance Sheets: A Study of Twenty Countries, 1688–1978*. Chicago: University of Chicago Press, appendix A.

industrialized, they developed the financial institutions and assets required for facilitating large-scale capital investments in industries and modern economies. Consequently, by the 1930s, for most of the nine major industrialized countries depicted in Figure 2.6, agricultural land fell to less than 10% of national wealth, and by the 1980s, less than 5%.[51]

Decline of natural capital?

The Industrial Revolution not only diminished the importance of agricultural land in national wealth but also ensured that fossil fuels displaced biomass as the main form of energy (see Figure 2.1). In addition, as economies modernized and industrialized in the 20th century, non-renewable mineral and material use rapidly replaced renewables (see Figure 2.3). Since World War II, all modern economies worldwide have become heavily dependent on fossil fuel energy use and non-renewable material use.

However, despite their overwhelming dependence on using fossil fuels, mineral and other non-renewable materials, much of the wealth accumulated by rich economies today does not consist of natural capital. As discussed previously, the main reason is that, in the post-war era, the lowering of trade barriers and transport costs led to the globalization of all fossil fuel, raw material and mineral commodity markets. Consequently, in order to develop and industrialize, an economy no longer needed to accumulate and exploit its own sources of natural resource wealth. In fact, since 1950, low and middle-income economies are predominantly the "suppliers" of natural resource commodities, whereas high-income economies are the main "consumers".[52]

In the modern world economy, as countries become richer, less of their economic wealth comprises natural capital, such as agricultural land, forests, minerals and fossil fuels. For example, as shown in Figure 2.7, in low-income and lower-middle-income countries, around 40% of their wealth consists of natural

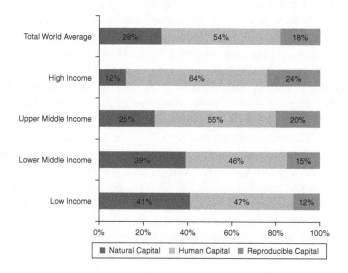

Figure 2.7   Contributions (%) to economic wealth by income group, 1990–2010 average

Notes: Natural capital includes fossil fuels (oil, natural gas and coal), minerals (bauxite, nickel, copper, phosphate, gold, silver, iron, tin, lead and zinc), forest resources (timber and non-timber forest resources), and agricultural land (cropland and pastureland). Human capital includes the education embodied in the population. Reproducible capital includes dwellings, factories, structures, road and other built infrastructure, equipment, inventories, consumer durables and so forth. All values are in 2005 US$; Low-income economies are those in which 2013 gross national income (GNI) per capita was $1,045 or less. Lower-middle-income economies are those in which 2013 GNI per capita was between $1,046 and $4,125. Upper-middle-income economies are those in which 2013 GNI per capita was between $4,126 and $12,745. High-income economies are those in which 2013 GNI per capita was $12,746 or more. Includes 26 low-income economies, 37 lower-middle-income economies, 35 upper-middle-income economies and 42 high-income economies.

Source: Based on United Nations University (UNU)-International Human Dimensions Programme (IHDP) on Global Environmental Change and United Nations Environment Programme (UNEP) (2014) *Inclusive Wealth Report 2014. Measuring Progress Toward Sustainability.* Cambridge: Cambridge University Press, table 3, p. 31.

capital. But for upper-middle-income countries, natural capital comprises 25% of economic wealth, and in all high-income countries just 12%.

Because wealthier countries are less dependent on exploiting their own sources of natural resources, their economies are also subject to less natural capital depreciation. In contrast, low and middle-income economies are much more dependent on natural capital depletion as they develop. For most countries since 1970, The World Bank provides estimates of the adjustments to national income, income growth and savings that allow for natural capital depreciation, which is the sum of valuations of net forest depletion, energy depletion and mineral depletion.[53] In the Appendix to this chapter, it is shown how national income can be adjusted to allow for both depreciation of reproducible capital and natural capital, resulting in a measure of *adjusted net national income*. Many economists believe that the latter is a better measure of the "net income" generated by an economy each year, as it accounts for the "using up" of two important stocks of capital – natural resources and reproducible assets – to produce more goods and services.

It is also interesting to see how much natural capital is degraded or depleted by an economy as it produces more net income each year. Figure 2.8 depicts the rate of natural capital depreciation as a percentage share of adjusted net national income over the past four decades for the eight richest countries, for developing economies and for the world. As Figure 2.8 indicates, the decline in natural capital has been consistently larger in developing economies compared to the eight richest countries. The average rate of natural capital depreciation over 1979–2012 was 7.0% in low and middle-income countries, which is five times greater than the average rate of 1.4% over 1970–2012 in the wealthy economies. In addition, although natural capital depreciation in all countries fell to its lowest levels in the 1990s, since then it has risen significantly again. There was a noticeable dip during the Great Recession of 2008–2009, but as the world economy has recovered, so has the rate of natural capital depreciation. This last trend is an important indicator of the overall dependence of the global economy on natural resource use, especially fossil fuels, minerals and other industrial materials.

Rise of finance

As economies industrialized, they developed the financial institutions and assets required for facilitating large-scale capital investments in industries and modern economies. As the economic historian Raymond Goldsmith has noted: "The creation of a modern financial superstructure, not in its details but in its essentials, was generally accomplished at a fairly early stage of a country's economic development, usually within five to seven decades from the start of modern economic growth. Thus it was essentially completed in most

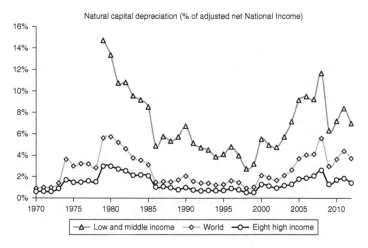

Figure 2.8 The rate of natural capital depreciation, 1970–2012

Notes: Low and middle-income (or developing) countries are economies with 2012 per capita income of $12,615 or less; The eight high-income countries are the United States, Japan, Germany, France, United Kingdom, Italy, Canada and Australia; The measure of natural capital depreciation is the annual value of net natural resource depletion as a % of adjusted net national income (constant 2005 US$). The World Development Indicators define the value of net natural resource depletion as the sum of net forest, fossil fuel and mineral depletion. Net forest depletion is unit resource rents times the excess of roundwood harvest over natural growth. Energy depletion is the ratio of the value of the stock of energy resources to the remaining reserve lifetime (capped at 25 years). It covers coal, crude oil, and natural gas. Mineral depletion is the ratio of the value of the stock of mineral resources to the remaining reserve lifetime (capped at 25 years). It includes tin, gold, lead, zinc, iron, copper, nickel, silver, bauxite and phosphate. Adjusted net national income is gross national income minus consumption of fixed capital and the value of net natural resources depletion, expressed in constant 2005 US$; The average rate of natural capital depreciation over 1970–2012 was 2.7% worldwide, 1.7% in the eight high-income countries and 7.0% in developing countries (1979–2012).

Source: The data used for these estimates are from the World Banks' World Development Indicators, available at: http://databank.worldbank.org/data

now-developed countries by the end of the 19th century of the eve of World War I, though somewhat earlier in Great Britain." Thus, industrialization in the richest economies was accompanied by "the rise of the share of financial in total assets from approximately one-fourth to one-half, and the increase in the share of financial institutions in total financial assets from about one-eighth to one-third."[54]

The "rise of finance" was directly related to the first phase of innovations spurred by the Industrial Revolution and the resulting global productivity boost from 1870 to the early 20th century (see Figure 2.2). In particular, the development of fossil fuel generated electricity and the invention of the telegraph, also allowed financial investments to flow more cheaply to all regions of the world. The telegraph reduced substantially the cost of transmitting commercial information and investments globally. Greater and faster information flows also lowered the business risks of investors and firms located in the major European and other financial centers of the world investing in subsidiary operations, production and inventories for distant markets.[55] As a consequence, the four decades from 1870 to 1914 saw an unprecedented boom in overseas foreign investment. At the beginning of the period, such investment amounted to 7% of world GDP, but by 1914 it jumped to almost 20% – an amount that would not be equaled again until 1980.[56]

Thus, the period 1870 to 1914 represented the "first global capital boom". During this era, the source of much of the global foreign investment that occurred during the boom was the leading industrial nations in Europe, such as Great Britain, France, Germany, Belgium, the Netherlands, Switzerland, and to a lesser extent, the United States. The major destination for these foreign investment flows outside of Europe (including Russia and Turkey) were North America, temperate Latin America and South Africa; in contrast, tropical regions received much less investment.[57] Great Britain was not only the biggest overseas investor during the era but also the majority of its investment flowed outside of Europe. Much of these investments overseas were aimed at exploiting the vast land and natural resource wealth of the rest of the world, especially in the temperate regions.[58]

With the onslaught of two world wars and the Great Depression, the global capital market largely collapsed in the middle third of the 20th century. However, since 1950 a "second global capital boom" has occurred.[59] This expansion corresponded with the general post-war boom in trade, especially in the commodity markets, and with the financial liberalization that began in the 1970s and has continued since. During the late 20th century, the United States emerged as the largest foreign investor, and even by 2000 it still accounted for one quarter of global foreign investment.[60]

However, there are two unique features of the post-war boom in global capital. First, as the economists Maurice Obstfeld and Alan Taylor note, "The new financial globalization is for the most part confined to rich countries. A handful of developing countries ('emerging markets') also participate to some degree, but most other developing countries are left out."[61] Second, the international financial liberalization that has occurred since the 1970s has also spurred domestic financial deregulation and expansion.[62] Not surprisingly, both trends have led to significant growth of the financial sectors of rich countries, so that the "modern financial superstructure" of these countries has expanded to dominate their national wealth and economies.

This "rise of finance" is reflected in the long-run trend from 1680 to 1980 in the ratio of financial assets to national wealth for six major economies – Great Britain, the United States, France, Germany, Italy and Japan (see Figure 2.9). Before industrialization, financial assets in these economies typically accounted for 15–20% of national wealth. However, as they started to develop the "modern

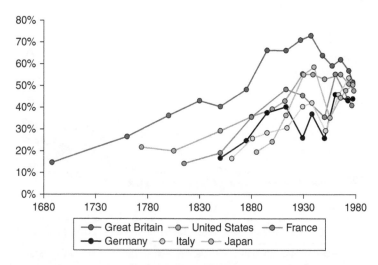

Figure 2.9   Financial asset share (%) of national wealth for six major economies, 1680–1980

Note: National wealth consists of all tangible and financial assets of an economy (see Chapter 1, and especially Figure 1.1). Total financial assets consist of claims against financial institutions, insurance and pension claims, loans by financial institutions, government domestic debt, corporate bonds, corporate stock, trade credit, other financial assets, plus net foreign assets.

Source: Raymond W. Goldsmith (1985) *Comparative National Balance Sheets: A Study of Twenty Countries, 1688–1978*. Chicago: University of Chicago Press, appendix A.

financial superstructure" necessary to support industrial growth and economic expansion, the financial asset share of wealth increased significantly. By the 1970s, this share in the six countries comprised 40% to 50% of national wealth.

Over the past five decades, the dominance of the financial sectors in the economies of high-income countries has continued. Since 1960, the ratio of the value of financial assets to national income has risen steadily in seven major economies – the United Kingdom, Japan, France, the United States, Canada, Germany and Australia (see Figure 2.10). Forty years ago, the financial asset–income ratio was approximately 800% in the UK, 300% in Germany and 400–500% in the other five countries. However, this ratio has increased gradually since, and rose more sharply in most economies from 1995 onwards. Despite the 2008–2009 Great Recession, which was precipitated by a financial crisis in the US that spread globally, by 2010 the financial asset–income ratio averaged nearly 1200% across the seven economies. All countries have experienced increases in this ratio, with the 2010 level ranging from 660% in Germany to nearly 2000% in the United Kingdom.

In sum, the "rise of finance" appears to be a definitive feature of both phases of the Industrial Revolution, which were in turn associated with two distinct productivity boosts to the world economy – from 1870 to 1900 and from 1900

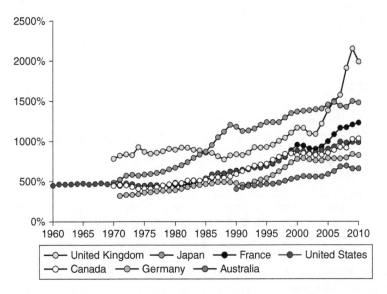

Figure 2.10   Financial asset share (%) of national income for seven major economies, 1960–2010

Note: National income (or gross national income) is gross domestic product (GDP), which measures the total of goods and services produced by a country in a given year, less any depreciation of capital that occurs through production, plus any net income from investments abroad. Financial assets are domestic financial assets (bank accounts, mutual funds, bonds, stocks, financial investments of all kinds, insurance policies, pension funds, etc.), less the total amount of domestic financial liabilities (debt); net foreign assets are not included.

Source: Thomas Piketty and Gabriel Zucman (2014) "Capital is Back: Wealth-Income Ratios in Rich Countries, 1700–2010", *Quarterly Journal of Economics*, 129(3): 1255–1310, appendix table A30: Gross financial assets of all domestic sectors 1960–2010 (% of national income), available at: http://piketty. pse.ens.fr/fr/capitalisback

to 1970 (see Figure 2.2). Only the disruptive impact of two world wars and the Great Depression during the early half of the 20th century seems to have separated this trend for financial wealth to dominate national wealth into two distinct "global capital booms". The first global capital boom appears to have occurred over a relatively short period of time, from 1870 to 1914. In contrast, the second global capital boom began in the 1950s and still continues today (see Figure 2.10). In fact, a remarkable feature of this second boom is that it actually accelerated *after* the second productivity boost of the Industrial Revolution petered out in the 1970s (see Figure 2.2). This important stylized fact is noted and described succinctly by the economist Thomas Piketty:

> Broadly speaking, the 1970s and 1980s witnessed an extensive "financialization" of the global economy, which altered the structure of wealth in the sense that the total amount of financial assets and liabilities held by various

sectors (household, corporations, government agencies) increased more rapidly than net wealth. In most countries, the total amount of financial assets and liabilities in the early 1970s did not exceed four to five years of national income. By 2010, this amount had increase to ten to fifteen years of national income (in the United States, Japan, Germany, and France in particular) and to twenty years of national income in Britain, which set an absolute historical record.[63]

Conclusion

This chapter has focused on how the structural changes brought about by the Industrial Revolution altered irrevocably the composition and accumulation of wealth in modern economies.

First, the Industrial Revolution comprised two distinct phases of innovations, with each phase associated with a core set of key innovations and pattern of energy use (see Figures 2.1 and 2.2). More importantly, the first phase propelled Great Britain to global economic and political dominance, and had lasting economic impacts on all industrializing economies up until 1900; and, the second phase spurred considerable industrial, transport and urban developments that boosted productivity until the 1970s, and led to the economic rise and worldwide dominance of the United States.

Second, the spread of industrialization ushered in the global fossil fuel era, which has continued uninterrupted since the mid-19th century. In addition, modern economic development is not only associated with rising (mainly fossil fuel) energy consumption (see Figure 2.1) but also increased non-renewable material use, such as minerals and ores, construction materials and non-renewable organics (see Figure 2.3).

Third, although in the modern era all economies have become entirely dependent on fossil fuel energy and non-renewable material use, since the 1950s the global integration of commodity markets has ensured that, in order to develop and industrialize, a country no longer needs to accumulate and exploit its own sources of natural resource wealth. Instead, any country can sustain its economic expansion by supplementing exploitation of its resource endowment with rising consumption of energy and other primary products purchased in international markets.

Consequently, in the modern world economy, as countries become richer, less of their economic wealth comprises natural capital, such as agricultural land, forests, protected areas, minerals and fossil fuels. In fact, since 1950, low and middle-income economies are predominantly the suppliers of natural resource commodities, whereas high-income economies are the main consumers, and there is a clear stratification between poor and rich countries in terms of the share of natural capital in total wealth (see Figure 2.7).

Finally, as economies develop and become wealthier, they develop the financial institutions and assets required for facilitating large-scale capital investments in industries and modern economies. However, over the past five decades, the dominance of the financial sectors in the economies of high-income countries has not only continued, it has actually accelerated since the 1970s (see Figure 2.10). In rich economies, financial wealth comprises more and more national wealth and income, and this trend has gone on well after the second global productivity boost of the Industrial Revolution.

These changes in the economic wealth of nations as a consequence of the Industrial Revolution have defined the unique structure of the modern world economy. In the next few chapters, we will explore some of the wider economic implications of this unique structure in more detail. For example, in Chapter 3 we will focus on how this structure has encouraged two types of economies that distinguish rich from poor countries: the emergence of carbon-dependent economies and resource-dependent economies. A second implication of the current structure of the world economy and its pattern of natural resource and environmental use is the problem of rising ecological scarcity, which is a focus of Chapter 4. Finally, a third major implication is the growing disparity of income and wealth inequality in the world economy, which is the theme of Chapter 5.

Appendix

Adjusting gross national income for natural capital depreciation

To estimate the total value of goods and services produced each year, as well as the income generated from this production, most countries follow the agreed United Nations' System of National Accounts (SNA). There are two main economic indicators of the SNA that are conventionally used, *gross domestic product* and *gross national income*.

Gross domestic product (GDP) is the market value of all goods and services produced by a country in a given year. However, the citizens and corporations of one country may own assets in other countries, and foreigners may also own some of the capital used for producing goods and services domestically. In any given year, some income earned from domestic production will flow overseas to foreigners as a return on their investments in domestic capital, and similarly, investments abroad will earn income for domestic residents and corporations. In the SNA, the measure of gross national income (GNI) of an economy adjusts GDP to account for these net income flows from overseas. Specifically,

Gross National Income (GNI) = total goods and services produced domestically (GDP) + net income from abroad

As we saw in Chapter 1, one of the most important forms of wealth in an economy is its *reproducible capital*, such as dwellings, factories, structures, road and other built infrastructure, equipment, inventories, consumer durables and so forth. This type of wealth is also called *domestic fixed capital*. During any given year, some of this capital may wear out, deteriorate and have to be replaced, as the economy uses it to produce more goods and services. In national accounts, such capital depreciation is referred to as the value of the *consumption of fixed capital*, which represents the replacement value of capital used up in the process of production. Adjusting NI for such reproducible capital depreciation is an estimate of *net national income* (NNI):

Net National Income (NNI) = GNI – the value of the consumption of domestic fixed capital

However, the SNA approach to national accounts does not account for the depreciation in natural resources essential to domestic production and national income, such as fossil fuels, minerals and forests. As discussed in the text, natural capital may be less important for rich countries, but a low-income country will typically have 41% of its economic wealth consist of natural capital, a lower-middle-income country 39% and an upper-middle-income country 25% (see Figure 2.7). Thus, adjusting net national income to account for natural capital depreciation is relevant to many developing countries, as they are more dependent on forest, energy and mineral depletion to produce goods and services each year. The resulting measure is *adjusted net national income*, which is estimated by subtracting from NNI any depletion of natural resources, which normally covers net forest depletion, energy depletion and mineral depletion. Such natural capital depreciation reflects the decline in asset values associated with the extraction and harvesting of these natural resources for use in the economy.[64] This is analogous to depreciation of fixed capital assets.

In sum, ANNI adjusts national income for both reproducible and natural capital depreciation:

Adjusted Net National Income (ANNI) = NNI – depreciation of natural capital

The figure below summarizes the various adjustments that are required to derive ANNI from the conventional economic indicators of GDP and gross national income.

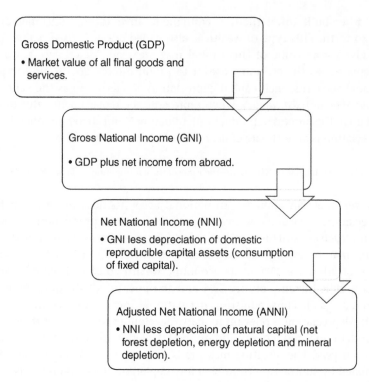

Figure 2.11 Adjusting gross national income (GNI) for reproducible and natural capital depreciation

3
Wealth, Structure and Functioning of Modern Economies

Introduction

In the previous two chapters, we learned that the economic wealth of a nation comprises three distinct assets: manufactured, or *reproducible, capital*, such as roads, buildings, machinery and factories; *human capital*, such as the skills, education and health embodied in the workforce; and *natural capital*, including land, forests, fossil fuels and minerals and ecosystems that provide valuable goods and services. However, the total or *national wealth* of an economy also includes the accumulation of sizable financial assets, such as monetary metals and currency, bank accounts, government bonds, corporate bonds and stocks, mutual funds, insurance policies, pension funds, trade credit, and foreign-owned assets (see Figure 1.1).

The purpose of this chapter is to explain how the composition and accumulation of economic wealth in today's global economy have influenced its structure and functioning. In particular this structure has encouraged two types of economies: rich and large emerging market countries that are *carbon-dependent* and developing countries that are mainly *resource-dependent*. Both types of economies are directly related to how natural resources are used to create wealth today.

In the modern world economy, as countries become richer, less of their economic wealth comprises natural capital, such as agricultural land, forests, protected areas, minerals and fossil fuels (see Figure 2.7). As a consequence, low and middle-income economies are predominantly the suppliers of natural resource commodities, whereas high-income economies are the main consumers. Developing economies therefore depend more on resource-based exports, which they export to the rest of the world, including rich and emerging market economies. Thus, many developing countries are characterized by a high ratio of primary product commodity exports – agricultural raw material, food, fuel, ore and metal commodities – to total merchandise exports. It is in this sense that economic development in low and middle-income countries can be considered *resource-dependent*.

In addition, modern economic development is not only associated with rising (mainly fossil fuel) energy consumption but also increased non-renewable material use, such as minerals and ores, construction materials and non-renewable organics. The result is that, as economies grow and become wealthier, they consume more fossil fuels and non-renewable materials, which release large amounts of carbon dioxide (CO_2) and other carbon-based gases, such as methane, nitrous oxides and various fluoro-carbons. Collectively, they are referred to as "greenhouse gas" (GHG) emissions, because these gases accumulate in the atmosphere and contribute to the "greenhouse effect" of trapping incoming solar radiation, thus leading to global warming and climate change. Rich countries are certainly responsible for rising global GHG emissions and past accumulation of these emissions in the atmosphere, but increasingly it is the largest and fastest growing emerging market economies that are becoming the main emitters. Because these rapidly growing economies are emulating the wealthy countries in consuming more products and resources that emit GHG, development in today's rich, large and more successful economies can be considered *carbon-dependent*. For example, as we shall see later, the 20 largest wealthy and emerging market economies account for around three quarters of the world's GHG emissions today.

This chapter explores these two dominant patterns of economic development. In subsequent chapters, we will examine some of the wider economic, social and environmental implications. For example, Chapter 4 will discuss how extensive natural resource and environmental use in the global economy the past several decades has contributed to a problem of rising ecological scarcity. There is also concern with how the underpricing of nature and the premium paid for increasingly scarce human capital has caused a structural imbalance in the world economy, which is the theme of Chapter 5.

Resource-dependent development

As less wealthy regions are the main source of the world's supply of mineral, energy and raw material commodities, the development of many low and medium-income economies remains largely resource-dependent – as measured by the ratio of primary products to total merchandise exports (see Figure 3.1). Although all types of economies have on average experienced a decline in primary product export share, resource dependency remains relatively high in low and middle-income economies compared to wealthy economies (see Figure 3.1A). For example, in recent years, primary products account for around 20% of the merchandise exports of high-income countries, whereas they amount to between 30% and 35% for low and middle-income countries.

However, among developing economies there are important regional differences (see Figure 3.1B). Since 1960, Asian countries have had the sharpest

A By type of economy

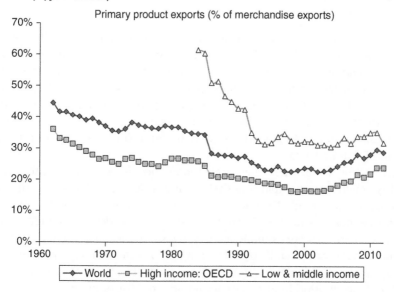

B Developing country regions

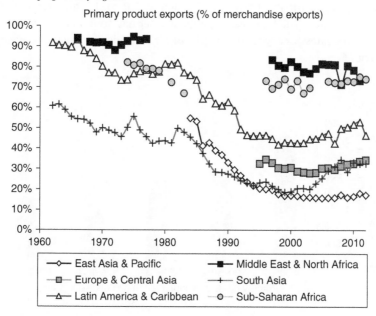

Figure 3.1 Resource dependency in exports, 1960–2012

Note: Primary product export share is the percentage of agricultural raw material, food, fuel, ore and metal commodities to total merchandise exports. Low and middle-income (or developing) countries are economies with 2013 per capita income of $12,745 or less. High-income OECD countries are members of the Organization for Economic Cooperation and Development (OECD) in which 2013 GNI per capita was $12,746 or more.

Source: World Bank, World Development Indicators, available from http://databank.worldbank.org/data

decline in resource dependency, as these economies have generally become more successful in diversifying their economies and developing labor-intensive manufacturing for exports. Latin America has also seen a decline in the ratio of primary products to total exports, especially in recent decades, but still around 50% of the exports from this region are resource commodities. In contrast, in Africa and the Middle East, resource dependency remains relatively high, around 80% for the Middle East and North Africa and over 70% for Sub-Saharan Africa.

Across the world, many low and middle-income economies still remain highly dependent on exploiting their natural resource endowments for commercial, export-oriented economic activities. For these economies, primary product exports – and often one or two main commodities – account for nearly all export earnings. For example, a study of resource dependency in developing economies indicates that 72 out of 95 low and middle-income economies have 50% or more of their exports from primary products, and 35 countries have an export concentration in primary commodities of 90% or more.[1]

Resource dependency may be linked to other structural economic features of developing countries. For example, Figures 3.2 to 3.5 indicate how gross domestic product (GDP) per capita, adjusted net national income and savings, and poverty rates vary with the degree of resource dependency of developing countries.[2]

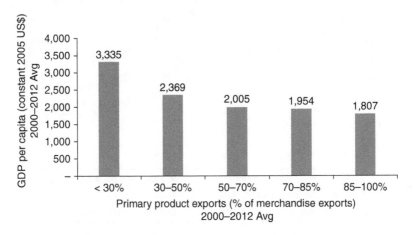

Figure 3.2   Resource dependency and GDP per capita in developing countries, 2000–2012

Note: 118 countries, of which 27 (< 30%), 20 (30–50%), 20 (50–70%), 26 (70–85%) and 25 (85–100%); Primary product export share is the percentage of agricultural raw material, food, fuel, ore and metal commodities to total merchandise exports (average 58.8%, median 64.0%). GDP per capita is gross domestic product divided by mid-year population (average $2,323, median $1,557); Low and middle-income (or developing) countries are economies with 2013 per capita income of $12,745 or less.

Source: World Bank, World Development Indicators, available from http://databank.worldbank.org/data

Figure 3.2 indicates how gross domestic product (GDP) per capita varies with resource dependency across low and middle-income countries. GDP per capita is the gross domestic product of an economy averaged over the entire population of a country.[3] GDP is calculated without making deductions for depreciation of reproducible capital, net additions to human capital or depletion and degradation of natural resources. As can be seen from Figure 3.2, developing countries that are extremely resource-dependent, i.e., with a large share of primary products in total merchandise exports, have much lower GDP per capita than countries that export relatively less resource commodities. In particular, those economies that have a primary product export share of less than 30% have 1.7 to 1.8 times more GDP per capita than countries with an export share of 70% or more.

As discussed previously, the economic wealth of most low and middle-income countries comprises natural capital, such as agricultural land, forests, protected areas, minerals and fossil fuels. Consequently, to grow and develop, these countries tend to "use up", through depletion and degradation, their endowment of natural resources. Similarly, in producing more goods and services each year, economies wear out roads, buildings, machinery, factories and other forms of fixed capital. Although the economy is generating income, which is a good thing, it is important to know how much of reproducible and natural capital is lost in this process. Adjusted net national income (ANNI) is a particularly useful indicator for monitoring this economic progress, as it estimates national income net of both reproducible and natural capital depreciation (see Chapter 2 Appendix). That is, by accounting for the depletion of fixed and natural capital, ANNI measures the remaining income available either for consumption or for investment that increases the country's wealth.

Figure 3.3 depicts how ANNI per capita varies with the resource dependency of developing countries. As the share of primary products in total merchandise exports rises across countries, ANNI per capita declines sharply. This decrease is even more striking than for the relationship between GDP per capita and resource dependency (see Figure 3.2). Economies with a low primary product export share (e.g., less than 30%) have at least twice the ANNI per capita of countries with a very large share (e.g., more than 70%). The latter group consists of 50 developing countries. The fact that ANNI per capita is much lower for these highly resource-dependent economies is worrisome. It means that a large proportion of the income generated each year involves considerable depreciation of natural capital, so that less income net of that depreciation is available for increased consumption or investment in other economic assets, such as human and reproducible capital.[4]

A more direct measure of the amount of funds available to increase a country's wealth is adjusted net savings. This is the amount of savings left over

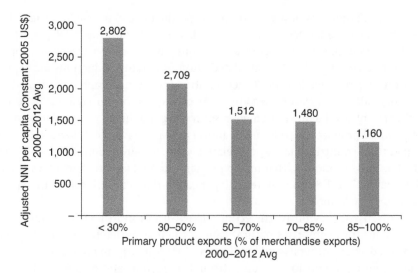

Figure 3.3   Resource dependency and adjusted NNI per capita in developing countries, 2000–2012

Notes: 114 countries, of which 26 (< 30%), 19 (30–50%), 19 (50–70%), 26 (70–85%) and 24 (85–100%); Primary product export share is the percentage of agricultural raw material, food, fuel, ore and metal commodities to total merchandise exports (average 58.9%, median 64.0%). Adjusted net national income (NNI) is gross national income (GNI) minus consumption of fixed capital and natural resources depletion (average $1,819, median $1,245). Net natural resource depletion is the sum of net forest, fossil fuel and mineral depletion. Net forest depletion is unit resource rents times the excess of roundwood harvest over natural growth. Energy depletion is the ratio of the value of the stock of energy resources to the remaining reserve lifetime (capped at 25 years). It covers coal, crude oil and natural gas. Mineral depletion is the ratio of the value of the stock of mineral resources to the remaining reserve lifetime (capped at 25 years). It includes tin, gold, lead, zinc, iron, copper, nickel, silver, bauxite and phosphate; Low and middle-income (or developing) countries are economies with 2013 per capita income of $12,745 or less.

Source: World Bank, World Development Indicators, available from http://databank.worldbank.org/data

after consumption; reproducible capital depreciation and natural resource depletion is deducted from the annual income of a country (see Chapter 3 Appendix). Adjusted net saving (ANS) should also include expenditures on education, health and training of the workforce that represent net additions to the human capital of an economy. When expressed as a percentage share of gross national income, ANS indicates what proportion of a country's annual income is available for investments to increase the human, natural and reproducible wealth of the economy.

Figure 3.4 shows that the adjusted net saving (ANS) rate, as a percentage of gross national income, declines sharply with the resource dependency of developing countries. Countries with less than 30% of the exports consisting of primary products have an ANS rate of 13.5%. However, this rate is almost halved for countries with a primary product export share of 30–50%, and it

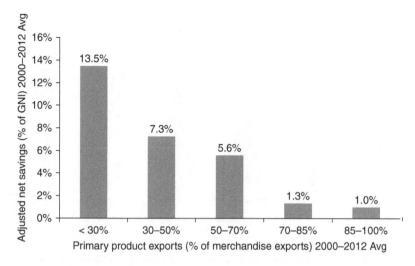

Figure 3.4 Resource dependency and adjusted net savings in developing countries, 2000–2012

Notes: 100 countries, of which 24 (< 30%), 15 (30–50%), 17 (50–70%), 22 (70–85%) and 22 (85–100%); Primary product export share is the percentage of agricultural raw material, food, fuel, ore and metal commodities to total merchandise exports (average 58.7%, median 63.8%); Adjusted net savings (ANS) are equal to net national savings plus education expenditure and minus energy depletion, mineral depletion and net forest depletion. ANS is expressed as the share (%) of gross national income (GNI). Average 5.8%, median 6.1%; Low and middle-income (or developing) countries are economies with 2013 per capita income of $12,745 or less.

Source: World Bank, World Development Indicators, available from http://databank.worldbank.org/data

falls to 5.6% for economies with an export share of 50–70%. For the 44 countries with more than 70% of their exports comprising resource commodities, the ANS rate is only 1%. This is again a disturbing trend. Developing countries that are heavily dependent on primary products for export are not only depreciating their natural capital but also not replacing this loss with sufficiently large net additions to either reproducible or human capital. In other words, the overall wealth of highly resource-dependent developing countries is barely increasing each year.

Finally, an important economic development objective is the alleviation of poverty, which is prevalent in all low and middle-income countries. However, as Figure 3.5 indicates, the poverty rate among developing countries varies considerably with resource dependency. For example, the percentage of the population that is poor is much higher for those countries that export at least 50% of their exports as primary products than for economies that have a lower export share. And, for those 21 economies that have a primary product export share of 85% or more, the majority of their populations are living in poverty.

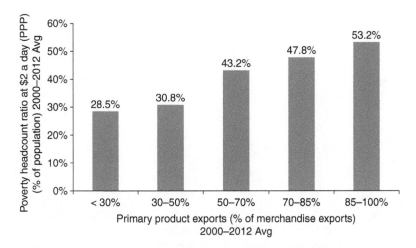

Figure 3.5   Resource dependency and poverty in developing countries, 2000–2012

Notes: 101 countries, of which 24 (< 30%), 18 (30–50%), 18 (50–70%), 20 (70–85%) and 21 (85–100%); Primary product export share is the percentage of agricultural raw material, food, fuel, ore and metal commodities to total merchandise exports (average 57.7%, median 58.6%). Population below $2 a day is the percentage of the population living on less than $2.00 a day at 2005 international purchase power parity (PPP) prices. For eight countries, the poverty headcount ratio is at national poverty line (% of population). Across all countries, the average poverty rate was 40.5%, and the median 35.5%; Low and middle-income (or developing) countries are economies with 2013 per capita income of $12,745 or less.

Source: World Bank, World Development Indicators, available from http://databank.worldbank.org/data

Table 3.1 indicates how different developing country regions have varied over 2000 to 2012 not only in terms of resource dependency but also gross domestic product (GDP) per capita, adjusted net national income and savings, and poverty rates. For example, the East Asia and Pacific region of developing countries has the lowest share of primary products in total exports – lower than that of high-income economies – and a very high rate of adjusted net savings, but it also has relatively low income per capita and high poverty compared to other regions. At the other extreme, over 70% of the exports from Sub-Saharan Africa came from resource commodities and also have the lowest level of adjusted net national income per capita of any region. Especially alarming is that Sub-Saharan Africa had on average a slightly negative adjusted net savings rate over 2000 to 2012, and the highest poverty rate (73%) of any developing region.

To summarize, resource dependency is a key structural feature of many developing economies. For example, primary products account for at least half of all merchandise exports in the majority of countries. In addition, resource

Table 3.1 Key development indicators by region, 2000–2012

Region	Primary product exports (% of merchandise exports)	GDP per capita (2005 US$)	Adjusted net national income per capita (2005 US$)	Adjusted net savings (% of GNI)	Poverty headcount ratio at US$2 a day (% of population)
East Asia & Pacific	16.5%	1,871	1,554	28.6%	38.5%
Europe & Central Asia	30.7%	3,933	3,303	5.0%	4.3%
Latin America & Caribbean	46.6%	5,037	4,081	6.1%	15.4%
Middle East & North Africa	78.7%	2,237	1,391	5.7%	15.8%
South Asia	26.9%	759	663	17.9%	72.1%
Sub-Saharan Africa	71.9%	878	627	-0.1%	72.7%
All low & middle income	**32.6%**	**1,849**	**1,502**	**15.5%**	**46.1%**
High income: OECD	19.5%	34,453	29,376	9.4%	–
World	25.6%	7,212	6,041	11.0%	–

The reported figures are the averages over 2000–2012 per region; Primary product export share is the percentage of agricultural raw material, food, fuel, ore and metal commodities to total merchandise exports; GDP per capita is gross domestic product divided by mid-year population. GDP is the sum of gross value added by all resident producers in the economy plus any product taxes and minus any subsidies not included in the value of the products. It is calculated without making deductions for depreciation of fabricated assets or for depletion and degradation of natural resources. Data are in constant 2005 US dollars; Adjusted net national income per capita is gross national income (GNI) minus consumption of fixed capital and natural resources depletion, divided by mid-year population; Gross national income (GNI) is the sum of value added by all resident producers plus any product taxes (less subsidies) not included in the valuation of output plus net receipts of primary income (compensation of employees and property income) from abroad. Data are in constant 2005 US dollars; Adjusted net savings are equal to net national savings plus education expenditure and minus energy depletion, mineral depletion and net forest depletion. This series excludes particulate emissions and carbon dioxide damage; Population below $2 a day is the percentage of the population living on less than $2.00 a day at 2005 international prices, using purchase power parity (PPP); Low and middle-income (or developing) countries are economies with 2013 per capita income of $12,745 or less. High-income OECD countries are members of the Organization for Economic Cooperation and Development (OECD) in which 2013 GNI per capita was $12,746 or more.

Source: World Bank, World Development Indicators, available from http://databank.worldbank.org/data

dependency is associated with other important structural features of "under-development" in these economies. More resource-dependent economies tend to have lower levels of GDP and adjusted net national income per capita, less savings and wealth accumulation, and higher poverty rates. Of particular concern is that highly resource-dependent developing countries appear to be degrading or depleting substantially their natural capital wealth, but not necessarily replacing it with more reproducible and human capital. In other words, resource dependency and natural capital depreciation are not leading to significant increases in wealth for those resource-rich developing economies that rely heavily on primary products for export.

Carbon-dependent development

If resource dependency is a key structural feature of developing countries in the modern world economy, carbon dependency is the attribute most associated with successful wealth accumulation.

As we saw in Chapter 2, as economies grow and become wealthier, they consume more fossil fuels and non-renewable materials, all of which release large amounts of carbon dioxide (CO_2) and other carbon-based "greenhouse gas" (GHG) emissions, such as methane, nitrous oxides and various fluoro-carbons. In effect, ever since the mid-19th century, the spread of industrialization and the rise of the global fossil fuel era have ensured that all economies have become structurally dependent on fossil fuel energy and non-renewable material use, which in turn has made them highly carbon-dependent. Certainly, the leading industrial countries, such as the United States, Japan, Western European countries, Australia and Canada, have been carbon-dependent for a long time, and still emit much of the world's GHG emissions today. But increasingly it is the largest, most populous and fastest growing developing economies, such as China, India, Russia, Brazil, Mexico and Indonesia, which have equaled, and in some cases surpassed, the emission levels of rich countries. Overall, as countries strive to industrialize, grow quickly and accumulate wealth, they cannot help but become more carbon-dependent.

Figure 3.6 depicts the changing regional pattern of carbon emissions in the world economy for over 150 years, from 1850 to 2011. This pattern reflects the spread of global industrialization and the rise of the fossil fuel era.

As discussed in Chapter 2, the first phase of innovations in the Industrial Revolution occurred from 1750 to 1830, and centered on steam power and coal. Until 1900 or so, these innovations propelled Great Britain to global economic dominance, and boosted the productivity of all industrializing nations, especially those in Western Europe and the United States, which followed Britain's example. As a consequence, in the latter half of the 19th century, carbon emissions were historically low but starting to rise, reflecting the growing carbon dependency of the leading industrialized economies. For example, in 1850 global emissions were approximately 200 million metric tonnes of carbon dioxide (MtCO$_2$), and almost all of these emissions were attributed to the United Kingdom and other countries of Western Europe (see Figure 3.6).

However, the mid-19th century onwards also corresponded to the second phase of the Industrial Revolution, and since the 1890s, coal, oil and gas have accounted for at least 50% of global energy consumption (see Figure 2.2). Thus, as the second phase of the Industrial Revolution progressed in the late 19th and early 20th century, the United States became the leading industrial power for the rest of the world to emulate. By 1920, it had exceeded Western Europe as the leading emitter of carbon, and by 1950, the US alone accounted for nearly half of the world's 5,700 MtCO$_2$ emissions (see Figure 3.6).

Since the 1950s, the rapid industrialization of major economies in Asia – first Japan and South Korea and followed more recently by China, India, Malaysia and Indonesia – has led this region to become the major global emitter. In 2011, Asia produced nearly 17,000 MtCO$_2$, which is more than double the combined

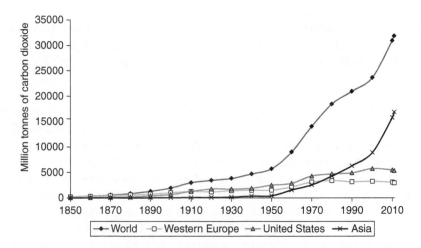

Figure 3.6   Carbon dioxide emissions by region, 1850–2011

Notes: Western Europe includes Austria, Belgium, Denmark, Finland, France, Germany, Greece, Ireland, Italy, Luxembourg, Netherlands, Portugal, Spain, Sweden and United Kingdom; Total carbon dioxide emissions in million tonnes of carbon dioxide (MtCO$_2$) excluding land use change and forestry; Emissions in 1850: World 197 MtCO$_2$, Western Europe 174 MtCO$_2$, United States 20 MtCO$_2$ and Asia 0.02 MtCO$_2$; Emissions in 1900: World 1,934 MtCO$_2$, Western Europe 1,011 MtCO$_2$, United States 663 MtCO$_2$ and Asia 27 MtCO$_2$; Emissions in 1950: World 5,698 MtCO$_2$, Western Europe 1,520 MtCO$_2$, United States 2,493 MtCO$_2$ and Asia 401 MtCO$_2$; Emissions in 2000: World 23,631 MtCO$_2$, Western Europe 3,249 MtCO$_2$, United States 5,748 MtCO$_2$ and Asia 8,890 MtCO$_2$; Emissions in 2011: World 31,855 MtCO$_2$, Western Europe 2,939 MtCO$_2$, United States 5,333 MtCO$_2$ and Asia 16,870 MtCO$_2$

Source: Climate Analysis Indicators Tool (CAIT) 2.0. ©2014. World Resources Institute, Washington, DC, available from http://cait2.wri.org

emissions of the US and Western Europe (about 8,300 $MtCO_2$), and well over half of the global total of around 32,000 $MtCO_2$ (see Figure 3.6).

Today, there are 20 economies that are considered to be the wealthiest and the most powerful and politically influential in the world. They are referred to as the "Group of 20", or "G20" for short. For example, the G20 economies account for around 90% of the global economy, 80% of international trade and 75% of the world population.[5] All are members of the G20 international policy forum, which has annual meetings that enable the governments and the central bank governors to discuss and coordinate their economic policies.

The members of the G20 include 19 countries (Argentina, Australia, Brazil, Canada, China, France, Germany, India, Indonesia, Italy, Japan, Mexico, Russia, Saudi Arabia, South Africa, South Korea, Turkey, the UK and the US), plus the European Union.[6] Thus, the G20 comprises:

- Ten of *the wealthiest and most advanced economies*, which have benefited from decades of industrialization and growth: Australia, Canada, the European Union, France, Germany, Italy, Japan, South Korea, the United Kingdom and the United States.
- Ten of *the wealthiest and largest emerging market economies*, which have experienced rapid growth and development in recent decades: Argentina, Brazil, China, India, Indonesia, Mexico, Russia, Saudi Arabia, South Africa and Turkey.

As Table 3.2 indicates, these 20 major world economies are responsible for most of the global greenhouse gas emissions from 1990 to 2011. By 2011, the G20 accounted for three quarters of the world's total GHG, and their annual emissions are rising faster than in the rest of the world. Although the ten high-income economies are still major contributors to global GHG emissions, in the United States and Japan emissions have grown only modestly, whereas in Germany, the United Kingdom, France, Italy and the European Union, they have actually fallen. Only South Korea, Australia and Canada had significantly high growth in carbon emissions. In contrast, the G20 emerging market economies had substantial growth in GHG emissions from 1990 to 2011. Among these countries, Brazil and Russia were the only ones with a decline.

Two other indicators can also be employed to reflect the degree of carbon dependency of an economy, *greenhouse gas intensity* and *per capita greenhouse gas emissions*. Greenhouse gas intensity is a measure of how much GHGs are emitted to produce a dollar's worth of goods and services produced each year by an economy. Per capita GHG emissions are the total annual emissions of an economy divided by the aggregate population of an economy, thus giving an indication of the average amount of GHGs emitted per person.

Table 3.2 Global greenhouse gas emissions, 1990–2011

	Million tonnes of CO_2 equivalent (MtCO$_2$e)			Average annual growth	Total growth	Share of 2011 world total
	1990	2011	Change			
China	3,047	10,216	7,213	11.3%	236.7%	22.3%
United States	5,696	6,135	988.5	0.4%	7.7%	13.4%
European Union	5,171	4,263	–907	–0.8%	–17.5%	9.3%
India	1,035	2,358	1,323	6.1%	127.7%	5.1%
Russia	3,130	2,217	–914	–1.4%	–29.2%	4.8%
Indonesia	1,077	2,053	976	4.3%	90.7%	4.5%
Brazil	1,739	1,419	–320	–0.9%	–18.4%	3.1%
Japan	1,123	1,170	47	0.2%	4.2%	2.5%
Canada	596	847	251	2.0%	42.0%	1.8%
Germany	1,107	806	–302	–1.3%	–27.2%	1.8%
Mexico	434	723	289	3.2%	66.7%	1.6%
South Korea	263	656	393	7.1%	149.6%	1.4%
Australia	438	595	158	1.7%	36.0%	1.3%
United Kingdom	743	541	–202	–1.3%	–27.2%	1.2%
Saudi Arabia	200	533	333	7.9%	166.4%	1.2%
France	506	463	–43	–0.4%	–8.6%	1.0%
Italy	470	458	–12	–0.1%	–2.6%	1.0%
South Africa	331	457	126	1.8%	38.0%	1.0%
Argentina	309	435	126	1.9%	40.6%	0.9%
Turkey	183	375	192	5.0%	105.2%	0.8%
G20 total	**24,771**	**34,496**	**9,725**	**1.9%**	**39.3%**	**75.1%**
Rest of world	**8,705**	**11,417**	**2,712**	**1.5%**	**31.2%**	**24.9%**
World	**33,476**	**45,914**	**12,437**	**1.8%**	**37.2%**	**100.0%**

Estimates of greenhouse gas (GHG) emissions, which are measured in million tonnes of carbon dioxide equivalent (MtCO$_2$e), include land use change and forestry; In 2011, world GHG emissions consisted of carbon dioxide (CO_2, 73.6% of total), methane (CH_4, 16.5%), nitrous oxide (N_2O, 8.5%), hydrofluorocarbons (HFCs, 1.0%), perfluorocarbons (PFCs, 0.3%) and sulfur hexafluoride (SF_6, 0.2%); G20 is the Group of 20 countries. The members of the G20 include 19 countries (Argentina, Australia, Brazil, Canada, China, France, Germany, India, Indonesia, Italy, Japan, Mexico, Russia, Saudi Arabia, South Korea, Turkey, the UK and the US), plus the European Union. The G20 total excludes Germany, United Kingdom, France and Italy, as their emissions are already included in the European Union aggregate

Source: Climate Analysis Indicators Tool (CAIT) 2.0. ©2014.World Resources Institute, Washington, DC, available from http://cait2.wri.org

The conventional way of estimating greenhouse gas intensity is to divide the total amount of GHG emissions by the gross domestic product (GDP) of an economy, which is the market value of all goods and service that a country produces in a given year. However, as argued previously, the gross national product or income of an economy should be adjusted for any depreciation of reproducible and natural capital that is "used up" in generating this production or income each year. The result is *adjusted net national income* (ANNI).[7] Thus a better measure of the greenhouse gas intensity of an economy is its total GHG emissions divided by its annual ANNI (see Table 3.3).

Table 3.3 indicates that over 1990 to 2011 the GHG intensity fell in the G20 major economies, and across the world generally. However, in 2011 the GHG intensity of the large emerging market economies was higher than for the United States, and in some cases, the world average. For example, the GHG intensity of China was three times the world average and six times the US level, in India two times the world average and four times that of the US, and in Russia 2.5 times the world average and five times the GHG intensity of the United States.

All ten high-income G20 countries were able to reduce the GHG intensity of their economies over 1990–2011. But in the case of Japan, Italy and France, which already had the lowest GHG intensity levels in 1990 among all rich economies, the reduction was much less. As countries reach levels around 250–350 tonnes of carbon emitted per million dollars of ANNI, the carbon dependency of their economies may make it increasingly difficult to reduce their GHG intensity much further.

Over 1990–2011, per capita GHG emissions rose across all G20 countries, due mainly to the rise in many large emerging market members (see Table 3.4). Per capita emissions in Argentina, Brazil, China, Indonesia, Russia, Saudi Arabia and South Africa are at 7–10 tonnes per person, or even higher, which match the levels among some rich countries, such as Japan, Germany, France, the UK and Italy. Already, the average per capita emissions of the G20 major economies are almost double the world average.

With the exception of Australia, Canada and Japan, the high-income G20 countries were able to reduce per capita GHG emissions over 1990–2011. But once again there may be structural limits on how much further these countries may be able to reduce emissions per person. For example, Japan and European countries had the lowest per capita GHG emissions among rich economies in 1990. Although the European countries reduced per capita emissions further by 2011, the decline was relatively small. Japan's per capita emissions were pretty much the same in 2011 as in 1990. This suggests that the carbon dependency of high-income economies may make it increasingly difficult for them to reduce per capita GHG emissions much further beyond 7–8 tonnes per person.

Table 3.3 Global greenhouse gas intensity, 1990–2011

| | Total GHG Emissions Per ANNI (tCO₂e / Million $ ANNI) | | | | | Ratio to world | Ratio to US |
	1990	2011	Change	Average annual growth	Total growth	2011	2011
China	6,556	3,141	−3,415	−2.5%	−52.1%	3.1	6.2
United States	799	504	−295	−1.8%	−36.9%	0.5	1.0
European Union	606	345	−261	−2.1%	−43.1%	0.3	0.7
India	3,502	2,065	−1,437	−2.0%	−41.0%	2.0	4.1
Russia	4,755	2,527	−2,229	−2.2%	−46.9%	2.5	5.0
Indonesia	8,657	6,256	−2,402	−1.3%	−27.7%	6.1	12.4
Brazil	3,488	1,475	−2,013	−2.7%	−57.7%	1.4	2.9
Japan	340	322	−18	−0.2%	−5.2%	0.3	0.6
Canada	954	802	−152	−0.8%	−15.9%	0.8	1.6
Germany	577	307	−270	−2.2%	−46.8%	0.3	0.6
Mexico	925	881	−44	−0.2%	−4.8%	0.9	1.7
South Korea	741	695	−46	−0.3%	−6.3%	0.7	1.4
Australia	1,308	906	−403	−1.5%	−30.8%	0.9	1.8
United Kingdom	605	259	−347	−2.7%	−57.3%	0.3	0.5
Saudi Arabia	–	–	–	–	–	–	–
France	354	235	−120	−1.6%	−33.8%	0.2	0.5
Italy	380	321	−59	−0.7%	−15.5%	0.3	0.6
South Africa	2,468	1,816	−651	−1.3%	−26.4%	1.8	3.6
Argentina	3,045	2,280	−765	−1.2%	−25.1%	2.2	4.5
Turkey	756	682	−74	−0.5%	−9.8%	0.7	1.4
G20 total	**1,064**	**879**	**−185**	**−0.8%**	**−17.4%**	**0.9**	**1.7**
Rest of world	3,535	2,133	−1,402	−1.9%	−39.7%	2.1	4.2
World	1,301	1,030	−271	−1.0%	−20.8%	1.0	2.0

Notes: Estimates of greenhouse gas (GHG) emissions, which are measured in million tonnes of carbon dioxide equivalent (MtCO₂e), include land use change and forestry; In 2011, world GHG emissions consisted of carbon dioxide (CO₂, 73.6% of total), methane (CH₄, 16.5%), nitrous oxide (N₂O, 8.5%), hydrofluorocarbons (HFCs, 1.0%), perfluorocarbons (PFCs, 0.3%) and sulfur hexafluoride (SF₆, 0.2%). GHG emissions from Climate Analysis Indicators Tool (CAIT) 2.0. ©2014.World Resources Institute, Washington, DC, available at: http://cait2.wri.org; Adjusted net national income (ANNI) is national income adjusted for both reproducible and natural capital depreciation (net forest, energy and mineral depletion), from World Bank, World Development Indicators available at: http://databank.worldbank.org/data; G20 is the Group of 20 countries. The members of the G20 include 19 countries (Argentina, Australia, Brazil, Canada, China, France, Germany, India, Indonesia, Italy, Japan, Mexico, Russia, Saudi Arabia, South Korea, Turkey, the UK and the US), plus the European Union. The G20 total excludes Germany, United Kingdom, France and Italy, as their emissions are already included in the European Union aggregate.

Table 3.4 Global greenhouse gas per capita, 1990–2011

	Total GHG emissions per capita (tCO₂e per person)			Average annual growth	Total growth	Ratio to world 2011	Ratio to US 2011
	1990	2011	Change				
China	2.7	7.6	4.9	8.8%	184.4%	1.2	0.4
United States	22.8	19.7	-3.1	-0.7%	-13.7%	3.0	1.0
European Union	10.6	8.5	-2.1	-1.0%	-20.2%	1.3	0.4
India	1.2	1.9	0.7	3.0%	62.0%	0.3	0.1
Russia	21.1	15.5	-5.6	-1.3%	-26.5%	2.4	0.8
Indonesia	6.0	8.4	2.4	1.9%	39.7%	1.3	0.4
Brazil	11.6	7.2	-4.4	-1.8%	-38.0%	1.1	0.4
Japan	9.1	9.2	0.1	0.0%	0.7%	1.4	0.5
Canada	21.5	24.7	3.2	0.7%	14.9%	3.7	1.3
Germany	13.9	9.9	-4.1	-1.4%	-29.3%	1.5	0.5
Mexico	5.0	6.1	1.0	1.0%	20.2%	0.9	0.3
South Korea	6.1	13.2	7.0	5.5%	114.9%	2.0	0.7
Australia	25.6	26.6	1.0	0.2%	3.9%	4.0	1.4
United Kingdom	13.0	8.5	-4.4	-1.6%	-34.1%	1.3	0.4
Saudi Arabia	12.3	19.2	6.8	2.6%	55.5%	2.9	1.0
France	8.7	7.1	-1.6	-0.9%	-18.3%	1.1	0.4
Italy	8.3	7.5	-0.7	-0.4%	-9.0%	1.1	0.4
South Africa	9.4	8.9	-0.5	-0.3%	-5.8%	1.3	0.5
Argentina	9.5	10.7	1.2	0.6%	12.6%	1.6	0.5
Turkey	3.4	5.1	1.7	2.5%	51.6%	0.8	0.3
G20 Average	11.1	11.9	0.8	0.3%	7.1%	1.8	0.6
World	6.3	6.6	0.2	0.2%	3.9%	1.0	0.3

Notes: Estimates of greenhouse gas (GHG) emissions per capita, which are measured in tonnes of carbon dioxide equivalent (MtCO₂e) per person, include land use change and forestry; In 2011, world GHG emissions consisted of carbon dioxide (CO₂, 73.6% of total), methane (CH₄, 16.5%), nitrous oxide (N₂O, 8.5%), hydrofluorocarbons (HFCs, 1.0%), perfluorocarbons (PFCs, 0.3%) and sulfur hexafluoride (SF₆, 0.2%); G20 is the Group of 20 countries. The members of the G20 include 19 countries (Argentina, Australia, Brazil, Canada, China, France, Germany, India, Indonesia, Italy, Japan, Mexico, Russia, Saudi Arabia, South Africa, South Korea, Turkey, the UK and the US), plus the European Union. The G20 average excludes Germany, United Kingdom, France and Italy, as their emissions are already included in the European Union average.

Source: Climate Analysis Indicators Tool (CAIT) 2.0. ©2014. World Resources Institute, Washington, DC, available from http://cait2.wri.org

Among the G20 economies, those with higher levels of per capita emissions tend to have lower levels of adjusted net savings (ANS) as percentage of national income (see Figure 3.7). Recall that the ANS rate indicates what proportion of a country's annual income is available for investments to increase the human, natural and reproducible wealth of the economy (see Chapter 3 Appendix). As indicated in Figure 3.7, economies with average 1990–2011 per capita GHG emissions around 6–7 tonnes per person or even less, displayed extremely high average ANS rates over 2000–2012. For example, China had savings rates of 33%, India 18.4%, Indonesia 16.5% and Turkey 14.2%. But none of the economies with per capita emission rates greater than 10 tonnes – which include Brazil, United Kingdom, Germany, Saudi Arabia, Russia, the United States, Canada and Australia – had average ANS rates of more than 10–11%. Greater carbon dependency in the form of higher per capita emissions, it seems, is not associated with more investments from annual income in the overall wealth of an economy.

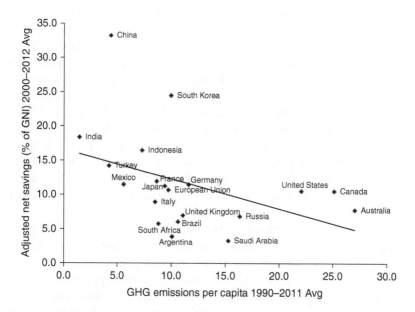

Figure 3.7 Greenhouse gas emissions per capita and adjusted net savings in major economies, 1990–2011

Notes: Estimates of greenhouse gas (GHG) emissions per capita, which are measured in tonnes of carbon dioxide equivalent (tCO$_2$e) per person, include land use change and forestry. The average GHG per capita across all 20 economies is 11.4 and the world average is 6.2. GHG emissions per capita estimates from Climate Analysis Indicators Tool (CAIT) 2.0. ©2014. World Resources Institute, Washington, DC, available at: http://cait2.wri.org; Adjusted net savings (ANS) are equal to net national savings plus education expenditure and minus energy depletion, mineral depletion and net forest depletion. ANS is expressed as the share (%) of gross national income (GNI). The average ANS share across all 20 economies is 11.7 and the world average is 12.3. ANS estimates from World Bank, World Development Indicators, available at: http://databank.worldbank.org/data.

Global implications

The continuing carbon dependency of large emerging market and rich economies is worrisome in several respects.

First, there is now significant scientific evidence that, if growth in aggregate GHG emissions is unchecked, there could be irreversible global climate change.[8] The resulting changes in global temperatures and precipitation are likely to contribute to sea level rise, and disrupt freshwater availability, ecosystems, food production, coastal populations and human health.

Second, the rich and large emerging economies that are responsible for the growing global GHG emissions are likely better able to adapt to the impacts of climate change than developing countries. The world's poor are especially vulnerable to the climate-driven risks posed by rising sea level, coastal erosion and more frequent storms. Around 14% of the population and 21% of urban dwellers in developing countries live in low elevation coastal zones that are exposed to these risks.[9] The livelihoods of billions – from poor farmers to urban slum dwellers – are threatened by a wide range of climate-induced risks that affect food security, water availability, natural disasters, ecosystem stability and human health. For example, many of the 150 million urban inhabitants that are likely to be at risk from extreme coastal flooding events and sea level rise are the poor living in developing country cities.[10] It is estimated that ten cities in developing countries will account for 67% of the future coastal population exposure to the risks from sea-level rise and storm surge.[11] Just 15 developing countries contain around 90% of the world's low-elevation coastal zone rural poor, who are highly vulnerable to the future risks to coastal GDP, agriculture and wetlands from sea-level rise and storm surge intensification.[12] Millions more poor inhabitants of drylands and other water-stressed agricultural areas will suffer from the risks and economic consequences of future climate change.

Third, if economies continue to become more carbon-dependent as they develop and become richer, then this does not bode well for controlling the growth in future GHG emissions. Given that many high-income economies are experiencing falling per capita emissions, and their populations are not expected to grow significantly, these countries will contribute less to overall global emissions. Instead, if future growth in aggregate GHG is to be slowed, "the bulk of the decreases in emissions will have to come from developing countries, especially those that are now catching up with the industrialized world, and that still have population growth to boot."[13] This will not happen as long as low and middle-income countries continue to emulate the carbon-dependent development path of today's rich, large and more successful economies.

Global ecosystems and freshwater sources are also endangered by the widespread environmental degradation that will accompany current patterns of economic development. Over the past 50 years, ecosystems have been modified more rapidly and extensively than in any comparable period in human history, largely to meet rapidly growing demands for food, fresh water, timber, fiber and fuel. The result has been a substantial and largely irreversible loss in biological diversity. Approximately 60% of the major global ecosystem services have been degraded or used unsustainably, including freshwater, capture fisheries, air and water purification, and the regulation of regional and local climate, natural hazards, and pests.[14]

Poor people in developing countries will be most affected by the continuing loss of critical ecological services worldwide. The rural poor in developing regions tend to be clustered in areas of ecologically fragile land, which are already prone to degradation, water stress and poor soils.[15] Already, nearly half of the developing world (2.9 billion people) live in cities, and by 2050, 5.2 billion people, or 63% of the population, will inhabit urban areas.[16] This brisk pace of urbanization means that the growing populations in the cities will be confronted with increased congestion and pollution and rising energy, water and raw material demands. Although such environmental problems are similar to those faced by richer countries, the pace and scale of urban population growth in developing countries is likely to lead to more severe and acute health and welfare impacts.

Conclusion

In the modern world economy, as countries become richer, less of their economic wealth comprises natural capital, such as agricultural land, forests, protected areas, minerals and fossil fuels. Paradoxically, however, this does not mean that economic development requires less exploitation of natural resources. To the contrary, as economies grow and become wealthier, they consume more energy – mainly fossil fuels – and more natural resources generally. Meanwhile, the vast majority of low and middle-income countries depend on exporting a large percentage of primary products relative to total merchandise exports. As a consequence, the current pattern and structure of modern global development encourages *carbon-dependent* rich and large emerging market countries, and *resource-dependent* developing countries.

In addition, the continuing natural resource exploitation and accompanying environmental degradation that is occurring on a growing scale worldwide may have three further economic implications.

First, as we shall discuss in the next chapter, carbon and resource-dependent development in the world economy also ensures that our endowment of ecological capital is declining rapidly. Over the past 50 years, ecosystems have been modified more rapidly and extensively than in any comparable period in human history, largely to meet rapidly growing demands for food, fresh water, timber, fiber and fuel. The result has been a substantial and largely irreversible loss in biological diversity, ecosystems and ecological services that they provide. Thus, an important source of economic wealth of all countries – not created by economies but endowed by nature – is disappearing quickly.

Second, as we have documented in the previous chapter and this one, greater natural capital depreciation and loss of ecological capital is not necessarily leading to significant increases in wealth in many economies – whether resource-dependent poor countries or carbon-dependent rich economies. Yet, almost all economies of the world are suffering problems of concentration of wealth – especially financially derived private wealth – in the hands of fewer and fewer extremely rich individuals, while at the same time, there is increasing "marginalization" of large segments of the labor force. Is it possible that these two trends are linked, if the same structural imbalances that are leading to the inefficient and unsustainable use of natural capital are also contributing to the economy-wide misallocation of labor and growing disparities in income and wealth? This is an important issue that is explored in some of the later chapters of this book.

Third, there is the growing threat of a warmer planet. As we have seen in this chapter, since the mid-19th century, global carbon dioxide emissions have continued to rise exponentially (see Figure 3.6). Since 1990, greenhouse gas emissions have already risen close to 40% (see Table 3.2). Over the next few decades, the continuing growth in aggregate GHG emissions could cause irreversible global climate change.[17] The resulting changes in global temperatures and precipitation are likely to contribute to sea level rise, and disrupt freshwater availability, ecosystems, food production, coastal populations and human health.

Appendix

Adjusted net savings and additions to economic wealth

As explained in the Appendix to Chapter 2, an important economic indicator for all countries is *gross national income* (GNI). Each year, this flow of national income can either be spent on current private and public consumption by individuals and government, respectively, or it can be saved as a source of investment. The latter is defined conventionally as *gross national saving* (GNS). Thus, by definition

Gross National Saving (GNS) = GNI – public and private consumption

Although GNS is an indicator of the total investment in an economy, not all of this investment may necessarily lead to an expansion in the capital stock.

Some of the savings generated must first replace any capital depreciation; i.e., the domestic fixed capital (reproducible capital) that is used up in the process of production each year. Thus, only gross national saving *less* the value of consumption of fixed capital will lead to a net increase in reproducible capital. The latter is conventionally defined as *net national saving* (NNS):

Net National Saving (NNS) = GNS – value of the consumption of domestic fixed capital

However, as explained in Chapter 1, the economic wealth of a country also comprises natural resources and human capital. Natural capital is especially important for developing economies, as it comprises around 25% of the total wealth of upper middle-income countries, 39% in lower middle-income countries, and 41% in low-income countries (see Figure 2.7). Human capital is also important, as it is a measure of the health and skills embodied in an economy's workforce. Unfortunately, the conventional measure of net national saving does not allow for depreciation of natural capital, which can arise through the depletion of forests, minerals and energy that occurs during the process of production each year. Similarly, NNS does not account for annual private and public expenditures, such as in education, health and training, that can lead to net additions to human capital (in standard national accounting these expenditures are instead treated as consumption). Modifying NNS for natural capital depletion and any expenditure that results in net additions to human capital is called *adjusted net saving*:

Adjusted Net Saving (ANS) = NNS – depreciation of natural capital + net additions to human capital

Often, it is more revealing to express ANS as a percentage share of gross national income (GNI) as this shows how much an economy is adding to its overall wealth out of the income it generates each year. In addition, one can also denote ANS as a percentage share of adjusted net national income (ANNI), which adjusts national income for both reproducible and natural capital depreciation (see Chapter 2 Appendix for further explanation of ANNI).

The figure below summarizes the various adjustments that are required to derive ANS from the conventional economic indicators of gross and net national saving.

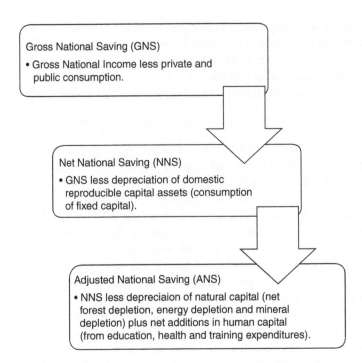

Figure 3.8   Adjusting gross national saving (GNS) for changes in reproducible, natural and human capital

4
The Age of Ecological Scarcity

Introduction

A critical problem facing humankind today is the rapid disappearance and deg-radation of many ecosystems worldwide. For the first time in history, fossil fuel energy and raw material use, environmental degradation and pollution has occurred on such an unprecedented scale that the resulting consequences in terms of global warming, ecosystem decline and environmental degradation are generating worldwide impacts. As a consequence, we are on the verge of a new era, the "Age of Ecological Scarcity".[1]

To overcome these problems, the pattern and structure of modern economies will need to change. As a starting point, we need to recognize that the basic unit of nature – the ecosystem – is also a special form of natural capital, which we can think of as *ecological capital*. Humans depend on and use ecosystems for a whole range of important benefits, including life support. Hence, our ecological wealth is extremely valuable, and must be protected and enhanced rather than wasted and degraded.

However, ecological capital is unique compared to other economic assets.[2] First, unlike skills, education, machines, tools and other types of reprodu-cible and human capital, we do not have to manufacture ecological capital; it is endowed by nature. Second, the provision of goods and services by many ecosystems is poorly understood, their values are often not marketed, and we are uncertain about their future importance. These include many vital benefits, such as natural hazard protection, nutrient uptake, erosion control, water purification and carbon sequestration. Third, although some degraded ecosystems can be restored, most are declining rapidly through habitat destruction, land conversion, pollution impacts and biological invasion. Finally, stressed ecosystems are vulnerable to unexpected, sudden and irre-versible collapse, which substantially impacts the quantity and quality of benefits provided.

Perhaps because ecological capital has been provided freely to us by nature, we tend to view it as limitless, abundant and always available for our use, exploitation and conversion at minimal cost. As a result, our remaining ecosystems and the various goods and services they provide still tend to be *undervalued*. The consequence is overexploitation of ecological capital in the pursuit of economic development, growth and progress. Over time, as ecological impacts and associated economic losses become apparent, the costs of irreversible ecosystem conversion, overexploitation and the risk of collapse may be significant. But, unfortunately, today's economies continue to exploit natural resources for raw material and energy inputs or use the environment to assimilate pollution and other waste by-products, while ignoring any consequences in terms of increasing ecological impacts and risks.

To overcome these problems, what is urgently required is better measurement of the contribution of ecological capital to current and future economic well-being, as well as better understanding of the economic consequences of its rapid decline. We also need to create the economic incentives for improved ecosystem management and use. The failure to do so may not only have important environmental impacts but also contribute to the current structural imbalance of the world economy. The purpose of this chapter is to discuss the environmental and economic consequences of growing ecological scarcity; Chapter 5 explains its role in the growing structural imbalance of the world economy.

Ecological scarcity

To understand why ecological scarcity is a fundamental economic problem, it is helpful to recap what has been learned in previous chapters about the modern economy's perspective on nature and wealth.

Although it is *economic wealth* that matters to current and future well-being, economies today focus on accumulating *national wealth*.[3] Recall from Chapter 1 that, as conventionally defined, national capital wealth comprises the total market value of everything owned by the residents and government of a given country at a given point in time. As depicted in the top half of Figure 4.1, we typically divide such national wealth into *tangible assets*, which are all the forms of marketable capital that can contribute to the current and future production of an economy, and *financial assets*, which are all marketable stores of, or claims on, wealth.

However, if we are interested in the economic wealth of an economy, we are interested in all forms of capital that can contribute to the current and future well-being of all those who depend on the economy for their livelihoods. All the tangible assets listed in Figure 4.1 – land, marketed natural resources and reproducible capital – are clearly very important forms of economic wealth as

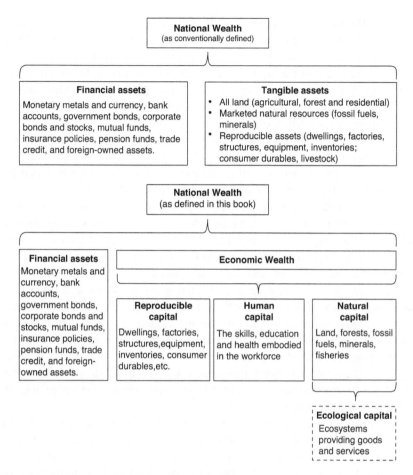

Figure 4.1   National wealth and economic wealth

they contribute to the current and future production of an economy. But they are not the only assets that support current and future well-being. Instead, as indicated in Figure 4.1, economic wealth should include three distinct assets: reproducible (or produced) capital: e.g., roads, buildings, machinery, factories, etc.; human capital: e.g., a healthy, better educated and more skilled workforce; and natural capital: e.g., land, forests, fossil fuels, minerals, fisheries. In addition, natural capital also consists of those ecosystems that through their natural functioning and habitats provide important goods and services to the economy, or ecological capital. Given the unique attributes of the latter asset, as shown in Figure 4.1, one could also consider ecological capital as a special type, or sub-set, of natural capital.

Despite the importance of reproducible, human and natural capital for the current and future well-being of people, modern economies do not maintain or even accumulate all of these assets. As countries become richer, less of their wealth comprises natural capital, such as agricultural land, forests, protected areas, minerals and fossil fuels, and instead, reproducible capital and financial assets have become the most important forms of wealth. In the richest economies, financial wealth accounts for more and more national wealth and income – a trend that has accelerated since the 1970s.[4] This is the pattern of wealth accumulation that the modern world economy encourages today.

Although in the modern era all economies have become entirely dependent on fossil fuel energy and non-renewable material use, the global integration of commodity markets has ensured that any economy can sustain its expansion by supplementing exploitation of its resource endowment with rising consumption of energy and other primary products purchased in international markets. Hence, the great paradox of modern economic development: as countries become richer, less of their economic wealth comprises natural capital, such as agricultural land, forests, protected areas, minerals and fossil fuels, but as economies grow and become wealthier, they consume more energy – mainly fossil fuels – and more natural resources generally. Meanwhile, the vast majority of low and middle-income countries depend on exporting a large percentage of primary products relative to total merchandise exports. As a consequence, the current pattern and structure of modern global development encourages *carbon-dependent* rich and large emerging market countries, and *resource-dependent* developing countries.

Finally, carbon and resource-dependent development in the world economy is having a major impact on our global endowment of ecological capital. Over the past 50 years, ecosystems have been modified more rapidly and extensively than in any comparable period in human history, largely to meet rapidly growing demands for food, fresh water, timber, fiber and fuel. The result has been a substantial and largely irreversible loss in biological diversity, ecosystems and the ecological services that they provide. In other words, our endowment of ecological capital is declining rapidly.

The consequence of this decline in ecological capital is the economic problem of ecological scarcity. For our purposes, *ecological scarcity* can be defined as the loss of the many contributions that ecosystems make to human wellbeing as these natural systems are exploited for human use and economic activity.

Ecological scarcity arises through a fundamental trade-off in our use of the natural environment, which relates directly to the current dependence of economies on ever-increasing natural resource depletion, pollution and ecological degradation. This trade-off can be depicted in a simple diagram (see Figure 4.2). Economic development cannot proceed without exploiting

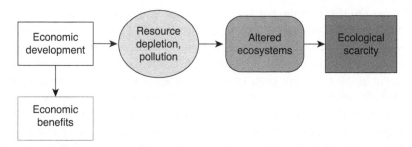

Figure 4.2 Ecological scarcity and the economy–environment trade-off

As economic development proceeds, it generates many economic benefits through the production and consumption of commodities. However, development also leads to natural resource depletion, pollution and the alteration of ecosystems. The latter can lead to ecological scarcity, i.e., the relative decline in beneficial ecosystem goods and services. Thus, the fundamental economy–environment trade-off is between the economic benefits arising from development and any resulting environmental and welfare impacts arising from natural resource depletion, pollution and ecological degradation.

natural resources for raw material and energy inputs or using the environment to assimilate pollution and other waste by-products. On the positive side, economic development also leads to the increased production and consumption of human-made goods and services. Technological change and innovation can also substitute for some of the raw material and energy inputs provided by natural capital. As these goods and services contribute to overall human welfare, they can be considered the "economic benefits" of development. However, the exploitation and use of the natural environment by humans for raw materials, energy and waste assimilation also leads to the alteration of many ecosystems. The disruption and destruction of ecosystems affect, in turn, their various contributions to human welfare, such as the use of aesthetic landscapes for recreation, the maintenance of beneficial species, the control of erosion, protection against floods or storms, and so forth. The loss of these "ecological benefits", or ecosystem goods and services, as the consequence of economic development can be considered increasing *ecological scarcity.*[5]

Once we begin to see ecological scarcity as an economic problem, it is not difficult to view ecosystems as ecological capital. Because many ecosystems generate goods and services that contribute to human welfare, they should be considered a form of economic wealth, as we have indicated in Figure 4.1. The trade-off of increased economic benefits versus increased ecological scarcity is therefore really about a trade-off between different assets. On the one hand, we are creating economic wealth by accumulating some assets – reproducible capital, financial assets and in some instances, human capital; on the other, we are sacrificing our available natural and ecological wealth to do so.

The rest of this chapter explains why the overexploitation of natural capital, and in particular ecological capital, in the pursuit of economic development, growth and progress is a major structural imbalance in the world economy today. To correct this imbalance will require better understanding and measurement of the economic costs of rising ecological scarcity, and ensuring that markets, institutions and policies include rather than hide these costs. These are the main themes that we will explore next. Before doing so, it is important to explain more clearly the key economic benefits provided by ecosystems, and how they arise through the normal structure and functioning of these important natural assets.

Ecological capital

The idea that ecosystems provide a range of "goods and services" that have value to humans is an important step in characterizing these systems as a special type of capital asset – *ecological capital*. That is, to be treated just like any other asset or investment in the economy, ecosystems must be capable of generating current and future flows of income or benefits.

For example, it is clear that what makes all the tangible and financial assets listed in Figure 4.1 valuable forms of *national wealth* is that they either support the economic production of marketable goods and services (tangible assets) or they are important stores of or claims on wealth that generate income as investments (financial assets). Consequently, people are willing to sell, purchase and hold on to these tangible and financial assets, which is why we can measure this "wealth" in terms of the total market value of all these two types of assets owned by the residents and government of a given country at a given point in time.

Similarly, we have argued that what makes reproducible, human and natural capital important assets comprising *economic wealth* is that they are forms of capital that can contribute to the current and future well-being of all those who depend on the economy for their livelihoods. In economics, we refer to these contributions to current and future well-being as "economic benefits", or *benefits*, for short.

A growing literature also suggests that ecosystems are assets that produce a flow of beneficial goods and services over time.[6] It is increasingly common to refer to these multiple benefits as *ecosystem services*. Or, as the Millennium Ecosystem Assessment defines them, "ecosystem services are the benefits people obtain from ecosystems".[7]

For example, the case for using ecosystem services to justify characterizing ecosystems as a form of capital has been made succinctly by Gretchen Daily and colleagues:

The world's ecosystems are capital assets. If properly managed, they yield a flow of vital services, including the production of goods (such as seafood and timber), life support processes (such as pollination and water purification), and life-fulfilling conditions. (such as beauty and serenity).[8]

In sum, the idea that ecosystems provide a range of goods and services that have value to humans is an important step in characterizing these unique assets as ecological capital. That is, just like any other asset in the economy, such as roads, building, machinery, financial wealth or job skills and education, ecosystems generate current and future flows of benefits, or *income*. In principle, then, ecosystems should be valued like other economic assets. The myriad goods and services they provide are essentially the beneficial flows of current and future "income". And, regardless, of whether or not there exists a market for the goods and services from ecological capital, it is an essential form of economic wealth.

Ecosystem goods and services

The way in which ecosystems provide their various benefits to humans is both complex and unique, which makes ecological capital unusual compared to other forms of economic wealth. Our failure to understand how this process works and how it contributes to the well-being of humans are major reasons why we tend to take ecosystems for granted and thus "undervalue" them.

Figure 4.3 summarizes this mechanism. *Ecosystems* comprise the abiotic (non-living) environment and the biotic (living) groupings of plant and

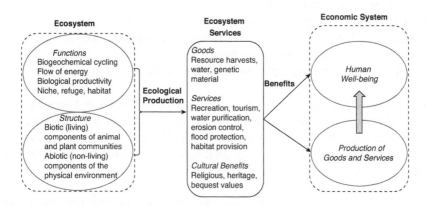

Figure 4.3 How ecosystems generate economic benefits

Note: The structure and functioning of ecosystems leads to the ecological production of ecosystem services. Some of these services benefit humans directly, whereas others indirectly benefit human well-being through supporting or protecting economic assets and production activities.

animal species called communities. The biotic and abiotic components, and the interactions between them, are often referred to as the *ecosystem structure*. In addition, essential *ecosystem functions* are carried out in every ecosystem: biogeochemical cycling and flow of energy. Important processes of biogeo-chemical cycling include primary production (photosynthesis), nutrient and water cycling, and materials decomposition. The flow, storage and transform-ation of materials and energy through the system are also influenced by proc-esses that link organisms with each other, such as the food web, which is made up of interlocking food chains. These food chains are often characterized by other key functions, such as pollination, predation and parasitism.

This basic structure and functions of an ecosystem are the source of many valuable goods and services, or benefits, to humans. For example, some of the living organisms found in an ecosystem might be harvested or hunted for food, collected for raw materials or simply valued because they are aesthet-ically pleasing. Some of the ecosystem functions, such as nutrient and water cycling, can also benefit humans through purifying water, controlling floods, recharging aquifers, reducing pollution, or simply by providing more pleasing environments for recreation. As noted above, these multiple and diverse bene-fits are now commonly called *ecosystem services*. As indicated in Figure 4.3, we can think of the structure and functioning of ecosystems as leading to the *eco-logical production* of ecosystem services.

Because of its broad interpretation, the term ecosystem services is used fre-quently to include a wide variety of benefits provided by ecosystems, which in economics would normally be classified under three different categories:

- "goods", e.g., products obtained from ecosystems, such as resource harvests, water and genetic material,
- "services", e.g., recreational and tourism benefits or certain ecological regu-latory and habitat functions, such as water purification, climate regulation, erosion control and habitat provision), and
- "cultural benefits", e.g., spiritual and religious beliefs, heritage values.[9]

Some of these benefits, such as resource harvests, recreation and even various cultural benefits, are well known to economists and have been the focus of environmental valuation efforts for some time. However, other ecosystem serv-ices, such as those arising from ecological regulatory and habitat functions, are less well understood and not have been always been assessed for the benefits they provide.

Although ecosystem services arise from the structure and functioning of ecosystems, the latter are not synonymous with the benefits provided to humans. Ecosystem structure and functions describe the components of an ecosystem and its biophysical relationship regardless of whether or not humans benefit from them. Only if they contribute to human well-being do these components and relationships generate an "ecosystem service".[10] As indicated in Figure 4.3, in some cases, ecosystem services can benefit human well-being directly, e.g., through enjoyment of recreation, cultural benefits and consumption of wild foods, or through protecting human health and lives through providing control of floods or reducing harmful pollutants. However, some ecosystem services also benefit humans indirectly, by providing protection or support of economic activities and other assets, which produce goods and services that humans enjoy or need. For example, the control of flooding may also reduce damages to production activities and property, and pollination may support the production of valuable agricultural crops.

Table 4.1 uses the example of a coastal wetland ecosystem, such as a salt marsh or mangrove, to illustrate more specifically how ecosystem structure and functioning can generate some important ecosystem services that benefit humans. Two of the most important ecosystem services are coastal protection, and support for offshore fisheries. Mangroves and marsh can reduce the energy of waves, thus protecting coastal populations, property and production activities from the damaging impacts of storm surge, and in the case of mangroves, high winds. However, the ability of these wetlands to provide coastal protection depends on the quality of vegetation, sea level and tides, beach slope, strength of winds and waves and other structural features. Similarly, mangroves and marsh provide breeding and nursery habitat for many fish species that are eventually harvested when they migrate offshore as adults. As indicated in Table 4.1, there are many structural components and functions of these ecosystems that make them a suitable habitat to support coastal and marine fisheries.

To summarize, ecosystems provide a number of valuable goods and services to humans. However, because most of these benefits are provided by ecosystems and endowed by nature, i.e., for free, they tend to be "undervalued". That is, there is no market for many important ecosystem goods and services, and so we have no information of the "price" people are willing to pay to have more of them, nor any incentive to manage ecosystems better. Moreover, because of the complex way in which the ecological production of ecosystem services occurs, we often do not know the consequences for human well-being when ecosystems are lost or degraded. Nor do we know the costs of replicating the ecological production of many ecosystem services, or if it is even technically feasible. These are important factors behind the widespread decline in ecological capital today.

The decline of ecological capital

Several indicators suggest that ecological scarcity is a growing problem worldwide.

Table 4.1 Examples of ecosystem functions and structure producing ecosystem services of salt marsh and mangroves

	Salt Marsh			Mangroves		
	Key ecosystem functions	Key structural components	Resulting ecosystem service	Key ecosystem functions	Key structural components	Resulting ecosystem service
	Biological productivity and diversity	Marsh species and density, habitat quality, inundation depth, healthy predator populations	Raw material and food	Biological productivity and diversity	Mangrove species and density, habitat quality, inundation depth, healthy predator populations	Raw material and food
	Attenuates and/or dissipates wave energy	Sea level, tides, coastal geomorphology, wave height and length, water depth, marsh area and width, wind velocity, marsh species and density	Coastal protection	Attenuates and/or dissipates wave and wind energy	Sea level, tides, coastal geomorphology, wave height and length, water depth, mangrove area and width, wind velocity, marsh species and density	Coastal protection
	Sediment stabilization and soil retention	Sea level, tides, coastal geomorphology, subsidence, fluvial sediment deposition and load, marsh species and density	Erosion control	Sediment stabilization and soil retention	Sea level, tides, coastal geomorphology, subsidence, fluvial sediment deposition and load, mangrove species and density	Erosion control
	Water flow regulation and control	Sea level, tides, coastal geomorphology, water depth, marsh area and width, marsh species and density	Flood protection	Water flow regulation and control	Sea level, tides, coastal geomorphology, water depth, mangrove area and width, mangrove species and density, mangrove root length	Flood protection

Ecosystem process	Marsh indicators	Ecosystem service
Nutrient and pollution uptake and retention, particle deposition	Marsh species and density, marsh quality and area, nutrient and sediment load, water supply and quality, healthy predator populations	Water purification and supply
Suitable reproductive habitat and nursery grounds, sheltered living space	Marsh species and density, marsh quality and area, primary productivity, healthy predator populations	Maintenance of fisheries, hunting and foraging activities
Biogeochemical activity, sedimentation, biological productivity	Marsh species and density, sediment type, primary productivity	Carbon sequestration
Biological productivity and diversity, healthy ecosystem functioning	Marsh species and density, habitat quality and area, prey species availability, healthy predator populations	Tourism, recreation, education and research

Ecosystem process	Mangrove indicators	Ecosystem service
Nutrient and pollution uptake and retention, particle deposition	Mangrove species and density, mangrove quality and area, nutrient and sediment load, water supply and quality, healthy predator populations	Water purification and supply
Suitable reproductive habitat and nursery grounds, sheltered living space	Mangrove species and density, mangrove quality and area, primary productivity, healthy predator populations	Maintenance of fisheries, hunting and foraging activities
Biogeochemical activity, sedimentation, biological productivity	Mangrove species and density, sediment type and deposition, primary productivity	Carbon sequestration
Biological productivity and diversity, healthy ecosystem functioning	Mangrove species and density, habitat quality and area, prey species availability, healthy predator populations	Tourism, recreation, education and research

An important indicator of the global decline in ecological capital was provided by the Millennium Ecosystem Assessment, which found that over 60% of the world's major ecosystem goods and services were degraded or used unsustainably (see Table 4.2).[11] Some vital benefits to humankind fall in this category, including fresh water, capture fisheries, water purification and waste treatment, wild foods, genetic resources, biochemicals, wood fuel, pollination, spiritual, religious and aesthetic values, and the regulation of regional and local climate, erosion, pests and natural hazards.

Almost all the degraded ecosystem goods and services listed in Table 4.2 are not marketed. Some goods, such as capture fisheries, fresh water, wild foods and wood fuel, are commercially marketed, but due to the poor management

Table 4.2 Global status of key ecosystem goods and services

Condition globally has been enhanced	Condition globally has been degraded	Condition globally is mixed
Crops	Capture fisheries	Timber
Livestock	Wild foods	Cotton, hemp, silk and other
Aquaculture	Wood fuel	fiber crops
	Genetic resources	Water regulation
	Biochemicals, natural medi-	Disease regulation
	cines and pharmaceuticals	Recreation and ecotourism
	Fresh water	
	Air quality regulation	
	Regional and local climate	
	regulation	
	Erosion regulation	
	Water purification and waste	
	treatment	
	Pest regulation	
	Pollination	
	Natural hazard regulation	
	Spiritual and religious values	
	Aesthetic values	
	Global climate regulation	

Notes: Enhancement is defined as either increased production of or change in the ecosystem good or service that leads to greater benefits for people; Degradation is defined as if current use exceeds sustainable levels, or a reduction in the benefits obtained from the good or service due to either some human-induced change or use exceeding its limits; Mixed status implies that the condition of the good or service globally has experienced enhancement in some regions but degradation in others.

Source: Millennium Ecosystem Assessment (MA) (2005) *Ecosystems and Human Well-being: Synthesis*. Washington, DC: Island Press, table 1. Although the MA reported that global climate regulation by ecosystems has been enhanced, recent scientific evidence reported by the Intergovernmental Panel on Climate Change (IPCC) suggests that this may no longer be the case. See Intergovernmental Panel on Climate Change (IPCC) Working Group II (2014) *Climate Change 2014: Impacts, Adaptation, and Vulnerability*. Philadelphia: Saunders. Available at: www.ipcc.ch/report/ar5/wg2/

of the biological resources and ecosystems that are the source of these goods, the market prices do not reflect unsustainable use and overexploitation. Nor have adequate policies and institutions been developed to handle the costs associated with worsening ecological scarcity globally. All too often, policy distortions and failures compound these problems by encouraging wasteful use of natural resources and environmental degradation.

One reason for the extensive habitat loss and degradation among terrestrial ecosystems globally is the ongoing conversion of forests and grasslands to agriculture, especially in tropical developing countries. As we saw in Chapter 2, over the past 50 years, agricultural land area in the tropics has expanded while forest area continues to decline (see Figure 2.4). Agricultural land expansion is also responsible for the loss of many tropical savannahs and grasslands.[12] In the major developing regions of Africa, Asia and Latin America, demand for new land for crop production shows little sign of abating in the near future. Feeding a growing world population is expected to require an additional 3 to 5 million hectares (ha) of new cropland each year from now until 2030, which could contribute to additional clearing of 150 to 300 million ha in total area of natural forests.[13]

Important marine ecosystems have also experienced alarming rates of loss over recent decades. Due to coastal development, population growth, pollution and other human activities, 50% of salt marshes, 35% of mangroves, 30% of coral reefs, and 29% of sea grasses have already been lost or degraded worldwide.[14] As much as 89% of oyster reefs may also have been lost globally.[15] Overfishing has been a persistent and growing problem in marine environments, and loss of fisheries is also linked to declining water quality through the increasing occurrence of harmful algal blooms, offshore pollution and oxygen depletion (hypoxia).[16] Finally, the disruptions in precipitation, temperature and hydrology accompanying climate change also impact marine fisheries and the key habitats that sustain them, such as wetlands, mangroves, coral and oyster reefs, and sea grass beds.[17]

Freshwater ecosystems are also under stress globally by a combination of interacting human-induced threats and global environmental change (see Table 4.3). Freshwater ecosystems, which comprise ponds, lakes, streams, rivers and wetlands, are the main source of accessible water supply for humans on our planet.[18] Other important human uses of freshwater ecosystems include inland capture fisheries, which contribute about 12% of all fish consumed by humans, irrigated agriculture, which supplies about 40% of the world's food crops, and hydropower, which provides nearly 20% of the world's electricity production.[19] The human-induced threats to freshwater ecosystems include modification of river systems and their associated wetlands, water withdrawals for flood control, agriculture or water supply, pollution and eutrophication, overharvesting of inland fisheries, and the introduction of invasive alien species; the significant environmental impacts are climate change, nitrogen deposition and shifts in precipitation and run-off patterns (see Table 4.3). These threats pose a grave risk to human water security by increasing water scarcity, endangering freshwater biodiversity, and in some cases are detrimental to both water security and biodiversity.

The state of global biological diversity also shows considerable decline. The Living Planet Index (LPI), which measures trends in thousands of the world's vertebrate species population, shows a decline of 52% from 1970 to 2010.[20] In effect, over the past 40 years, the number of mammals, birds, reptiles, amphibians and fish has been halved. For freshwater species, the decline has been even worse (76%). For tropical countries, the LPI shows a 56% fall in species, with Latin America experiencing the worst drop (83%). The main causes of the loss in species globally appear to be habitat loss and degradation, hunting and fishing, and climate change.

In sum, every major indicator of the health and status of the world's most important ecosystems indicates that ecological capital is in serious decline. Moreover, the problem seems to have been worsening over recent decades. This deterioration in ecological capital worldwide is the clearest evidence that we have entered an Age of Ecological Scarcity.

Table 4.3   Main threats to and impacts on freshwater ecosystems

	Negative impacts on:	
Type of threat:	**Freshwater biodiversity**	**Water security**
Human-induced		
Modification of river systems and their associated wetlands	Yes	No
Water withdrawals for flood control, agriculture or water supply	Yes	No
Pollution and eutrophication	Yes	Yes
Overharvesting of inland fisheries	Yes	No
Introduction of invasive alien species	Yes	No
Environmental change		
Climate change	Yes	Yes
Nitrogen deposition	Yes	Yes
Shifts in precipitation and run-off patterns	Yes	Yes

Sources: W. R. T. Darwall, et al. (2008) "Freshwater Biodiversity – A Hidden Resource Under Threat", in J.-C. Vié, C. Hilton-Taylor and S. N. Stuart (eds), *The 2008 Review of The IUCN Red List of Threatened Species*. Gland, Switzerland: IUCN; D. Dudgeon, et al. (2006) "Freshwater Biodiversity: Importance, Threats, Status and Conservation Challenges", *Biological Review*, 31: 163–182; C. Revenga, et al. (2005) "Prospects for Monitoring Freshwater Ecosystems Towards the 2010 Targets", *Philosophical Transactions of the Royal Society B-Biological Sciences*, 360: 397–413; and C. J. Vörösmarty, et al. (2012) "Global Threats to Human Water Security and River Biodiversity", *Nature*, 467: 555–561.

Accounting for ecological capital

As previous chapters have shown, because the accumulation of natural capital is considered no longer vital to the overall economic wealth of successful modern economies – and certainly a less important form of national wealth than before the Industrial Revolution – we routinely fail to account for how much natural capital is "depreciated", or "used up", by an economy to produce more goods and services each year.

What we have shown in this chapter is that an important sub-set of natural capital – ecological capital – is especially endangered by current patterns of economic development. Over the past 50 years, ecosystems have been modified more rapidly and extensively than in any comparable period in human history, largely to meet burgeoning demands for food, energy, raw materials and other resource products and to serve as a "sink" to absorb waste. Unfortunately, ecological capital, being unique, poorly understood and difficult to measure, tends to be undervalued. Nevertheless, ecological capital remains an important source of economic wealth, because it contributes to current and future human well-being. Accounting for the economic contributions of ecological capital is therefore just as important as any other asset that generates essential benefits.

Recall that the Appendix to Chapter 2 demonstrated how national income can be adjusted to allow for both depreciation of reproducible capital and natural capital, resulting in a measure of *adjusted net national income*. Many economists believe that the latter is a better measure of the "net income" generated by an economy each year, as it accounts for the "using up" of two important stocks of capital – natural resources and reproducible assets – to produce more goods and services. In this chapter, we have argued that the concept of economic wealth should be extended to include ecological capital. It follows that, if the economy is also degrading or converting ecosystems to produce more goods and services each year, then the net income generated should also account for any losses to this type of economic wealth. Thus, the Appendix to this chapter shows the measure of adjusted net national income could be further extended to allow for any such changes in ecological capital, as well as the direct benefits to human well-being provided by the remaining ecosystems.

Consider the example of mangroves in Thailand over 1970 to 2009.[21] Thailand is estimated to have lost around a third of its mangroves since the 1960s, mainly to shrimp farming expansion and other coastal development. Yet mangroves provide four essential ecosystem benefits – collected wood and non-wood products (e.g., shellfish, plants, honey, medicines, etc.), nursery and breeding grounds for offshore fisheries, storm protection and carbon sequestration. Estimates of these benefits can be used to determine the annual net gain or loss in mangrove value that results from conversion to other land uses (see Figure 4.4). This net mangrove value has two components. The remaining

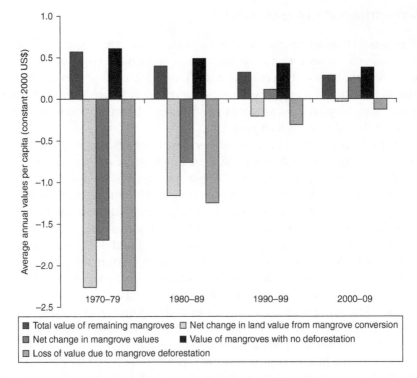

Figure 4.4   Accounting for mangrove capital, Thailand, 1970–2009

Notes: Total value of remaining mangroves are the net subsistence benefits to local coastal communities from mangrove nursery and breeding ground support for offshore fisheries and from wood and non-wood products collected from mangrove forests (e.g., shellfish, plants, honey, medicines, etc.), and carbon sequestration benefits. As storm protection value is based on expected damages to economic property, it is assumed that this benefit is already accounted for in the current market values of property; Net change in land value from mangrove conversion is the difference between the capitalized value of mangroves converted to shrimp farms less the capitalized value of these mangroves if they were not converted. The latter valuation includes all current and future mangrove benefits from collected wood and non-wood products, nursery and breeding grounds for offshore fisheries, storm protection, and carbon sequestration; Value of mangroves with no deforestation assumes that the mangrove area remains unchanged since 1970. The total value of mangroves in 1970 was $25.2 million (constant 2000 US$) and the population of Thailand was 36.9 million. The decline in per capita values over 1970–2009 is therefore due to population growth; Based on the annual losses from deforestation, the total per capita losses in Thailand from mangrove deforestation from 1970 to 2009 amount to $39.79 per person (constant 2000 US$). Based on the 2009 population of 68.7 million, the total cumulative losses from mangrove deforestation from 1970 to 2009 are over $2.73 billion (constant 2000 US$).

Source: Adapted from Edward B. Barbier (2014) "Account for Depreciation of Natural Capital", *Nature*, 515: 32–33.

mangroves generate extra benefits each year that do not appear in the national accounts, such as net subsistence for local coastal communities and economy-wide carbon sequestration benefits. But from these values must be subtracted the net loss in land value that arises from converting mangroves each year to some other economic activity, such as shrimp farming.

The economic impacts are significant. During the 1970s and 1980s, when mangrove deforestation was rapid, Thailand lost $1.69 and $0.76 respectively in mangrove net values per person per year. By 2009, around one-third of the 1970 mangrove area was deforested and Thailand's population had grown rapidly. As a result, the total value from the subsistence and carbon benefits of the remaining mangroves has halved, from $0.57 to $0.28 per person per year (see Figure 4.4). This means that, even though mangrove loss slowed in the 1990s and 2000s, the net values of mangroves were very modest, only $0.11 and $0.25 respectively.

To put it another way, cumulative mangrove deforestation over the past four decades in Thailand has cost each Thai citizen $40. This debit amounts to losses of more than $2.73 billion, which has never appeared in Thailand's national accounts.

Halting the decline in natural capital – including ecosystem loss – worldwide will require many more examples for different countries and regions, and for other key ecosystems, such as tropical forests, coral reefs, freshwater wetlands, grasslands, and so on. In addition, there are clearly intrinsic values and other important cultural benefits to preserving unique natural resources, species and ecosystems, as well as the biological diversity contained in these systems, which have so far proven difficult to capture by current approaches to accounting for ecological capital. Other benefits of many important ecosystem services are also proving difficult to value, such as pollution control, pollination, climate regulation and watershed protection.

The UN and the World Bank have begun pilot studies to construct adjustments to income and wealth that include changes in ecological capital, as well as other types of natural capital besides minerals, energy and timber harvests. The UN *Inclusive Wealth Report 2012* has developed accounts from 1990 to 2008 for 20 countries that include non-timber benefits from forests, carbon sequestration, fisheries (for four countries only), carbon damages and agricultural land, as well as minerals, energy and timber.[22] The follow up *Inclusive Wealth Report 2014* has extended this analysis to 140 countries.[23] The World Bank is expanding pilot studies on ecosystem accounting from 8 to 15 developing countries, which cover water, forest and mangrove ecosystems.[24] To move beyond these pilot studies, the UN systems of national accounts must adopt a more systematic approach, that all countries can follow, to account for losses of natural capital and ecological capital, as we already do for depreciation of reproducible capital.

Global implications

The example of Thailand's mangroves illustrate why accounting for the growing problem of declining ecological capital and increasing ecological scarcity is so important. As long as the resulting economic costs remain hidden, we have little idea how much the current and future well-being of people are affected. Only by accounting for the depreciation of natural capital, including the loss and degradation of ecosystems, can we see how much we are using up of our natural endowment to produce more goods and services in the economy each year.

Because many of the goods and services provided by ecosystems are not marketed, their rising ecological scarcity is not reflected in everyday transactions and policy decisions. This underpricing of nature is a major structural imbalance in the world economy today. To correct this imbalance will require better understanding and measurement of the economic costs of rising ecological scarcity, and ensuring that markets, institutions and policies include rather than disregard these costs.

If instead the growing scarcity of vital ecosystem goods and services were not ignored but reflected in the markets, policies and institutions of modern economies, then these "price signals" would stimulate improvements to the management and use of ecosystems. These incentives would also encourage restoration of degraded ecosystems, where it is cost-effective, as well as technological change and innovation that would facilitate substitution for ecologically damaging production and development activities.

Conclusion

Previous chapters have documented the rapid loss in natural capital that has occurred in recent decades. These trends show little sign of abating, especially as economies grow and accumulate other forms of wealth, principally reproducible capital and financial assets. Since the 1970s, natural capital depreciation has been on the rise in all countries, except perhaps for a brief respite during the Great Recession of 2008–2010. In addition, the decline in natural capital has been five times greater in developing countries compared to the eight richest economies.

In addition, as this chapter has shown, over the past several decades, the world has seen dramatic declines in ecological capital – ecosystems such as wetlands, coral reefs, grasslands and freshwater systems that also provide valuable goods and services to economies. The results have been the loss of some important current and future benefits to humankind, such as freshwater, capture fisheries, water purification and waste treatment, wild foods, genetic resources, biochemicals, wood fuel, pollination, spiritual, religious and aesthetic values, and the regulation of regional and local climate, erosion, pests and natural hazards.

However, because most of these benefits are provided by ecosystems for free, they tend to be "undervalued". There are no markets for many important ecosystem goods and services, and because of the complex way in which the ecological production of ecosystem services occur, we often do not know the consequences for human well-being when ecological capital is depleted or degraded. Nor do we know the costs of replicating the ecological production of many ecosystem services, or if it is even technically feasible. These are important factors behind the widespread decline in ecological capital today.

As highlighted in this chapter, the decline in ecological capital is a major structural feature embedded in the workings of the modern world economy. What is more, the economy cannot automatically correct for this problem, because the increasing costs associated with this rising ecological scarcity are not routinely reflected in markets. Nor have adequate policies and institutions been developed to handle the costs associated with worsening ecological scarcity globally; in fact, too often, existing policies and institutions compound the problem by encouraging wasteful use of natural resources and environmental degradation.

In Chapter 6, we discuss further how the underpricing of nature leads to excessive use and degradation of natural resources and the environment, and thus the continuing and rapid decline in global ecosystems and the important benefits that they provide. However, we also begin our exploration of how this trend is linked to another structural imbalance in the economy: the premium paid for increasingly scarce human capital, which is contributing to the growing gap between rich and poor in all economies of the world.

Appendix

Extending adjusted net national income for ecological capital

As explained in the Appendix to Chapter 2, an important economic indicator for all countries is *gross national income* (GNI). Each year, this flow of national income can either be spent on current private and public consumption by individuals and government, respectively, or it can be saved as a source of investment. Thus, in that appendix, we how showed how national income can be adjusted to allow for both depreciation of reproducible capital and natural capital, resulting in a measure of *adjusted net national income* (ANNI). Many economists believe that the latter is a better measure of the "net income" generated by an economy each year, as it accounts for the "using up" of two important stocks of capital – natural resources and reproducible assets – to produce more goods and services.

If ecosystems are also considered capital assets – or *ecological capital* for short – then ANNI should be modified to account for the contributions of ecosystems as well, including any changes that occur to this asset. Accounting for changes in ecological capital should involve similar rules for estimating the depreciation and appreciation of other assets in an economy.[25] First, accounting for ecosystems and their services leads to adjusting net national income for the direct benefits provided by the current stock of ecosystems, but not for their indirect contributions to human well-being in terms of supporting economic activity, or protecting the value of other capital assets in the account. The reason for not including these latter contributions is that they are already accounted for in our measure of ANNI. Second, when ecosystems are irreversibly converted for economic development, ANNI must be further modified to reflect any capital revaluation that occurs with the current conversion of ecological capital to other land uses. Similarly, if ecosystems are restored from other land uses, then ANNI must also account for any subsequent gains in ecological capital.[26]

In sum, ANNI should adjust national income for both reproducible and natural capital depreciation, and for the benefits of and changes in ecological capital:

> Adjusted Net National Income (ANNI) = GNI – the value of the consumption of domestic fixed capital – depreciation of natural capital + value of the direct benefits provided by the current stock of ecosystems and any capital revaluation due to ecosystem conversion or restoration.

The figure below summarizes the various adjustments that are required to derive ANNI from the conventional economic indicators of gross domestic product (GDP) and gross national income (GNI).

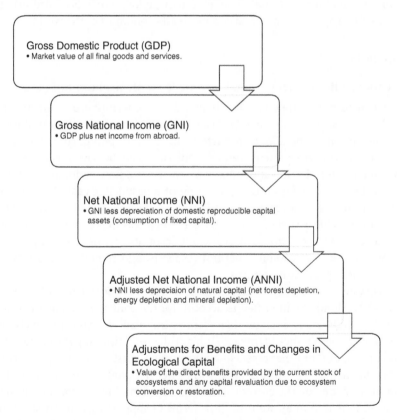

Figure 4.5 Adjusting gross national income (GNI) for reproducible, natural and ecological capital depreciation

5
Structural Imbalance

Introduction

As previous chapters have explored, there is a growing structural imbalance in the world economy, which has at its core a fundamental misalignment between our exploitation of *nature* and the creation of *economic wealth*. One aspect of this misalignment is that rich and large emerging market economies become carbon-dependent, whereas the majority of low and middle-income countries are resource-dependent. Another is the increasing dependence on exploiting more natural resources, such as fossil fuels, minerals, forests and non-renewable material use. But the most dramatic declines in recent decades have been in ecological capital – ecosystems such as wetlands, coral reefs, grasslands and freshwater systems that also provide valuable goods and services to economies. In addition, with greenhouse gas emissions continuing to grow, the Earth's ability to absorb these emissions is diminishing.

This excessive use and degradation of natural resources and the environment is symptomatic of the *underpricing of nature*. We are overusing the environment because the costs associated with increasing natural resource degradation and rising ecological scarcity are not routinely reflected in the markets, institutions and policies of our economies.

However, the structural imbalance of modern economies has another dimension to it. Whereas natural capital (including ecological capital) is underpriced, and hence overly exploited, the *underinvestment in human capital* in economies is making this important asset scarce. Human capital does not just reflect the basic time and effort of labor but represents the skills, education and health embodied in the workforce. Human capital is a unique asset that cannot be detached from the person in whom it is embodied. Thus, when human capital becomes scarce, highly skilled labor receives much higher wages than those with little or no skills.

If nature is underpriced at the same time that insufficient human capital accumulation is occurring, then highly skilled and educated workers become *relatively more expensive* to employ in production compared to natural resources that are used as energy and raw material inputs. This chapter makes the case that this outcome is a pervasive problem in all economies, which has three important consequences for the structure of production. First, all sectors of an economy will use too many natural resources relative to skilled labor. Second, the skilled workers throughout the economy will have higher real incomes and thus will be better off. Third, wealth inequality will increase, as the income gap between skilled and unskilled workers widens. The result is a profound structural imbalance in the modern world economy; global production today uses natural capital excessively, skilled workers are made much better off, and wealth inequality is increasing.

To begin our explanation of how these distortions are linked, we need first to examine the role of human capital in economic wealth. In Chapter 6, we will explore in more detail the key factors underlying the underpricing of natural and ecological capital, and similarly, in Chapter 7, what causes insufficient human capital accumulation and the growing wealth disparity between rich and poor.

Human capital

As explained in Chapter 1, a key asset comprising economic wealth is *human capital*, which consists of the skills, education and health embodied in the workforce (see Figure 1.1). As Chapter 2 demonstrated, national income can be adjusted to allow for both depreciation of reproducible capital and natural capital, resulting in a measure of *adjusted net national income* (ANNI). In Chapter 4, we also showed how ANNI could be further extended to allow for any such changes in ecological capital, as well as the direct benefits to human well-being provided by the remaining ecosystems. It follows that, if we add human capital as an additional component of the stock of economic wealth, then we should also adjust net national income for investments that are contributing to net increases in human capital.

The Appendix to this chapter shows that our concept of adjusted net national income should therefore be further extended to include net additions in human capital from education, health and training investments. As such expenditures lead to a healthy, better educated and more skilled workforce, they are clearly adding to any economy's stock of human capital, and thus serve as a proxy measure of the direct and indirect benefits to human well-being of increases in this vital asset. Note that, with the inclusion of adjustments for net additions to human capital in our concept of ANNI, the latter measure now accounts for all the adjustments to the conventional indicator of an economy's national income for our full stock of economic wealth – reproducible, human, and natural capital (including ecological capital). These adjustments to conventional economic indicators to derive our final measure of fully adjusted net national income are summarized in the figure at the end of this chapter's Appendix.[1]

However, a key feature that distinguishes human capital from the other assets comprising economic wealth is that human capital is "embodied" in labor; that is, one cannot separate the level of health, skills and education from each person or worker. Thus, when we talk about "accumulating" human capital, what we really mean is improvements in the health, education and training of the workforce of an economy.[2] Consequently, it is common to consider the level of human capital to be the acquired skills and knowledge that distinguish *skilled* from *unskilled* labor in an economy. Whereas unskilled labor has only a minimal level of education and training, skilled labor is embodied with much more human capital. Thus, the higher the amount of human capital accumulated in an economy, the higher the level of education and skills of the average worker.

Trends in human capital

Figure 5.1 depicts the trends in the rate of human capital investment (educational expenditure) as a percentage share in adjusted net national income from 1970 to 2012 for the eight wealthiest countries, for developing economies and the world.[3] Over these four decades, the average rate of educational expenditure was 5.7% in the eight rich countries, 5.4% worldwide and 4.0% in developing countries. But the rate of human capital investment appears to be lower in recent years for all countries. For example, in the wealthiest countries, since 2000 the rate of educational expenditure has stayed mainly around 5.5%, whereas from 1975 to 1985 it was well over 6.0%. In developing economies, the rate of educational expenditure climbed to above 4.5% in the early 1990s, but since 1995 has hovered around 4.0%.

Overall, it appears from Figure 5.1 that economies are not increasing human capital investment significantly as they produce more net income each year. Yet, as we saw in Chapter 2, the rate of natural capital depreciation has been rising in all countries since the 1990s (see Figure 2.8). Of particular concern is the rapid increase in the rate of natural capital depreciation in developing countries since the late 1990s, to 8–9% on average, whereas the rate of educational expenditures has remained at 4.0% (see Figure 5.1). This suggests that low and middle-income economies are depleting their fossil fuel, mineral and forest resources at twice the rate at which they are investing in human capital. In other words, in these economies, the decline in natural capital is not being compensated by expansion in human capital.

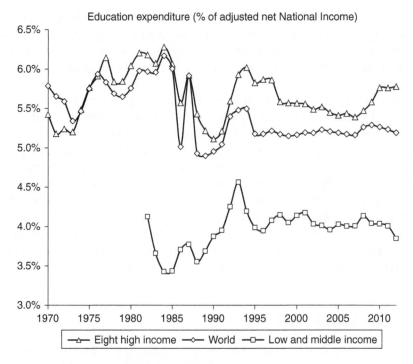

Education expenditure (% of adjusted net National Income)

Figure 5.1　The rate of human capital investment, 1970–2012

The data used for these estimates are from the World Banks' World Development Indicators, available at: http://databank.worldbank.org/data; Low and middle-income (or developing) countries are economies with 2012 per capita income of $12,615 or less; The eight high-income countries are the United States, Japan, Germany, France, United Kingdom, Italy, Canada and Australia; Human capital investment is measured by education expenditure, which refers to the current operating expenditures in education, including wages and salaries and excluding capital investments in buildings and equipment. Adjusted net national income is gross national income minus consumption of fixed capital and the value of net natural resources depletion, expressed in constant 2005 US$; The average rate of education expenditure over 1970–2012 was 5.4% worldwide, 5.7% in the eight high-income countries and 4.0% in developing countries (1982–2012).

Given that the accumulation of human capital is about investing in improvements to the health, education and training of people, a useful indicator is the level of human capital investment per person. Figure 5.2 depicts trends in real educational expenditures per capita from 1970 to 2012 in the eight wealthiest economies, developing countries and the world. Over this period, human capital investment in the rich economies was $119,176 per person, which was 15 times the expenditure worldwide ($7,961) and 25 times the investment in developing countries ($4,694). However, in all countries, education expenditure per capita rose substantially over the past four decades. In the eight high-income countries, the amount doubled so that by 2012 it reached $156,562 per

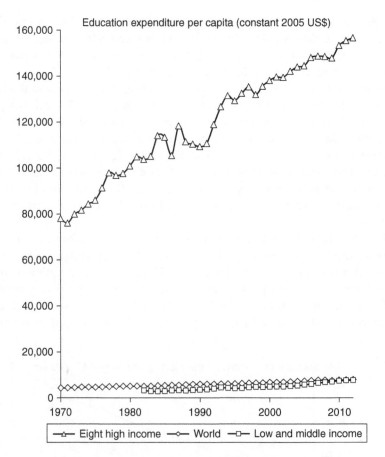

Figure 5.2   Human capital investment per person, 1970–2012

The data used for these estimates are from the World Banks' World Development Indicators, available at: http://databank.worldbank.org/data/views/variableselection/selectvariables.aspx?source=world-development-indicators; Low and middle-income (or developing) countries are economies with 2012 per capita income of $12,615 or less; The eight high-income countries are the United States, Japan, Germany, France, United Kingdom, Italy, Canada and Australia; Human capital investment is measured by education expenditure, which refers to the current operating expenditures in education, including wages and salaries and excluding capital investments in buildings and equipment. Education expenditure per capita is education expenditure divided by mid-year population. Data are in constant 2005 US dollars; The average education expenditure per capita (constant 2005 US$) over 1970–2012 was $7,961 worldwide, $119,176 in the eight high-income countries and $4,694 in developing countries (1982–2012).

person. In developing economies, real education expenditure per person more than doubled from 1970 to 2012, and rose to $7,615 by 2012, which is close to the worldwide average. Clearly, though, the level of human capital investment per person in low and middle-income economies has a considerable way to go to reach the spending levels of rich countries.

These long-run trends in human capital investment have had an impact on educational attainment globally. Figure 5.3 summarizes the findings of Robert Barro and Jong Wha Lee of the average years of schooling of adult populations in high-income countries, developing countries and worldwide since 1950. As shown in Figure 5.3, average years of schooling have grown steadily in all countries. In 2010, the world population aged 15 and above had an average of 7.9 years of schooling, compared to 5.3 years in 1980 and 3.1 years in 1950. In high-income countries, the adult population had 11.3 years of schooling in 2010 in contrast to 6.1 in 1950, and developing countries 7.2 years in 2010 compared to 2.0 in 1950. However, there is also considerable variation in the educational attainment by region; for example, in 2010 the adult population in Sub-Saharan Africa and South Asia had only 5.3 years of schooling on average.[4]

However, Figure 5.3 also indicates that the gap between developing and high-income countries in average years of schooling of the adult population has not diminished over the past 60 years. In 1950, the gap in educational attainment between rich and poor economies was around 4.1 years of schooling, and this disparity is still the same in 2010. A key factor in sustaining this gap is the continued increase in the proportion of the population in advanced

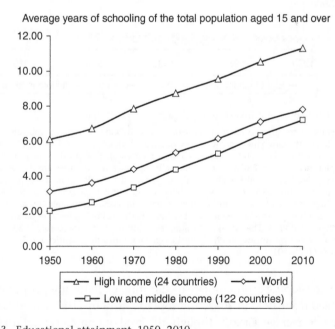

Figure 5.3 Educational attainment, 1950–2010

Source: Robert J. Barro and Jong Wha Lee (2013) "A New Data Set of Educational Attainment in the World, 1950–2010", *Journal of Development Economics*, 104: 184–198.

countries reaching higher levels of education, whereas most of the increase in educational attainment in low and middle-income countries is attributed to improving basic literacy and higher primary and secondary education completion and enrollment ratios.[5] Overall, the current level and distribution of educational attainment in developing countries is comparable only to that of rich countries in the late 1960s.

In sum, human capital is the acquired skills and knowledge that distinguish skilled from unskilled people in an economy. Trends in human capital investment and educational attainment over recent decades confirm that richer countries have a much greater share of skilled to unskilled workers compared to developing economies. The amount of education spending and years of schooling per person is rising in all economies, but clearly in high-income countries, a much higher level of educational attainment is reached on average by the adult population. Thus, wealthier economies spend more than 25 times more on educating each person than do low and middle-income economies. Advanced modern economies not only require a more skill-intensive workforce, but also as a result of prolonged high levels of human capital investment, are endowed with a relatively large supply of skilled workers.

Economic wealth and the structure of production

Throughout this book, we have emphasized that there are three basic assets that constitute the economic wealth of an economy – reproducible, human and natural capital. These three forms of capital should be considered the real wealth of an economy, because they can either benefit the well-being of humans directly (e.g., people are better off if they are healthy; they enjoy a cleaner environment and well-functioning ecosystems, etc.), or they benefit humans indirectly through contributing to current or future production (e.g., more machines, raw material and energy inputs and better skilled workers can increase the output of the goods and services that people want). In considering how the distribution of economic wealth affects the structure of an economy, it is especially relevant to examine how these various assets influence production activities.

First, it should be noted that each asset serves as a primary factor or input in production, in that it is a stock providing services that contribute to production.[6] Although all three assets influence production in this way, not all of these primary factors determine the structure of the various production activities in an economy. Following a long tradition in economics, we consider that the key structural characteristic that distinguishes these production activities is how much of one factor is used as opposed to another. Economists refer to this characteristic as the *factor intensity of production*. For example, if more raw materials, energy and other natural resources are used relative to any other possible inputs to produce goods and services, then production would be relatively *resource-intensive*. Alternatively, if relatively more human capital is used compared to other inputs, then production would be relatively *skill-intensive*.

Economists also maintain that the key influence determining the factor intensity, and thus structure, of production is the relative supply, or *factor endowment*, of assets that are *immobile* between countries.[7] Here, we will suggest that, of the three assets that comprise economic wealth, only human and natural capital are truly factor endowments of economies, as they are specific to each country and cannot be shifted quickly to other economies. In contrast, reproducible capital is still vitally important as an input to production, but because it is highly mobile internationally, it cannot be considered part of the factor endowment of any one country. Thus, reproducible capital does not determine what type of production activities different countries adopt. Instead, only the immobile primary factors – human and natural capital – do this.

The main reason for excluding reproducible capital as one of the factor endowments that determine the structure of production is stated by Adrian Wood: "The exclusion of capital in this context thus calls for some rather strong justification, of which the most obvious and empirically plausible is that capital is internationally mobile. Machines are traded, and finance flows freely around the world, which makes capital different from other factors such as land and most sorts of labour."[8]

The key point made by Wood is that, because "finance flows freely around the world", investments in reproducible capital are highly mobile, and thus can shift very quickly from one country to another throughout most of the world. As we saw in Chapter 2, the global integration of international financial markets has accelerated since the 1950s, further reinforcing this trend.[9] This has two implications. First, domestic financial asset markets are linked to international markets, so that the cost of capital borrowing and lending is similar in most countries.[10] It follows that international capital mobility ensures that the rate of return to reproducible capital tends to be equalized across countries. Second, if the cost of reproducible capital is similar in most countries, and is highly mobile between them, then no one country has potentially a large fixed endowment of capital that determines its comparative advantage in terms of producing certain type of goods and services.

In comparison, human capital and natural capital are primary factors that are also endowments specific to each country. It is true that some human capital may be internationally mobile; for example, some workers that are highly educated and skilled do leave their country of origin and take jobs in other countries. But generally the human capital of an economy is largely a factor supply that stays within its country of origin.[11] The human capital accumulated in an economy, and "embodied" in the skill level of the workforce through education and training – is a primary factor endowment that can influence the structure of production.

Of course, natural assets (and especially ecosystems) are completely immobile factors; geography, geology and nature determine each country's endowment of natural capital. However, there are some important distinctions between how ecosystems, or ecological capital, support production as opposed to other types of natural resources.

As we have seen in Chapter 4, the various goods and services, or benefits to humans, provided by ecosystems are mostly not bought and sold on markets. Although many ecosystem services, such as freshwater supply, coastal protection, flood control, maintenance of habitats, and so forth, provide valuable support and enhancement to production activities in the economy producers do not purchase or pay for using these services. Thus, ecological capital is a primary factor contributing to production, but as this contribution is not paid for, changes in the endowment of ecological capital and its services will not influence the structure of production. As we saw in Chapter 4, even if ecosystem conversion and degradation is causing increasing ecological scarcity, because ecosystem inputs are free, this rising scarcity will have little impact on the production input and output choices of an economy.

However, some other types of natural capital provide marketed energy and raw material inputs into production. These include fossil fuels and other energy supplies, minerals, timber and other forest products, and so on. Land is also a viable asset that is important for agricultural production and for building structures, dwellings, factories and other uses. Consequently, land and some natural resources are not only primary factors contributing to production, but owners of this natural capital are compensated for their use. As the availability of these primary factors does influence their cost and use in production, natural capital is a primary factor endowment that can also influence the structure of production.

To summarize, of the three assets comprising economic wealth, only different endowments of natural and human capital influence the structure of production in modern economies. Reproducible capital is also a primary factor that is vital for production, but because it is highly mobile between countries and thus earns a similar rate of return worldwide, reproducible capital does not determine the fundamental differences in factor intensity that define the structure of production across economies.[12] Ecological capital is an important immobile factor endowment for economies, but because ecosystem services are virtually free, its relative abundance or scarcity has little impact on the structure of production.

The relative price of human to natural capital

Having established that natural and human capital are the primary factors of an economy that influence its pattern of production, we are now able to explore how underpricing of natural capital, combined with the scarcity of human capital, can lead to structural distortions. To show this explicitly, the following section develops a simple model of an economy's production, based on the two main factor endowments: natural and human capital.

Recall that human capital is a unique asset as it is embodied in labor, and thus is viewed as the acquired skills and knowledge that distinguish skilled from unskilled labor. It follows that, if H is the human capital stock in an economy, then we can define $H = hL$, where h represents the amount of human capital per worker and L is the total number of workers. Thus, h approximates the skill level of the workforce, and if the amount of human capital per worker is increasing, then labor in the economy is becoming more skilled. That is, unskilled labor has only a minimal level of education and training (a very low h), whereas skilled labor has accumulated much more human capital through education and training (a very high h).

As investments in human capital translate into a workforce that has better education, training and health, then we can consider the wage rate w paid to relatively skilled labor to be the returns to human capital. But as these returns are paid out as wages to the labor embodied with human capital, w also represents the cost of using relatively skilled labor in the economy. That is, w is the wage paid to skilled labor relative to that of unskilled workers, who have only a minimal level of education and training. Finally, an economy that has higher levels of human capital per worker h will have higher output and pay its workers more income.[13]

Similarly, we can denote as N as the aggregate stock of natural capital that is marketed and used as raw material and energy inputs in an economy (e.g., fossil fuels, forests used as timber, agricultural land for crops and livestock, minerals and other non-renewable sources of material inputs, etc.). Let us assume that all these natural resources have an average market price or rental rate r, which reflects the cost of using these resources in production as well as the returns to natural capital. For shorthand, we will follow convention and refer to r as resource rents.

As maintained previously, human capital H and natural capital N are the two primary factors of the economy that determine the relative factor-intensity, and thus structure, of production activities. To show this, we can think of the economy producing two distinct types of goods and services, which we will call "goods" for short.[14] Both goods use raw material and energy inputs from natural resources, as well as skilled labor (i.e., labor embodied with a relatively high level of human capital per worker). However, the production of one type of good uses more natural as opposed to human capital, and thus can be considered relatively *resource-intensive*. The second good uses more human than natural capital, and consequently is more *skill-intensive*.[15]

However, the input choice that producers actually make in each sector will depend on the relative costs of using its human as opposed to natural capital stock. If resource costs are high and wages low, producers will choose to use relatively little natural capital and a lot of human capital (i.e., skilled labor); if r is low and w high, they will use more natural resources and less skilled labor. An increase in the input cost ratio w/r will therefore lead to a rise in the use of natural relative to human capital N/H in production, regardless of whether it is resource or skill-intensive.[16]

Finally, assume that all goods produced in the economy are sold on markets. Let P^R be the average market price for all resource-intensive goods and P^S the price of skill-intensive goods. It follows that there will be a one-to-one relationship between the input cost ratio of human to natural capital w/r and the relative price of skill-intensive to resource-intensive goods P^S/P^R. That is, the higher the relative cost of using human capital (i.e., skilled labor) compared to natural capital, the higher must be the relative price of the skill-intensive good. If human capital becomes relatively more expensive to use, then producers of the skill-intensive good will need to receive a higher price to cover this increased cost.[17]

The implication of these relationships for the structure of production in an economy is indicated in Figure 5.4. In the right panel of the figure, the curve SS shows the natural-human capital ratio choices N^S/H^S in producing the skill-intensive good, and the curve RR the corresponding N^R/H^R choices in producing the resource-intensive good. At any given wage-rental ratio w/r, the resource-intensive good uses a higher natural-human capital ratio, whereas for the skill-intensive good, N^S/H^S is always lower. In the left panel of Figure 5.4, the curve PP shows the one-to-one relationship between the input cost ratio w/r and the relative price of skill-intensive to resource-intensive goods P^S/P^R. With an initial relative price $(P^S/P^R)^0$, the corresponding ratio of the wage rate to the rental rate must equal $(w/r)^0$.[18] The amount of natural relative to human capital used to produce the skill-intensive good is $(N^S/H^S)^0$, and for the resource-intensive good $(N^R/H^R)^0$.

Suppose there is underpricing of natural capital, and because human capital is scarce, skilled workers receive a premium wage. In the economy, this means that natural resources are cheaper to use than skilled labor as inputs into production. As shown in Figure 5.4, we can represent this by an increase in the ratio of the wage to resource rents from $(w/r)^0$ to $(w/r)^1$. One effect of this change in input costs is that the relative price of the skill-intensive good goes up (see the left panel of Figure 5.4). Another impact is to raise the amount of natural resources, as opposed to skilled labor, used in production in both sectors. Because natural capital is now relatively cheaper, more of it is used to make both the skill-intensive good $(N^S/H^S)^1$ and the resource-intensive good $(N^R/H^R)^1$. Thus, one key outcome of natural capital becoming less expensive to use than skilled labor is that production throughout the economy uses relatively more natural resources (see the right panel of Figure 5.4).

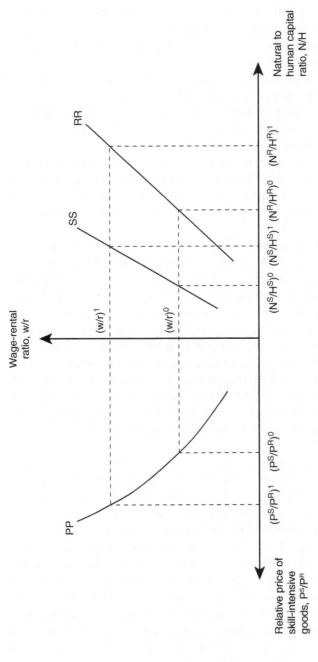

Figure 5.4 The structural effects of increasing the price of human to natural capital

The curve SS shows the natural–human capital ratio choices in producing the skill-intensive good, and the curve RR the corresponding choices in producing the resource-intensive good. The curve PP shows the one-to-one relationship between the input cost ratio of human to natural capital w/r and the relative price of skill-intensive to resource-intensive goods P^S/P^R. If the wage-rental ratio rises from its initial level $(w/r)^0$ to $(w/r)^1$, then the relative price of skill-intensive goods must also increase to $(P^S/P^R)^1$. This will cause the natural–human capital ratio used in the production of both goods to rise.

Despite the increased resource use, it is the skilled workers in the economy that are better off. Because the ratio of natural to human capital rises in producing both types of goods, the share of this additional production that is paid as wages to skilled labor is higher than that paid as rent to the owners of natural resources. As a result, skilled workers find their real wages higher throughout the economy, which means that their wages rise relative to any price.[19] The underpricing of natural capital and the scarcity of human capital ensures that skilled workers gain in terms of higher real incomes.

This outcome also leads to greater wealth inequality, especially between highly skilled and unskilled labor. Recall that the wage rate w represents the returns to human capital as well as the wage paid to skilled as opposed to unskilled labor. Also, workers with higher levels of human capital per worker h, and thus embodied with more skills, will be paid higher real incomes. Thus, if the real wages of skilled workers throughout the economy increase, high-skilled workers will gain much more compared to low or unskilled labor. The income gap between skilled and unskilled workers will therefore become larger as a result of human capital being more expensive to use compared to natural capital.[20] The widening of this income gap will mean greater inequality in accumulated assets, or wealth, of skilled compared to unskilled workers.

To summarize, if there is a structural imbalance across economies so that natural capital is relatively cheaper to use than human capital, then there are three major consequences. First, the economy will use too much natural resources relative to skilled labor in all sectors, regardless of whether they are resource-intensive or skill-intensive. Second, the skilled workers throughout the economy will have higher real incomes and thus will be better off. Third, wealth inequality will increase, as the income gap between skilled and unskilled workers widens. Finally, as emphasized throughout this book, these effects occur not just in a few economies but throughout the world economy.[21] The result is that global production tends to use natural capital excessively, skilled workers are made better off, and wealth inequality has increased.

Natural capital expansion

Of course, overuse of natural resources for production in the world economy has another consequence, which is high rates of natural capital depreciation, especially in those economies that supply most of the world economy with its energy and material inputs. As we saw in Chapter 2, the rate of natural capital depreciation over the past three decades has been five times greater in developing economies than in the richest countries (see Figure 2.7). And, as noted in Chapter 3, many low and middle-income economies still remain highly dependent on exploiting their natural resource endowments for commercial, export-oriented economic activities. In some of these economies, primary product exports – and often one or two main commodities – account for nearly all export earnings.

If all economies expand their use of natural capital, and these natural resources become increasingly depleted through production, then new sources of raw material and energy inputs need to be found and exploited. The most likely sources of new natural resources are those countries that are relatively abundant in such supplies. These tend to be the resource-dependent developing countries, which currently supply the world economy with much of its raw material and energy inputs. This explains why such countries are experiencing rapid rates of natural resource exploitation and land conversion. As they increasingly supply more primary products for exports, resource abundant economies deplete their natural capital, which means that they must replenish these diminishing assets by finding new sources of natural resources to exploit.

Finding and exploiting new sources of raw material and energy supplies for the rest of the world has two further effects on the economic structure of low and middle-income economies. First, the expansion of natural capital perpetuates the resource dependency of these economies, as measured by the share of primary products to total exports. In addition, they are likely to attract more financial and physical capital, which is internationally mobile, to assist in the expansion of natural resource supplies.

Natural capital may be an immobile primary factor of production, but an economy's endowment (i.e., supplies) of natural resources of an economy is rarely "fixed" forever. This is especially true of the aggregate stock of natural capital that is marketed and used as raw material and energy inputs in an economy, such as fossil fuels, forests used as timber, agricultural land for crops and livestock, minerals and other non-renewable sources of material inputs, which we have designated as the primary factor N in our analysis. Rather than remaining immutably fixed, the supply of natural capital available to an economy can be expanded over time through investments that lead to the discovery of new reserves, innovations that make less accessible natural resources more profitable to exploit, and conversion of forests, wetlands and other habitats into land for agriculture and other economic activities.[22] This has been facilitated by the increasing global integration of financial markets since the 1950s, which as noted earlier in the chapter, accounts for the mobility of reproducible capital investments worldwide and tends to equalize, across countries, the rate of return on these investments.[23]

In most economies today, whether rich or poor, the main investment used to expand supplies of natural capital is in reproducible capital, especially machinery, equipment, tools, transport infrastructure and similar items. This is true both historically, for instance with the expansion of global discovery, extraction and production of resource-based commodities since the mid-19th century, and more recently, with the increasing land and resource extraction activities that have occurred worldwide over the past several decades.[24] Much of the conversion of forests to agricultural and the expansion of mineral and energy production in developing countries are occurring through capital investments by large-scale resource-extractive and commercial agricultural activities.[25]

The effects of increasing the supply of natural capital in a relatively resource-abundant economy are indicated in Figure 5.5. We begin with the hypothesis that we have maintained throughout this chapter: natural capital is under-priced and human capital is scarce, leading to a premium wage paid for skilled labor. Because of this prevailing structural imbalance in the world economy, natural resources are cheaper to use than skilled labor as inputs into production. Thus, the input cost ratio is $(w/r)^1$, and the corresponding relative world price of skill-intensive to resource-intensive goods is $(P^S/P^R)^1$. The small economy takes the latter world price as given, but nonetheless, expands its resource supply. Figure 5.5 shows the consequences of this expansion.

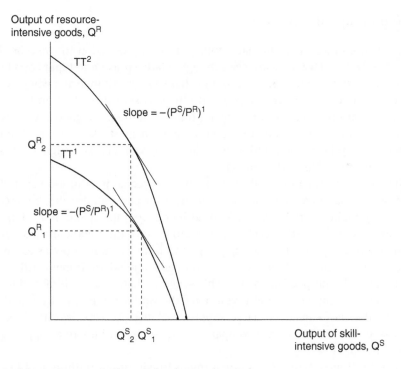

Figure 5.5 An increase in the supply of natural capital

An increase in the supply of natural resources biases production towards resource-intensive goods. The economy switches to producing more of those goods and less of skill-intensive goods.

The curve TT[1] indicates all the possible production combinations of skill-intensive and resource-intensive goods that the economy is capable of making, using natural and human capital. At the relative world price of skill-intensive goods $(P^S/P^R)^1$, the economy will allocate natural resources and skilled labor to make Q^S_1 amount of skill-intensive goods and Q^R_1 resource-intensive goods. As illustrated in Figure 5.5, the country produces more of the latter type of goods, reflecting that it is relatively abundant in natural as opposed to human capital.

However, now suppose that the economy increases its supply of land and natural resource assets. As shown in the figure, even though relative prices have not changed, the economy will produce even more resource-intensive goods.[26] In contrast, output of skill-intensive goods will decline. The economy remains resource-dependent, and may export a greater share of primary products to total exports. Thus natural capital expansion, driven largely by investments in internationally mobile financial and reproducible capital, will lead to more natural and human capital inputs allocated to produce increased amounts of resource-intensive goods.

Human capital expansion

Similarly, an increase in human capital will bias production in the economy towards skill-intensive goods, even though relative prices and input costs have not changed (see Figure 5.6). Output of these goods will increase, whereas the amount of resource-intensive goods declines as skilled workers and natural resources are reallocated to producing more skill-intensive goods. As we saw earlier in this chapter, human capital expansion most likely occurs through greater expenditures on training and education, which leads to higher levels of schooling and skills in the population.[27]

The level of human capital investment, as reflected in education spending per person, has increased in all countries over the past four decades, but is considerably higher in rich countries. Wealthier economies spend more than 25 times more on educating each person than do low and middle-income economies. Average years of schooling per person have therefore grown steadily in all countries since 1950, but a large gap in educational attainment still exists between rich and poor countries. This suggests that, as a result of prolonged high levels of human capital investment, the workforce in advanced modern economies has a relatively large supply of skilled workers. Wealthier economies, on the whole, have a comparative advantage in human as opposed to natural capital.[28]

The continued high levels of investment in education, training and health improvements also mean that the wealthier countries are continuing to increase their supply of investments. Although we have only examined expenditures on

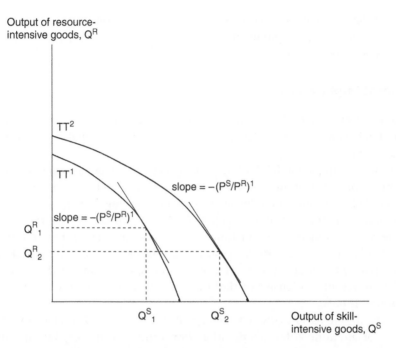

Figure 5.6 An increase in the supply of human capital

An increase in the supply of human capital biases production towards skill-intensive goods. The economy switches to producing more of those goods and less of resource-intensive goods.

education and schooling levels, evidence suggests that, if educational attainment levels are increasing, then other investments in human capital, such as expenditures on health and training, are also likely to be rising. Increasing average years of schooling per person is therefore a pretty good indicator that the supply of human capital is expanding.[29]

In Figure 5.6, we again assume initially that the input cost ratio is $(w/r)^1$, and the corresponding relative world price of skill-intensive to resource-intensive goods is $(P^S/P^R)^1$. Given these input and goods prices, the economy will allocate natural resources and skilled labor to make Q^S_1 amount of skill-intensive goods and Q^R_1 resource-intensive goods. As illustrated in Figure 5.6, the country produces more of the former type of goods, as it is relatively abundant in human as opposed to natural capital.

Now suppose the economy invests in education and training. As shown in the figure, the production possibilities curve shifts out from TT^1 to TT^2. Production of skill-intensive goods increases substantially to Q^S_2 and resource-intensive goods decline to Q^R_2. Thus human capital expansion, spurred by expenditures in education, training and health, will lead to more natural and human capital inputs allocated to produce increased amounts of skill-intensive goods. The relative human capital abundant country continues to have a comparative advantage in producing goods and services that rely relatively more on skilled labor.

Global implications

We will leave much of the discussion of the global implications of this structural imbalance to the next chapters. However, it is worth making a few observations here.

First, the simple model developed in this chapter explains some of the key features of the structural imbalance that we have explored previously. One example is the continuing dependence of all economies – rich and poor – on using more natural resources, such as fossil fuels, minerals, forests and non-renewable materials in production. If these raw material and energy inputs are underpriced, then natural resources are cheaper to use than skilled labor as inputs into production. As Figure 5.4 shows, all sectors of the economy, whether resource-intensive or skill-intensive, will use relatively more natural resource inputs.

Second, one reason why natural capital is underpriced is that many of the costs of environmental deterioration from using natural capital, and especially degrading and converting ecosystems, is largely ignored by economies. In particular, although ecological capital is a primary factor contributing to production, its economic contribution is not paid for, and thus changes in the endowment of ecological capital and its services will not influence the structure of production. Even if ecosystem conversion and degradation is the cause scarcity of vital services globally, such as freshwater supply, coastal protection, flood control, maintenance of habitats, and so forth, this rising ecological scarcity will have little impact on the production input and output choices of an economy. Similarly, even though the world economy continues to emit more greenhouse gases, so that the Earth's assimilative capacity for absorbing more emissions is increasingly limited, any potential economic impacts of future climate change are not included as part of the costs of carbon-dependent production today.

Third, if the marketed raw material and energy inputs in production are underpriced, and thus overused, then more sources of these inputs need to be found. The most likely sources of new natural resources that can be exploited for these inputs are those countries that are relatively abundant in such supplies. These tend to be the resource-dependent developing countries, which supply the world economy with much of its raw material and energy inputs. As shown in Figure 5.5, increased investment in expanding the supply of energy and other natural resources in a resource-abundant economy will further increase its output, and thus exports, of primary products and decrease production of skill-intensive goods. Consequently, the overuse of natural resources for production in the world economy, because they are artificially cheap, reinforces the tendency of many low and middle-income countries to remain resource-dependent.

Finally, if human capital is scarce, then skilled labor will receive premium wages. As this is occurring throughout the world economy, then the income gap between skilled and unskilled workers grows and wealth inequality increases. Because this is occurring at the same time as the underpricing of natural capital inputs, such as raw material and energy, the larger and richer economies are, on the one hand, using more of these inputs, and on the other, investing more in education and training to increase the supply of human capital. As shown in Figure 5.6, these increased investments in wealthy economies that are already relatively abundant in human capital means that production becomes even more biased towards skill-intensive goods. Hence the paradox of production in most rich economies: their overuse of raw material and energy inputs keeps them fundamentally carbon-dependent, whereas their structure of production becomes oriented towards skill-intensive goods and skill-biased technological change. As we shall see in Chapter 7, unfortunately, the latter bias simply increases the demand for more skilled labor, which means that human capital still remains scarce, skilled workers receive higher relative wages, and wealth inequality increases.

Conclusion

We started this chapter with the premise that a key structural imbalance in the world economy is the underpricing of natural capital, and at the same time, insufficient investment in human capital to meet its growing demand. We then explored the implications of this imbalance for the structure of production in economies.

We found that, if there is a structural imbalance across all economies so that natural capital is relatively cheaper to use than human capital, then there are three major consequences. First, the economy will use too many natural resources relative to skilled labor in all sectors, regardless of whether they are resource-intensive or skill-intensive. Second, the skilled workers throughout the economy will have higher real incomes and thus will be better off. Third, wealth inequality will increase, especially the income gap between skilled and unskilled workers. As these effects are pervasive throughout the world economy, global production tends to use natural capital excessively, skilled workers are made better off, and inequality has increased.

In the next two chapters, we will explore more fully the hypothesis that natural capital is underpriced and there is substantial underinvestment in human capital in modern economies. We also examine further the economic consequences of this structural imbalance.

For example, in Chapter 6, we will see that the underpricing of nature not only leads to the overuse and degradation of natural resources and ecosystems but also means that excessive rents, or returns, are generated from finding and exploiting new sources of natural capital. This produces a vicious cycle where, the additional costs of environmental degradation, natural resource depletion and increasing ecological scarcity are not reflected in the market prices for natural capital exploited for raw material and energy inputs and used in production. The consequent underpricing of natural capital leads to excessive raw material and energy use in all economies, and the resulting additional returns from supplying new sources of these inputs perpetuates this entire process.

In Chapter 7 we will explore further why insufficient human capital accumulation is occurring in economies today. We will also see that the consequence of making human capital relatively more expensive to use explains an importance paradox: Although economies invest in training and education to increase their supply of skilled labor, this supply cannot keep up with the demand for human capital due to the pace of skill-biased technological change. The result is that in all economies there is a growing gap between rich and poor, which as we have shown in this chapter is fostered by skilled labor becoming more expensive to use than natural resources in production. In addition, workers with little or no skills are either relegated to low-paying jobs that are less likely to be displaced by skill-biased innovation, or become chronically unemployed. Developing countries face the additional problem of persistent rural poverty, especially the tendency of the very poor to be concentrated in remote and less favored lands that suffer from low agricultural productivity and degradation, and growing numbers of urban poor clustered in less desirable and polluted neighborhoods. As we shall see, these trends are linked to the structural imbalance identified in this chapter, as the inefficient and unsustainable use of natural capital contributes to the economy-wide misallocation of labor.

Appendix

Extending adjusted net national income for human capital

So far in this book, we have shown how *gross national income* (GNI) can be adjusted to allow for both depreciation of reproducible and natural capital (see the Appendix to Chapter 2), and that the resulting measure of *adjusted net national income* (ANNI) can be further extended to allow for the contributions of and changes in ecological capital (see the Appendix to Chapter 4).

However, economies and people are also better off as a result of improvements to *human capital*, where the latter is defined as the skills, education and health embodied in the workforce. Thus, expenditures in the economy that lead to such improvements are contributing to net increases in human capital. It follows that an improved indicator of an economy's progress would be to extend the measure of ANNI that allows for any net additions to human capital.[30]

However, a key feature that distinguishes human capital from other forms of economic wealth, such as natural, ecological and reproducible capital, is that "human capital cannot be detached from the person in whom it is embodied, nor can it be transacted separately and in its own right in the market like conventional fixed capital."[31] Because human capital is embodied in labor, a common approach in the economics literature is to consider human capital as the acquired skills and knowledge that distinguish *skilled* from *unskilled* (i.e., raw) labor in an economy.[32] That is, unskilled labor has only a minimal level of education, skills and training (if any), whereas skilled labor is embodied with varying degrees of accumulated human capital.

If investments in human capital lead to a healthy, better-educated and more skilled workforce, how does one measure the direct and indirect benefits to human well-being of increases in human capital? Ideally, one would want to estimate these economic contributions in a similar way as for other forms of wealth, namely by measuring the discounted value of all current and future benefits derived from investments in that asset. In the case of human capital, one economic application of this approach would involve measuring the stream of future earnings that human capital investment generates in the person embodied with more health, education or skills.[33] Another would be to measure how certain levels of human capital, such as educational attainment or health status, increase the value-added contributions of the labor that is embodied with that accumulated human capital.[34] However, both approaches are fraught with measurement difficulties that make them difficult to apply to a wide range of economies and over time.

Instead, a consensus is emerging that, rather than treating them as expenditures in measures of national income for an economy, education and other spending that increases human capital should be considered as investments.[35] That is, expenditures on human capital that increase the education, training and health of the workforce should be treated as net additions, or investments, in the economy. Such an approach may serve only as a proxy for measuring the direct and indirect benefits to human well-being of increases in human capital, but it nonetheless at least reflects how key expenditures in the economy are contributing to net increases in human capital.

In sum, ANNI should adjust national income for reproducible and natural capital depreciation, for the benefits of and changes in ecological capital, and for net additions to human capital:

> Adjusted Net National Income (ANNI) = GNI – the value of the consumption of domestic fixed capital – depreciation of natural capital + value of the direct benefits provided by the current stock of ecosystems and any capital revaluation due to ecosystem conversion or restoration + net additions in human capital from education, health and training investments.

The figure below summarizes the various adjustments that are required to derive ANNI from the conventional economic indicators of gross domestic product (GDP) and gross national income (GNI).

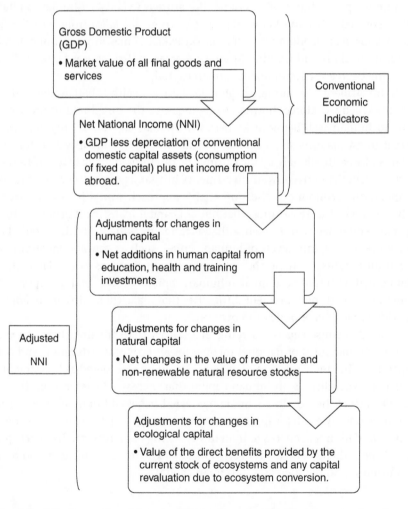

Figure 5.7 Adjusting national income (NI) for reproducible, human, natural and ecological capital

6
The Underpricing of Nature

Introduction

At the heart of structural imbalance in the world economy is the underpricing of nature. In this chapter, we explore the factors underlying this pervasive problem. In particular, we focus on a key question: If natural and ecological capital are valuable sources of economic wealth, why are we squandering these assets? In addition, if ecological scarcity and natural capital depreciation are on the rise, why are we are we doing so little to address these problems?

One persistent difficulty is that the increasing costs associated with many environmental problems – climate change, freshwater scarcity, declining ecological services and increasing energy insecurity – are not routinely reflected in markets. Nor have we developed adequate policies and institutions to handle these costs. This means that economies do not have the correct price signals or incentives to adjust production and consumption activities. All too often, policy distortions and failures compound ecological scarcity and natural capital depreciation by encouraging wasteful use of natural resources and environmental degradation.

As depicted in Figure 6.1, this process has become a vicious cycle.[1] The failure of environmental values to be reflected in markets and policy decisions leads to economic development with excessive environmental degradation. This in turn leads to the costs of natural capital depreciation, environmental losses, and rising ecological scarcity in terms of current and future human well-being continuing to be ignored in decision making. The result is that the vicious cycle is reinforced, and the current pattern of economic development persists. Over time, the ongoing loss of natural and ecological capital constrains economic progress and adversely impacts both current and future human well-being.

A further effect, as described in Chapter 5, is that the structural imbalance in production becomes ingrained. The underpricing of nature leads to excessive use and degradation of natural resources and ecosystems, but the overuse of energy and raw material inputs also puts pressure on finding and exploiting new sources of these inputs. This is also an outcome of the vicious cycle depicted in Figure 6.1, as the additional costs of environmental degradation, natural resource depletion and increasing ecological scarcity are not reflected in the market prices for natural capital exploited for raw material and energy and used in production. Consequently, the persistent underpricing of natural capital leads to the overuse of natural capital in all economies, thus perpetuating this entire process.

Economists for some time have warned about the "hidden costs" associated with the producing and consuming goods and services, when their market

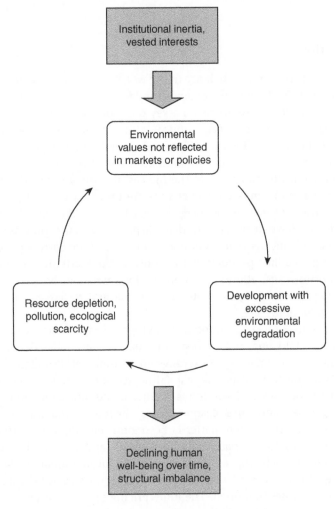

Figure 6.1 The vicious cycle of excessive environmental degradation

price does not reflect fully environmental damages, such as those caused by pollution or overexploitation of natural resources.[2]

More recently, economists have called attention to the economy-wide impacts of failing to correct the persistent "undervaluation" of the environment.[3] Overall, there appears to be two main distortions:

- the failure to "internalize" the environmental damages into the final prices paid for marketed goods and services, and
- the failure to curb subsidies to environmentally damaging activities.

The first failure is at the core of the vicious cycle depicted in Figure 6.1. The second further compounds the problem; such subsidies encourage production activities to cause even more environmental damage. To illustrate the economic, environmental and social implications of these two failures underlying the underpricing of nature, we focus on two examples: fossil fuels and mangrove ecosystems.

As we discussed in Chapter 2, we are still in the midst of the fossil fuel era, and as a consequence, all economies remain highly dependent on coal, oil and natural gas supplies for energy consumption (see Figures 2.1 and 2.2). Thus, fossil fuels represent the most important natural asset exploited in the world economy, yet the failure to curb subsidies or to internalize environmental costs in fossil fuel markets has led to excessive emissions of local pollutants, more greenhouse gas emissions, and a general misallocation of resources. In addition, the environmental and social costs of the environmental damages attributed to underpricing fossil fuels are disproportionately borne by the poor. In this chapter, we will look at this phenomenon, especially with respect to the 20 largest advanced and emerging market economies, which have set the pace of carbon-dependent development that the rest of the world is following.

Mangrove ecosystems are an important source of ecological capital, which as we saw in Chapter 4 generate a wide range of valuable goods and services (see Table 4.1). We also showed that accounting for the mangrove capital lost to Thailand has led to considerable costs to the economy and people (see Figure 4.4). Here, we explore further how the failure to curb subsidies for shrimp aquaculture or to include mangrove damages in the net returns to shrimp production has contributed to excessive mangrove deforestation in Thailand. In addition, these resulting losses impact mainly coastal households and communities, who rarely benefit from the conversion of mangroves to shrimp farming.

Finally, this chapter explores why the underpricing of nature remains a persistent problem across all economies. If we are able to quantify and estimate the "hidden costs" of excessive environmental damages – as the examples of fossil fuels and mangroves illustrate – why is it proving so difficult to remove any environmentally harmful subsidies and ensure that those responsible for generating additional environmental costs pay for them? As shown in Figure 6.1, the main underlying cause appears to be institutional inertia and vested interests. As the vicious cycle of excessive environmental degradation persists, social institutions that reinforce this process are established, maintained and even expand. Vested political and economic interests that benefit from the process are also built up and become entrenched. The result is that it becomes very difficult and costly to overcome the institutional inertia and vested interests that prevent economy-wide reform of the underpricing of nature.

Fossil fuels

Chapter 2 documented how cheap and accessible fossil fuels – first coal and then oil and natural gas – were essential to the two phases of innovation that characterized the long process of industrialization that began around 1750. It was during this process, approximately around the middle of the 19th century, that the global spread of industrialization and the growing dependence of virtually every economy on the new sources of energy ushered in the fossil fuel era. Inexpensive and more accessible fossil fuel energy also sparked a dramatic fall in the costs of shipping bulk raw material goods across oceans and continents. After World War II, further falls in transport costs and trade barriers in the post-war era fostered the global integration of commodity markets, which has allowed all economies to have better and cheaper access to natural resources than reliance on just their own endowments would allow. Thus, in the modern era, all economies have become entirely dependent on fossil fuels, and access to inexpensive supplies of these natural assets is considered strategically essential to economic development worldwide. Carbon-dependent development, mainly through the consumption of fossil-fuel energy, is the model of successful economic development to which all economies aspire.

Perhaps because of the association of fossil fuel energy use and economic development, underpricing of coal, oil and natural gas remains a significant and widespread practice in the world economy. Yet, the result has also considerable impacts on the environment and human health, with considerable economic costs. For example, researchers from the International Monetary Fund (IMF) have estimated some of these impacts and costs:

- Increased outdoor air pollution, which comes primarily from fossil fuel combustion, and causes more than 3 million premature deaths each year worldwide, costing about 1% of annual gross domestic product (GDP) in the United States and 4% in China.

- Increased motor vehicle use, which leads to crowded roads, accidental deaths and injuries; traffic accidents already account for 1.2 million deaths worldwide.
- Greater greenhouse gas emissions, which is causing global climate change.[4]

Current markets for coal, oil and natural gas, as well as for their key products – electricity generation, diesel and gasoline – not only exclude these environmental damages and other impacts but also the prices in these markets are frequently subsidized. Subsidies to consumers lower the prices paid for fossil fuels used in transport (e.g., gasoline and diesel), kerosene and natural gas used in homes, or fuels used in electricity generation or by domestic industries. In recent years, these subsidies have ranged between $480 billion and $548 billion globally, or approximately 0.7% of global GDP and 2% of all government revenues.[5]

Subsidies to producers occur when suppliers of fossil fuels receive higher than market prices in domestic markets, and include tax breaks, allowances for accelerated depreciation, and reduced royalty payments. These producer subsidies have proven more difficult to measure, although estimates suggest that they may range from $80 billion and $285 billion annually in developing and emerging market economies.[6] Oil and gas production subsidies in Russia are around $14.4 billion annually, in Norway $4 billion, Canada $2.8 billion and Indonesia $1.8 billion.[7] In the United States, fossil fuel production subsidies have grown from $12.7 billion in 2009 to $18.5 billion in 2014.[8]

Related to production subsidies is government-provided support for fossil fuel exploration, which aims to find new oil, natural gas and coal resources and reserves. Between 2010 and 2013, the Group of 20 (G20) countries – the 20 largest and richest economies in the world – provided each year $49 billion for investment by state-owned enterprises in these activities, $23 billion in subsidies of direct spending and tax breaks, and $16 billion in other forms of public finance for exploration.[9]

Table 6.1 summarizes estimates of subsidies and underpricing of fossil fuels in the G20 countries. Support for exploration amounts to approximately $88 billion per year in these economies, and annual fossil fuel subsidies are a further $187 billion, or approximately 39% of the global total. However, when further underpricing is accounted for – tax breaks and the failure to take into account environmental damages such as the costs of climate change, local pollution, traffic congestion, accidents and road damage – the losses in G20 economies amount to nearly $1.3 trillion, which is over two-thirds of the world total. The United States alone accounts for $502 billion in underpricing, or over a quarter of the world total, followed by China with $257 billion, or 14% of the world total.

Fossil fuel subsidies comprise just over 1% of the world's annual adjusted net national income (ANNI), and for 0.5% of ANNI in the G20 (see Table 6.1).[10]

Table 6.1 Underpricing of fossil fuels, Group of 20 economies

	Annual exploration subsidies (US$ billion) 2010–2013[a]	Annual fossil fuel subsidies (US$ billion) 2011[b]	Share (%) of world total	Annual fossil fuel subsidies, tax breaks and environmental costs (US$ billion) 2011[b]	Share (%) of world total	Annual fossil fuel subsidies share (%) of ANNI 2011	Annual subsidies, tax breaks and environmental costs share (%) of ANNI 2011
Argentina	6.5	3.4	0.7%	7.7	0.4%	1.8%	4.0%
Australia	3.6	38.1	7.9%	26.5	1.4%	5.8%	4.0%
Brazil	12.0	0.0	0.0%	5.0	0.3%	0.0%	0.5%
Canada	3.5	21.1	4.4%	26.4	1.4%	2.0%	2.5%
China	11.5	0.0	0.0%	257.4	13.5%	0.0%	7.9%
France	0.06	0.0	0.0%	4.7	0.2%	0.0%	0.2%
Germany	0.5	2.7	0.6%	21.6	1.1%	0.1%	0.8%
India	4.6	25.8	5.4%	74.8	3.9%	2.3%	6.6%
Indonesia	0.5	21.8	4.5%	39.2	2.1%	6.6%	11.9%
Italy	0.7	0.0	0.0%	7.5	0.4%	0.0%	0.5%
Japan	6.0	0.0	0.0%	46.0	2.4%	0.0%	1.3%
Mexico	3.0	0.0	0.0%	27.6	1.5%	0.0%	3.4%
Russia	6.0	20.2	4.2%	92.8	4.9%	2.3%	10.6%
Saudi Arabia	17.0	44.5	9.3%	83.2	4.4%	–	–
South Africa	0.004	0.1	0.0%	14.4	0.8%	0.0%	5.7%
South Korea	3.1	0.2	0.0%	16.7	0.9%	0.0%	1.8%
Turkey	1.0	0.2	0.0%	7.5	0.4%	0.0%	1.4%
United Kingdom	2.0	0.0	0.0%	10.9	0.6%	0.0%	0.5%
United States	6.5	8.8	1.8%	502.1	26.4%	0.1%	4.1%
G20 Total	87.9	186.9	38.9%	1,272.0	66.9%	0.5%	3.6%
World	–	480.0		1,900.0		1.1%	4.3%

G20 is the Group of 20 countries. The members of the G20 include 19 countries (Argentina, Australia, Brazil, Canada, China, France, Germany, India, Indonesia, Italy, Japan, Mexico, Russia, Saudi Arabia, South Africa, South Korea, Turkey, the UK and the US), plus the European Union. The G20 total excludes the European Union; [a] Elizabeth Bast, Shakuntala Makhijani, Sam Pickard and Shelagh Whitley (2014) The Fossil Fuel Bailout: G20 subsidies for Oil, Gas and Coal Exploration. Washington, DC: Overseas Development Institute, London and Oil Change International. Exploration subsidies include government subsidies for exploration, public investment on exploration through state-owned enterprises, and public finance from domestic and international sources for exploration; [b]Benedict Clements, David Coady, Stefania Fabrizio, Sanjeev Gupta, Trevor Alleyne and Carlo Sdalevich (eds) (2013) Energy Subsidy Reform: Lessons and Implications. Washington, DC: International Monetary Fund (IMF). The costs include annual fossil fuel subsidies plus tax breaks for fossil fuels and the failure to price (tax) negative externalities, such as the costs of climate change, local pollution, traffic congestion, accidents and road damage; Adjusted net national income (ANNI) is gross national income minus consumption of fixed capital and the value of net natural resources depletion, expressed in constant 2005 US$), from World Development Indicators, available from http://databank.worldbank.org/data

However, the effects of overall underpricing of fossil fuels amounts to over 4% of ANNI per year in the world economy, and just under 4% of annual ANNI in the G20. But the economic costs are even higher in individual economies: 12% in Indonesia, 11% in Russia, 8% in China, 7% in India and 6% in South Africa. Note that these latter countries are not the richest members of the G20 but large emerging market economies. As these economies strive to industrialize and develop, the underpricing of fossil fuels is actually imposing significant hidden costs on their populations.

The burden of the environmental damages caused by underpricing of fossil fuels is also borne by the poorer and less advantaged populations within countries. This is especially the case for local pollution effects, such as deteriorating air quality. Studies across a wide range of countries consistently show that, among the general population, it is the disadvantaged groups – such as the poor and minorities – that are exposed to sources of air pollution and more susceptible to any resulting health effects.[11]

For example, in metropolitan areas of the United States, exposure to air pollution is generally higher for households that are poor, unemployed or from racial minorities.[12] In China, rural residents, and especially rural migrants to urban areas, are disproportionately exposed to industrial pollution from burning fossil fuels.[13] Across European cities, poorer people are also more exposed to air pollution, and in general, households of lower socioeconomic status experience greater adverse health impacts from lower air quality.[14]

The environmental burden of fossil fuel pollution is also disproportionately affecting the poor in the cities of developing countries. One quarter of the world's poor live in urban areas, and that proportion appears to be rising over time as cities in developing countries expand.[15] The urban poor are especially vulnerable to a range of air quality impacts associated with cities, such as outdoor and indoor air pollution from burning fossil fuels. Many strategies for reducing greenhouse gas emissions also decrease emissions of health-damaging air pollutants as well as other urban health risks, which may especially benefit the poor located in the cities of developing countries.[16]

Mangroves

As we saw in Chapter 4, mangrove ecosystems provide a wide range of valuable goods and services, including raw material and food, coastal protection from storms, nursery and habitat support for offshore fisheries, and carbon sequestration (see Table 4.1). In Chapter 4, we used the example of mangrove loss in Thailand from 1970 to 2009 to estimate the economic costs of this decline in valuable ecological capital. Here, we explore how excessive mangrove conversion to shrimp farming is directly related to how this land use decision ignores the value of important ecosystem benefits. In addition, we show that the impacts of mangrove losses fall mainly on less well-off rural coastal communities.

Since the 1960s, Thailand has lost around a third of its mangroves, mainly to shrimp farming and coastal development.[17] Although declining in recent years, conversion of mangroves to shrimp farm ponds and other commercial coastal developments continues to be a major threat to Thailand's remaining mangrove areas.[18] Thus, the choice between conserving versus developing mangroves is an important land use policy decision in Thailand as well as many other tropical countries.

As shown in Figure 6.2, when this decision is made on the basis of the private benefits of investing in a commercial shrimp farm compared to retaining mangroves, it looks as if the aquaculture option should be preferred. For a typical shrimp farm, the present value of commercial profits is around $9,600 per hectare (ha), whereas the value to local coastal communities of exploiting mangroves directly for a variety of products, such as fuelwood, timber, raw materials, honey and resins, and crabs and shellfish, is only about $580 per ha. But this comparison of private benefits is misleading. Many of the conventional inputs used in shrimp pond operations are subsidized below border-equivalent prices, thus increasing artificially the prices that producers receive from shrimp farming, and thus the money that they earn. A further problem is that intensive shrimp farming lasts for only a short period of time, usually five years or even less. After this period, yields decline and disease outbreaks can occur; shrimp farmers then abandon their ponds and create new ones elsewhere on the coast. As Figure 6.2 indicates, once the generous subsidies to shrimp farming are accounted for, the actual value of the private benefits of aquaculture, when discounted over the five-year period of normal operation, amount to $1,220 per ha.

During their operation, intensive shrimp farming also generates substantial water pollution, as the ponds are often flushed with water that is then discharged into the surrounding environment. The cost of this pollution is estimated to be around $1,000 per ha in present value terms. There is also the problem of the highly degraded state of abandoned shrimp ponds after the five-year period of their productive life. Across Thailand those areas with abandoned shrimp ponds degenerate rapidly into wasteland, since the soil becomes very acidic, compacted and too poor in quality to be used for any other productive use, such as agriculture. To rehabilitate the abandoned shrimp farm site requires treating and detoxifying the soil, replanting mangrove forests and maintaining and protecting mangrove seedlings for several years. These restoration costs are considerable, and are estimated to be $9,318 per ha. As indicated in Figure 6.2, when pollution and restoration costs are included, the *net public costs* of shrimp farming are about $9,100 per hectare.

But there are also additional *public benefits* from mangroves beyond the direct private benefits to local communities from using the resources. Mangroves serve as nursery and breeding habitats for many species of fish that are important to offshore fisheries. Mangroves also have an important role as natural "storm barriers" to periodic coastal storm events, such as windstorms, tsunamis, storm surges and typhoons. The present value of mangroves as habitat in support of fisheries is $987 per ha, and for protection against coastal storms is $10,821 per ha. After adding these two public benefits of mangroves their value increases to nearly $12,400 per ha (see Figure 6.2). Unfortunately, these benefits are all lost when mangroves are converted to shrimp farming, and so these lost benefits can be considered part of the "hidden costs" of producing and selling shrimp in this way.

The Thailand mangrove case study illustrates how basing a land use decision solely on comparing the *private benefits* of conservation versus development options is misleading. The irreversible conversion of mangroves for aquaculture results in the loss of ecological services that generate significantly large

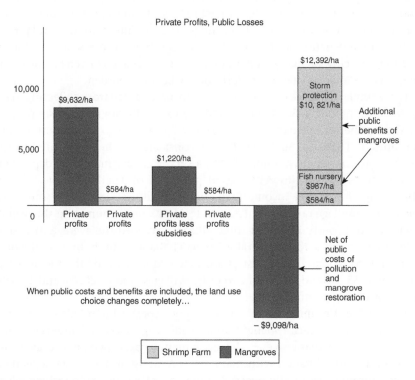

Figure 6.2 The underpricing of mangroves and their conversion to shrimp farms, Thailand

Source: Edward B. Barbier (2007) "Valuing ecosystems as productive inputs", *Economic Policy*, 22: 177–229.

economic benefits. This loss of benefits should be taken into account in land use decisions that lead to the widespread conversion of mangroves, but typically these environmental costs are ignored. This is an indication that farmed shrimp and other commercial products resulting from mangrove deforestation are underpriced when they are sold in markets. The high costs of restoring mangroves also reflect that "reversing" mangrove conversion is difficult and expensive. Nevertheless, these restoration costs again suggest that the use of mangroves to create shrimp farms is underpriced, and should be included as part of the overall costs of shrimp aquaculture based on mangrove conversion. Finally, other environmental damages that occur during the operation of the shrimp farm, such as pollution, should also be considered a form of "environmental subsidy" to shrimp production, and is yet another part of its additional costs.

There is growing evidence from Thailand and other tropical developing countries that the rural poor in coastal areas are especially affected by the loss of mangroves. Mangroves not only benefit the coastal rural poor by supporting fishing or protecting agriculture through buffering coastlines from erosion and saltwater intrusion, but also protect against storm surge and other coastal hazards, provide raw materials, food and forage, and filter sediment and pollutants.[19] These benefits can be significant to poor coastal households. Thus, if the underpricing of mangroves leads to their excessive conversion, it is the poor in coastal areas that disproportionately bear the burden.

For example, in Figure 6.2, the estimated income earned from collecting mangrove forest products ($584 per ha) and the value of mangroves in supporting offshore fisheries by mangroves ($987 per ha) accrue to local coastal communities in Thailand. Such benefits are considerable when compared to the average incomes of coastal households; a survey of four mangrove-dependent communities in two different coastal provinces of Thailand indicates that the average household income (including agricultural and other sources of income) per village ranged from $2,606 to $6,623 per annum, and the overall incidence of poverty in all but three villages exceeded the average incidence rate of 8% found across all rural areas of Thailand.[20] Excluding the income from collecting mangrove forest products would have raised the incidence of poverty to 55.3% and 48.1% in two of the villages, and to 20.7% and 13.64% in the other two communities.

The Thailand example is not unusual; poor coastal households across the developing world typically benefit from a wide range of ecosystem services that are derived from mangroves.[21] However, many coastal people also associate important cultural values with mangroves. A study of mangrove-dependent coastal communities in Micronesia demonstrated that the communities "place some value on the existence and ecosystem functions of mangroves over and above the value of mangroves' marketable products."[22]

The rural poor in coastal areas are especially vulnerable to natural disaster shocks, such as hurricanes, tsunamis, floods and other extreme coastal events.[23] In addition, the inadequate protection infrastructure in rural areas, such as storm shelters, seawalls and embankments, means that poor rural households are often reliant on mangroves as a "natural barrier" to protect them from frequent tropical storms. For example, two studies based on the 1999 cyclone that struck Orissa, India found that mangroves significantly reduced the number of deaths as well as damages to property, livestock, agriculture, fisheries and other assets.[24] Without mangroves to protect coastal villages, there would have been 1–2 additional deaths per village during the cyclone.[25] Losses incurred per household were greatest ($154) in a village that was protected by an embankment but had no mangroves compared to losses per household ($33) in a village protected only by mangrove forests.[26] In many developing regions, poor households rely on coastal systems such as mangroves not just for protection against storms and other environmental shocks but as insurance and coping strategies for avoiding the income and subsistence losses associated with such disasters.[27]

Institutional inertia

The above examples of fossil fuels and mangroves illustrate how the underpricing of key natural and ecological assets imposes significant costs on economies – which are often borne by the poorest and most vulnerable members of the population in rich and poor countries. There are many other examples of similar misuse of other important natural resources and ecosystems, such as freshwater resources, coral reefs, fertile soils, fisheries, forests, and so on. So, returning to the question posed at the beginning of this chapter: why are we are we doing so little to address these problems?

One reason why these environmental problems seem so intractable is the numerous market, policy and institutional failures that prevent recognition of the economic significance of these problems. Although we have the economic tools to correct many of these failures, one possible obstacle is the difficulty of modifying many important social institutions, once they have been established for a long time.[28] This rigidity, or *institutional inertia*, tends to reinforce the vicious cycle of underpricing natural resources, as depicted in Figure 6.1.

We can think of *institutions* as all the mechanisms and structures for ordering the behavior and ensuring the cooperation of individuals within society. They are the formal and informal "rules" that govern and organize social behavior and relationships, including reinforcing the existing social order, which is a stable system of institutions and structure that characterizes society for a considerable period of time.

Consequently, as societies develop, they become more complex, and their institutions are more difficult to change. Institutions help structure the means of production, and how goods and services are produced influence the development of certain institutions. This is a cumulative causative, or mutually reinforcing, process. But the build-up of this institutional inertia also means that it is easier to conform to existing markets, policies and institutions than to try to reform them.

As we have chronicled throughout this book, the way in which modern economies view the relationship between nature and wealth has evolved significantly since the Industrial Revolution. This perspective was shaped in turn by the process of economic development through industrialization, which has changed how we view wealth and how it is created. This transformation in the creation of wealth is the primary reason why our social institutions have become "fixed" (or perhaps even "fixated") on reinforcing the vicious cycle of underpricing nature. In the world economy today, as countries become richer, less of their wealth comprises natural capital, such as agricultural land, forests, protected areas, minerals and fossil fuels, and instead, reproducible capital and financial assets have become the most important forms of wealth. In addition, the current pattern and structure of modern global development encourages carbon-dependent rich and large emerging market countries, and resource-dependent developing countries. Finally, carbon and resource-dependent development in the world economy is having a significant impact on major ecosystems globally, and this rising ecological scarcity is mostly ignored in our markets and policies. Therefore, it is not surprising that, as we have evolved this process of wealth creation over the past several centuries, we have developed a set of institutions that reinforces this process, thus making policy, market and institutional reform difficult.

It follows that our existing economic process of creating economic wealth from nature has evolved a stable set of economic institutions, which in turn determines how production is organized and how all inputs are combined and used. This includes how natural capital is used with human capital, reproducible capital, technology and knowledge to create goods and services. Our existing institutions are therefore geared towards continuing the same production patterns, including replicating the pattern of finding, exploiting and using the same set of natural resources and ignoring the consequences of rising ecological scarcity. Or to put it in economic terms, it is more cost-effective to maintain the same way in which we find, exploit and use natural capital than it is to change the market, policy and institutional processes that reinforce the vicious cycle of underpricing nature. Thus, institutional inertia is built up around maintaining the *existing production and exchange relationships* rather than making it easier to introduce new policies and incentives to reduce energy and resource use, pollution and ecological degradation.

Figure 6.3 illustrates the difficulty often confronted in overcoming such institutional inertia when instigating policies to correct environmental degradation. When a new policy is implemented, such as a tax on pollution, removal of perverse subsidies that are environmentally damaging, implementing licenses for resource harvest or establishing a new protected area, there are additional *transaction costs* incurred through search and information, political bargaining, negotiating and decision-making, and policing and enforcement (Area A).[29]

However, implementing market-based instruments and trading mechanisms, such as taxes, tradable permit systems and new resource markets, will also require the establishment or reallocation of property rights to facilitate these instruments, and the setting up of new public agencies and administrative procedures to record, monitor and enforce trades. Thus the costs of overcoming institutional inertia to implement the new policy will be areas A and B in the figure. Finally, if additional changes in the institutional environment and legal system are required, the full costs of overcoming institutional inertia will be larger still, including areas A, B and C.

All three types of costs depicted in Figure 6.3 have proven to be barriers to implementing a wide range of environmental policies. They may be especially relevant for policies to combat the carbon-dependency of economies. As several studies have shown, transaction costs and the other barriers to overcoming institutional inertia are attributed to delaying or inhibiting the implementation of carbon taxes or tradable permits, adding to the costs of technological change and greenhouse gas (GHG) abatement, and reducing the

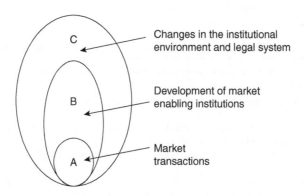

Changes in the institutional environment and legal system

Development of market enabling institutions

Market transactions

Figure 6.3 The costs of overcoming the institutional inertia to environmental policy change

Source: Adapted from L. McCann, B. Colby, K. W. Easter, A. Kasterine and K. V. Kuperan (2005) "Transaction Cost Measurement for Evaluating Environmental Policies", *Ecological Economics*, 52: 527–542, figure 1.

effectiveness of the Clean Development Mechanism that funds the adoption of carbon abatement in developing countries.[30]

The high costs of overcoming institutional inertia have also been an obstacle to implementing innovative policies, such as water markets and trading, for reducing freshwater scarcity (see Table 6.2).[31] Most policy recommendations for tackling water scarcity emphasize the need for more efficient water allocation and trading to conserve supplies and moderate demand. The use of water markets and market-based reforms for a wide range of water sector applications is growing globally. Active markets are emerging in Australia, Canada and the United States, but also in Brazil, Chile, China, Mexico, Morocco, South Africa and Turkey, as well as in many other countries and regions. But as listed in Table 6.2, the magnitude and incidence of the institutional inertia barriers associated with such allocation mechanisms are often significant. Establishing and enforcing water rights and trading schemes, as well as putting in place mechanisms to resolve conflicts over water rights and use, are some of the more prohibitive costs to effective water markets and trading.

For example, one reason why establishing irrigation water pricing in Egypt, India and Indonesia has proved less successful than in Morocco is that the irrigation system in the former countries is not designed for the use of volumetric charges and tradable water rights whereas the system in Morocco is. There are also no legally defined groundwater rights in Egypt and India.[32] In the Ukraine, there are problems with the smaller scale of privatized farms relative to the larger "block" supply of irrigation water. Finally, in many countries, farmers are resistant to switching to water markets when the predominant method of allocation has been the rationing of irrigation water, which does not involve charges to recover costs.[33]

Table 6.2   Institutional inertia barriers to establishing water markets and trading

- Water rights or water usage rights are not well established, quantified and separated from the land.
- Water rights are not registered, and people are not well informed about water trading.
- Organizational or management mechanisms are not in place to ensure that the traded water reaches the owner or owners.
- The infrastructure for conveying water is insufficiently flexible for water to be rerouted to the new owner.
- Mechanisms are not in place to provide "reasonable" protection against damages caused by water sale for parties not directly involved in the sale.
- Mechanisms are not in place to resolve conflicts over water rights and changes in water use.

Source: Based on K. W Easter and S. Archibald (2002) "Water Markets: The Global Perspective", *Water Resources Impact*, 4(1): 23–25.

Vested interests

Vested interests and political lobbying reinforces institutional inertia and further strengthens the vicious cycle of underpricing nature. Governments can be influenced by powerful interest groups to block policy reforms that redistribute costs and benefits against their interests. In effect, the role of vested interests, political lobbying, and in some cases outright corruption and bribery, is to "expand" each of the cost "bubbles" A, B and C illustrated in Figure 6.3. The result is that it becomes even more difficult to implement a new environmental policy, such as removing perverse subsidies that are environmentally damaging or imposing a tax on pollution.

Figure 6.4 demonstrates why there are strong economic incentives for vested interests to resist such policy reforms. Recall that we have suggested that the underpricing of nature occurs through the failure to incorporate the environmental damages from economic activities into the market prices derived for their goods and services, and also from subsidies to environmentally damaging activities. Figure 6.4A illustrates the latter case of a perverse subsidy, whereas Figure 6.4B shows the imposition of an environmental tax.

In Figure 6.4A, the upward-sloping curves S and S' represent the costs of supply of a quantity of goods Q to market, whereas the curve D represents the demand for these goods. However, as more goods are sold and purchased, environmental damages E also rise. If there is a subsidy to production, costs are lower, and thus the market supply shifts from S to S'. The market price falls from P to P' (although producers receive a higher price P″ because of the subsidy), the amount of goods produced and bought increases from Q to Q', and thus environmental damages also rise from E to E'. It would seem, then, that eliminating the subsidy would be an ideal means to reducing the latter damages.

However, Figure 6.4A shows that vested interests have a strong incentive to maintain the existing subsidy. The removal of a perverse subsidy causes a shift in market supply from S' to S. The quantity sold declines from Q' to Q, and the market price rises from P' to P. The government and taxpayers save (P″-P')*Q', there is a gain from more efficient production and consumption c, and environmental damages are reduced by area d. Although consumers face higher prices, the public as a whole will gain c+d as economic inefficiency is reduced and the environment improves. However, as a special interest group profiting from the subsidy, producers might feel differently. They suffer a substantial producer surplus, or profit, loss a+b. As indicated in the diagram, they have a strong economic incentive to block the policy change, as they experience a high relative *political cost* from the subsidy removal, which amounts to (a+b)/(c+d).

Of course, even if the subsidy is successfully eliminated, there is still a lingering environmental damage E. Suppose such damages arise from the

A. Removal of a perverse subsidy

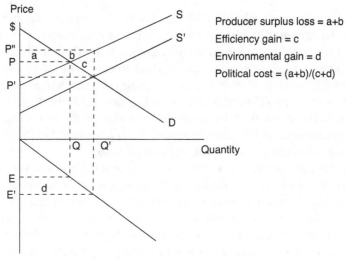

Producer surplus loss = a+b
Efficiency gain = c
Environmental gain = d
Political cost = (a+b)/(c+d)

Marginal environmental damages

B. Environmental tax

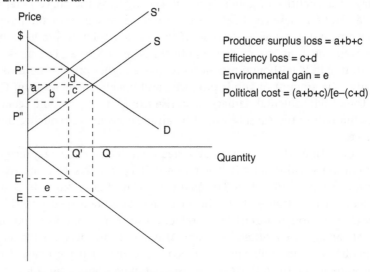

Producer surplus loss = a+b+c
Efficiency loss = c+d
Environmental gain = e
Political cost = (a+b+c)/[e−(c+d)]

Marginal environmental damages

Figure 6.4   The political cost of overcoming vested interests
A. Removal of a perverse subsidy B. Environmental tax

pollution generated from producing the quantity of goods Q. As shown in Figure 6.4B, this damage can be reduced further, if an environmental tax is imposed on pollution. But vested interests also have strong incentives to resist such a pollution tax. The tax raises production costs and thus shifts the supply curve from S to S'. As a result, Q declines to Q', and the market price rises from P to P'. The government gains tax revenue equal to (P'-P")*Q', but there is still an efficiency loss equal to c+d. The environmental improvement, which is e, may compensate for this loss; however, producers will still be worse off by a+b+c. Thus, the political cost of the environmental tax is (a+b+c)/e-(c+d).

The incentive of vested interests to lobby against policy change is therefore strong. In economics, a growing literature is examining the role of such lobbying in influencing environmental policy outcomes.[34] In all cases, the influence of lobbying by powerful vested interests fosters outcomes that work against the greater social interest and perpetuate environmental damages. The greater the political bargaining power of special interests, the more difficult it is to implement reform. Yet there are many examples where such reforms could yield improvements in both environmental outcomes and economic efficiency.

For example, as indicated previously in Table 6.1, subsidies, tax breaks and environmental damages from fossil fuels impose additional costs globally of $1.9 trillion annually. These costs comprise 2.5% of global GDP, and 8% of total government revenue worldwide; ending such underpricing of fossil fuels would reduce global energy demand significantly, encourage alternative energy options, and could lead to a 13% reduction in carbon emissions worldwide.[35] Yet, the combination of institutional inertia and vested interests remains a potent obstacle to realizing these economic and environmental gains from correcting the distorted pricing of fossil fuels in the world economy.

In the past few decades, powerful vested interest in terms of large-scale plantations, farms, ranching, timber and mining operations, and agribusiness enterprises, have become the dominant cause of much of the world's defor-estation, which is occurring primarily in tropical developing countries.[36] According to Thomas Rudel, "to facilitate their plans for expansion, large land-owners lobbied for the construction of improved and expanded networks of roads. Local politicians and bankers joined the landowners to form 'growth coalitions' that lobbied federal and provincial governments for improved infrastructure." These governments were soon "won over by powerful interest groups of landowners whose agendas involved agricultural expansion at the expense of forests."[37]

Global implications

The vicious cycle depicted in Figure 6.1 has unfortunately become the norm for modern economies. Institutional inertia and vested interests have been built up to block reform of this process, or at least to make it prohibitively expensive.

Globally, this vicious cycle lies at the heart of the rising costs of environmental degradation, ecological scarcity and natural capital depreciation experienced by all economies. However, as long as these costs remain hidden and difficult to assess, then economies lack the proper incentives, price signals, policies and institutions to control the underpricing of nature and the excessive overuse of natural capital.

Finally, as we have seen throughout this book, the global impacts of environmental degradation are becoming a pressing problem. Thus, overcoming these worldwide market failures and environmental threats, especially climate change, ecological scarcity and declining freshwater availability, has become a priority. However, the bigger and more widespread the environmental problem, the harder it appears to overcome institutional inertia and vested interests to instigate reforms. Nevertheless, Chapters 8 and 9 outline a strategy of policies that, if successfully implemented, could end the current practice of underpricing and overuse of natural capital, thus reducing excessive environmental degradation worldwide.

Conclusion

In this chapter we have explored how the chronic underpricing of nature in the world economy has become a vicious cycle. The failure of markets and policies to reflect the environmental damages and rising ecological scarcity imposed by economic development means that we are depreciating valuable natural and ecological capital much too quickly. The widespread prevalence of subsidies to environmentally damaging activities further compounds this problem. The ensuing environmental and economic costs are substantial, rising significantly, and increasingly borne by the most disadvantaged and vulnerable populations. Yet overcoming the market, policy and institutional failures underlying this vicious cycle seem even more prohibitively expensive. Powerful vested interests also coalesce to block policy reforms that change existing institutional and production patterns, as such actions will inevitably redistribute costs and benefits. The outcome is a replication of the same patterns of production that are reliant on the underpricing of nature, even though we may be aware of the rising ecological scarcity associated with over-reliance on fossil fuels and ecological degradation.

In the next chapter, we examine another key structural problem in the world economy, which is underinvestment in human capital. As we shall see, this problem is associated with its own self-reinforcing vicious cycle. Institutional inertia and vested interests also underlie this process, making reform difficult and costly to implement. Nevertheless, the social and economic implications of insufficient human capital accumulation have become significant, as it is contributing to increasing wealth inequality and structural imbalance in all economies. As we will explore in the final chapters of this book, correcting both the underpricing of natural capital and the underinvestment in human capital is the only way to address the major structural ills that are inhibiting sustainable development in modern economies.

7
Wealth Inequality

Introduction

Up to now, this book has focused on how nature is used to create wealth. Here, we explore how that wealth is distributed, and its economic implications.

A key threat facing the world today is the growing gap between rich and poor. In this chapter, we will argue that this wealth disparity represents another major structural imbalance in the world economy. This imbalance is related, in turn, to an economic distortion that has become widespread in recent decades: the overpricing of skilled labor through insufficient human capital accumulation.

Human capital represents the skills, education and health embodied in the workforce. Thus, when the human capital embodied in workers is not sufficient to meet the growing demand for better-educated and trained labor, then skilled workers will receive higher real wages than less-skilled workers. Since human capital varies across the workforce, this disparity in wages can be considerable; only those workers with high skills and better education have the potential to receive premium wages.

As we shall explore in this chapter, the main mechanism through which this wage disparity arises in modern economies is through the "race" between education and technology.[1] Education and technology affect, respectively, the supply and demand of human capital in economies. The demand for human capital rises through *skill-biased technological change*.[2] If the technological innovations accompanying reproducible capital accumulation require increasingly more skills, then the demand for more highly skilled workers will increase throughout the economy. In contrast, investments in the education, training and health of workers in the economy boost the supply of human capital.

In the race between technological change and education, whether the demand for skilled and educated workers outpaces the supply determines the degree to which human capital accumulation is sufficient to prevent the wages for skilled labor from escalating. If the demand for more skilled labor is not met through rising supply, then workers embodied with more skills and education will increasingly attract a premium wage compared to less-skilled labor. This scarcity of human capital not only leads to redundancy and under-employment for workers with the wrong set or little skills but also allows those with the right set of skills, education, and training to capture a bigger share of the wealth created in an economy. The consequence is the growing wealth gap between rich and poor.

This process is also exacerbated, as we showed in Chapter 5, by skilled labor becoming more expensive to use than natural resources in production. In Chapter 5, we argued that the pervasive underpricing of natural capital combined with the overpricing of human capital have three important conse-quences for the structure of production in all economies. First, all sectors of the economy will use too many natural resources relative to skilled labor. Second, the skilled workers throughout the economy will have higher real incomes and thus will be better off. Third, wealth inequality will increase, as the income gap between skilled and unskilled or less-skilled workers expands. The result is a profound structural imbalance in the modern world economy; global pro-duction today uses natural capital excessively, skilled workers are made much better off, and wealth inequality is increasing.

Throughout the world today, the disparity in incomes and wealth has grown steadily over recent decades. Developing countries face the additional problem of persistent rural poverty, especially the tendency of the very poor to be concentrated in remote and less favored lands, which suffer from low agri-cultural productivity and degradation, or in poor urban areas, which become "poverty sinks" of deprivation and worsening environmental quality. Growing wealth inequality in economies also increases the risk of financial instability and crisis, and perpetuates global imbalances. Unemployment is also on the increase worldwide. Only by understanding how insufficient human capital accumulation has led to higher relative wages for skilled labor and rising wealth inequality can we begin to consider the policies needed to overcome this structural imbalance.

The demand and supply for human capital

Recall from Chapter 5 that a key feature that distinguishes human capital from natural and reproducible capital is that human capital is "embodied" in labor; that is, one cannot separate the level of health, skills and education from each person or worker. Thus, when we talk about "accumulating" human capital, what we really mean is improvements in the health, education and training of people, and especially the workforce, of an economy. Consequently, it is common to consider the level of human capital to be the acquired skills and knowledge that distinguish *skilled* from *unskilled* labor in an economy. Whereas unskilled labor has only a minimal level of education and training, skilled labor is embodied with varying degrees of accumulated human capital. Thus, the higher the amount of human capital accumulated in an economy, the higher the level of education and skills of the average worker.

In Chapter 5, we also defined the human capital stock in an economy as $H = hL$, where h represents the amount of human capital per worker and L is the total number of workers. It follows that, if human capital increases in an economy, so does the skill level of the average worker. Thus, h approximates the skill level of the workforce: unskilled labor has only a minimal level of education and training (a very low h), whereas skilled labor has accumulated much more human capital through education and training (a very high h).

As investments in human capital translate into a workforce that has better education, training and health, then the wage rate w paid to relatively skilled labor is also the returns to human capital. But as these returns are paid out as wages to the labor embodied with human capital, w also represents the cost of using relatively skilled labor in the economy. Thus, we can consider w to be the *relative wage paid to skilled versus unskilled workers.*

In Chapter 5, we suggested that human capital is scarce relative to demand in most economies, which means that w is very high, without explaining how this has occurred. One reason for this outcome might be the "race between education and technology", which as shown by the economists Claudia Goldin and Lawrence Katz, has occurred in the United States since the early 20th century.[3]

Goldin and Katz maintain that, if technological change in modern economies is largely skill-biased, then technological progress through reproducible capital accumulation will lead to higher wages being paid to skilled as opposed to unskilled workers.[4] In essence, this type of technological innovation increases the demand for relatively more skilled labor. Unless the resulting rise in demand is matched by increases in the supply of human capital, then relative wages paid to skilled labor will go up. As we saw in Chapter 5, human capital expansion most likely occurs through greater expenditures on training and education, which leads to higher levels of schooling and skills in the population. Hence, the "race" between education and technology: education raises the supply of human capital in economies, whereas skill-biased technological change increases the demand for more skilled relative to unskilled labor. If technological change wins this "race", then human capital ends up "overpriced"; i.e., increasingly higher wages will be paid to skilled as opposed to unskilled or less-skilled workers in the economy.

Figure 7.1 illustrates how this supply and demand for human capital determines relative wages in the economy. The horizontal axis in the figure measures the number of skilled workers relative to the number of unskilled workers.

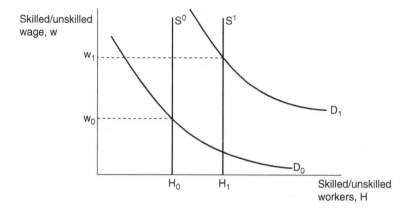

Figure 7.1 The supply and demand for human capital

Skilled biased technological change increases the relative demand for skilled, as opposed to unskilled, workers in the economy from D_0 to D_1. Although education and training investments may increase the relative supply of skilled to unskilled workers from S_0 to S_1, the increase is not enough to match the rise in demand. The result is higher wages w_1 will be paid to skilled as opposed to unskilled or less-skilled workers in the economy.

This measure approximates the amount of human capital H accumulated in the economy.[5] The vertical axis indicates w. Thus, the intersection of the relative demand and supply for these two types of workers, D_0 and S_0 respectively, determines their initial relative wage w_0.[6]

As shown in Figure 7.1, education can increase the supply of human capital in the economy, from S_0 to S_1. However, if skill-biased technological change increases the demand even more, from D_0 to D_1, then the relative wage paid to skilled workers must go up to w_1. It follows that, if the growth in the demand for skills driven by technological advances continues to outpace the growth in the supply of human capital driven by educational investment, the relative wage of skilled workers will continue to go up. Eventually, this must result in a growing income gap between relatively high compared to low-skilled workers in the economy.

The detailed analysis by Goldin and Katz of the education, technology and relative wages in the United States over the past century or so confirms that the "race" between education and technology has shifted in recent decades. In particular, they find that skill-biased technological change occurred rapidly and almost continuously in the US economy over much of the 20th century and into the early decades of the 21st century. In contrast, "the growth in the relative supply of educated and skilled workers was rapid from the early to mid-twentieth century, but became lethargic in the late twentieth century."[7]

The consequence is that "the inequality story of the twentieth century contains two parts: an era of initially declining inequality and a more recent one of rising inequality."[8] That is, for much of the 20th century, skill-biased technological progress in the United States did not widen the gap of inequality in wages and income between skilled and unskilled workers, because it was countered by increases in the supply of human capital. Instead, the rise in inequality over the last three or so decades was the result of human capital accumulation not keeping pace with skill-biased technological change; i.e., "the rise in educational wage differentials and wage inequality since 1980 resulted from an acceleration in demand shifts from technological change, or a deceleration in the growth of the supply of skills, or some combination of the two."[9]

What happens to the unskilled and less-skilled labor in the economy? One outcome is that workers with the wrong set of, or little, skills will find themselves without jobs or chronically "underemployed", meaning that they accept jobs for low pay or work less than they would like. However, another possibility is that workers who are displaced from jobs that have become more skill-intensive find alternative employment in less-skilled occupations in the service sector. As shown by the economists David Autor and David Dorn, this polarization of the low-skill labor market has occurred in the United States in recent decades.[10] Between 1980 and 2005, real earnings and employment have been stagnant or declining in most low-skill occupations, but not in the service sector. Skill-biased technological change has displaced routine tasks performed by low-skill workers, many of whom have moved to service jobs that are less susceptible to such innovations.[11]

Although the strongest evidence of the growing income gap in recent decades between relatively high compared to low-skilled workers in the economy is for the United States, it appears that other economies have been experiencing similar trends. For example, a study by the Organization for Economic Cooperation and Development (OECD) found that "the evolution of earnings inequality across OECD countries over the past few decades could be viewed mainly as the difference between the demand for and supply of skills...the outcome of a 'race between education and technology'."[12] Similarly, as developing economies increasingly adopt the skill-biased technologies of advance economies and the demand for skilled labor rises globally, there is also the increasing pressure of the relative wages of skilled workers and income inequality worldwide.[13] Thus, the rising demand for skilled labor, and the subsequent inequality in income earnings and wealth, appears to be a global phenomenon.

Insufficient human capital accumulation

To summarize, the race between education and technology is clearly at the center of the vicious cycle that leads to the pervasive higher premium for the wages of skilled labor in modern economies. This is especially the case, as we have just seen, if the demand for human capital grows faster than education, training and similar investments can supply relatively more skilled workers.

However, in Chapter 5, we also saw a second dimension to this problem. As levels of human capital investment increase in the economy, such as through expenditures in education, training and health, it will lead to greater production of skill-intensive goods and services, such as high-tech items, advanced financial services and other products that require relatively more skilled-labor inputs (see Figure 5.5). Over time, the economy will develop a comparative advantage in human as opposed to natural capital, and thus will specialize in producing more skill-intensive rather than resource-intensive goods. This is especially notable in wealthier economies today; as a result of prolonged levels of human capital investment, their workforces have relatively more skilled labor, and they dominate the production of skill-intensive goods and services in the world economy. But as we also saw in Chapter 5, the educational attainment levels of the workforce in most countries has grown steadily in recent years, and so more economies worldwide are experiencing at least some expansion in the production of skill-intensive goods.[14]

Over the long run, the process of rising skill levels, increasing bias towards skill-intensive goods production, and the failure of education to keep pace with technological change results in a vicious cycle of insufficient human capital accumulation that leads to relatively higher wages for skilled labor and increasing wealth inequality.[15] This vicious cycle is depicted in Figure 7.2. As long as education keeps up with skill-biased technological change, the supply of human capital will match the growth in demand, and the relative wages of skilled labor will not change significantly. But even if relative wages remain stable, continued human capital growth will itself change the process of production; it will drive the economy to produce relatively more skill-intensive goods and services. As a result, the economy will invest even more in skill-biased technological change through reproducible capital accumulation.[16] As this process continues, eventually human capital accumulation cannot keep up with demand, and higher prices for skilled labor, rising wealth inequality and structural unemployment for those potential workers with too little or the wrong set of skills will ensue.

In sum, the evidence discussed in Chapter 5 and in this chapter suggests that underinvestment in human capital and rising inequality have become chronic problems in the world economy over the past several decades:

- Average years of schooling per person have grown steadily in all countries since 1950, but a large gap in educational attainment still exists between rich and poor countries.
- Wealthier economies spend more than 25 times more on educating each person than do low and middle-income economies.

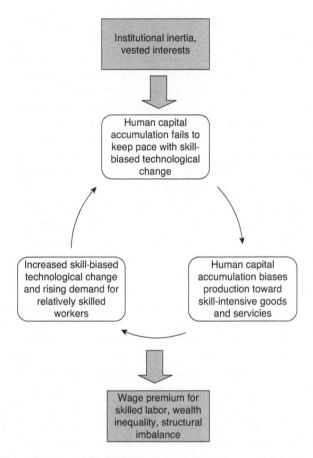

Figure 7.2   The vicious cycle of insufficient human capital accumulation

- Rising human capital in wealthier economies has given them a relatively large supply of skilled workers, and thus a comparative advantage in producing skill-intensive as opposed to resource-intensive goods.
- These economies therefore invest heavily in reproducible capital that induces skill-biased technological change, a process that began decades ago for some countries (e.g., the United States).
- In recent decades, as developing economies increasingly adopt the skill-biased technologies of advance economies, the demand for skilled labor rises globally.
- All economies have difficulty in expanding human capital fast enough to keep pace with the rising demand for relatively skilled labor.
- Insufficient human capital accumulation becomes chronic; the relative wages of skilled labor rises; and increasing wealth inequality becomes pervasive globally.

As we saw in the case of the underpricing of nature in Chapter 6, once this structural imbalance is established in the world economy, it becomes ingrained. As the vicious cycle of insufficient human capital accumulation persists, social institutions that reinforce this process are created, maintained and even expanded.[17] Vested political and economic interests that benefit from the process are also built up and become entrenched. The result is that it becomes very difficult and costly to overcome the institutional inertia and vested interests that prevent economy-wide reform of chronic underinvestment in human capital.

To explain how difficult it is to correct this structural imbalance, and the institutional inertia and vested interests reinforcing it, we finish this chapter by exploring the role of natural capital in this process, the increasing concentration of wealth globally, the rise of finance, and the political economy of wealth inequality. We then examine the resulting global implications of the continuing under-investment in human capital.

The role of natural capital

The roots of the vicious cycle of insufficient human capital accumulation are very much connected to the relationship between natural capital and economic development in modern economies. To see this connection, recall from Chapter 2 that the Industrial Revolution represented a major shift in the innovation, productivity and structure of economies, which irrevocably changed the role of natural wealth in economic activity.

For example, the first phase of the Industrial Revolution occurred from 1750–1830, and centered on key inventions during this period, such as the steam engine, cotton spinning, railroads and steamships (see Figure 2.2). Such innovations helped propel Great Britain to global economic and political dominance, and they had lasting economic impacts on all industrializing economies up until 1900. The second phase of the Industrial Revolution centered on key innovations from 1870–1900, such as electricity, the internal combustion engine, water and sanitation systems, refrigerated transport, and oil and gas refining (see Figure 2.2). These innovations spurred considerable industrial, transport and urban developments that boosted productivity until the 1970s, and led to the economic rise and worldwide dominance of the United States. Both phases of the Industrial Revolution also led to the emergence of the global fossil fuel age, which began in the 1890s when coal, oil and natural gas first accounted for more than half of energy consumption worldwide, and has continued to this day (see Figures 2.1 and 2.2).

One of the more important insights from Goldin and Katz's study of the rise of skill-biased technological change in the United States is that it is directly related to the key innovations and structural changes that launched the second phase of the Industrial Revolution. Specifically, Goldin and Katz maintain that "the technological shift from factories to continuous-process and batch methods, and from steam and water-power to electricity, were at the root of the increase in the relative demand for skilled labor in manufacturing in the early twentieth century. These technological changes provide the origins of the transition to technology-skill complementarity, which we believe to be in full blossom today."[18]

Moreover, as we discussed in Chapter 2, because the United States emerged as the leading economy from the second phase, the pattern of material and energy use in the US became the model for global industrialization development after World War II.[19] This process of industrialization therefore emulated and adopted many important US innovations, including centralized electricity generation, the internal combustion engine and petro-chemicals. In addition, the globalization of commodity markets and trade has allowed all economies to have better and cheaper access to natural resources than reliance on just their own endowments would allow. As we can now see, this has had two consequences: first, the overall dependence of the global economy on natural resource use, especially fossil fuels, minerals and other industrial materials, and second, the spread of skill-biased technological change through the emulation of US industrial development throughout the world economy.

Thus, the same economic forces, and especially the way in which natural wealth is used in modern economies, are responsible for the underinvestment in human capital and the underpricing of nature that are prevalent today. These forces have their roots in the changes in the pattern of innovation, productivity and structure of economies that were launched during the second phase of the Industrial Revolution, and which have perpetuated the fossil fuel era. As argued throughout this book, how modern economies use nature to create wealth is at the heart of this pattern, and until we change this process of wealth creation, both insufficient human capital accumulation and excessive environmental degradation will continue to be the main symptoms of the resulting structural imbalance that we see in the world economy today.

We have become so accustomed to this prevailing pattern of economic development that we have failed to see the root cause of it. One of the few exceptions is the analysis, provided by Ramón López, of the causes of the financial crisis that lead to the 2008–2009 Great Recession.[20] Although there have been many in-depth economic analyses of this crisis, what distinguishes López's approach is that he considers the structural dependence of the world's economy on natural resource exploitation to be central to the cause of the crisis. He argues that the key to understanding the financial crisis, and the threat of future global crises, is the increasing "commodity and energy-intensity of global economic growth", which, coupled with the fact that "the world is now experiencing scarcity of environmental resources", makes "commodity supply less responsive" to the growth in demand; consequently, "economic growth is now more closely tied to rising commodity prices than in the twentieth century."[21]

According to López, the increasing commodity and energy-intensity of global growth has occurred at the same time as another important structural trend, which is the increasing concentration of wealth in the world economy. This has not only made global growth less inclusive but also means that economic policies have focused on expanding credit to fuel consumer demand to sustain growth and on restricting this credit when that growth threatened to turn inflationary.[22] Hence, López argues, the world economy becomes vulnerable to financial and economic crises, as "the persistent rise in commodity prices fuelled by rapid world growth eventually feeds into core inflation, thereby forcing governments to adopt restrictive monetary policies."[23]

Although López focuses on how the use of natural resources in the world economy makes it more crisis-prone in the short run, it is clear that the long-run implications of his analysis are similar to the arguments developed in this book. Over the long term, the response of the world economy to increasing environmental and ecological scarcity is not to change the structure of production to make it less dependent on natural resource exploitation but to persist with the underpricing of nature to match the commodity dependence of global growth. Similarly, this same structural imbalance is fueling the underinvestment in human capital and even greater concentration of wealth. As the latter phenomenon is an important feature of the world economy, the next section describes this trend in more detail.

The concentration of wealth

Much attention in recent years has focused on the highly concentrated distribution of wealth in all economies, and especially among the so-called "one percent" of the population that is super-rich, i.e., the wealthiest 1% of all adults. Most analysts agree that, although data on long-run trends are available for only a handful of countries, the wealth of the super-rich has been increasing since the early 1970s for some economies and since 1980 for others.[24] More importantly, worldwide:

- the top 1% today account for almost half of the all the wealth in the world,
- the richest 10% own 87% of all assets, and
- the lower half of the global population possess less than 1% of global wealth.[25]

Figure 7.3 provides a snapshot of the current global wealth distribution. Just over 3 billion people in the world, nearly 70% of the world's population, have

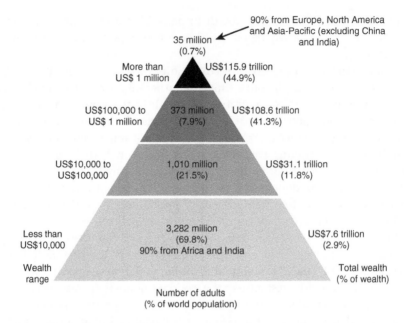

Figure 7.3 The global wealth pyramid, 2014

Note: For the 35 million at the apex, the wealth of 30.8 million ranges from US$1 million to 5 million, 2.5 million from US$5 to 10 million, 1.4 million from US$10 to 50 million, and 128,200 more than US$50 million.

Source: Markus Stierli, Anthony Shorrocks, Jim Davies, Rodrigo Lluberas and Antonios Koutsoukis (2014) *Global Wealth Report 2014*. Zurich: Credit Suisse Research Institute. figure 1, p. 24, figure 4, p. 26, and pp. 24–26.

wealth of less than US$10,000. Among this group, 90% are located in Africa and India. In comparison, people who are millionaires or richer comprise less than 1% of the population yet they own 45% of global assets. Of these wealthy individuals, 90% live in Europe, North America and the Asia–Pacific (excluding China and India). Among the global rich, just 128,000 have wealth that exceeds US$50 million.

However, it is the recent rise in wealth inequality – and its spread throughout the world economy – that is the most significant trend. Table 7.1 depicts the level of inequality in 46 major economies, and also indicates whether the level has been rising or falling from 2000 to 2014. Wealth inequality is high or very high in 30 of these countries. Moreover, since 2000, nine countries have experienced a rapid rise in inequality, five have seen a rise, and three a slight rise. Of particular concern is that nine of these countries are members of the Group of 20, which comprises the largest and most populous economies.

Table 7.1 Trends in wealth inequality across countries, 2000–2014

	Change in wealth share of the top decile, 2000–2014						
	Rapid fall	Fall	Slight fall	Flat	Slight rise	Rise	Rapid rise
Top decile wealth share, 2014							
>70% Very high inequality (US ca. 1910)		Malaysia Philippines	Switzerland	Peru *South Africa* Thailand *United States*		*Brazil* *Indonesia*	*Argentina* Egypt Hong Kong *India* *Russia* *Turkey*
>60% High inequality (US ca. 1950)	Poland *Saudi Arabia*	Colombia *Mexico*	Denmark *Germany*	Austria Norway Sweden	Chile	Czech Republic Israel	*China* *South Korea* Taiwan
>50% Medium inequality (Europe ca. 1980)		*Canada* *France* New Zealand Singapore		*Australia* Finland Greece Ireland *Italy* Netherlands Portugal	United Arab Emirates	*United Kingdom*	Spain
<50% Low inequality			*Japan*	Belgium			

Note: The top decile is the wealthiest 10% of all adults; 46 countries, with the Group of 20 (G20) countries indicated in italics. The members of the G20 include 19 countries (Argentina, Australia, Brazil, Canada, China, France, Germany, India, Indonesia, Italy, Japan, Mexico, Russia, Saudi Arabia, South Africa, South Korea, Turkey, the UK and the US), plus the European Union.

Source: Markus Stierli, Anthony Shorrocks, Jim Davies, Rodrigo Lluberas and Antonios Koutsoukis (2014) *Global Wealth Report 2014*. Zurich: Credit Suisse Research Institute, table 1, p. 30 and table 2, p. 33.

The good news to emerge from Table 7.1 is that 14 countries saw at least some reduction in wealth inequality from 2000 to 2014, with Poland and Saudi Arabia showing a rapid fall. However, in the near future, it is unlikely that many of the countries in Table 7.1 will reach the historically low wealth inequality levels that only Japan and Belgium appear to have attained.

Finally, given that both financial capital and wealthy people are inherently mobile, perhaps more revealing in the changes in wealth inequality is how much wealth the global super-rich are accumulating compared to the average individual. For example, based on estimates by Thomas Piketty compiled from data on billionaires' wealth in *Forbes* magazine, Table 7.2 indicates how the wealth of the very rich increased from 1987 to 2013 compared to average world wealth per adult. The richest billionaires in the world consisted of 30 adults out of 3 billion people in the 1980s, and their average wealth was US$3.4 billion in 1980. Their accumulated assets grew each year by 6.8% to 2013, totaling US$32.3 billion. Billionaires numbered 150 adults out of 3 billion in the 1980s, and their average wealth grew at 6.4% per year between 1987 and 2013, from US$1.6 billion to US$14.0 billion. In comparison, average world wealth per adult increased by only 2.1% annually from 1987 to 2013, and average income per person by just 1.4%. Thus, the wealth of the global rich appears to be growing much faster than that of the average individual.

Table 7.2 Increase in wealth of the world's rich, 1987–2013

	Wealth or Income in:		Average annual growth (%) 1987–2013
	1980	2013	
The richest billionaires[a]	$3.4 billion	$32.3 billion	6.8%
Billionaires[b]	$1.6 billion	$14.0 billion	6.4%
Average world wealth per adult	$26,065	$76,628	2.1%
Average world income per adult	$7,759	$19,187	1.4%
World adult population	2.85 billion	4.68 billion	1.9%
World gross domestic product (GDP)	$22,119 billion	$89,719 billion	3.3%

Note: All values are in US dollars, and adjusted net of inflation (2.3% per year from 1987 to 2013); [a] About 30 adults out of 3 billion in the 1980s, and 45 adults out of 4.5 billion in 2010; [b] About 150 adults out of 3 billion in the 1980s, and 225 adults out of 4.5 billion in 2010.

Source: Thomas Piketty (2014) *Capital in the Twenty-First Century*. Cambridge, MA: Harvard University Press, table 12.1 and supplementary table S12.3. Available at: http://piketty.pse.ens.fr/capital21c

The role of finance

Wealth inequality is therefore a notable feature of the world economy today. It is also linked to another important trend in recent decades, which is the rise of finance.

In Chapter 2, we saw how over the past five decades the financial sector has dominated the economies of high-income countries. For example, since 1960, the ratio of the value of financial assets to national income has risen steadily in seven major economies – the United Kingdom, Japan, France, the United States, Canada, Germany and Australia (see Figure 2.9). By 2010, the value of financial assets had increased to 20 years of national income in the United Kingdom, and ten to 15 years in the other six economies.[26]

Not surprisingly, one implication of the growth of the finance sector is that it has attracted many of the high skilled, and as a consequence, their wages have risen significantly. For example, in the United States, in 1980 a financial services employee earned about the same wages as a counterpart in other industries, but by 2006, the wages of the financial services employee was 70% higher.[27] Across most countries, since the 1970s, financial services have become more skill-intensive, and wages have grown relative to wages in the economy as a whole.[28] In addition, the higher relative wages in finance are associated with the adoption of information and communications technology, indicating once again that, by driving up the demand for skilled workers, skill-biased technological change is a major factor leading to the increased wage premium paid to these workers.[29] Thus, it appears that it is the highly skilled employees of the financial sector that are among the major beneficiaries of the resulting rise in relative wages due to the economy-wide underinvestment in human capital.

As the financial sector has boomed and financial assets dominate national wealth, more of the income and wealth of the rich is from this sector. In recent decades, the income earned by the wealthiest 1% of adults in France, Germany, the United Kingdom and the United States increasingly comes from financial asset-based earnings (capital gains, dividends, interest and rents).[30] For many top executives, their earned income (income received in return for work) and bonus payments are frequently in the form of financial-asset compensations, such as stock options.[31] This may explain why, for example, in the United States individuals in the top 1% of earned income also comprised 80% of the top 20% receiving income from financial assets, and similarly, those in the top 1% of financial capital income consisted of 60% of those in the top 20% of earned income.[32]

Josh Bivens and Lawrence Mishel report that, in the United States, households who were headed by executives or financial sector employees accounted for 58% in the expansion of income for the 1% wealthiest households between 1979 and 2005, and two-thirds of the income growth for the top 0.1% households.[33]

Overall, Bivens and Mishel find that from 1979 to 2007, the share of earned income in the total income of the top 1% wealthiest households increased from 4% to nearly 9%, but the share of financial capital income rose from 32% to 56%.

Compensation of financial sector employees and executives is also increasing relative to other workers. From 1952 to 1982, in the United State the ratio of financial sector pay relative to the pay of workers in the rest of the economy never exceeded 1.1. But since then, the ratio has risen steadily, reaching 1.83 by 2007.[34] Between 1989 and 2010, the compensation (capital and earned income) paid to chief executive officers grew from 1.14 to 2.06 times that of the average incomes of the wealthiest 0.1% households; from 1978 to 2012, executive compensation grew 876%, more than double the real growth in the stock market. In comparison, the hourly compensation of a private sector production or non-supervisory worker increased by only 5%.[35] As Bivens and Mishel conclude, "the overall pay of financial sector workers relative to others in the economy has risen substantially", and both these employees and executives (whose pay is increasingly based on financial capital income) are able to extract excessively high compensation well beyond what they should be paid as returns to their skills and abilities, due to the scarcity of human capital.[36]

Finally, a major factor in the rise of finance in recent decades has been global financial deregulation. Many attribute this trend to a political "ideological shift toward acceptance of a form of free market capitalism which, among other characteristics, offers less support for government provision of transfers, lower marginal tax rates for those with high incomes, and deregulation of a number of industries."[37] Given that the resulting financial sector boom worldwide has overwhelmingly benefited the wealthy, it is not surprising that many commentators maintain that "financial deregulation, in particular, has been a source of income inequality."[38]

Political economy of wealth inequality

If insufficient human capital accumulation is leading to the overpricing of skilled labor and increased wealth inequality, why not simply invest more in education?

This is certainly the policy prescription offered by Claudia Goldin and Lawrence Katz. They suggest that three main types of policies are needed to increase the growth rate of educational attainment in the United States, and thus increase the supply of human capital:

- Create greater access to quality pre-school education for children from disadvantaged families;

- Improve the operation of kindergarten through high-school education so that more students graduate from high school and are prepared for higher education; and,
- Make financial aid sufficiently generous and transparent so that those who are ready for higher education can complete a four-year university undergraduate degree or gain marketable skills at a community college.[39]

Although these policies are geared towards the US educational system, they are sufficiently general that they could also easily apply to improving educational attainment in other countries. From the standpoint of ensuring continued investment in human capital accumulation, the three policies seem to be a reasonable and justifiable economic strategy.

Unfortunately, they are also unrealistic, given the political economy of wealth inequality in the world today. For example, as argued by Daron Acemoglu and David Autor: "Research by political scientists and economists alike (e.g., summarized in Bartels, 2008) suggests that the US political system has been giving much more weight to the rich and wealthy and much less to the poor. If the political voice of minority and low-income Americans remains limited, it is unlikely that the sort of broad-based and far-reaching investments in the schooling of the most disadvantaged that Goldin and Katz advocate will be undertaken."[40]

There are several reasons why Acemoglu and Autor may be correct, not only for the United States but for other countries as well.

For one, Goldin and Katz's policies to increase educational opportunities will require significant public investments, which for most modern economies today means more taxes on income to fund these investments. As such policies appear to be redistributing income and wealth opportunities, they could be resisted by the wealthy, especially if they are asked to pay for the additional public expenditures on education. Or, as Adam Bonica and colleagues succinctly put it, "as the 1 percent get relatively richer, they turn against redistribution."[41]

In addition, the wealthy do not need public investments to increase their earning and income potential; they can afford to pay the rising private costs of educational, health care and other human capital investments in modern economies. At the top private colleges and universities in the United States, the costs of four years of higher education are now a quarter of a million dollars.[42] As a review in *The Economist* magazine found, such institutions are increasingly affordable only to the wealthy, and as a result, students are predominantly from richer and better-educated households.[43] Even the costs of attending public institutions such as state universities and community colleges have been rising significantly. The result is that 69% of graduating seniors at US institutions in 2013 incurred at least some debt, with an average of $28,400 in loan debt per student.[44]

There is increasing evidence that wealth inequality is affecting educational attainment in other ways. Students from US families within the top 25% income bracket with low college entrance test scores are more likely to graduate from college than students with high test scores from the bottom 25% income bracket.[45] Although more students from all income groups are graduating from college in the United States, the difference in college graduation between the top and bottom groups has widened by nearly 50% over the past two decades.[46] The main reason for this growing gap is that, while the college graduation rates of wealthy students increased significantly, there was little increase in the graduation rates of the poor. Two decades ago, 36% of the children from upper-income families graduated from college, whereas only 5% of children from low-income families graduated. Currently, 54% of students from wealthy families are graduating from college, as opposed to just 9% from poorer families. The rising costs of educational expenditures do not appear to be a deterrent for wealthy families investing in human capital, but poorer families may be more affected.

Another factor is that the political influence of the wealthy is growing. For one, their numbers are increasing very quickly worldwide; for example, the Credit Suisse *2014 Global Wealth Report* indicates that between 2008 and mid-2014, there was a 54% rise in millionaires worldwide (now almost 35 million individuals), a 106% increase in people with wealth above US$100 million, and more than double the number of billionaires.[47] For the foreseeable future, if there are more wealthy people in economies, they will gain more political clout; or, as Tyler Cowen puts it: "The wealthy will grow in numbers, and that also means that the wealthy will grow in influence."[48]

Already, the political influence of the wealthy is being felt, especially in the United States. For example, Adam Bonica and colleagues have suggested that, among the reasons "why the US political system has during the last few decades failed to counterbalance rising inequality" is that "the rich have been able to use their resources to influence electoral, legislative, and regulatory processes through campaign contributions, lobbying and revolving door employment of politicians and bureaucrats", whereas "immigration and low turnout of the poor have combined to make the distribution of voters more weighted to high incomes than is the distribution of households."[49] In short, the political influence of the wealthy is not only increasing but their influence is also disproportionately large compared to their relatively small number.

Finally, taxing the wealthy to raise funding for educational expenditure may not be effective. With their political and economic clout, richer households are able to avoid taxes and possibly shift them to others. As argued by Cowen, it is not easy to extract more money from the very wealthy, because they have access to "tax shelters, write-offs, tax deductions, untaxed workplace perks, and overseas accounts, all backed by the best lawyers and accountants money can buy", and "you can levy a greater tax on a top earner, but there is no guarantee that they will have to bear the entire burden...a lot of taxes end up getting passed on to other parties."[50]

In sum, because the wealthy benefit the most from the high returns to skilled labor and rising wealth inequality, they have a vested interest in maintaining the existing system. Using their growing political influence, the wealthy may oppose policies to increase human capital accumulation, such as higher taxes and public spending on education, as being too redistributive. As we shall see in Chapters 8 and 9, however, there may be other ways of overcoming under-investment in human capital accumulation that do not involve direct taxation of the income or wealth of the rich.

Global implications

Insufficient human capital accumulation that has led to higher relative wages for skilled labor and rising wealth inequality has several additional implications for the world economy:

- greater risk and instability in financial markets and institutions,
- increasing global imbalances,
- concentration of the poor, especially in developing countries, in urban and rural "pockets of poverty", and
- rising global unemployment, with many unemployed remaining jobless for longer periods of time.

An important implication of the growing inequality of wealth worldwide, and the increasing interdependence between the wealthy and financial markets, is that it may be introducing greater risk and instability into these markets and the institutions that dominate them.

This argument is summarized in Credit Suisse's *2014 Global Wealth Report*:

> Some commentators have claimed that rising equity prices are a conse-quence – as well as a cause – of rising inequality. It is suggested that rising income inequality in the United States from the 1970s onwards raised the disposable income of the top groups, who typically save a higher proportion of their income...this led to an increase in funds seeking investment opportunities, driving down interest rates and raising stock prices, which in turn created further capital gains for the top income groups, propelling income inequality to even higher levels. In addition, the fall in interest rates encouraged the housing bubble that developed in the United States in the early 2000s and fuelled the unsustainable growth of debt, which triggered the financial crisis of 2007–2008. If this account is even partially true, it raises concerns about the implications of the wide-spread rise in wealth inequality since 2008, and about the implications for equity markets once low interest rates are no longer regarded as a priority by central banks.[51]

Figure 7.4 illustrates this process. As more of the income and wealth of the global rich takes the form of financial capital, this leads to more investments funds flowing into financial markets. The result is that interest rates are lowered, and stock prices rise. The ensuing capital gain for the rich simply adds to their accumulated wealth, and further spurs wealth inequality. As the process continues, financial expansion leads to more risk and instability. The failure to curb this process suggests that growing wealth inequality in the world economy is not just a symptom of structural imbalance but could be the cause of inherent instability and the risk of repeated global crises within the system.[52]

The process depicted in Figure 7.4 may be further exacerbated by the chronic *global imbalances* that are another structural feature of the world economy today. According to the International Monetary Fund, "The phrase 'global imbalances' refers to the pattern of current account deficits and surpluses that built up in the global economy starting in the late 1990s, with the United States and some other countries developing large deficits (United Kingdom; southern Europe, including Greece, Italy, Portugal, and Spain; central and eastern Europe), and others large surpluses (notably, China, Japan, other east Asian economies, Germany, and oil exporters)."[53] These global imbalances are now believed to be a major contributing factor to the 2008–2009 Great Recession, and the

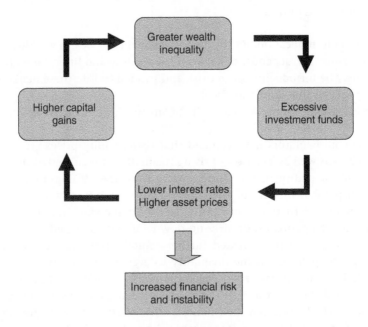

Figure 7.4   Wealth inequality and increasing financial risks

Source: Adapted from Markus Stierli, Anthony Shorrocks, Jim Davies, Rodrigo Lluberas and Antonios Koutsoukis (2014) *Global Wealth Report 2014*. Zurich: Credit Suisse Research Institute, figure 3, p. 34.

persistence of such imbalances continues to add uncertainty and risk to the future stability of the world economy.[54] The reason is that, in the years leading up to the Great Recession, those economies with chronic trade deficits received large and sustained capital inflows from surplus economies seeking safer assets as investments. The massive credit flows arising from these global imbalances may have precipitated the credit bubble and subsequent bust in financial markets. Consequently, the continuing persistence of such imbalances after the Great Recession adds to the uncertainty and instability of the world economy.

One consequence of global imbalances is the emergence and proliferation of *sovereign wealth funds*. A sovereign wealth fund (SWF) is a state-owned investment fund or entity that is commonly established from balance of payment surpluses or large accumulations of export earnings, such as from oil and other resource commodity exports. Thus, as global imbalances continue, and chronic surplus economies accumulate more and more trade revenues, they accumulate in SWFs.[55] These state-owned investment funds are then ploughed back to purchase assets in global financial markets, often in the chronic deficit countries in the United States, United Kingdom and Europe.

There is nothing inherently wrong with SWFs, which can offer important economic and financial benefits. For example, in chronic trade surplus countries, SWFs facilitate the saving of proceeds from non-renewable resource exploitation and help reduce boom and bust cycles driven by changes in commodity export prices. These investment funds also allow for a greater portfolio diversification, as they are usually invested in a broad range of financial and other economic assets. From the viewpoint of international financial markets, SWFs can facilitate a more efficient allocation of revenues from commodity surpluses across countries and enhance market liquidity, including at times of global financial stress.

However, realizing these various economic and financial benefits requires that SWFs do not add to the wealth inequality burden on financial markets, as depicted by the process in Figure 7.4. Unfortunately, there are signs that this might be happening.

For example, Piketty has argued that the continuing growth of SWFs and their rising dominance of international financial markets may potentially be causing more stress on these markets than dampening it.[56] In recent years, high oil prices, financial globalization, and sustained, large global imbalances have resulted in the rapid accumulation of foreign assets particularly by oil exporters and several Asian countries. As a result, the number and size of SWFs are rising fast and their presence in international capital markets is becoming more prominent. By 2013, SWFs had total investments worth a little over US$5.3 trillion, of which about US$3.2 trillion belongs to the funds of oil-exporting states.[57]

Given the continuing structural dependence of the world's economy on natural resource exploitation, and the high rate of natural capital depreciation globally (see Chapters 2 and 3), SWFs are likely to increase rather than diminish in size. For example, Piketty observes that globally, since the 1970s, the annual rent derived from the exploitation of natural resources (i.e., the difference between the revenues from selling extracted natural resources and the costs of extraction), has been increasing. In, the early 1970s, the rents earned from fossil fuels, minerals and timber were less than 1% of global national income, rising to about 2% in the 1990s and reaching 5% since the mid-2000s – half of which is oil rent and the rest rent on other natural resources.[58]

Thus, Piketty concludes: "If a sufficiently large faction of the corresponding rent is invested in sovereign wealth funds every year (a fraction that should be considerably larger than it is today) one can imagine a scenario in which the sovereign wealth funds would own 10–20 percent or more of global capital by 2030–2040...In any event, it is almost inevitable that the sovereign wealth funds of the petroleum exporting countries will continue to grow and that their share of global assets in 2030–2040 will be at least two to three times greater than it is today – a significant increase."[59]

Another important global implication of insufficient human capital accumulation and the growing wealth inequality worldwide is the creation of *pockets of poverty*. These often take the form of *spatial* or *geographical poverty traps*, which occur when the characteristics of a specific geographical region or location are such that people living there cannot easily escape from poverty and poor environmental conditions, whereas similar people living in a different, better-endowed area might be able to have better economic opportunities.[60]

As we saw in Chapter 6, one such pocket of poverty encompasses the poor neighborhoods of the growing metropolitan areas and cities around the world. One quarter of the world's poor live in urban areas, and that proportion appears to be rising over time as cities in developing countries expand.[61] In both rich and poor countries, it is the households that are poor, unemployed, or from disadvantaged groups (e.g., ethnic or racial minorities) that are increasingly clustered into the urban areas that suffer not only from deteriorating environmental conditions but also have poor schools, health facilities, high crime and inadequate public services. Not surprisingly, these urban locations have become "poverty sinks" of deprivation and worsening environmental quality.

Developing countries face the additional problem of persistent rural poverty, especially the tendency of the very poor to be concentrated in remote and less favored lands, which suffer from low agricultural productivity and degradation. As noted by Aart Kraay and David McKenzie, "The evidence most consistent with poverty traps comes from poor households in remote rural regions".[62]

Since 1950, the estimated population in developing economies has doubled in such areas, which comprise uplands, converted forests, drylands and other poor quality lands, reaching nearly 1.3 billion in 2000.[63] Almost half of the people in these fragile environments (631 million) consist of the rural poor, who throughout the developing world outnumber the poor living on favored lands by 2 to 1.[64] In addition, around 430 million people in developing countries live in remote rural areas, which are locations that are five or more hours of travel away from any market town of significant size.[65] Estimates for 2010 suggest that there are around 1.5 billion rural people in developing countries found on less favored agricultural land, being over 35% of the rural population.[66] Nearly a quarter of the rural population (22%) on marginal lands in developing countries is located in remote areas with poor market access. The regions with the largest share of their rural population in marginal and remote areas are Sub-Saharan Africa (29%), East Asia and Pacific (24%) and South Asia (16%). These three regions also tend to have the highest incidence of poverty.

As we saw previously in this chapter, skill-biased technological change and the overpricing of human capital is displacing workers with no or little skills. Some of these workers are finding alternative employment in less-skilled occupations in the service sector.[67] However, for many others around the world, finding work has proven increasingly difficult.

Global unemployment trends continue to rise steadily, with the prospects of future jobs for younger workers especially bleak.[68] Increasingly, the jobless are out of work for longer periods of time. For example, in the member countries of the Organization for Economic Cooperation and Development (OECD), over 16 million people – more than one in three of all unemployed – were out of work for 12 months or more in 2014. This group of long-term unemployed has increased by 85% since 2007.[69] Allowing a larger share of the work force to remain chronically unemployed is a worrisome indicator of insufficient human capital accumulation. Some of the long-term jobless eventually exit the work force, retiring long before their capacity and willingness to work ends. Others may find employment, but in jobs that do not match their skills and experience. These losses in human capital have consequences for every economy, reducing potential output and increasing the burden on costly transfer and social welfare programs.[70]

Conclusion

Growing wealth inequality poses a major threat to the world economy. The main cause of this imbalance is the failure of education investments and human-capital accumulation to keep pace with skill-biased technological change. The result is that those workers with better skills, education and access to the high returns from the booming financial sector are able to amass huge personal fortunes. With growth in wealth also comes extraordinary political and economic influence, or as Daron Acemoglu and James Robinson put it, there is an "inequality multiplier" at work: as wealth inequality increases, the rich are able to influence government regulation and policy further in their favor, thus creating even more inequality.[71]

The global implications of insufficient human capital accumulation and growing wealth inequality in economies are increased risk of financial instability and crisis, and the perpetuation of global imbalances. Meanwhile, the increasing numbers of those left out of the wealth creation process of modern economies will find themselves isolated to pockets of poverty – undesirable urban and rural locations have become "poverty sinks" of deprivation, poor education, health and other public services, and worsening environmental quality. There is also rising global unemployment, with the jobless increasingly out of work for longer periods of time.

Thus, both economies and societies will become even more polarized. The wealthy do not need public investments to increase their earning and income potential; they can afford to pay the rising private costs of educational, health care and other human capital investments in modern economies, protect themselves against crime and other social ills, and can afford to live in the most desirable locations with clean environments and other amenities. Because their wealth is highly mobile between countries and regions, the wealthy can also protect themselves from financial instability and crises. Thus, they have little interest or need to change the existing political and economic system to ensure more widespread human capital accumulation. At the other extreme, the less skilled, unemployed and poor do not have sufficient private wealth or income to pay for the increasing costs of obtaining more education or skills training. If accumulating human capital increasingly requires more private investment, a large and growing segment of the population may be increasingly priced out of the market.

To summarize, combined with the underpricing of natural capital, underinvestment in human capital is a pervasive problem throughout the world economy, which has three important consequences. First, modern economies end up using too many natural resources relative to skilled labor. Second, the skilled workers throughout the economy will have higher real incomes and thus will become better off compared to those with less or no skills. Third, as the gap between rich and poor widens, wealth inequality will increase. The result is a profound structural imbalance in the modern world economy; global production today uses natural capital excessively, human capital accumulation is insufficient to keep up with skill-based technological change, and wealth inequality is increasing. In the next two chapters, we discuss the policies that are necessary to address underinvestment in human capital and the underpricing of nature, thus leading to more structurally balanced and sustainable economic development.

8
Redressing the Structural Imbalance

Introduction

The world economy today is facing two major threats: increasing environmental degradation and a growing gap between rich and poor. Drawing on historical and contemporary evidence, this book has argued that these two threats are symptomatic of a growing structural imbalance in all economies, which is how *nature* is exploited to create *wealth*, and how this wealth is distributed among the population. The root of this imbalance is that natural capital is underpriced, and hence overly exploited, whereas human capital is insufficient to meet demand, thus encouraging wealth inequality.

The purpose of the following chapter is to discuss various policy strategies that could redress this structural imbalance. To provide a context for this discussion, we first recap some of the key findings and trends concerning the structure of the world economy today, and the resulting implications for the accumulation and use of wealth. We then review two popular perspectives on correcting the economic and social problems of modern economies.

First, some maintain that recent innovations in computing and information and communication technology (ICT), perhaps combined with emerging technologies for renewable energy sources, portends the start of a Third Industrial Revolution that will propel the world economy onto a path of renewed innovation, development and prosperity. Another perspective is that a new era of economic development lies in the transition to a green economy, and that this transition has already begun with the expansion of key green sectors and innovation within major economies.

These approaches are instructive but insufficient. On their own they fall short of addressing the key failures in wealth accumulation that are behind the structural imbalance in the world economy today. In addition, as we have seen throughout this book, the global impacts of environmental degradation are becoming a pressing problem, especially with respect to climate change, ecological scarcity and the availability of fresh water. Only by adopting policies to correct these economy-wide and global market failures can we overcome the structural imbalance between nature and wealth that is inhibiting innovation, growth and prosperity. The chapter concludes by outlining the broad policy strategy required to redress this structural imbalance. We call this the Balanced Wealth Strategy. In the next chapter, we explore the specific policy mechanisms and steps to implement this Strategy.

Key trends

As we saw in Chapter 2, the current structure of production in the world economy was determined by the second phase of innovations of the Industrial Revolution. These innovations occurred from 1870 to 1900, and were based largely on electricity and the internal combustion engine, which were in turn made possible by the new hydrocarbons, oil and gas, along with coal. Harnessing these technological and economic changes eventually led to the rise of the United States, which became the model for 20th century industrialization. As industrialization spread worldwide, fostered by trade in energy and resources, there was a large boost to global productivity, which lasted until the 1970s (see Figure 2.2).

However, the second phase of the Industrial Revolution was also rooted in the fossil fuel era. Since the 1890s, coal, oil and gas have accounted for at least half of global energy consumption. And, despite the rise in renewable energy and nuclear power, fossil fuels still account for 80% of energy use worldwide (see Figure 2.1). In addition, as economies became more energy-intensive during the second phase, they also increased non-renewable material use, such as minerals and ores, construction materials and non-renewable organics, which currently comprise 95% of material consumption (see Figure 2.2).

Thus, by the 1970s, the world economy was still in the midst of the fossil fuel age, the productivity boost of the second phase of innovations was waning, despite continuing skill-biased technological change, and the growth and structure of production carried on using more resources and energy. Consequently, starting in the 1970s, a number of economic trends symptomatic of a growing structural imbalance in the world economy began emerging.

Figure 8.1 summarizes these key timelines of the second phase of the Industrial Revolution since 1870. Two long-term trends that accompanied the second phase of industrialization have occurred since the early 20th century: skill-biased technological change and increased resource and energy use. As we have seen in previous chapters, both long-run trends are not only fundamental

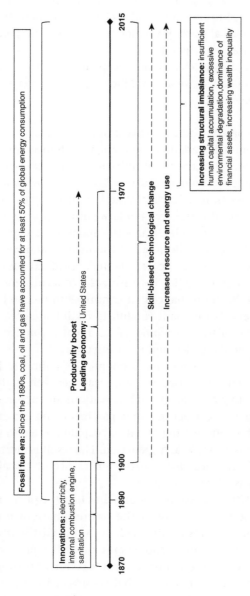

Figure 8.1 Key timelines of the second phase of the Industrial Revolution, 1870–2015

Note: These innovations occurred from 1870 to 1900, and were based largely on electricity and the internal combustion engine. These innovations led to the economic rise of the United States, which became the model for contemporary industrialization from the 20th century onwards, and boosted global productivity until 1970. This phase has been assisted by the rise of fossil fuel and non-material use associated with the fossil fuel era. Since the 1970s, however, a number of trends have emerged indicating a structural imbalance within the world economy.

to understanding the structural imbalance that has arisen since the 1970s, in addition, as we have argued, this imbalance is being made worse today by:

- the chronic underpricing of nature and underinvestment in human capital;
- rather than face the rising economic and social costs of increasing natural resource use and ecological scarcity, we hide these costs by perpetuating the underpricing of natural capital; and,
- rather than investing in sufficient human capital to keep pace with skill-biased technological change, we allow skilled labor to become scarce and thus attract excessive wages.

It seems that we are prepared to accept the economic and social consequences of excessive environmental degradation and rising wealth inequality.

As shown in Figure 8.2, this structural imbalance is increasingly reflected in how modern economies accumulate and use their wealth. Economic wealth consists of three main assets: reproducible capital, human capital and natural capital. Along with financial assets, economic wealth comprises the overall wealth of countries. In recent decades, financial capital has become the dominant form of economic wealth, and more of the income and wealth of the rich is from the financial sector. Moreover, its unchecked expansion has led to greater financial risk and instability, increasing the concentration of wealth and global imbalances. Reproducible capital continues to be overly resource and energy-intensive, and is the main conduit for skill-biased technological change. As a result, accumulation of reproducible capital encourages more use of natural capital and the rising demand for relatively skilled labor. However, human capital accumulation in modern economies is failing to keep pace with this demand, which has caused the wage gap between highly skilled and less skilled workers to grow. The global implications are increasing wealth inequality, pockets of poverty, structural unemployment, and increased social polarization. Finally, the underpricing of natural capital has led to increasing overuse and excessive environmental degradation. The result is increasing ecological and natural resource scarcity, and the emergence of global environmental problems, such as climate change.

In sum, since the 1970s, the world economy has been gripped in a *second phase malaise*: The productivity boost of the second phase of innovations of the Industrial Revolution has diminished, yet we persist with the same pattern and structure of resource and energy-intensive production and growth that were fostered by these innovations. It is not surprising that the outcome of this second phase malaise is that we are facing the increasing economic, social and environmental costs of maintaining the same pattern and structure of production, which has led in turn to a profound structural imbalance.

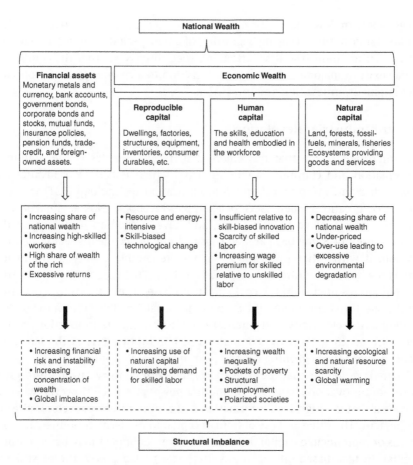

Figure 8.2 Structural imbalance and wealth

Clearly, then, the starting point to end the current structural imbalance in most modern economies today is to tackle these twin problems of excessive environmental degradation and insufficient human capital accumulation. As we have seen throughout this book, most of the current economic ills – whether it is ecological scarcity and climate change, or the growing gap between rich and poor and rising unemployment – can be traced back to these key symptoms of structural imbalance. Thus, a policy strategy to end this imbalance must target the fundamental distortion in modern economies, which is the underinvestment in human capital and the underpricing of natural capital.

Later in this chapter we outline this broad policy strategy, our Balanced Wealth Strategy. However, before doing so, it is worth examining first an alternative perspective, which is that the structural imbalance we observe today may represent less the continuance of the "second phase malaise" of the Industrial Revolution but the beginning of a new period of industrial takeoff, i.e., a "Third" Industrial Revolution. We then discuss whether the conditions today exist in major economies for a transition to a greener path of economic development, innovation and prosperity.

A third Industrial Revolution?

An important sector that has emerged in recent decades is the high-tech information and communications industry, which is based on advances in computing and information and communication technology (ICT). Notable global corporations, such as Google, Apple, Facebook, Nokia, Amazon and Verizon, have evolved in this sector, and have exerted an influence on the world economy. Some have argued that the emergence of this sector, perhaps combined with other innovations such as renewable energy technologies, offers the hope of a Third Industrial Revolution.[1] That is, if the First Industrial Revolution resulted from the coal and steam-based innovations that occurred in the late 18th century and the Second Industrial Revolution from the hydro-carbon-based electricity and internal combustion engine innovations of the late 19th century, then the computer and ICT innovations of the late 20th century mark the beginning of the Third Industrial Revolution.

There is no doubt that that the end of the 20th century saw a "third great wave" of innovations based on computing power and ICT.[2] However, whereas it is clear that the high-tech information and communications sector is already influencing the value and use of human capital in modern economies, and key forms of reproducible capital, it is unclear what its impact may be on natural capital. In fact, based on the arguments made in Chapter 7, the most likely impact of recent computing and ICT innovations is to boost further skill-biased technological change, thus raising the demand for relatively skilled labor. If human capital accumulation continues to fall well short of this rising demand, then the wage gap between highly skilled and less skilled workers will still widen and wealth inequality will worsen.[3]

In fact, some commentators, notably Robert Gordon, have acknowledged that the wave of computing and ICT innovations in the late 20th century did constitute the beginning of a Third Industrial Revolution, but that its impact in terms of boosting productivity over subsequent years has been rela-tively limited.[4] The main innovations began with the first commercial uses of computers around 1960 and reached its climax in the dot.com era of the late 1990s through the development of the Internet, the web and e-commerce. As argued by Gordon: "Initially computers shared with the steam engine, the internal combustion engine, and the electric motor the many-faceted benefits of replacing human effort, making jobs easier, less boring, and less repetitive."[5]

But unlike the previous innovations, ICT and computing had only a short-lived impact on growth. For example, Gordon compares the productivity impacts in the United States of the 1960–1990s innovations with the productivity boost from the Second Industrial Revolution (what we have called in this book the second phase of the Industrial Revolution). From 1891 to 1972, the average annual growth in US labor productivity was 2.33%, which is directly related to the productivity boost from the second phase of the Industrial Revolution (see Figure 8.1). In contrast, the boost from the 1960–1990s computing and ICT innovations occurred from 1996 to 2004 only, which saw US labor productivity grow annually by 2.46%. But from 2004 to 2012, productivity growth fell to 1.33% annually.[6] Consequently, if there was a Third Industrial Revolution associated with the late 20th century ICT and computing innovations, its boost to productivity lasted less than a decade.

Gordon offers three principal reasons why the boost to productivity was so brief.[7] First, the ICT and computing innovations were one-time inventions, which had diminishing impacts on productivity once all the subsidiary and complementary developments took place. This happened very quickly after the initial innovations occurred. Second, the new ICT and computing innovations impacted consumption more than production. The main use of the computing and robotic inventions that began in the 1960s was to save on labor in industries, commerce and some services. However, the ICT and computing innovations in the 1990s focused on entertainment, e-commerce and communication, which "provided new opportunities for consumption on the job and in leisure hours rather than a continuation of the historical tradition of replacing human labor with machines".[8] Third, the ICT and computing innovations were not as fundamental to the structure and pattern of production in modern economies, compared to the major 1870 to 1900 innovations, such as electricity, the internal combustion engine and improved sanitation.

In fact, one could argue that the more recent ICT and computing innovations are subsidiary and complementary developments – albeit extremely important ones – compared to the second phase innovations. For example, computers, robots, personal devices and the web all require electricity to function, and the principal way in which electricity is produced in all modern economies is centrally generated power through burning fossil fuels.

In sum, the biggest problem with viewing the late 20th century ICT and computing innovations as heralding a Third Industrial Revolution – or even a third phase of the Industrial Revolution – is that these innovations have yet to change fundamentally how nature is used to create wealth. In particular, their implementation has not altered the fossil fuel age, nor the major economic trends that have occurred since the 1870s that have led to the structural imbalance in the world economy today (see Figure 8.1). The computing and ICT innovations have also not changed the way in which our economies accumulate and distribute wealth, which is also a manifestation of this imbalance (see Figure 8.2). Instead, as Chapter 7 discussed, ICT innovations and computing appear to be accelerating the pace of skill-biased technological change. Above all, overcoming the second phase malaise that has gripped the world economy requires tackling the two fundamental distortions causing structural imbalance: the underpricing of natural capital that is leading to excessive environmental degradation and insufficient accumulation of human capital relative to demand that is contributing to wealth inequality.

The limits to green growth

There is also a prevailing view that the risks, instabilities and recent crises faced by the world economy, most notably the 2008–2009 Great Recession, may also stimulate a transition to a "greener" economy.[9] According to this view, a *green economy* results in "improved human well-being and social equity, while significantly reducing environmental risks and ecological scarcities".[10] Consequently, the transition from the economy today to a green economy is often referred to as *green growth*, which means "fostering economic growth and development while ensuring that natural assets continue to provide the resources and environmental services on which our well-being relies".[11]

Proponents of green growth suggest that the transition is already on the way, and point to the use of green fiscal measures during the Great Recession and the emergence and expansion of green sectors as evidence. Although such progress is encouraging, a review of the impacts of the green stimulus policies, their aftermath and the current challenges facing the expansion of green sectors suggests that we are still a long way from an economy-wide green growth transition. In other words, the nascent green economy today is at a crucial crossroad: Will "green" sectors remain a small niche within an overall "brown" economy, or will these sectors foster a new wave of sustainable industrial innovation, research and development (R&D), and employment that ultimately replaces the brown economy? As we shall see, fostering green growth can help instigate a new wave of innovations, productivity and economic prosperity, but only if a policy strategy is implemented to overcome the structural imbalances and economic distortions that we have identified in this book.

A unique feature of the global policy response to the 2008–2009 recession is that, as part of their efforts to boost aggregate demand and growth, some governments adopted expansionary policies that also incorporated a sizable "green fiscal" component. Such measures were wide ranging, including support for renewable energy, carbon capture and sequestration, energy efficiency, public transport and rail, and improving electrical grid transmission, as well as other public investments and incentives aimed at environmental protection.

Table 8.1 indicates the total green stimulus worldwide and by ten major economies that adopted these measures plus the European Union, which adopted its own package separately from its member countries. Of the $3.3 trillion allocated worldwide to fiscal stimulus over 2008–2009, $522 billion was devoted to such green expenditures or tax breaks.[12] Almost the entire global green stimulus was by the Group of 20 (G20), which comprise the world's twenty largest and richest countries. In fact, just four economies – China, the United States, South Korea and Japan – accounted for around 85% of the global green stimulus over 2008–2009. China (42%) and the United States (23%) contributed

Table 8.1   Green stimulus during the Great Recession, 2008–2009

| Economies | Green stimulus ($US billion) | | | | Share (%) of green stimulus in: | | |
	Low carbon power[a]	Energy efficiency[b]	Waste and water[c]	Total	Global total	Fiscal stimulus	GDP[d]
China	1.6	182.4	34.0	218.0	41.8%	33.6%	3.1%
United States	39.3	58.3	20.0	117.7	22.5%	12.0%	0.9%
South Korea	30.9	15.2	13.8	59.9	11.5%	78.7%	5.0%
Japan	14.0	29.1	0.2	43.3	8.3%	6.1%	1.0%
European Union[e]	13.1	9.6	0.0	22.8	4.4%	58.7%	0.2%
Germany	0.0	13.8	0.0	13.8	2.6%	13.2%	0.5%
Australia	3.5	6.5	0.0	9.9	1.9%	22.7%	1.3%
France	0.9	5.1	0.2	6.2	1.2%	18.2%	0.3%
United Kingdom	0.9	4.9	0.1	5.8	1.1%	16.3%	0.3%
Canada	1.1	1.4	0.3	2.8	0.5%	8.7%	0.2%
Italy	0.0	1.3	0.0	1.3	0.3%	1.3%	0.1%
Total G20	105.3	330.1	78.1	513.5	98.3%	17.1%	0.8%
Global total	107.6	335.4	79.1	522.1	100%	15.7%	0.7%

Notes: [a] Support for renewable energy (geothermal, hydro, wind and solar), nuclear power, and carbon capture and sequestration; [b] Support for energy conservation in buildings; fuel efficient vehicles; public transport and rail; and improving electrical grid transmission; [c] Support for water, waste and pollution control, including water conservation, treatment and supply; [d] Based on 2007 estimated Gross Domestic Product (GDP) in terms of purchasing power parity, from the US Central Intelligence Agency The World Factbook, available at: https://www.cia.gov/library/publications/the-world-factbook/rankorder/2001rank.html; [e] Only the direct contribution by the European Union is included; The members of the Group of 20 (G20) include 19 countries (Argentina, Australia, Brazil, Canada, China, France, Germany, India, Indonesia, Italy, Japan, Mexico, Russia, Saudi Arabia, South Africa, South Korea, Turkey, the UK and the US), plus the European Union.

Sources: Edward B. Barbier (2010) *A Global Green New Deal: Rethinking the Economic Recovery.* Cambridge: Cambridge University Press; Nick Robins, Robert Clover and Charanjit Singh (2009) "Taking stock of the green stimulus", 23 November. New York: HSBC Global Research; and Nick Robins, Robert Clover and D. Saravanan (2010) "Delivering the green stimulus", 9 March. New York: HSBC Global Research.

nearly two-thirds of the global expenditure on green fiscal stimulus, followed by South Korea (12%) and Japan (8%). In comparison, the European Union contributed just over 4%, and Germany almost 3%, which was the most by any individual European economy.

Only a handful of economies devoted much of their total fiscal spending to green stimulus (see Table 8.1). South Korea launched a "Green New Deal" as its fiscal response to the global recession, which when supplemented by additional green stimulus spending, comprised 5% of its GDP. China apportioned around a third of its total fiscal spending to green measures, or 3% of GDP. Although low-carbon investments accounted for the majority of fiscal spending by the European Union, total EU fiscal spending in general was small ($22.8 billion), only 0.2% of GDP. Green stimulus amounted to just 12% of total fiscal stimulus of the United States and 0.9% of GDP.

Despite the Great Recession, over the past decade, progress in green growth in some economies has been promising. This may be due, at least in part, to the green stimulus enacted during 2008–2009. However, even before the recession, nascent green sectors were emerging. Today, there are five key sectors that are considered part of the burgeoning green economy:

- energy from renewable resources
- energy efficiency
- pollution abatement and materials recycling
- natural resources conservation and ecological restoration and
- environmental compliance, education, training and public awareness.[13]

In North America, the United States was an early leader. Between 1998 and 2007, jobs in the clean energy sector grew more quickly than overall US employment growth, and by 2007, accounted for over 770,000 jobs, or approximately 0.5% of employment in the United States.[14] The green sectors in the United States may now employ more than 3 million workers (ca. 3% of US employment), produce around 3% of gross domestic product (GDP), and have exceeded economy-wide GDP growth every year since 2000.[15]

In Canada, between 2007 and 2009, clean technology investments boomed by 47%, and by 2010 this sector employed 45,000 jobs.[16] In 2013, there were over 730,000 environmental professionals in Canada, just over 4% of the labor force (ECO Canada, 2013). The number of jobs in this area have grown tenfold since 1993 and nearly tripled in the past ten years; in comparison, total Canadian employment from 2003 to 2013 grew by only 13%.[17]

Even before it adopted green fiscal measures, China viewed promotion of green sectors as sound industrial policy, aiming to be the world market leader in solar panels, wind turbines, fuel-efficient cars, and other clean energy industries.[18] By 2008, its renewable energy sector already had a value of nearly

US$17 billion and employed close to 1 million workers.[19] From 2006 to 2010, the expansion of renewable energy in China may have resulted in a further 472,000 net employment gains, and in 2010, for every 1% increase in the share of solar photovoltaic generation there could be a 0.68% increase in total employment, larger than any other power generation technology in China.[20] In December 2013, China announced that it would modify further the 12th Five-Year Plan (2011–2015), which already contains binding environmental targets such as a 17% reduction in carbon intensity, to give even more weight to environmental protection, resource efficiency, and other goals compatible with supporting green sectors.[21]

South Korea also sees its industrial strategy tied to green growth.[22] In addition to the Green New Deal adopted during the Great Recession, the South Korean government established a US$72.2 million renewable energy fund to attract private investment in solar, wind and hydroelectric power projects. In July 2009, South Korea launched a five-year Green Growth Investment Plan, spending an additional US$60 billion on reducing carbon dependency and environmental improvements, with the aim of creating 1.5–1.8 million jobs and boosting economic growth through 2020.[23]

Despite its relatively modest green stimulus during the Great Recession compared to China and South Korea, as early as the 1990s Japan developed a lead position in green manufacturing, especially for consumer durables, motor vehicles, parts and accessories, electrical equipment and other special purposes machinery.[24] This has allowed Japan to maintain a leading edge in these industries, and in green innovation overall.

In Europe, manufacturing in Germany appears to have benefited from green innovation, whereas other economies, notably Italy, may be lagging behind.[25] For example, Germany has used its existing capacity and innovations in high-precision machining to develop an early comparative advantage in wind turbines. After Japan, Germany has the strongest international record in green innovation, and continues to be well ahead of other European countries.[26] Germany is also well known for adopting a feed-in-tariff system to promote electricity production from renewables, especially the adoption of solar power by homeowners.[27]

However, if these green economic developments are to be successful in generating economy-wide innovation and prosperity, they must eventually foster a degree of structural transformation and industrial development that is well beyond the simple expansion of the five green sectors identified above. For example, Sam Fankhauser and colleagues suggest that, if we "interpret green growth as an economy-wide transformation, rather than the expansion of the environmental goods and services sectors", then there are several strategic sectors whose transformation is central to the creation of a green economy.[28] These areas include industrial processes, which need to become cleaner and more resource efficient (e.g., iron and steel); sectors that are important for energy efficiency on the supply side (electricity distribution systems) and the demand side (domestic appliances); the energy supply chain for electricity generation and other industrial processes (steam generators; engines and turbines; electric motors and transformers); and car manufacturing (low-emission and electric vehicles) and key components (accumulators, primary cells and batteries).

Fankhauser and colleagues find that the "green race" to become global competitive leaders in these industries is between eight high-income or large emerging market economies – China, France, Germany, Italy, Japan, South Korea, the United Kingdom and the United States. Of the North American and East Asian economies, only Japan has a large number of sectors (61) with above-average green innovation, which accounts for two-thirds of the country's manufacturing output. In contrast, in the other seven economies, green innovation is occurring in at most 20–40% of manufacturing. Japan also has the highest green innovation in its 15 largest manufacturing sectors, although as noted above, Germany is showing great promise. In addition, China has significant green innovation in its fabricated metal products, and Fankhauser and colleagues conclude "that we should expect China's performance to improve as the objectives of the five-year plan are implemented".[29] Among other economies, South Korea has a competitive advantage with green innovation in basic chemicals (excluding fertilizer) and special purpose machinery; the United States leads in electronic equipment, basic chemicals, automobile parts and accessories, measuring, testing and navigating appliances, and aircraft manufacture; Germany and France lead in motor vehicles; and the United Kingdom in pharmaceuticals.

Overall, Fankhauser and colleagues find that, in developing a competitive advantage in green transformation and innovation, "public policy is important. A key challenge for the green economy is to overcome persistent market failures (e.g., on innovation) and externalities (e.g., pricing the environment), which requires well-designed and consistent public policy intervention. Business decisions on investment and R&D in particular respond to such policy signals."[30]

Unfortunately, as we have maintained throughout this book, such a policy strategy appears to be lacking, even in the major economies that have shown signs of emerging green sectors and innovation. With the exception of China and South Korea, a principal obstacle to green structural transformation in these economies is the "policy void" present since the enactment during the Great Recession of the green stimulus policies. In North America especially, the expansion of the green economy could remain confined to a few niche sectors rather than lead to sustained, economy-wide green growth. Key difficulties include outdated utility business models, inadequate transmission infrastructure for renewables, and complications caused by decreasing energy and resource prices.[31] The clean technology industry in Canada is also underfunded by venture capitalism and public R&D financing.[32] China also faces unique obstacles, such as overcoming the reluctance of some provincial policy-makers to meet key environmental and green sector targets.[33] In addition, there is concern that, in the absence of implementing an economy-wide carbon tax and other complementary policies, China may have difficulty in achieving its ambitious green industrial strategy and greenhouse gas reduction targets.[34] South Korea may also incur significant economic costs, if it tries to achieve its mid-term green growth targets without introducing policies that support economy-wide green innovation and technological change.[35] In Europe, recovery of employment and growth since the Great Recession is still sluggish, which has limited the political will to overcome concerns about the social and economic costs of adopting green fiscal reform and other policies to support economy-wide green growth.[36]

To summarize, although current expansion of green sectors and innovation in major economies offers the promise of a new wave of structural transformation and innovations, in the current policy climate the prospects of this occurring seem limited. It is therefore unlikely that a new era of green growth will emerge and overcome the structural imbalances and economic distortions that we have identified in this book. This is due to several reasons.

First, the boost to green sectors provided by the green stimulus measures enacted during the 2008–2009 Great Recession is waning quickly. Almost two-thirds of the global green stimulus was devoted to energy efficiency (see Table 8.1), much of which was aimed at boosting short-term employment and not the promotion of long-term structural transformation. In the major European economies, virtually all the green stimulus was for energy efficiency; in China over 80%; in Japan and Australia around two-thirds; and in the US and Canada, around half of green stimulus spending. Although very important to reduce overall energy use, energy efficiency investments not only have short-lived impacts on the economy but also are one-time investments. Once they have occurred and impacted productivity and jobs, these benefits are not repeated, and there is little subsequent generation of sustained and complementary green developments and innovations in the economy.

Second, major market disincentives to long-term development of the green economy exist in the form of distortionary policies. These include environmentally harmful subsidies, the absence of pollution taxes and other market-based incentives, and the lack of public investments to support private green R&D. As we have argued throughout this book, and especially in Chapter 6, these distortions represent the underpricing of natural capital, a leading cause of the current structural imbalance in the world economy. Unless a greater effort is made to remove these major market disincentives, then the long-term prospects for green innovation and transformation will be severely hindered.

Third, the prevalence of underpricing natural capital through these market distortions creates another problem for the transition to a green economy. They provide the rationale for implementing *environmentally motivated subsidies* as the main policy for fostering the green economy: First, to counter the price advantage that underpricing of fossil fuels gives to the brown economy, and second, to promote expansion of and employment in the emerging sectors of the green economy. But as such environmentally motivated subsidies become more pervasive, they fail to establish the appropriate incentives for efficient and sustainable use of natural capital.

The use of environmentally motivated subsidies, in the form of tax discounts, grants and soft loans, and tariff subsidies, to promote various green sectors in major economies is already large and increasing in number as well as in coverage.[37] Table 8.2 indicates the subsidies used to promote a variety of green sectors and activities in ten major economies.[38] For example, the United States employs the most such subsidies across a range of activities. Mexico has just begun introducing environmentally motivated subsidies, and although Japan and Germany have the next lowest amount, their use in these countries has increased in recent years.

Fourth, it appears that most of the green sector developments and innovations are occurring largely among advanced and large emerging market economies. To be relevant to the majority of developing countries, green growth must be reconciled with the two key structural features of natural resource use and poverty in these countries. The first key feature, as we saw in Chapter 3, is that most low and middle-income economies remain predominantly resource-dependent. Primary products account for the majority of their export earnings, and they are unable to diversify from primary production. The second feature, as discussed in Chapter 7, is that many of these economies contain large pockets of poverty. They have a substantial share of their rural population located on less favored agricultural land and in remote areas, thus encouraging "geographic" poverty traps, as well as large numbers of the urban poor clustered in neighborhoods that suffer from pollution, crime and limited economic opportunities. If green growth is to be a catalyst for economy-wide transformation and poverty alleviation in developing countries, then it must be accompanied by policies aimed directly at overcoming these two structural features.[39]

Fifth, as we discussed previously, even among the major economies involved in the "green race" to become competitive leaders globally, economy-wide green innovation falls well short of the level necessary to generate structural transformation. That is, underinvestment in research and development (R&D) leading to widespread technological change may be a serious obstacle to the development of the green economy.[40] Moreover, overcoming this disincentive cannot be achieved solely by the use of market-based incentives to correct

Table 8.2 Environmentally motivated subsidies in selected economies

Type of subsidy and activities supported	Australia	Canada	France	Germany	Italy	Japan	Mexico	South Korea	United Kingdom	United States
Grant										
Clean-up of earlier pollution	X	X						X		X
Energy saving	X	X		X	X			X	X	X
Investment in physical capital	X	X	X	X	X	X		X	X	X
Market penetration of clean products	X	X		X	X	X			X	X
Operation of treatment facilities						X			X	X
Research and Development (R&D)	X	X	X	X	X			X	X	X
Training of employees	X	X		X						X
Other				X	X	X			X	X
Soft Loan										
Clean-up of earlier pollution		X	X					X		
Energy saving	X	X	X							X
Investment in physical capital	X	X	X			X		X	X	X
Market penetration of clean products	X							X	X	X
Operation of treatment facilities						X		X		
Research and Development (R&D)								X	X	X
Other										X
Tax Reduction										
Clean-up of earlier pollution	X						X			X
Energy saving		X	X		X			X	X	X
Investment in physical capital	X	X	X		X	X	X	X	X	X
Market penetration of clean products		X	X		X	X		X	X	X
Operation of treatment facilities			X					X	X	X
Research and Development (R&D)			X					X	X	X
Other					X		X			X
Other										
Clean-up of earlier pollution		X								
Energy saving	X	X	X	X	X			X	X	X
Investment in physical capital	X	X	X	X	X		X	X	X	X
Market penetration of clean products	X	X			X				X	X
Operation of treatment facilities	X							X		
Research and development (R&D)	X							X		
Other				X					X	X
Total	**16**	**16**	**12**	**9**	**12**	**8**	**4**	**17**	**18**	**24**

Source: Organization for Economic Cooperation and Development (OECD). Database on instruments used for environmental policy. Environmental subsidies: Activities supported. Available at: http://www2.oecd.org/ecoinst/queries/#.

inefficient pricing but requires the simultaneous implementation of "technology-push policies", such as research and development (R&D) subsidies, public investments, protecting intellectual property, and other initiatives.[41] Market-based incentives may reduce pricing distortions that put green goods and services at a competitive advantage. However, only technology-push policies directly address the tendency of firms and industries to underinvest in green R&D. As studies for reducing greenhouse gas emissions in the United States, Asia and Europe have shown, combining the two types of policies substantially lowers the costs of meeting the targets, with the optimal portfolio of policies including some form of subsidies and other public support for technology R&D and learning along with carbon pricing and other direct emissions policies.[42] Although some economies have initiated R&D grants, loans, tax breaks and other subsidies to spur innovation in some green activities (see Table 8.2), a concerted strategy of combining technology-push policies with market-based incentives to foster economy-wide green innovation has yet to be adopted.

Finally, it is unclear what impact current green sector expansion and innovations, including the environmentally motivated subsidies used to support them, may be having on the other major structural problem – the growing gap between rich and poor. It is likely that most of the green technological innovations implemented tend to be skill-biased, and thus will further exacerbate the problem of insufficient human capital accumulation to meet demand, thus worsening the problem of increasing wealth inequality. In addition, the "green race" to become global competitive leaders is between eight high-income or large emerging market economies – China, France, Germany, Italy, Japan, South Korea, the United Kingdom and the United States. As just discussed, it is unclear how this "green race" will benefit the vast majority of resource-dependent developing countries or end the significant pockets of poverty in these economies.[43]

A balanced wealth strategy

The only way to end the second phase malaise that has gripped the world economy is to devise a policy strategy that addresses simultaneously the two key sources of structural imbalance: that natural capital is underpriced, and hence overly exploited; whereas human capital is insufficient to meet demand, thus encouraging wealth inequality. In addition, such a strategy needs to be inclusive, which means that it must be accompanied by policies aimed directly at benefiting the large number of resource-dependent economies and ending the significant pockets of poverty found especially in rural areas worldwide. Finally, as we have seen throughout this book, the global impacts of environmental degradation are becoming a pressing problem. Most of the impending environmental crises facing the world economy – climate change, ecological scarcity and declining availability of water – are examples of market failures on a global scale, which need to be addressed.

Such a Balanced Wealth Strategy must contain four key elements:

- Ending the persistent underpricing of natural capital that leads to its overuse in all economies;
- Ending insufficient human capital accumulation that contributes to increasing wealth inequality;
- Adopting policies targeted at inefficient natural resource use and poverty in developing economies; and
- Creating markets to address key global environmental impacts.

In the next chapter, we will discuss in detail each element of this Balanced Wealth Strategy. Here, we will simply outline the overall approach.

As we saw in Chapter 6, the chronic underpricing of natural capital leading to excessive environmental damage, such as that caused by pollution or over-exploitation of natural resources, can be linked to two main economic distortions: the failure to "internalize" the environmental damages into the final prices paid for marketed goods and services, and the failure to curb subsidies to environmentally damaging activities. In addition, as we have discussed in this chapter, these two market disincentives plus insufficient public support for private green R&D and technological change are likely to limit the potential of a new wave of economy-wide innovation, employment and green growth. In other words, to end the second phase malaise and usher in a new era of innovation and structural transformation – the third phase of the Industrial Revolution (or, as some might call it, a Third Industrial Revolution) – then we must end the underpricing of natural capital and the underinvestment in green innovation. This is the only way to transition out of the fossil fuel age and head towards a long-term boost in economic productivity.

Consequently, a comprehensive approach for promoting green innovation and structural transformation requires a three-part policy strategy:

- phasing out environmentally harmful subsidies, and where possible, rationalizing or eliminating unnecessary environmentally motivated subsidies;
- implementing various market-based incentives to correct any remaining underpricing of natural capital; and finally
- using any resulting financial savings and revenues to fund public support for private green R&D and investments.

However, as we have discussed, green growth and innovations may not be sufficient to address the other major structural problem confronting the world economy – increasing wealth inequality. As we saw in Chapter 7, a major cause of this problem is that human capital accumulation in modern economies is insufficient to keep pace with the rising demand for skilled labor caused by ongoing skill-biased technological change. The result is not only greater redundancy and underemployment for labor with the wrong set or little skills but also those with the right set of skills, education, and training capture a bigger share of the wealth created in an economy. The consequence is the growing wealth gap between rich and poor. As more of the income and wealth of the global rich takes the form of financial capital, financial assets begin to dominate overall wealth of economies, and continued financial expansion leads to more risk and instability (see Figure 7.4). The failure to curb this process is worrisome, as it suggests that growing wealth inequality in the world economy is not just a symptom of structural imbalance but could be the cause of inherent stability and the risk of repeated global crises within the system.

Thus, one way to address the problem of insufficient human capital accumulation, and also curb the potential risk and instability of financial expansion that is increasingly driven by growing wealth inequality and global imbalances, is to implement a two-part strategy:

- adopting levies on the activities of financial institutions to raise revenue and reduce financial market risk, and
- using the additional revenues to increase human capital accumulation that improves the educational attainment, health and training of more potential workers, thus better matching the pace of skill-biased technological change.

The steps outlined above to end the underpricing of nature and improve human capital accumulation should be adopted by all economies. However, as we have argued in this chapter, an additional set of policies needs to be formulated to address the two key structural features of resource dependency and poverty in these countries. First, primary products account for the majority of their export earnings, and they are unable to diversify from primary production. Second, many economies have a substantial share of their rural population located on less favored agricultural land and in remote areas, thus encouraging "geographic" poverty traps. Economy-wide transformation and poverty alleviation in developing countries therefore requires policies aimed directly at overcoming these two structural features.

Addressing the unique structural conditions of natural resource use and poverty in developing countries would involve the following two sets of policies, whereby:

- policies and reforms should foster forward and backward linkages of primary production, enhance its integration with the rest of the economy, and improve opportunities for innovation and knowledge spillovers, and

- additional targeted policies and investments, and where necessary, policies to promote rural-urban migration should be adopted to address the persistent concentration of the rural poor on less favored agricultural lands and in remote areas.

The problem of environmental degradation has reached such epic proportions on a global scale that all economies worldwide must grapple with the consequences. In particular, three environmental problems – climate change, ecological scarcity and declining availability of fresh water – are examples of market failure on a global scale. In the case of climate change, the uncompensated damages are truly global, in that all economies are contributing to the problem, without paying fully for the costs, and the economic consequences of the market failure will be felt worldwide; in the case of ecological scarcity, it is the scale and pace of the loss of ecosystems and their services that has created a global market failure; and, finally, in the case of freshwater scarcity, it is the chronic underpricing of vital water resources worldwide, and the increasing dependence of many countries on shared sources of water supply.

To address these worldwide market failures and environmental threats, the creation of global markets is required, needing in the first instance the establishment of:

- a long-term and credible price signal for carbon across world markets, so as to provide the economic incentive for all economies worldwide to invest in clean energy and reduce their carbon dependency;
- a system of international payment of ecosystem services that allows individuals in one part of the world who value these services to compensate those in other parts of the world for managing ecosystems; and
- renewing and negotiating commitments by countries sharing transboundary water resources to cooperate on governance and pricing arrangements to manage joint supply relative to demand.

As aforementioned, in Chapter 9 we discuss each of the four elements of the Balance Wealth Strategy in more detail, including outlining the specific policy mechanisms and steps to implement this Strategy.

9
Making the Transition

Introduction

As outlined in the previous chapter, in order to end the current structural imbalance in the world economy, all economies need to address simultaneously the two key sources of this imbalance: the underpricing of natural capital that leads to its overexploitation, and the insufficient accumulation of human capital to meet the demand, which contributes to wealth inequality. Also, there must be additional policies aimed at encouraging structural transformation in resource-dependent developing economies and ending the significant pockets of rural poverty found worldwide. Finally, as we have seen throughout this book, the global impacts of environmental degradation are becoming a pressing problem. Thus, overcoming these worldwide market failures and environmental threats, especially climate change, ecological scarcity and declining freshwater availability, requires creating global markets.

Chapter 8 proposed a Balanced Wealth Strategy for overcoming environmental scarcity and wealth inequality to usher in a new global era of innovation, structural transformation and economic prosperity:

- Ending the persistent underpricing of natural capital that leads to its overuse in all economies;
- Ending insufficient human capital accumulation that contributes to increasing wealth inequality;
- Adopting policies targeted at inefficient natural resource use and poverty in developing economies; and
- Creating markets to address key global environmental impacts.

This chapter discusses each of these four elements of the Balanced Wealth Strategy in more detail, including the specific policy mechanisms and main steps involved. Obtaining political support for implementing this Strategy is of course extremely difficult. For example, in Chapter 6 we outlined the many vested interests and the institutional inertia that reinforce the current practice of underpricing natural capital and excessive environmental degradation. In Chapter 7, we also examined the political economy of wealth inequality, which underlies the chronic underinvestment in human capital and perpetuates the growing gap between rich and poor. Equally, there are many pervasive economic and political obstacles to addressing the specific natural resource use and poverty problems of developing countries and to creating markets to mitigate global environmental problems.

However, rather than focus on the various barriers to making the transition to a more innovative, productive and inclusive world economy, this chapter explores in greater depth the four main elements of the Balanced Wealth Strategy that can foster such a transition. Implementation is clearly not costless in the short term, and will require substantial commitments by policy-makers worldwide. But unless such a Strategy is adopted, and the world economy makes the transition to a new era of innovation and growth, the current global threats of environmental scarcity and inequality will continue to worsen.

Greener innovation and growth

As we saw in Chapter 8, the underpricing of natural capital not only leads to excessive environmental damage, such as through pollution and overexploitation of natural resources, but also is a major obstacle to *green innovation and growth*, which is necessary for an economy-wide transformation to a new era of economic productivity and wealth creation. However, three major market disincentives are limiting this potential structural transformation: environmentally harmful subsidies, inadequate market-based incentives, and insufficient public support for private research and development (R&D). In other words, to remove the limits to green growth and transition out of the fossil fuel age, we must end the underpricing of natural capital and the underinvestment in green innovation. Consequently, a comprehensive approach for promoting green innovation and structural transformation requires a three-part policy strategy, namely:

- phasing out environmentally harmful subsidies, and where possible, rationalizing or eliminating unnecessary environmentally motivated subsidies;
- implementing various market-based incentives to correct any remaining underpricing of natural capital; and finally,
- using any resulting financial savings and revenues to fund public support for private green R&D and investments.

This three-part strategy is outlined in Figure 9.1.

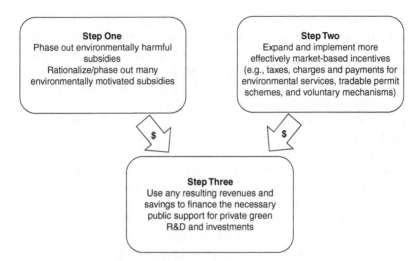

Figure 9.1   Policy strategy for green innovation and structural transformation

Step one: Phasing out environmentally harmful subsidies

As we saw in Chapter 6, with the case of fossil fuels, annual subsidies worldwide amount to just under US$500 billion annually, with around US$190 billion occurring in the Group of 20 (G20) comprising the twenty richest and large emerging market economies (see Table 6.1). These subsidies account for just over 1.1% of the world's annual adjusted net national income (ANNI), and for 0.5% of ANNI in the G20. Support for fossil fuel exploration amounts to an additional $90 billion per year spent in the G20 economies. According to one estimate, phasing out all fossil fuel consumption and production subsidies by 2020 could result in a 5.8% reduction in global primary energy demand and a 6.9% fall in greenhouse gas emissions.[1]

Environmentally harmful subsidies are also pervasive in other sectors, notably agriculture and fishing.

In 2013, support provided to agricultural producers totaled US$258 billion in the countries of the Organization for Economic Cooperation and Development (OECD), which amounts to around 18% of gross farm receipts.[2] In 2012, seven other major agricultural producers – Brazil, China, Indonesia, Kazakhstan, Russia, South Africa and Ukraine – had farm subsidies totaling US$227 billion, with China alone accounting for US$165 billion in subsidies.[3] As these seven countries plus the OECD members produce almost 80% of global agricultural value added, this suggests that agricultural output worldwide is heavily subsidized – with payments totaling around US$485 billion annually.[4] Removal of such subsidies would improve the efficiency of agricultural production, boost the competitiveness of smaller producers and poor economies, and reduce environmental degradation, such as excessive conversion of forests, wetlands and other natural habitats to agriculture and pollution runoff from overuse of fertilizers, pesticides and other inputs.

Globally, marine fisheries receive around US$27 billion in subsidies annually, around 60% of which are considered environmentally harmful.[5] One of the most damaging fishing activities globally is sea-bottom trawling, and it is estimated that fleets that engage in this activity receive about US$152 million per year, which constitutes around one quarter of the total landed value of the fleet.[6]

As discussed in Chapter 8, the persistence of fossil fuel, agricultural, fishing and other environmentally damaging subsidies creates another problem for economies today. They provide the rationale for implementing environmentally motivated subsidies as the main policy for fostering the green economy: first, to counter the price advantage that environmentally harmful subsidies give to the brown economy, and second, to promote expansion of and employment in the emerging sectors of the green economy. The use of environmentally motivated subsidies, in the form of tax discounts, grants and soft loans, and tariff subsidies, to promote various green sectors in major economies is already large and increasing in number as well as in coverage (see Table 8.2).

Employing subsidies to foster temporarily the expansion of nascent green sectors and industries may seem like a reasonable policy. Unfortunately, as the persistence and spread of subsidies for fossil fuels, agriculture and fishing illustrate, once any subsidy is implemented, it becomes difficult to remove and thus often remains in place indefinitely. Consequently, the growing and widespread use of environmentally motivated subsidies in many economies is worrisome, as they may become an obstacle to green economic development over the long term. Just like any other subsidy, they can lead to distortionary incentives and inefficiencies, lack of competitiveness and overuse. They may also, perversely, cause some environmental damages. For example, biofuel subsidies in the United States have been directly related to increased nitrate runoff, and energy efficient subsidies across North America, especially to households or for technology changes in transport, have sometimes led to increased energy use.[7] In other cases, subsidies might increase adoption rates of a green good or service, but without producing all the desired environmental and green development impacts. For example, a study of the German feed-in-tariff for renewable energy contributions to the electricity grid found that the subsidy did lead to a massive growth in renewable electricity production; however, the policy did not reduce greenhouse gas emissions substantially, as renewable expansion led to too little abatement from other mitigation opportunities such as fuel switching, nor was there a significant boost to clean energy innovation.[8] The equivalent subsidy used widely across North America – the Renewable Portfolio Standards (RPS) – could be producing similar outcomes.

Step two: Implementing market-based incentives

The second step in the strategy outlined in Figure 9.1 is to implement various market-based incentives to correct any remaining underpricing of natural capital. These include: taxes and charges for environmental services, tradable permit schemes, payments for environmental service (PES), and voluntary mechanisms.

A variety of environmental taxes and charges are currently employed in many high-income economies, including emissions charges, product charges (including deposit/refund schemes for recycling), and user fees for environmental services, natural resource use or waste disposal.[9] However, most of these incentives are currently set at low rates or subject to many exemptions, so they do not reduce environmental damages significantly or provide sufficient incentives for economy-wide green investments. In addition, many taxes and charges are designed principally for raising revenues rather than for generating incentive effects. There are fewer cases of environmental taxes and charges in developing countries. Although taxes on petroleum products are the most common form of instrument, there is growing use of charges for pollution, solid waste and water supply use.[10]

The benefits to many economies of implementing more effectively taxes, charges and other environmental market-based incentives could be substantial. For example, as discussed in Chapter 6, the environmental damages imposed by underpricing fossil fuels are significant, and include the costs of climate change, local pollution, traffic congestion, accidents and road damage. When these costs are added to fossil fuel subsidies, the overall global cost of underpricing fossil fuels amounts to US$1.9 trillion annually, or over 4% of the world's annual adjusted net national income (ANNI) (see Table 6.1).[11] The economic costs are even higher in rapidly developing, large emerging market economies: 12% of ANNI in Indonesia, 11% in Russia, 8% in China, 7% in India and 6% in India. Moreover, the burden of the environmental damages caused by the underpricing of fossil fuels is also borne by the poorer and less advantaged populations within countries. This is especially the case for local pollution effects, such as deteriorating air quality.

Similar inefficient pricing exists in markets for key goods and services throughout many economies, including agriculture, water supply and use, natural resources and transport. To take one example – inefficient water pricing – this problem may best be tackled by a variety of market-based incentives, such as establishing water markets, tradable permit schemes, taxes and charges for water use and pollution, and payments for watershed services. Although the use of water markets and market-based reforms for a wide range of water sector applications is growing, as we discussed in Chapter 6, there remain fundamental barriers to instigating such market-based incentives in many countries. Nevertheless, water pricing and institutional reforms, especially in agriculture, will be essential to controlling the growing problem of freshwater availability in many developing economies.[12] In addition, greater efforts need to be made in all economies on developing and implementing water pollution charges, including permit fees, discharge levies and fines, as a means to discouraging excessive effluent discharges from point and non-point sources. The use of water quality trading schemes is occurring in some river basins in Canada and the United States, but the geographic coverage remains small.[13]

Payments for environmental services (PES) are also emerging worldwide, but are still underutilized. PES are agreements whereby a user or beneficiary of an environmental service provides payments to individuals or communities whose management decisions influence the provision of that service. The main purpose of introducing payments for environmental services is to influence land use decisions by enabling landholders to capture more of the value of these services than they would have done in the absence of the mechanism. However, existing PES schemes have largely focused on four services: carbon sequestration, watershed protection, biodiversity benefits and landscape beauty. Hydrological services from watershed protection tend to predominate, although land use and geological carbon sequestration schemes have expanded in recent years.[14]

Step three: Using financial savings and revenues to support green innovation

The final step in fostering green innovation and structural transformation is to allocate the revenues saved or generated from eliminating or reducing subsidies and implementing various market-based incentives to overcome under-investment in green innovation (see Figure 9.1). Phasing out environmentally harmful subsidies, and rationalizing or removing many environmentally motivated subsidies should provide funds to finance the necessary public support for private sector green R&D and investments as well as other public infrastructure and programs necessary for green innovation and structural transformation. In addition, many market-based incentives, notably taxes, fees, charges, levies and auctioned permits, would raise revenues that could also be used to support green R&D and investments. For example, just based on the estimates for fossil fuels, agriculture and fisheries discussed here, removal of subsidies and employing market-based incentives would raise globally:

- US$1.9 trillion annually from ending the underpricing of fossil fuels,
- US$485 billion annually from eliminating agricultural subsidies, and
- US$27 billion annually from eliminating subsidies to marine fisheries.

As we discussed in Chapter 8, there are two reasons why using these additional revenues to support private R&D would foster economy-wide green innovation and structural transformation.

First, an important impetus for rapid economy-wide innovation is *technology spillovers*, which occur when the inventions, designs and technologies resulting from the R&D activities by one firm or industry spread relatively cheaply and quickly to other firms and industries. However, such technology spillovers also undermine the incentives for a private firm or industry to invest in R&D activities. The private investor bears the full costs of financing R&D, and may improve its own technologies and products as a result, but the investor receives no returns from the subsequent spread of these innovations throughout the economy. The consequence is that private firms and industries routinely underinvest in R&D, and the result is less economy-wide innovation overall.[15] As underinvestment in R&D may be a serious obstacle to green innovation in economies, there is a role for public support to encourage private R&D and economy-wide technology spillovers through R&D subsidies, public investments, protecting intellectual property and other initiatives.

Second, such *technology-push policies* are especially effective when used in combination with the market-based incentives that are implemented to end the underpricing of natural capital. For example, Larry Goulder finds that reducing the costs of low-carbon energy adoption in the United States stems both from the boost to private sector R&D and from learning-by-doing as firms gain familiarity with new low-carbon technologies, products and processes.[16] He identifies both a set of technology-push policies and a set of market-based incentives that consistently induce additional technological change by supporting private R&D and learning-by-doing (see Table 9.1). However, Goulder also finds that the market-based incentives on their own cannot induce sufficient private-sector investment in innovations and learning-by-doing; rather, there needs to be complementary technology-push policies implemented as well. Similar studies for environmental and green growth policies in the

Table 9.1 Induced innovation and public policies for reducing carbon dependency

Market-based incentives	Technology-push policies
Carbon taxes	Subsidies to R&D in clean energy technologies
Carbon quotas	Public-sector R&D in clean energy technologies
Cap-and-trade for greenhouse gas (GHG) emissions	Government-financed technology competitions (with awards)
Subsidies to GHG emission abatement	Strengthened patent rules

Source: Lawrence H. Goulder (2004) *Induced Technological Change and Climate Policy*. Arlington, VA: Pew Center on Global Climate Change.

United States, Asia and Europe have shown that the most effective outcome is from combining some form of subsidies and other public support for technology R&D and learning, along with carbon pricing and other market-based incentives.[17]

In sum, the biggest obstacles to sustaining green growth and innovation in economies today are major market disincentives, especially the underpricing of natural capital and market failures to spur green innovation. A three-part strategy to overcome these obstacles would involve, first, removing environmentally harmful subsidies, second, employing market-based instruments to further reduce the economic and social costs of natural capital use, and third, allocating any resulting revenue to public support for green innovation and investments. Such a strategy would ensure that green growth is not about promoting niche green sectors but instigating economy-wide innovation and structural transformation.

Inclusive wealth and human capital accumulation

As we have seen throughout this book, the underpricing of nature combined with insufficient human capital accumulation to meet demand has led to growing wealth inequality. In addition, the process of wealth creation itself becomes more exclusive, and it is increasingly distorted towards the expansion of the financial sector and its assets. Unchecked financial expansion may also be leading to more risk and instability. Increasing wealth inequality in the world economy is not just a symptom of structural imbalance but could be the cause of inherent instability and the risk of repeated global crises within the system, and possibly even social conflicts. Consequently, to address the problem of insufficient human capital accumulation, and also curb the potential financial risk and instability arising from growing wealth inequality and global imbalances, requires implementing a two-part strategy:

- adopting levies on the activities of financial institutions to raise revenue and reduce financial market risk; and
- using the additional revenues to increase human capital accumulation that improves the educational attainment, health and training of more potential workers, thus better matching the pace of skill-biased technological change.

In recent years, interest in implementing some form of new taxation on financial institutions has grown, given the widespread concern over the costliness to governments of the financial crisis that led to the 2008–2009 Great Recession. In addition, there is a general perception that the financial sector is undertaxed, as their crises impose large negative effects on the overall economy. Financial institutions benefit from underpriced bailout guarantees, they receive cheap funding from central banks, and in some countries they enjoy low, or exemption from, value-added taxation.[18]

Three types of levies on financial institutions or their activities have been proposed:

- *Financial transaction tax* – a tax collected on the sale of specific financial assets, such as stocks, bonds, currencies and derivatives.
- *Bank levy* – a tax on a financial institution's balance sheets, either on their total liabilities or their assets.
- *Financial activities tax* – a tax imposed on the combined profits and wage bill of a financial institution.

Interest in a financial transaction tax (FTT) on stocks, bonds or derivatives is gaining ground, especially in Europe, as one possible long-term funding source for additional revenues because of its relative ease of implementation. A variant is a currency transaction tax (CTT), or Tobin tax, named after the economist James Tobin who first proposed it in the 1970s. This is a tax applied to any foreign currency exchange transaction. For example, a small tax of 0.10% on equities and 0.02% on bonds could bring in about \$48 billion from G20 member states.[19] Foreign exchange transactions total around US\$800 trillion annually, which means that a CTT of only 0.05% could raise \$400 billion in revenues.[20]

An FTT is usually seen as a tax that would be implemented nationally, and in fact, such taxes already exist. However, over 1990–2009, France, Italy, Japan and Germany, which ended FTTs over this period, collected at most 0.2% of gross domestic product (GDP) since 1990; India, the United Kingdom, South Africa, South Korea and Switzerland raised cumulative revenues in the range of 0.2% to 0.7% of GDP; and Hong Kong and Taiwan 1% to 2% of GDP.[21] A proposal by the European Union (EU) to adopt an EU-wide FTT was put forward in 2011, but failed to obtain the necessary support among member states.[22] This led to a revised proposal in 2013 from the European Commission, with just 11 countries agreeing to implement jointly an FTT by the end of 2016. Estimates suggest that annual revenues from the FTT would be around US\$33 to US\$38 billion, or 0.4 to 0.5% of the GDP of the 11 participating EU states.

Although proponents believe that an FTT would both generate revenue for governments and also help to stabilize financial markets by curbing short-term speculative trading, the latter claim has been questioned.[23] As the estimates above indicate, an FTT needs only to be set at a very low level to raise substantial revenue, yet such a low rate will have little impact on trading volumes, thus limiting its effectiveness in reducing speculation. As a broad-based tax on all transactions, an FTT would not be able to distinguish between trading that is speculative and day-to-day activities of financial institutions that facilitate investments. Thus, FTTs could be a potentially inefficient instrument for reducing financial instability and risk. Financial institutions would also likely pass the cost of an FTT on to their clients, which include not only wealthy individuals, corporations and sovereign wealth funds, but also charities and pension and mutual funds.

At their Pittsburgh meeting in September 2009, the leaders of the Group of 20 (G20) economies asked the International Monetary Fund (IMF) to explore a range of options for ending the undertaxation of financial institutions. The IMF proposed a two-tier system.[24]

First, the IMF recommended imposing bank levies on financial institutions, called a *financial stability condition* (FSC), with the goal of ensuring that each institution contributes to a reasonable share of direct costs associated with failure, which might involve their sale, transfer, or liquidation during a crisis.[25] The FSC would be initially levied at a flat rate for all financial institutions, but then adjusted to reflect each institution's riskiness and contribution to the overall instability of the financial sector.

Second, the IMF suggested imposing a financial activities tax (FAT) on the sum of the profits and wages of financial institutions, to raise revenue from the financial sector's activities more generally. In effect, such an FAT would be a levy on the value added by a financial institution, and thus if the institution was earning excessive profits or overpaying its employees and providing them with unwarranted bonuses, then such a tax would discourage these practices.[26]

Given the evidence discussed in Chapter 7 that financial sector executives and employees appear to extract excessively high compensation well beyond what they should be paid as returns to their skills and abilities, that overinvestment in the financial sector may be contributing to its instability, and that the resulting financial sector boom worldwide has overwhelmingly benefited the wealthy, it seems that the two-tier system of taxation proposed by the IMF is a sensible approach to addressing the undertaxation of financial institutions.[27] In addition, the revenues raised by the FAT should be allocated to increase the human capital accumulation that improves the educational attainment, health and training of more potential workers, thus better matching the pace of skill-biased technological change. Over the long term, this should lead to more inclusive wealth creation in economies.

Table 9.2 summarizes the possible revenues that could be raised by a 5% FAT in 21 major economies, using estimates provided by the IMF. Such an FAT would raise US$4.7 billion on average in each economy, or approximately 0.24% of GDP, and the total amount collected by the 21 countries would be US$99 billion per year. However, the revenues would vary significantly by country. For example, the United States would accrue US$45 billion each year, and Japan

Table 9.2   Potential revenues from a financial activity tax, selected countries

| Country | Financial Sector Value Added (% of GDP)[a] | | | | Annual Revenues from 5% FAT | |
	Profits (1)	Fixed Capital Formation (2)	Wages (3)	Tax Base (1–2+3)	% of GDP[b]	US$ billion
Australia	3.2	0.7	3.8	6.4	0.32	2.6
Austria	2.1	0.8	2.7	4.0	0.20	0.7
Belgium	2.2	0.8	2.8	4.2	0.21	0.9
Canada	3.0	1.3	3.9	5.6	0.28	3.5
Denmark	1.8	0.4	2.5	4.0	0.20	0.5
Finland	1.1	0.3	1.2	1.9	0.10	0.2
France	1.4	0.8	2.7	3.3	0.17	3.8
Germany	1.5	0.3	2.3	3.6	0.18	5.5
Hungary	2.1	0.3	1.9	3.6	0.18	0.2
Iceland	3.2	0.9	4.2	6.5	0.33	0.1
Ireland	5.9	0.6	3.2	8.4	0.42	0.9
Italy	1.7	0.4	2.3	3.6	0.18	3.3
Japan	4.6	..	2.2	6.8	0.34	15.8
Korea, Republic of	4.5	0.6	2.5	6.4	0.32	3.5
Netherlands	2.7	1.1	3.3	4.9	0.25	1.8
Norway	1.8	0.4	1.4	2.7	0.14	0.4
Portugal	3.8	1.6	2.6	4.8	0.24	0.5
Spain	2.1	0.7	2.1	3.5	0.18	2.1
Sweden	1.2	0.6	1.9	2.5	0.13	0.5
United Kingdom	2.8	0.7	3.9	6.1	0.31	7.6
United States	3.2	0.9	4.4	6.6	0.33	44.9
Average all countries	**2.7**	**0.7**	**2.8**	**4.7**	**0.24**	**4.7**
Total revenues						**99.1**

Notes: GDP = Gross Domestic Product; FAT = Financial Activities Tax; [a] International Monetary Fund (IMF) (2010) A Fair and Substantial Contribution by the Financial Sector. Final Report for the G-20, June. Washington DC: IMF, table A6.1, p. 70. Available at: http://www.imf.org/external/np/g20/pdf/062710b.pdfjenny check all links in this chapter; [b] Based on GDP in 2010 (constant 2005 US$). From World Bank, World Development Indicators. Available at: http://databank.worldbank.org/data

US$16 billion.[28] A 5% FAT is a very modest tax rate, which is much lower than comparable value-added taxes in most economies. However, as Table 9.2 indicates, even a relatively low FAT would raise significant additional revenues.

The revenues raised from an FAT should be allocated for human capital accumulation, which may vary depending on the various educational, health and training needs of a country. Some of the options include:

• increase availability and affordability of pre-school education to more families

- improve primary and secondary school education (i.e., kindergarten through high school) to increase the number of students and prepare them better for higher education
- provide generous and affordable financial aid for higher education (e.g., four-year universities, community colleges, technical schools)
- provide better health care and more coverage
- increase skills training and re-training of workers, and
- reduce distorting labor taxes that discourage hiring and training of workers.

The first three options are similar to those proposed by Claudia Goldin and Lawrence Katz to end the "race between education and technology" in the United States (see Chapter 7).[29] The revenues raised by an FAT in the United States could go a long way towards meeting these objectives. For example, the additional revenues of US$45 billion each year from a 5% FAT in the United States (see Table 9.2) amounts to approximately half of the US$98 billion in annual average loans issued in the US over 2010 to 2014 from all public and private sources.[30]

However, other countries may also choose other human capital investment priorities for their revenues, such as improved health care and removal of distortionary labor taxes. For example, Germany has high labor taxes that are thought to discourage the hiring and training of workers. Thiess Büttner and Katharina Erbe estimate that a very low FAT of 3% in Germany would generate US$1.4 billion in additional annual revenue, and if it were used to lower distortionary labor taxes, there would be a welfare gain of US$1.2 billion.[31]

Finally, there will clearly be an overlap between some of the human capital investments, especially in education and training, and some of the public expenditure in support of green R&D and other "technology-push" policies discussed earlier (see Figure 9.1 and Table 9.1). Ultimately, such an overlap can only be a win-win for economies, as it creates synergies and economy-wide spillovers between the goals of encouraging, on the one hand, green innovation and structural transformation, and on the other, more inclusive human capital and wealth accumulation. From a financing perspective, there are also likely to be gains from such an overlap and synergies. If the additional financial support for technology-push policies also covers many of the key educational and training needs of an economy, then more of the revenues from an FAT could be allocated to improving health care and its access or removing distortionary labor taxes.

To summarize, Figure 9.2 depicts the overall strategy for addressing the problem of insufficient human capital accumulation, and also curbing the potential financial risk and instability arising from growing wealth inequality and undertaxation of the financial sector. Bank levies on the liabilities of

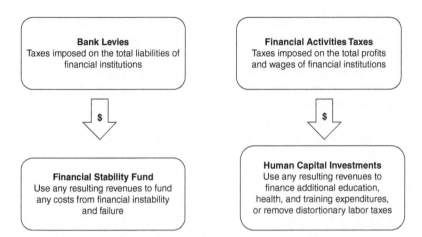

Figure 9.2 Policy strategy for reducing financial risk and increasing human capital accumulation

financial institutions are most appropriate for establishing a fund to ensure that each institution contributes to a reasonable share of direct costs associated with failure, which might involve their sale, transfer, or liquidation during a crisis. A financial activities tax (FAT) on the sum of the profits and wages of financial institutions would raise additional revenue and also discourage the financial sector from earning excessive profits or overpaying its employees. The revenues raised from an FAT should be allocated to a variety of human capital investments, which may vary depending on the various educational, health and training needs of a country. The revenues could also be used to eliminate distortionary labor taxes, which discourage the hiring and training of workers.

Additional policies for developing countries

The above strategies for ending the underpricing of natural capital, expanding human capital accumulation and making wealth creation more inclusive should be implemented by all economies. However, as outlined in Chapter 8, additional policies need to be adopted by developing countries to address the two key structural features of resource dependency and poverty in these countries. First, primary products account for the majority of their export earnings, and they are unable to diversify from primary production. Second, many economies have a substantial share of their rural population located on less favored agricultural land and in remote areas, thus encouraging "geographic" poverty traps. Consequently, to foster economy-wide transformation and poverty alleviation in developing countries will require policies aimed directly at overcoming these two structural features:

- policies and reforms should foster forward and backward linkages of primary production, enhance its integration with the rest of the economy, and improve opportunities for innovation and knowledge spillovers; and
- additional targeted policies and investments and, where necessary, policies to promote rural–urban migration, should be adopted so as to address the persistent concentration of the rural poor on less favored agricultural lands and in remote areas.

Table 9.3 summarizes the key structural features of developing countries that have been emphasized in this book. Not only do poorer economies have lower per capita incomes and higher poverty rates, but they also are more resource-dependent and have a higher share of their rural population located on remote less favored agricultural land. But Table 9.3 also indicates that resource dependency and the concentration of some rural populations in remote and marginal agricultural areas remains widespread across all developing countries, including many at the upper-middle-income level.

Table 9.3 Summary of key structural features of developing economies

	GDP per capita (2005 US$) 2000–2012 avg	Poverty head-count ratio (% of population) 2000–2012 avg	Primary product exports (% of merchandise exports) 2000–2012 avg	Share (%) of rural population on remote less favored agricultural land 2010
Low income	537	64.1%	66.6%	10.2%
Lower-middle income	2,409	23.4%	53.5%	7.8%
Upper-middle income	6,101	15.3%	43.7%	6.7%
All developing	2,077	40.9%	58.1%	8.8%

Notes: 98 countries, of which 45 are low income, 39 are lower-middle income and 14 are upper-middle income; Low-income economies are those in which 2013 GNI per capita was $1,045 or less. Lower-middle-income economies are those in which 2013 GNI per capita was between $1,046 and $4,125. Upper-middle-income economies are those in which 2013 GNI per capita was between $4,126 and $12,745.

Source: World Bank, World Development Indicators, available from http://databank.worldbank.org/data and Edward B. Barbier and Jacob P. Hochard (2014) "Land Degradation, Less Favored Lands and the Rural Poor: A Spatial and Economic Analysis", A Report for the Economics of Land Degradation Initiative. University of Wyoming: Department of Economics and Finance. Available at: www.eld-initiative.org

The persistence of these features in poorer countries suggests that they cannot be overcome by emphasizing solely structural transformation that promotes growth of high-productivity industries and highly commercialized agricultural and service activities. Such structural transformation – "green" or otherwise – is unlikely to benefit the rural poor on less favored lands and in remote areas. It is also unlikely to end the "enclavism" predominating in primary production and resource-based activities. Instead additional policies are required to address resource dependency and rural poverty. First, there is the need for specific policies aimed at improving the efficiency and sustainability of primary production for economy-wide gains, and second, additional targeted policies are needed for the rural poor on less favored agricultural lands and in remote areas.

Various examples of successful and sustainable resource-based development, from the late 19th century to the present, highlight the three key factors in this process:

- resource-enhancing technological change in primary production activities;
- strong forward and backward linkages between the resource-based primary production sector and the rest of the economy; and
- substantial knowledge spillovers in primary production and across resource-based activities.[32]

First, country-specific knowledge and technical applications in the resource extraction sector can effectively expand what appears to be a "fixed" resource endowment of a country. For example, Gavin Wright and Jesse Czelusta document this process for several successful mineral-based economies over the past 30 to 40 years: "From the standpoint of development policy, a crucial aspect of the process is the role of country-specific knowledge. Although the deep scientific bases for progress are undoubtedly global, it is in the nature of geology that location-specific knowledge continues to be important... the experience of the 1970s stands in marked contrast to the 1990s, when mineral production steadily expanded primarily as a result of purposeful exploration and ongoing advances in the technologies of search, extraction, refining, and utilization; in other words by a process of learning."[33]

Second, there must be strong linkages between the resource sector and frontier-based activities and the rest of the economy. For example, Ron Findlay and Mats Lundahl note the importance of such linkages in promoting successful "staples-based" development during the 1870–1914 era: "not all resource-rich countries succeeded in spreading the growth impulses from their primary sectors... in a number of instances the staples sector turned out to be an enclave with little contact with the rest of the economy... The staples theory of growth stresses the development of linkages between the export sector and an incipient manufacturing sector."[34]

Third, there must be substantial knowledge spillovers arising from the extraction and use of resources and land in the economy. For example, the rise of the American minerals-based economy from 1879 to 1940 can be at least partly attributed to the infrastructure of public scientific knowledge, mining education and the "ethos of exploration".[35] Creating knowledge spillovers across firms is one of the crucial "components of successful modern-regimes of knowledge-based economic growth" in several successful mineral-based economies over the past 30 to 40 years.[36] There is also evidence of this occurring in successful resource-based industries in some developing economies, such as Malaysia, Thailand and Botswana.[37]

In sum, as examples of successful resource-based development illustrate, the type of natural resource endowment and primary production activities is not necessarily an obstacle to implementing a successful strategy. Neither the abundance of natural resources nor the type of resources exploited for primary production are inherently a "curse" or a "blessing" on economic development; instead, it is the institutions and policies of an economy that determine whether or not resource-based development will be successful in the long run.[38] Or, as Maria Sarraf and Moortaza Jiwanji have argued, "the natural resource curse is not necessarily the fate of resource abundant countries ... sound economic policies and good management of windfall gains can lead to sustained economic growth."[39]

However, encouraging more efficient and sustainable resource-based development in developing economies may not alone eliminate the persistent problem of widespread rural poverty. Specific policies need to be targeted at the poor where they live, especially the rural poor clustered on less favored agricultural lands and remote areas. Even developing economies that have pursued successful resource-based development are still grappling with these structural poverty problems.

Thus, there is a need for targeted policies to these households to raise real wages and alleviate poverty concentrated on those less favored agricultural lands and remote areas, which involves:

- targeting investments and policies to improve the livelihoods and productivity of traditional agricultural in these locations;
- targeting research, extension and agricultural development to improve the livelihoods of the poor, increase employment opportunities and reduce environmental degradation; and
- better market integration for the rural poor through developing public services and infrastructure in remote and less favored agricultural regions, such as extension services, roads, communications, protection of property, marketing services and other strategies to improve smallholder accessibility to larger markets.[40]

Such a strategy supports recent efforts to target investments directly to improving the livelihoods of the rural poor in remote and fragile environments.[41] For example, in Ecuador, Madagascar and Cambodia poverty maps have been developed to target public investments to geographically defined sub-groups of the population according to their relative poverty status, which could substantially improve the performance of the programs in terms of poverty alleviation.[42] A World Bank study that examined 122 targeted programs in 48 developing countries confirms their effectiveness in reducing poverty, if they are designed properly.[43] A review of poverty alleviation programs in China, Indonesia, Mexico and Vietnam also finds evidence of "the value in specifically targeting spatially disadvantaged areas and households", although the benefits are larger when programs, such as PROGRESA in Mexico, were successful in employing second-round targeting to identify households in poor locations and thus reducing leakages to non-poor households.[44]

Appropriate targeting of research, extension and agricultural development has been shown to improve the livelihoods of the poor, increase employment opportunities and even reduce environmental degradation.[45] Empirical evidence of technical change, increased public investments and improved extension services in remote regions indicates that any resulting land improvements that do increase the value of homesteads can have a positive effect on both land rents and reducing agricultural expansion.[46]

Improving market integration for the rural poor may also depend on targeted investments in a range of public services and infrastructure in remote and ecologically fragile regions, such as extension services, roads, communications, protection of property, marketing services and other strategies to improve smallholder accessibility to larger markets.[47] For example, for poor households in remote areas of a wide range of developing countries, the combination of targeting agricultural research and extension services to poor farmers combined with investments in rural road infrastructure to improve market access appears to generate positive development and poverty alleviation benefits.[48] In Mexico, poverty mapping was found to enhance the targeting of maize crop breeding efforts to poor rural communities in less favorable and remote areas. In the Central Highlands of Vietnam, the introduction of fertilizer, improved access to rural roads and markets, and expansion of irrigation dramatically increased agricultural productivity and incomes.[49]

However, any policy strategy targeted at improving the livelihoods of the rural poor located in remote and less favored agricultural regions should be assessed against an alternative strategy, which is to encourage greater out-migration from these areas. Rural development is essentially an indirect way of deterring migration to cities, yet because of the costliness of rural investments, "policies in developing countries are increasingly more concerned with influencing the direction of rural to urban migration flows – for example, to particular areas – with the implicit understanding that migration will occur anyway and thus should be accommodated at as low a cost as possible."[50] Rarely, however, are the two types of policy strategies, investment in poor rural areas and targeted outmigration, directly compared. In addition, only recently have the linkages between rural out-migration, smallholder agriculture and land use change and degradation in remote and marginal areas been analyzed.[51] Researching such linkages will become increasingly important to understanding the conditions under which policies to encourage greater rural out-migration should be preferred to a targeted strategy to overcome poverty in remote and fragile areas. It may be, as argued by the World Bank, that "until migration provides alternative opportunities, the challenge is to improve the stability and resilience of livelihoods in these regions". As this paper has pointed out, this may become a critical feature in the design of structural transformation policies to overcome widespread rural poverty in many developing economies.[52]

In sum, to tackle the type of structural features of developing countries indicated in Table 9.3 will require specific policies for improving the efficiency and sustainability of primary production for economy-wide gains and investments to be targeted at the poor where they live, especially the rural poor clustered on less favored agricultural lands and remote areas. The overall aim should be to improve their health and welfare, provide more economic opportunities to escape from poverty, and to increase their accumulation of human capital. This strategy will require a rethinking of aid policy priorities by both developing countries and the international community.

Creating global markets

Throughout this book we have identified three environmental problems – climate change, ecological scarcity and declining availability of freshwater – which have pervasive environmental impacts worldwide. They are also examples of market failure on a global scale. In the case of climate change, the uncompensated damages are truly global, in that all economies are contributing to the problem, without paying fully for the costs, and the economic consequences of the market failure will be felt worldwide. In the case of ecological scarcity, it is the scale and pace of the loss of ecosystems and their services that have created a global market failure. And, finally, in the case of freshwater scarcity, it is the chronic underpricing of vital water resources worldwide, and the increasing dependence of many countries on shared sources of water supply. Consequently, the most efficient solution for combating such worldwide market failures is to create global markets, which in the case of these three environmental problems requires:

- establishing a long-term and credible price signal for carbon across world markets, so as to provide the economic incentive for all economies worldwide to invest in clean energy and reduce their carbon dependency;

- establishing a system of international payment of ecosystem services that allow individuals in one part of the world who value these services to compensate those in other parts of the world for managing ecosystems; and
- renewing and negotiating commitments by countries sharing transboundary water resources to cooperate on governance and pricing arrangements to manage joint supply relative to demand.

A key priority is the need to reach agreement on a post-Kyoto global climate change framework. Many of the low carbon investments and innovations needed to reduce the carbon dependency of the world economy will be affected by the growing uncertainty over the future global carbon market in the aftermath of the Kyoto treaty. Both uncertainty over future global climate policy and the delay caused by inaction also increase sharply the costs of an agreement. Delay in adopting effective climate policies will affect the cost of future agreements that will be required to abate an even larger amount of greenhouse gas (GHG) emissions. Such inaction in the short term increases significantly the costs of compliance in the long term, which is compounded by the effects of uncertainty on investment and policy decisions.

One encouraging sign that a post-Kyoto climate deal might be attainable is the recent agreement on climate change between the United States and China. Under the terms of the bilateral pact, the United States has pledged to reduce greenhouse gas (GHG) emissions to 17% below 2005 levels by 2020, and 26 to 28% below these levels by 2025. China aims to cap its total GHG emissions by 2030, if not sooner.[53] Another positive sign is that the third largest global emitter of GHGs – the European Union of 28 countries – has also pledged to cut greenhouse gas pollution by 40% below 1990 levels by 2030. Some commentators take the view that these steps improve the chances of reaching a post-Kyoto climate change agreement under the auspices of the United Nations.[54]

However, perhaps a more promising way forward is to extend the two-nation agreement between China and the United States to a four-party deal, and then perhaps to a larger group of twenty major emitters.[55] The two additional partners in the four-nation agreement should be countries that also have close economic ties with the US and China, are major global economies, and are responsible for a large share of global GHG emissions. The two economies that fit these criteria are the European Union and Japan. Also, the United States, China, the EU and Japan are leading members of the Group of 20 (G20), which is an international policy forum for the governments and central bank governors from the world's 20 wealthiest, most populous and powerful economies.[56] As we saw in Chapter 3, they also account for three quarters of the world's GHG emissions (see Table 3.2). Because the G20 is already an established international policy forum for its members to negotiate and cooperate on economic issues of mutual interest and benefit, using this forum to agree common yet differentiated commitments by the twenty economies to long-term GHG reduction is a viable goal. In addition, such a process of negotiation is more likely to be successful in establishing an international trading scheme for carbon among participating countries, or mutually agreed carbon taxes, thus establishing a long-term and credible price signal for carbon across world markets. Such a global carbon market could be easily extended to allow developing economies to finance their mitigation measures and would also achieve attainment of global GHG emission reduction targets, much like the current Clean Development Mechanism established under the Kyoto climate change agreement.

A second priority for creating global markets is to overcome the funding challenge for global ecosystem and biodiversity conservation. There remains a huge gap between the global benefits that humankind receives from ecosystems and what we are willing to pay to maintain and conserve them. For example, over ten years ago, David Pearce pointed out that the global benefits of ecosystem goods and services are likely to be "hundreds of billions of dollars", yet currently the world spends at most $10 billion annually on ecosystem conservation.[57] Overcoming this funding gap is critical if we are to stop the current decline in global ecosystems and the benefits they provide. But there are a number of economic disincentives that have so far prevented successful international negotiation and agreement to halt biodiversity loss and ecosystem degradation worldwide. Financing and implementing international mechanisms to combat this global funding problem is a major obstacle.

The wide gap between the global benefits that humankind receives from ecosystems and what we are willing to pay to maintain and conserve them is a critical symptom of how oblivious we are to the risks arising from the excessive ecological deterioration arising from the current pattern of economic development. Yet, there are many disincentives working against the creation of such schemes. Although progress has been made in establishing international payments for global ecosystem services, most notably a nascent financial mechanism to Reduce Emissions from Deforestation and forest Degradation (REDD+), several important concerns have arisen.[58] Monitoring and verifying changes in deforestation rates in developing countries and their impacts on carbon emissions could increase substantially the transaction costs of implementing a REDD+ scheme on a global scale. In addition, a carbon market for avoided deforestation may not necessarily be the best way of protecting forests that yield other global ecosystem services. There is also concern over the high opportunity costs faced by many developing countries from losses in foregone agricultural and timber benefits. These issues need to be resolved if there is to be a successful REDD+ financial mechanism implemented on a global scale.

With regard to negotiating and implementing a more comprehensive international scheme to cover a wider range of ecosystems yielding global benefits, the best outcome that we can hope for currently is a scheme that is underwritten by only a handful of rich countries, and which is capable of providing a level of global ecosystem protection that is only slightly more than current efforts.[59] Although they may be supported through multilateral and bilateral assistance, developing countries will continue to bear the direct and opportunity costs of ecosystem conservation for the foreseeable future. Clearly, this perpetuates the unsustainability problem, especially given the rising global ecological scarcity. But to overcome the economic disincentives that are reinforcing such an outcome, the international community needs to think more creatively as to how to agree, design, implement and verify international mechanisms for payment of ecosystem services. We also need to develop more innovative ways of financing such schemes, other than the traditional methods of development assistance or transfers.

Table 9.4 outlines actual and potential funding mechanisms for global ecosystem conservation. Only three mechanisms in operation are in the process of implementation. These include the Global Environmental Facility (GEF) of the United Nations (UN), which has been in operation since 1991; REDD+, which has been operating as a pilot initiative; and various adaptation funds, which are really for climate change adaptation rather than ecosystem conservation. The other financing mechanisms listed in Table 9.4 have yet to be implemented, but have been discussed and debated as potential ways of providing substantial additional funding for the GEF, REDD, new international payment for ecosystem service (IPES) schemes, or possibly a direct source of financing ecosystem conservation globally.

A comparison between how much funds are currently being raised by the current mechanisms versus what could be potentially financed by the other mechanisms is listed in Table 9.4.[60] Even if one adds total GEF, REDD+ and multi-lateral climate change adaptation funds together, plus include total global energy development assistance and Millennium Development Goals assistance, the amount spent each year is US$161.6 billion. In contrast, if the other potential methods of funding are used, they could raise US$1.1 trillion per year. Even if a carbon tax is omitted, because of political infeasibility, the amount of new financing would be almost US$600 billion each year – almost four times what is currently being spent on environment and development from existing sources.

A further complication in global water management is that many countries share their sources of water, as river basins, large lakes, aquifers and other freshwater bodies often cross national boundaries. Such transboundary water sources are important for global supply; for example, two out of five people in the world live in international water basins shared by more than one country.[61] Three or more countries share the water of 53 river basins worldwide; the Amazon River has seven countries sharing it, the Nile ten countries, and

Table 9.4 Financing mechanisms for funding global ecosystem conservation

Mechanism	Description
Global Environmental Facility (GEF)*	A multi-donor global mechanism to meet the additional costs of developing countries in achieving global environmental benefits from biological diversity, climate change, international waters, ozone layer depletion, reduced land degradation and abatement of persistent organic pollution.
Adaptation Fund (e.g., Green Climate Fund, etc.)*	A fund financing adaptation projects and programs in developing countries; funded with 2% of the Certified Emission Reduction credits issued for projects of the Clean Development Mechanism and from other sources.
Reduced emissions from deforestation and forest degradation (REDD+) scheme*	A specific international payment scheme aimed at reducing greenhouse gas (GHG) emissions from deforestation and forest degradation in developing countries, while improving biodiversity conservation.
Global carbon tax	Taxes applied to carbon-equivalent GHG emissions.
International Finance Facility (IFF)	Mobilizes financing from international capital markets by issuing long-term bonds repaid by donor countries.
Sovereign wealth fund (SWF) tax	Tax applied to a state-owned investment fund or entity that is commonly established from balance of payment surpluses or large accumulations of export earnings, such as from oil and other resource commodity exports.
Financial transaction tax (FTT)	Tax applied to the sale of specific financial assets, such as stock, bonds or futures.
Currency transaction tax (CTT or Tobin tax)	Tax applied to currency exchange transactions.
Airline travel tax	Tax applied to international airline ticket sales.
Aviation or shipping fuel tax	Tax applied to international aviation and shipping fuel use.
Arms trade tax	Tax applied to international exports of armaments.
Tobacco excise tax	Tax applied to sales of tobacco products, a proportion of which is allocated to global funds.

Note: *Mechanism is in operation or is being implemented.

Source: Adapted from Edward B. Barbier (2012) "Tax 'societal ills' to save the planet", *Nature*, 483: 30.

the Danube 17.[62] Sometimes transboundary water resources are equally distributed across countries, making it reasonably easy for the countries to agree on sharing arrangements. Alternatively, the external sources of water may not be the most important source of supply for countries. But as Table 9.5 indicates, 39 countries currently receive most of their water from outside their borders. All but two of the countries are developing economies. The freshwater impacts of climate change are especially likely to pose a challenge for such economies.[63]

While most countries have institutional mechanisms and policies for allocating internal water resources and resolving water disputes, negotiating and implementing workable agreements to manage and share international water resources has proved more difficult. Currently, there are around 200 treaties and agreements that govern transboundary water allocation.[64] Such agreements are necessary because of the interdependencies that such shared resources imply. For example, how an upstream country uses a river will affect the availability, timing and quality of water downstream. Countries that share an aquifer or lake are also affected by the common water use. In recent years, the international community has adopted conventions, declarations and legal statements concerning the management of international transboundary water bodies, while countries sharing river basins have established integrated basin management initiatives. However, many international river basins and other shared water resources still lack any type of joint management structure, and some international agreements and joint management structures need to be updated or improved. Although the potential for armed conflict between countries over shared water resources remains low, cooperation to resolve disputes

Table 9.5 Transboundary water availability

Region	Countries receiving 50–75% of their water from external sources	Countries receiving >75% of their water from external sources
Middle East	Iraq, Israel, Syria	Bahrain, Egypt, Kuwait
East Asia and the Pacific	Cambodia, Vietnam	
Latin America and the Caribbean	Argentina, Bolivia, Paraguay, Uruguay	
South Asia		Bangladesh, Pakistan
Sub-Saharan Africa	Benin, Chad, Congo, Eritrea, Gambia, Mozambique, Namibia, Somalia, Sudan	Botswana, Mauritania, Niger
Eastern Europe and Central Asia	Azerbaijan, Croatia, Latvia, Slovakia, Ukraine, Uzbekistan	Hungary, Moldova, Montenegro, Romania, Serbia, Turkmenistan
High-Income OECD	Luxembourg	Netherlands

Source: United Nations Development Programme (UNDP) (2006) *Human Development Report 2006. Beyond Scarcity: Power, Poverty and the Global Water Crisis*. New York: UNDP.

over water is often lacking.[65] In some cases, like the shrinkage of Lake Chad in Sub-Saharan Africa, the lack of cooperation is having a detrimental effect on the shared water system.[66] In South Asia, the 1996 Ganges River Treaty between India and Bangladesh may be in serious jeopardy because of projected future water uses relative to basin supply, unless the treaty is extended to allow augmentation of river flows through water transfers from Nepal.[67]

Given the high and increasing dependency of many countries on transboundary water resources, the need to reduce potential conflicts and increase cooperation over jointly managing these resources is paramount. Modification of freshwater ecosystems and watersheds to meet human water security needs and global environmental threats such as climate change will also put pressure on existing arrangements to manage transboundary water resources. Fostering more cooperation and international sharing of water resources will be important, and creating mutual incentives to do so will be important. Two general types of reciprocal benefits appear to be relevant.[68] First, as water is a multi-functional resource, there are opportunities for linking water supplies with hydroelectricity trade, using water transfers as an incentive to conclude multi-party river basin agreements, and linking water quality with controls over unilateral diversion by an upstream country or countries. Second, there is also the scope of linking water sharing agreements with mutual benefits outside of the water sector, including improved trade, agricultural, industrial, political and military relations. Both types of incentives appear to be important to many transboundary water sharing arrangements, and they should be explored as a way of tying economic incentives and benefits to successful negotiation of such agreements.

In sum, creating global markets has become essential for environmental problems that are beyond the scope for any single country to manage. Climate change, ecological scarcity and transboundary water allocation are three examples where such markets are needed. Without sufficient cooperation on establishing a long-term and credible global price signal for carbon; implementing and financing a system of international payment of ecosystem services; and creating viable transboundary water sharing arrangements, these global environmental problems will continue to worsen, perhaps with irrevocable consequences for humankind.

Conclusion

The world economy today is at a crossroads. As Mahatma Gandhi once said, "Earth provides enough to satisfy every man's need, but not every man's greed."

As this book has shown, the current global threats of environmental scarcity and rising wealth inequality are proving Gandhi to be correct. These threats arise because of the way we currently mismanage and accumulate wealth in our economies, and specifically, how nature is used to create wealth and who benefits from this wealth.

The Balanced Wealth Strategy outlined in this book offers a way forward to correct the current structural imbalance. In recent decades, this imbalance has emerged after a long period of global economic development, resulting from the *second phase* of the Industrial Revolution. This phase was initiated by a series of innovations, such as electricity and the internal combustion engine, which occurred from 1870 to 1900. These innovations were in turn the outcome of the discovery and use of the new hydrocarbons, oil and gas, along with coal. Harnessing these technological and economic changes led to the rise of the United States, which became the model for 20th century industrialization. As this structural transformation spread worldwide, fostered by trade in energy and resources, there was a large boost to global productivity, which lasted until 1970.[1]

The second phase of the Industrial Revolution was firmly rooted in the *fossil fuel era*, which continues to this day. Since the 1890s, coal, oil and gas have accounted for at least half of global energy consumption. And, despite the rise in renewable energy and nuclear power, fossil fuels still account for 80% of energy use worldwide. In addition, as economies have become more energy-intensive, they have also increased non-renewable material use, such as minerals and ores, construction materials and non-renewable organics, which currently comprise 95% of material consumption.

Since the early 20th century, economic expansion worldwide has been accompanied by a steady rise in resource and energy use as well as increased skill-biased technological change, which requires more use of skilled rather than unskilled labor in production. As long as human capital accumulation could keep pace with such innovations, and natural resources were cheap and accessible, the world economy could expand rapidly while the gap between rich and poor would narrow.

However, beginning in the 1970s, new stresses emerged. Human capital accumulation and educational attainment started to lag behind skill-biased technological change, and increasing environmental degradation and natural capital depreciation fostered ecological scarcity. Rather than face the rising economic and social costs of increasing natural resource use and ecological scarcity, modern economies have chosen to hide these costs by underpricing natural capital. And, rather than investing in sufficient human capital to keep pace with skill-biased technological change, we allow skilled labor to become scarce and thus attract excessive wages. Meanwhile, less skilled labor faces barriers to appropriate training and education.

Hence, the period from the 1970s onward can be termed the *second phase malaise*. In recent decades, financial capital has become the dominant form of wealth, and more of the income and wealth of the rich is from the financial sector. Moreover, its unchecked expansion has led to greater financial risk and instability, increasing concentration of wealth, and global imbalances. Reproducible capital continues to be overly resource and energy-intensive, and is the main conduit for skill-biased technological change. As a result, accumulation of reproducible capital encourages more use of natural capital and the rising demand for relatively skilled labor. However, human capital accumulation in modern economies is failing to keep pace with this demand, which has caused the wage gap between highly skilled and less-skilled workers to grow. The global implications are increasing wealth inequality, pockets of poverty, structural unemployment, and greater social polarization. Finally, the underpricing of natural capital has led to increasing overuse and excessive environmental degradation. The result is greater ecological and natural resource scarcity, and the emergence of global environmental problems, such as climate change and freshwater availability. The hallmark of the second phase malaise, it seems, is that we are prepared to accept the economic and social consequences of excessive environmental degradation and rising wealth inequality.

These consequences could weigh heavily on the world economy. The largest and most populous emerging market and rich economies, such as those comprising the Group of 20 (G20), may fare reasonably well.[2] So might a few other high-income and smaller emerging economies. But, as the productivity boost from the second phase of innovations continues to wane, and the transition from the fossil fuel age is postponed, long-run growth even for these economies will be modest. However, many smaller and developing countries may struggle to take off into sustained economic progress. In addition, there will be the ongoing risk to all economies from financial instability, global imbalances, and environmental problems such as ecological scarcity, climate change and freshwater availability. The world economy will have to cope with these dangers as well as the needs of an expanding global population, which will likely grow from 7.2 billion today to 8.1 billion in 2025 and 10.9 billion by 2050.[3]

Wealth inequality will continue, if not worsen. The numbers of the wealthy may rise, but their proportion of the overall population will remain relatively low. The benefits of modest growth will also tend to spread unevenly, so that those with sufficient skills for high-wage employment will disproportionately gain. Thus, as Tyler Cowen suggests, "I imagine a world where, say, 10 to 15 percent of the citizenry is extremely wealthy and has fantastically comfortable and stimulating lives, the equivalent of current-day millionaires, albeit with better health care."[4] Of course, the rich and super-rich, those with 1% or even 0.1% of all wealth, will do even better.

The wealthiest 10–15% of the population will have the means to protect themselves from many of the economic and social consequences of an unstable world. They will increasingly use their privately accumulated wealth to live in the more prosperous economies, inhabit clean and safe neighborhoods with good schools, hospitals and other services, invest in private education and healthcare for their families, and ultimately, secure for themselves the most highly skilled and lucrative employment opportunities. They will also continue to have a disproportionate political influence in the countries where they reside, which will translate into determining which public policies and investments are ultimately adopted.

However, the prospects for the remaining 85% of the population are less promising. Worldwide the top 1% today account for almost half of the all the wealth in the world, and the richest 10% own 87% of all assets. The lower 50% of the global population possess less than 1% of global wealth.[5] Thus, most people will not have accumulated sufficient private wealth to protect themselves from environmental scarcities, to avoid the fallout from financial crises, or to invest in private education and healthcare for their families. The failure to obtain the necessary skills to compete in the workforce where both the availability and types of jobs are increasingly determined by new technologies will severely constrain income-earning opportunities.

A vast number of people at the bottom of the wealth scale will still inhabit the pockets of poverty worldwide. These include the poor neighborhoods of the growing metropolitan areas and cities around the world, remote and less favored agricultural lands in developing countries, and low-elevation coastal zones exposed to coastal storms, sea-level rise and other climate change impacts. For the poor living in these and other disadvantaged locations, their vulnerability to increasing environmental and economic risks will compound their inability to escape from poverty.

The polarization of society that may result from this growing disparity in wealth and income could lead to political instability, increased violence, regional conflicts and ethnic, religious and racial tensions. Particularly for those disenfranchised and disadvantaged groups, civil conflict, rebellion and even terrorism might be seen as attractive political options. As environmental scarcities worsen, they will lead increasingly to more and more local, regional and global conflicts. As a report by the United Nations concludes, "Depletion of renewable natural resources, combined with environmental degradation and climate change, pose fundamental threats to human security."[6] These threats are likely to increase in a world of growing environmental scarcity, inequality and population expansion.

However, as outlined in this book, there is another way forward for the world economy – a Balanced Wealth Strategy. Ending the persistent underpricing of natural capital and spurring additional human capital accumulation offers the promise of a new era of innovation and structural transformation that both transcends the fossil fuel age and will lead to a new boost of long-term productivity worldwide. Eventually, the outcome would be a *third phase* of the Industrial Revolution, or as some would call it, a Third Industrial Revolution. To be inclusive and beneficial to all economies, the transition period may require implementation of supplementary policies that are consistent with many developing countries' key structural features of natural resource use and poverty. In addition, it will be necessary to create global markets to facilitate the incentives to combat the most pressing environmental problems, such as climate change, ecological scarcity and freshwater availability.

Implementing the Balanced Wealth Strategy is of course extremely difficult. Throughout this book we have identified many vested interests and the institutional inertia that reinforce the current practice of underpricing natural capital and chronic underinvestment in human capital. Equally, there are pervasive economic and political obstacles to addressing the specific natural resource use and poverty problems of developing countries, to creating markets to mitigate global environmental problems, and to cooperating on ending such problems.

But unless the world economy makes the transition to a new era of innovation and growth, the current threats of environmental scarcity and inequality will continue to worsen. As suggested in this book, overcoming these threats by redressing the structural imbalance between nature and wealth is the only way to usher in a new era of innovation, sustained growth and inclusive prosperity. Hence, the call for the Balanced Wealth Strategy proposed in this book.

As Gandhi also said, "The future depends on what we do in the present."

Notes

Introduction

1. "Beijing Population 2014", *World Population Review*, 19 October 2014. Available at: http://worldpopulationreview.com/world-cities/beijing-population/
2. Based on air quality monitoring data released by the US Embassy Beijing, as reported in Lily Kuo, "Six years of Beijing air pollution summed up in one scary chart", *Quartz*, 10 April 2014. Available at: http://qz.com/197786/six-years-of-bejing-air-pollution-summed-up-in-one-scary-chart/
3. Avraham Ebenstein, et al. (2015) "Growth, Pollution, and Life Expectancy: China from 1991–2012", HKUST IEMS Working Paper No. 2015–10, February 2015.
4. As reported by Jonathan Kaiman, "Beijing smog makes city unliveable, says mayor", *The Guardian*, 28 January 2015. Available at: http://www.theguardian.com/world/2015/jan/28/beijing-smog-unliveable-mayor-wang-anshun-china
5. Chunbo Ma (2010) "Who bears the environmental burden in China? An analysis of the distribution of industrial pollution sources", *Ecological Economics*, 69: 1859–1875; Ethan D. Schoolman and Chunbo Ma (2012) "Migration, Class and Environmental Inequality: Exposure to Pollution in China's Jiangsu Province", *Ecological Economics*, 75: 140–151; Sqi Zheng and Matthew E. Kahn (2013) "Understanding China's Urban Pollution Dynamics", *Journal of Economic Literature*, 51(3): 731–772.
6. Zheng and Kahn (2013), *op. cit.*, pp. 746–747. Ironically, when air pollution regulations are enforced, it is also the less-skilled workers in urban and surrounding areas whose incomes are most affected by the reduction in industrial and mining jobs; see "The cost of clean air", *The Economist*, 7 February 2015. Available at http://www.economist.com/news/china/21642214-measures-combat-air-pollution-are-biting-hard-industrial-areas-already-hit-economic
7. Zheng and Kahn (2013), *op. cit.*
8. Oliver Wainwright, "Inside Beijing's airpocalypse – a city made 'almost uninhabitable' by pollution", *The Guardian*, 16 December 2014. Available at http://www.theguardian.com/cities/2014/dec/16/beijing-airpocalypse-city-almost-uninhabitable-pollution-china
9. "Free exchange: the real wealth of nations", *The Economist*, 30 June 2012. Available at: http://www.economist.com/node/21557732. See also United Nations University (UNU)-International Human Dimensions Programme (IHDP) on Global Environmental Change and United Nations Environment Programme (UNEP) (2012) *Inclusive Wealth Report 2012. Measuring Progress Toward Sustainability*. Cambridge: Cambridge University Press.
10. Edward B. Barbier (2011) *Capitalizing on Nature: Ecosystems as Natural Assets*. Cambridge: Cambridge University Press.
11. Millennium Ecosystem Assessment (MEA) (2005) *Ecosystems and Human Well-being: Current State and Trends*. Washington, DC: Island Press.
12. R. Dirzo and P. H. Raven (2003) "Global State of Biodiversity and Loss", *Annual Review of Environment and Resources*, 28: 137–167.

13. This concern explains the worldwide acclaim and interest in the book on income and wealth disparity by Thomas Piketty (2014) *Capital in the Twenty-First Century*. Cambridge, MA: Harvard University Press.
14. World Economic Forum (2013) *Global Risks 2013. Eighth Edition*. World Economic Forum, Geneva. Available at: http://www3.weforum.org/docs/WEF_GlobalRisks_Report_2013.pdf
15. Organization for Economic Cooperation and Development (OECD) (2011) *An Overview of Growing Income Inequalities in OECD Countries: Main Findings*. Paris: OECD. Available at: http://www.oecd.org/els/soc/49499779.pdf
16. Claudia Goldin and Lawrence F. Katz (2008) *The Race Between Education and Technology*. Cambridge, MA: Harvard University Press.
17. Edward B. Barbier (2010) "Poverty, Development and Environment", *Environment and Development Economics*, 15: 635–660.
18. Edward B. Barbier et al. (2015) "Debt, Poverty and Resource Management in a Rural Smallholder Economy", *Environmental and Resource Economics*, published online 26 February 2015; Edward B. Barbier and Jacob P. Hochard (2014) "Poverty and the Spatial Distribution of Rural Populations", Policy Research Working Paper No. 7101. Washington, DC: The World Bank, November; and Edward B. Barbier and Jacob P. Hochard (2014) "Land Degradation, Less Favored Lands and the Rural Poor: A Spatial and Economic Analysis", A Report for the Economics of Land Degradation Initiative, Bonn, Germany. Available at: www.eld-initiative.org
19. Piketty (2014), *op. cit.*; Edward B. Barbier (2011) *Scarcity and Frontiers: How Economies Have Developed Through Natural Resource Exploitation*. Cambridge and New York: Cambridge University Press; Raymond W. Goldsmith (1985) *Comparative National Balance Sheets: A Study of Twenty Countries, 1688–1978*. Chicago: University of Chicago Press.

1 The Origins of Economic Wealth

1. Thomas Piketty (2014) *Capital in the Twenty-First Century*. Cambridge, MA: Harvard University Press, p. 46.
2. Piketty (2014), *op. cit.*, p. 48.
3. Raymond W. Goldsmith (1985) *Comparative National Balance Sheets: A Study of Twenty Countries, 1688–1978*. Chicago: University of Chicago Press.
4. Piketty (2014), *op. cit.*, p. 48.
5. Thus, in the system of national income accounts of economies, it is assumed that the financial balance of an economy, i.e., the net acquisition of financial assets (new assets acquired less new liabilities) should be zero. The rationale behind this assumption is explained by Dudley Jackson (1982) *Introduction to Economics: Theory and Data*. London: The Macmillan Press, p. 543: "...it appears to make common sense that the sum of *all* the sectors' financial balances must in principle sum to zero because a financial asset (a claim on someone) cannot be acquired without a corresponding acceptance of a financial liability by someone else: for the system as a whole the total of – new – financial assets acquired (plus) and total – new – financial liabilities accepted (minus) must in principle match each other exactly, so that their algebraic total is zero." As Jackson further explains (p. 85), this assumption of a zero financial balance between new assets and new liabilities in an economy is essential to the economic principle that all investments in an economy must equal all savings: "Thus any system of financial balance equations can be rearranged to

show the equivalence of the total flow of saving to the total flow of investment. To subtract total investment from total saving, as does the equation for the sum of financial balances, must therefore give a total of zero." Of course, including net foreign-owned assets in the aggregate financial assets of an economy is important. For example, if new domestic-owned assets exceed new domestic-owned liabilities in an economy, then a person or enterprise in the economy is clearly accumulating foreign assets abroad (accepting a financial liability incurred by someone located overseas). Conversely, if new liabilities exceed new assets in the domestic economy, then someone is clearly borrowing overseas; i.e., foreign residents or enterprises are accumulating domestic financial assets.

6. "Free exchange: the real wealth of nations." *The Economist*, 30 June 2012. Available at http://www.economist.com/node/21557732. See also United Nations University (UNU)-International Human Dimensions Programme (IHDP) on Global Environmental Change and United Nations Environment Programme (UNEP) (2012) *Inclusive Wealth Report 2012. Measuring Progress Toward Sustainability.* Cambridge: Cambridge University Press,

7. Edward B. Barbier (2011) *Capitalizing on Nature: Ecosystems as Natural Assets.* Cambridge: Cambridge University Press.

8. See Eric Alden Smith, et al. (2010) "Wealth Transmission and Inequality among Hunter-Gatherers", *Current Anthropology*, 51(1): 19–34. This article is one of a series of papers appearing in a special section of *Current Anthropology* from a detailed and comprehensive study of the transmission of wealth and inequality in prehistoric societies, including hunter-gatherer and early agricultural societies.

9. The classic treatise on the domestication of animal and plant societies and its impact on early human society is Jared Diamond (1997) *Guns, Germs, and Steel: The Fates of Human Societies.* New York: WW Norton & Co. See also Peter Bellwood (2005) *First Farmers: The Origins of Agricultural Societies.* Oxford: Blackwell Publishing. In chapter 2 of my book, Edward B. Barbier (2011) *Scarcity and Frontiers: How Economies Have Developed Through Natural Resource Exploitation.* Cambridge and New York: Cambridge University Press, I document the role of natural resource scarcity, innovation and the availability of new "farming" frontiers in explaining the Agricultural Transition. That is, natural resource scarcity and frontier land expansion played a pivotal role in both the development of early agriculture and its spread from the primary areas of origin to other regions in the world. Climate change, the extinction of large prey, and population pressure may have confined populations of hunter-gatherers to isolated but resource-rich ecological zones near rivers, lakes and other aquatic systems. These populations were the first to try early farming. The development and spread to other regions was facilitated both by trade and the migration and settlement of farmers into nearby sparsely populated or unpopulated territories with suitable soils, rainfall and other environmental conditions for agriculture. The availability of such land in neighboring regions was clearly an important "pull factor". One important "push factor" was population pressure and environmental degradation in previously cultivated and grazed areas. A second "push factor" was the evolution of farming technologies and agro-pastoral systems that made the early farmers more mobile and allowed them to transfer these systems to new lands and regions. In favorable areas such as the rich and productive floodplains of Southwest Asia, new agronomic techniques, irrigation and the development of new agricultural commodities created food and raw material surpluses that were instrumental to urbanization, manufacturing and trade, and of course, the basis of the creation and accumulation of wealth.

10. Samuel Bowles, Eric Alden Smith and Monique Borgerfhoff Mulder (2010) "The Emergence and Persistence of Inequality in Premodern Societies: Introduction to the Special Section", *Current Anthropology*, 51(1): 7–17.

11. Herbert Kaufman (1988) "The Collapse of Ancient States and Civilizations as an Organizational Problem", in Norman Yoffee and George L. Cowgill (eds), *The Collapse of Ancient States and Civilizations*. Tucson, Arizona: University of Arizona Press, chapter 9, p. 231.

12. J. J. Spengler (1980) *Origins of Economic Thought and Justice*. Carbondale, IL: Southern Illinois University Press, p. 40.

13. Gordon V. Childe (1950) "The Urban Revolution", *Town Planning Review*, 21(1): 3–17. There is no doubt that, once launched circa 3000 BC, the process of urbanization has continued unabated globally ever since. For example, in his study of the emergence of important world cities over the past 5000 years, George Modelski (2003) *World Cities – 3000 to 2000*. Washington DC: Faros 2000,.p. 111, concludes that "the human experience of the past 5000 years" with urbanization "can be understood in a unitary perspective as one continuous process, with considerable ups and downs but one that can be portrayed and understood in one uninterrupted sequence."

14. See, for example, Azar Gat (2002) "Why City-States Existed? Riddles and Clues of Urbanization and Fortifications", in Mogens H. Hansen (ed.) *A Comparative Study of Six City-State Cultures*. Copenhagen: The Danish Royal Academy, pp. 125–138. The author does acknowledge that that fortification for defense was not a principal factor in the cities of Ancient Egypt, although Gat (p. 130) suggests that the geographical isolation of the kingdom may have been a possible explanation why: "Finally, where the defensive motive barely existed at all, as in the kingdom of Egypt, which had been unified on a grand scale very early in the development of civilization in the Nile Valley and which was largely sheltered by geography, the peasants continued to live in the countryside and around un-walled market towns, whereas cities were few and functioned as 'consumptive' metropolitan administrative and religious centers."

15. Rondo Cameron and Larry Neal (2003) *A Concise Economic History of the World: From Paleolithic Times to the Present*. Oxford: Oxford University Press, pp. 26–28; Gat (2002) "Why City-States Existed? Riddles and Clues of Urbanization and Fortifications", in Mogens H. Hansen (ed.), *A Comparative Study of Six City-State Cultures*. Copenhagen: The Danish Royal Academy, pp. 125–138; George Modelski (1999) "Ancient World Cities 4000–1000 BC: Centre-Hinterland in the World Systems", *Global Society*, 13(4): 383–392; and George Modelski (2003) *World Cities – 3000 to 2000*. Washington DC: Faros 2000, chapter 2.

16. William Easterly, Diego Comin and Erick Gong (2007) "Was the Wealth of Nations Determined in 1000 BC?", Global Economy and Development Working Paper #10. Washington, DC: The Brookings Institute, September 2007.

17. See, for example, Stephen Mithin (2003) *After the Ice: A Global Human History: 20,000–5,000 BC*. Cambridge, MA: Harvard University Press; Andrew Sherratt (1997) *Economy and Society in Prehistoric Europe: Changing Perspectives*. Princeton, NJ: Princeton University Press.

18. Sherratt (1997, pp. 10–11), *op. cit.* provides a wonderful description of this early core-periphery pattern of trade based on Sumer and the other first civilizations of Mesopotamia: "...in an otherwise rather unattractive region (the lower Mesopotamian plain) the opportunity arose to concentrate on added-value

production, principally in the form of textiles, supporting its labour-force by an expansion of irrigated farming. This created an increasing contrast... between a manufacturing core area and a raw-material supplying hinterland, altering the economic and political character of the interaction. Within the core, it produced a technological explosion as a whole range of new manufacturing processes were explored, from the mass-production of wheelmade pottery to more elite products such as wheeled vehicles or granulated goldwork. These, in turn, required increasing quantities of raw materials from the (mostly highland) periphery, which could only be acquired by the active setting up of colonial stations to alter local tastes and mobilise supplies. This was what happened in the Uruk period, which saw the emergence of true cities, writing systems and the formal characteristics of civilisation... The scale of this expansion, which drew in valuable materials like lapis lazuli from as far afield as eastern Afghanistan, began to involve two new alluvial agrarian cores which rapidly developed into independent centres of activity with their own immediate peripheries: Egypt and the Indus valley."

19. For further discussion of core-periphery trade in Ancient Egypt, see Jerry H. Bentley (1993) *Old World Encounters: Cross-Cultural Contacts and Exchanges in Pre-Modern Times.* Oxford: Oxford University Press; Rondo Cameron and Larry Neal (2003), *op. cit.*; Donald J. Hughes (2001) *An Environmental History of the World: Humankind's Changing Role in the Community of Life.* London: Routledge; and Peter Temin (2005) "Mediterranean Trade in Biblical Times", in Ronald Findlay, Rolf G. H. Henriksson, Håkan Lindgren and Mats Lundahl (eds) *Eli Heckscher, International Trade, and Economic History*, Cambridge, MA: MIT Press, chapter 6, pp. 141–156.

20. See Patrick T. Culbert (1988) "The Collapse of Classic Maya Civilization", in Norman Yoffee and George L. Cowgill (eds), *The Collapse of Ancient States and Civilizations.* Tucson, Arizona: University of Arizona Press, chapter 4, pp. 69–101; Donald J. Hughes (2001), *op. cit.*; and Kevin J. Johnson (2003) "The Intensification of Pre-Industrial Cereal Agriculture in the Tropics: Boserup, Cultivation Lengthening, and the Classic Maya", *Journal of Anthropological Archaeology*, 22: 126–161.

21. See Justin Jennings (2006) "Core, Peripheries and Regional Realities in Middle Horizon Peru", *Journal of Anthropological Archaeology*, 25: 346–370 and Darrell La Lone (2000) "Rise, Fall, and Semi-Peripheral Development in the Andean World-System", *Journal of World-Systems Research*, 6(1): 67–98.

22. For example, the empires that participated in the Silk Road trade included the Roman Empire (circa 300 BC to 476 AD), the Parthian Empire (250 BC to 226 AD), the Middle Indian Kingdoms of the Mauryan Empire (circa 322 to 185 BC), the Satavahana Empire (circa 230BC to 220 AD), the Kushan Empire (circa 1 to 270 AD), and the Gupta Empire (320 to 486 AD), and the Chinese Qin and Han Dynasties (221 BC to 220 AD).

23. For further discussion of the global expansion and significance of the Silk Road trade routes, see Jerry H. Bentley, (1993) *op. cit.*; Christopher K. Chase-Dunn and Thomas D. Hall (1997) *Rise and Demise: Comparing World-Systems.* Boulder, Colorado: Westview Press; David Christian (2000) "Silk Roads or Steppe Roads? The Silk Roads in World History", *Journal of World History*, 11(1): 1–26; Philip D. Curtin (1984) *Cross-Cultural Trade in World History.* Cambridge: Cambridge University Press; and Liu Xinru (1995) "Silks and Religions in Eurasia: c. A.D. 600–1200", *Journal of World History*, 6: 25–48. Although many commodities were ultimately traded through these routes, silk (in exchange for gold and silver) was the principal and most important

good, and the *de facto* medium of exchange. This is highlighted by Chase-Dunn and Hall (1997, p. 164), op. *cit.*: "Silk did not travel directly from China to Rome. Rather, it passed through several stages. At the eastern end of the trade many local lords, either nomad leaders or rulers of the 'Western countries' acquired more silk than they could consume, either themselves or as 'gifts' to followers or payment for other goods or services. Hence many local states and nomad leaders acquired a great deal of surplus silk, and they actively sought new markets for it. Indeed, silk was so common, it was often used for money... Silk was often processed, including unraveling and reweaving, in Syria or on the borderlands between the Parthian Empire and the Roman Empire."

24. The growth in international trade during 1000–1500 may have heralded the emergence of a world economy, but full integration of world markets, or "globalization", would be a process that would take many centuries to occur. See Kevin H. O'Rourke and Jeffery G. Williamson (2002) "When Did Globalisation Begin?", *European Review of Economic History*, 6: 23–50. A similar sentiment is expressed by Janet Abu-Lughod (1989) *Before European Hegemony: The World System A.D. 1250–1350*. New York: Oxford University Press, pp. 352–353, who refers to the rise of "an incipient world system" over 1250–1350. She notes that "although it was not a *global* system, since it did not include the still-isolated continental masses of the Americas and Australia, it represented a substantially larger system than the world had previously known. It had newly integrated an impressive set of interlinked subsystems in Europe, the Middle East (including the Northern portion of Africa), and Asia (coastal and steppe zones)."

25. Based on Angus Maddison (2003) *The World Economy: Historical Statistics*. Paris: Organization for Economic Cooperation and Development, tables 8a and 8b.

26. See Maddison (2003, Table 8b), *op. cit.*

27. See Barbier (2011, table 4.2), *Scarcity and Frontiers, op. cit.* and Modelski (2003), *op. cit.*

28. For economic analysis and overview of the core-periphery, or North–South, trade relationships of the emerging world economy of 1000–1500, see Barbier (2011) *Scarcity and Frontiers, op. cit.*, chapter 4; Ronald Findlay (1998) "The Emergence of the World Economy", in Daniel Cohen (ed.), *Contemporary Economic Issues: Proceedings of the Eleventh World Congress of the International Economics Association, Tunis. Volume 3. Trade Payments and Debt*. New York: St Martin's Press, pp. 82–122; and Ronald Findlay and Kevin H. O'Rourke (2007) *Power and Plenty: Trade, War, and the World Economy in the Second Millennium*. Princeton, NJ: Princeton University Press, chapter 3.

29. See chapter 5 "Global Frontiers and the Rise of Western Europe (from 1500 to 1914)", in Barbier (2011) *Scarcity and Frontiers, op. cit.*

30. Several scholars have noted the relationship between global frontier and economic expansion and the rise of the West. One of the earliest was Walter P. Webb (1964) *The Great Frontier*. Lincoln: University of Nebraska Press, who suggested (p. 13) that exploitation of the world's "Great Frontier", present-day temperate North and South America, Australia, New Zealand and South Africa, was instrumental to the "economic boom" experienced in the "Metropolis", or modern Europe: "This boom began when Columbus returned from his first voyage, rose slowly, and continued at an ever-accelerating pace until the frontier which fed it was no more. Assuming that the frontier closed in 1890 or 1900, it may be said that the boom lasted about four hundred years." See also William H. McNeill. 1982. *The Great Frontier: Freedom and Hierarchy in Modern Times*. Princeton, NJ: Princeton University Press; Eric L. Jones (1987) *The European Miracle: Environments, Economics and Geopolitics in the History*

of Europe and Asia, 2nd edn. Cambridge: Cambridge University Press; and Kenneth Pomeranz (2000) *The Great Divergence: Europe, China, and the Making of the Modern World Economy.* Princeton, NJ: Princeton University Press.

31. On the history of coinage and money in relationship to early modern economies and trade, see Fernand Braudel (1967) *Capitalism and Material Life 1400–1800.* New York: Harper & Row; and John Kenneth Galbraith (1975) *Money: Whence It Came, Where It Went.* London: Andre Deutsch.

32. This view of European motives for overseas expansion and "empire", especially the initial imperial forays of Portugal and Spain, is also stressed by the historian Franklin Knight (1991, p. 71): "Wealth in the early modern world was closely identified with the possession of gold and silver. If one purpose of the establishment of empire was the creation of wealth not only for individuals but also for the emergent nation-states, then the Iberians thought only two ways to acquire it: by trade and by mining for precious metals."

33. For the pre-1500 African slavery statistics, see R. A. Austen (1979) "The Trans-Saharan Slave Trade: A Tentative Census", in H. A. Germany and J. S. Hogendorn (eds) *The Uncommon Market: Essays in the Economic History of the Atlantic Slave Trade.* New York: Academic Press. For a discussion of the history of slavery in Africa before 1500, see Christopher Ehret (2002) *The Civilizations of Africa: A History to 1800.* Charlottesville: University Press of Virginia.

34. This estimate is from Colin McEvedy and Richard Jones (1978) *Atlas of World Population History.* London: Penguin Books, p. 215. Note that over this same period, 1500–1810, the authors suggest that the traditional "Arab" supply of African slaves to the Middle East was about 1.2 million. Actual shipping records indicate that Europeans sent almost eight million slaves to the New World between 1500 and 1867. See David Eltis, Stephen D. Behrendt, David Richardson and Herbert S. Klein (1999) *The Trans-Atlantic Slave Trade: A Database on CD-ROM.* Cambridge: Cambridge University Press. There was also considerable undocumented and illegal trade in slaves over this period, so historical shipping records are likely to underestimate the true volume of the slave trade and should be considered a minimum number. Thus the estimate of ten million slaves shipped by McEvedy and Jones may be close to the actual trade figures.

35. As described by Ronald Findlay (1993) "The 'Triangular Trade' and the Atlantic Economy of the Eighteenth Century: A Simple General-Equilibrium Model", in R. Findlay (ed.), *Trade, Development and Political Economy: Essays of Ronald Findlay.* London: Edward Elgar, p. 322, "the pattern of trade across the Atlantic that prevailed from shortly after the time of the discoveries down to as late as the outbreak of the American Civil War came to be known as the 'triangular trade', because it involved the export of slaves from Africa to the New World, where they produced sugar, cotton, and other commodities that were exported to Western Europe to be consumed or embodied in manufactures, and these in turn were partly exported to Africa to pay for slaves."

36. Patrick K. O'Brien and Stanley L. Engerman (1991) "Exports and the Growth of the British Economy from the Glorious Revolution to the Peace of Amiens", chapter 8 in Barbara L. Solow (ed.), *Slavery and the Rise of the Atlantic System.* Cambridge: Cambridge University Press, p. 207. See also Barbier (2011) *Scarcity and Frontiers, op. cit.*, chapter 6; and Joseph E. Inikori (1992) "Slavery and Atlantic Commerce", *American Economic Review,* 82(2): 151–157.

37. Based on available demographic and slave trade statistics for 1500 to 1860, Barbier (2011, chapter 6) *Scarcity and Frontiers, op. cit.* estimates that a minimum of over

7.9 million slaves were shipped from Africa during the triangular trade era, and it is likely that the actual figure was closer to 10 million if not higher. In 1500, the total population of Africa was around 46.6 million. Thus, the slave trade accounted for around 17 to 20% of the African population at the beginning of the era. Although the population of Africa did grow over the next two and a half centuries, reaching 74.2 million in 1820 and 90.5 million in 1870, the rate of expansion was considerably smaller compared to other regions. For example, total world population nearly doubled over 1500 to 1820, from 438 million to over 1.04 billion, and increased again to nearly 1.3 billion by 1870.

38. See especially Nathan Nunn (2008) "The Long-Term Effects of Africa's Slave Trades", *Quarterly Journal of Economics*, 123(1): 139–176. During the trans-Atlantic slave trade, the three regions where slaves were taken in greatest numbers correspond to a specific group of modern-day African states: the "Slave Coast" (Benin and Nigeria), West Central Africa (Zaire, Congo and Angola), and the "Gold Coast" (Ghana). Nunn finds that the slave trade adversely affected the long-term economic development of these states and others in the interior who supplied slaves for export. In addition, because the African regions that were most severely impacted by the slave trade tended to have the least developed political systems, after independence these countries continued to have weak and unstable states, as well as slower economic growth.

39. Findlay (1993, p. 342), *op. cit.* However, David Eltis and Stanley L. Engerman (2000) "The Importance of Slavery and the Slave Trade to Industrializing Britain", *The Journal of Economic History*, 60(1): 123–144, pp. 137–138, note that Britain's export expansion could have just as much been a result of the Industrial Revolution as a cause of it: "A striking feature of the markets for British goods between 1775 and 1850 is their wide geographic range, suggesting an ability to sell in whatever markets happened to become available. This in turn indicates that the late expansion of the British plantation sector and the subsequent strengthening of connections between the British economy and the world outside its empire are more plausibly seen as results of industrialization than as causes. In short, export expansion should be seen as the result of an outward shift in supply as well as a growth of demand."

40. Barbier (2011) *Scarcity and Frontiers, op. cit.*, chapter 6.

41. Daron Acemoglu, Simon Johnson and James A. Robinson (2005) "The Rise of Europe: Atlantic Trade, Institutional Change, and Economic Growth", *American Economic Review*, 95(3): 546–579. See also Daron Acemoglu and Simon Johnson (2012) *Why Nations Fail: The Origins of Power, Prosperity and Poverty.* New York: Crown Publishers.

42. Piketty (2014), *op. cit.*, pp. 158–160.

43. See, for example, Ronald Bailey (1992) "The Slave(ry) Trade and the Development of Capitalism in the United States: The Textile Industry in New England", in Joseph E. Inikori and Stanley L. Engerman (eds), *The Atlantic Slave Trade: Effects on Economies, Societies, and Peoples in Africa, the Americas, and Europe.* Durham, NC: Duke University Press, chapter 8, pp. 205–246; Stephen J. Hornsby (2005) *British Atlantic, American Frontier: Spaces of Power in Early Modern British America.* Hanover and London: University Press of New England; Donald W. Meinig (1986) *The Shaping of America: A Geographical Perspective on 500 Years of History, vol. 1, Atlantic America, 1492–1800.* New Haven: Yale University Press; and Donald W. Meinig (1993) *The Shaping of America: A Geographical Perspective on 500 Years of History, vol. 2, Continental America, 1800–1867.* New Haven: Yale University Press; and David Meyer (2003) *The Roots of American Industrialization.* Baltimore: Johns Hopkins University Press.

44. See, for example, Peter Temin (1991) "Free Land and Federalism: A Synoptic View of American Economic History", *Journal of Interdisciplinary History*, 21(3): 371–383.

45. Goldsmith (1985), *op. cit.* and Barbier (2011) *Scarcity and Frontiers, op. cit.*

2   Natural Capital and Economic Development

1. Edward B. Barbier (2011) *Scarcity and Frontiers: How Economies Have Developed Through Natural Resource Exploitation*. Cambridge and New York: Cambridge University Press.

2. World Bank (2011) *The Changing Wealth of Nations: Measuring Sustainable Development in the New Millennium*. Washington DC: World Bank.

3. Gavin Wright (1990) "The Origins of American Industrial Success. 1879–1940", *American Economic Review*, 80: 651–668, p. 666.

4. See Figure 2.7.

5. For example, based on historical records of the trends in capital/income ratios for a handful of countries in Europe and North America since the 18th century, Thomas Piketty (2014) *Capital in the Twenty-First Century*. Cambridge, MA: Harvard University Press, p. 164 concludes: "Over the long run, the nature of wealth was totally transformed: capital in the form of agricultural land was gradually replaced by industrial and financial capital and urban real estate. Yet the most striking fact was surely that in spite of these transformations, the total value of the capital stock, measured in years of national income – the ratio that measures the overall importance of capital in the economy and society – appears not to have changed very much over a very long period of time."

6. See C. Anthony Wrigley (1988) *Continuity, Chance and Change: The Character of the Industrial Revolution in England*. Cambridge: Cambridge University Press; and Brinley Thomas (1985) "Escaping from Constraints: The Industrial Revolution in a Malthusian Context", *Journal of Interdisciplinary History*, 15: 729–753.

7. David Landes (1998) *The Wealth and Poverty of Nations: Why Some are Rich and Some are Poor*. New York: W.W. Norton, p. 200.

8. Vaclav Smil (2005) *Creating the Twentieth Century: Technical Innovations of 1867–1914 and Their Lasting Impact*. Oxford: Oxford University Press, p. 29 makes a strong case for dating the start of the current global fossil fuel era as "sometime during the 1890s", as stated in the following paragraph: "This legacy of the pre-WWI era is definitely most obvious as far as energy sources and prime movers are concerned. As already stressed, no two physical factors are of greater importance in setting the pace and determining the ambience of a society than its energy sources and prime movers. Global fossil fuel era began sometime during the 1890s when coal, increasing volumes of crude oil, and a small amount of natural gas began supplying more than half of the world's total primary energy needs.... By the late 1920s biomass energies (wood and crop residues) provided no more than 35% of the world's fuels, and by the year 2000 their share was about 10% of global energy use. The two prime movers that dominate today's installed power capacity – internal combustion engines and steam turbines – were also invented and rapidly improved before 1900. And an extremely new system for the generation, transmission and use of electricity – by far the most versatile form of energy – was created in less than 20 years after Edison's construction of first installations in London and New York in 1882." See also Bouda Etemad, Jean Lucini, Paul Bairoch and Jean-Claude Toutain (1991) *World Energy Production 1800–1995*. Centre National de la Recherche Scientifique and Centre

D'Histoire Economique Internationale, Geneva, Switzerland; Roger Fouquet (2008) *Heat, Power and Light: Revolutions in Energy Services*. Cheltenham: Edward Elgar; and Vaclav Smil (2010) *Energy Transitions: History, Requirements, Prospects*. Santa Barbara, CA: Praeger.

9. Smil, Vaclav. 1994. *Energy in World History*. Westview Press, Boulder, CO.especially figure 6.5 and pp. 232–233. See also Etemad et al. (1991), *op. cit.*; Fouquet (2008), *op. cit.*; and Smil (2010), *op. cit.*

10. In depicting the Industrial Revolution as two distinct phases (see also Figure 2.2), I am following the pioneering long-run analysis by Robert J. Gordon (2012) "Is U.S. Economic Growth Over? Faltering Innovation Confronts the Six Headwinds", NBER Working Paper 18315, National Bureau of Economic Research, Cambridge, MA. Gordon refers to these two phases as Industrial Revolution (IR) #1 and IR#2. In addition, he contends that there was an IR#3 with the computer and Internet revolution that began around 1960 and reached its climax in the dot.com era of the late 1990s, but its main impact on productivity was short-lived, lasting until the 2010s. I believe that Gordon is also correct about this third phase of the Industrial Revolution, and I will be discussing its economic and natural resource implications in subsequent chapters.

11. See, for example, Gregory Clark (2007) *A Farewell to Alms: A Brief Economic History of the World*. Princeton, NJ: Princeton University Press; Ronald Findlay and Kevin H. O'Rourke (2007) *Power and Plenty: Trade, War, and the World Economy in the Second Millennium*. Princeton, NJ: Princeton University Press; M. W. Flinn (1978) "Technical Change as an Escape from Resource Scarcity: England in the 17th and 18th Centuries", in William Parker and Antoni Maczak (eds), *Natural Resources in European History*. Resources for the Future, Washington, DC, pp. 139–159; Eric L. Jones (1987) *The European Miracle: Environments, Economics and Geopolitics in the History of Europe and Asia*, 2nd edn. Cambridge: Cambridge University Press; Landes (1988), *op. cit.*; Angus Maddison (2003) *The World Economy: Historical Statistics*. Paris: Organization for Economic Cooperation and Development; Joel Mokyr (ed.) (1999) *The British Industrial Revolution: An Economic Perspective*. Boulder: Westview Press; Patrick K. O'Brien (1986) "Do We Have a Typology for the Study of European Industrialization in the XIXth Century?" *Journal of European Economic History*, 15: 291–333; and P. H. H. Vries (2001) "Are Coal and Colonies Really Crucial? Kenneth Pomeranz and the Great Divergence", *Journal of World History*, 12(2): 407–446.

12. For instance, Nicholas Crafts and Terence C. Mills (2004) "Was 19th Century British Growth Steam-powered? The Climacteric Revisited", *Explorations in Economic History*, 41: 156–171, find that the contribution of steam power to industrial output and labor productivity growth in 19th century Britain was at its strongest after 1870. Sean Adams (2003) "US Coal Industry in the Nineteenth Century", EH.Net Encyclopedia, edited by Robert Whaples. 24 January 2003. This URL http://eh.net/encyclopedia/article/adams.industry.coal.us documents how expansion of the coal industry in the latter half of the 19th century became central to the "take off" into industrialization in the United States. In Japan, the proto-industrial center of Osaka became the focal point for industrialization by harnessing steam and coal, investing heavily in integrated spinning and weaving steam-driven textile mills during the 1880s. See Carl Mosk (2001) *Japanese Industrial History: Technology, Urbanization, and Economic Growth*. Armonk, New York: M.E. Sharpe.

13. For example, as summarized by Findlay and O'Rourke (2007), *op. cit.*, p. 382, "it seems clear that the four decades leading up to World War I did indeed witness

an unprecedented, dramatic, and worldwide decline in intercontinental transport costs – especially when declines in overland rates are taken into account." See also C. Knick Harley (1988) "Ocean Freight Rates and Productivity 1740–1913: The Primacy of Mechanical Invention Reaffirmed", *The Journal of Economic History*, 48: 851–876; Kevin H. O'Rourke and Jeffrey G. Williamson (1999) *Globalization and History: The Evolution of a Nineteenth-Century Atlantic Economy*. Cambridge, MA: MIT Press. Patrick K. O'Brien (1997) "Intercontinental Trade and the Development of the Third World Since the Industrial Revolution", *Journal of World History*, 8(1): 75–133; and Jeffrey G. Williamson (2006) *Globalization and the Poor Periphery Before 1950*. Cambridge, MA: MIT Press.

14. Findlay and O'Rourke (2007), *op. cit.*, pp. 384–385.
15. From O'Brien (1997), *op. cit.*, p. 79, who also notes the importance of this railway expansion in terms of reducing the cost of shipping bulk commodities and integrating global markets: "Worldwide, kilometers of rails grew from around eight thousand in the 1840s to well over a million by World War I. Easily the most famous invention of the period, railways did a great deal to integrate markets and to open up the interior of continents, especially for regions within Europe and North America poorly serviced by rivers and canals. For heavy and bulky goods (or where speed mattered for the delivery of perishable produce and for the movement of passengers), costs could be reduced dramatically by shifting goods and people from road to rail."
16. See Barbier (2011), *op. cit.*, table 7.3, p. 378.
17. Findlay and O'Rourke (2007), *op. cit.*, p. 411.
18. Barbier (2011), *op. cit.*, table 7.2, p. 376.
19. See, for example, Paul A. David and Gavin Wright (1997) "Increasing Returns and the Genesis of American Resource Abundance", *Industrial and Corporate Change*, 6: 203–245; Ronald Findlay and Ronald Jones (2001) "Input Trade and the Location of Production", *American Economic Review*, 91: 29–33; Douglas A. Irwin (2003) "Explaining America's Surge in Manufactured Exports, 1880–1913", *Review of Economics and Statistics*, 85(2): 364–376; and Wright (1990), *op. cit.*
20. As summarized by O'Brien (1997), *op. cit.*, p. 89, "before 1914 mineral ores exported by the independent countries and colonies of the Third World to Europe amounted to not more than 4 percent of the total exports from South America, Asia, and Africa. The importance of these mines and energy supplies for European development emerged when crude oil came on stream around the turn of the century. Before World War I – and indeed until after World War II with the exception of tin and copper – European dependence on the other hemispheres for supplies of energy and minerals remained negligible."
21. C. Knick Harley (1978) "Western Settlement and the Price of Wheat, 1872– 1913", *Journal of Economic History*, 38(4): 865–878; and C. Knick Harley (1980) "Transportation, the World Wheat Trade, and the Kuznets Cycle, 1850–1 913", *Explorations in Economic History*, 17: 218–250.
22. See, for example, Barbier (2011), *op. cit.*; John C. Weaver (2003) *The Great Land Rush and the Making of the Modern World, 1650–1900*. Montreal: McGill-Queen's University Press; and Williamson (2006), *op. cit.*
23. The methodology for determining the historical land use trends depicted in Table 2.1 is explained in N. Ramankutty and Jon A. Foley (1999) "Estimating Historical Changes in Global Land Cover: Croplands From 1700 to 1992", *Global Biogeochemical Cycles*, 13: 997–1027. To reconstruct historical croplands, the authors

first compiled an extensive database of historical cropland inventory data, at the national and sub-national level, from a variety of sources. Then they used actual 1992 cropland data within a simple land cover change model, along with the historical inventory data, to reconstruct global 5 min resolution data on permanent cropland areas from 1992 back to 1700. The reconstructed changes in historical croplands are consistent with the history of human settlement and patterns of economic development. By overlaying the historical cropland data set over a newly derived potential vegetation data set, the authors determined the extent to which different natural vegetation types have been converted for agriculture. Similar methods were used to examine the extent to which croplands have been abandoned in different parts of the world.

24. Barbier (2011), *op. cit.*, table 7.5, pp. 382–383.
25. Raymond W. Goldsmith (1985) *Comparative National Balance Sheets: A Study of Twenty Countries, 1688–1978*. Chicago: University of Chicago Press; and Piketty (2014), *op. cit.*
26. For example, in 1860 the United States accounted for only 7.2% of world manufacturing output, but by 1913 its share was 32.0%. In contrast, in 1860 the United Kingdom was the leading world manufacturer, with 19.9% of world output, but by 1913 its share had fallen to 13.6%. See Barbier (2011), *op. cit.*, table 7.8, p. 391.
27. See, for example, Adams (2003), *op. cit.*; Barbier (2011), *op. cit.*; David and Wright (1997), *op. cit.*; Findlay and Jones (2001), *op. cit.*; Irwin (2003), *op. cit.*; Douglas W. Meinig (1998) *The Shaping of America: A Geographical Perspective on 500 Years of History. Volume 3 Transcontinental America 1850–1913*. New Haven, CT: Yale University Press; Paul M. Romer (1996) "Why, Indeed, in America? Theory, History, and the Origins of Modern Economic Growth", *American Economic Review*, 86(2): 202–212; Wright (1990), *op. cit.*; and Gavin Wright and Jesse Czelusta (2004) "Why Economies Slow: The Myth of the Resource Curse", *Challenge*, 47(2): 6–38.
28. Irwin (2003), *op. cit.* By 1913, raw cotton was still the leading US export, accounting for 22.5% of the total, but compared to the resource-based industries such as iron and steel, Irwin (2003), *op. cit.*, p. 374 notes that "cotton was easily traded and was exported in great quantities from the United States. The domestic cotton textile industry had no international cost advantage, despite the presence of local cotton production. By contrast, the Lake Superior iron ores could not be easily exported, and America's resource abundance manifest itself in exports of the intermediate and final goods embodying those resources."
29. Wright (1990), *op. cit.*
30. See, for example, Barbier (2011), *op. cit.*; Findlay and Jones (2001), *op. cit.*; Irwin (2003), *op. cit.*; Meinig (1998), *op. cit.*; Wright (1990), *op. cit.*; and Wright and Czelusta (2004), *op. cit.*
31. Irwin (2003), *op. cit.*, p. 375.
32. Giovanni Federico (2005) *Feeding the World: An Economic History of Agriculture, 1800–2000*. Princeton, NJ: Princeton University Press, table 8.11, p. 168.
33. From Federico (2005), *op. cit.* Total factor productivity is usually measured as a residual; i.e., the difference between the rate of growth of output and aggregate inputs, weighting the rates of change in inputs with the respective shares on production. Federico (2005), *op. cit.*, pp. 74–75 discusses the methods, and inherent difficulties, of applying such a total factor productivity measure in agriculture. Federico (2005), *op. cit.*, table IV, p. 240 indicates that historical estimates of total factor productivity growth in US agriculture averaged around 0.4% before 1870,

ranged from 0.17 to 0.53% between 1870 to 1910 and rose to a range of from 0.5 to 1.08% from 1910 to 1938. However, Federico (2005), *op. cit.*, p. 79 also notes that total factor productivity in US agriculture actually declined from 1900 to 1920, so much of the growth in the 1910–1938 period occurred during the upheavals of the Great Depression and Dust Bowl of the 1930s. Bruce L. Gardner (2002) *American Agriculture in the Twentieth Century: How It Flourished and What It Cost.* Cambridge, MA: Harvard University Press, figure 1.3, p. 6 shows that US real agricultural gross domestic product per person in farming (farmers and agricultural workers) grew at a long-run trend rate of 1.0% per year, excluding the Great Depression, from 1880 to 1940. But immediately after World War II, and for the next four decades, the trend rate of growth was 2.8% annually.

34. The source of these data is the US Department of Agriculture National Agricultural Statistics Service, available at: http://www.nass.usda.gov/Publications/index.asp

35. Peter J. Hugill (1988) "Structural Changes in the Core Regions of the World-Economy, 1830–1945", *Journal of Historical Geography*, 14(2): 111–127, table 2, p. 121.

36. The statistics for central electricity generation are from Arthur G. Woolf (1984) "Electricity, Productivity, and Labor Saving: American Manufacturing, 1900–1929", *Explorations in Economic History*, 21: 176–191. Woolf confirms the findings of earlier studies that the large increase in total factor productivity that occurred in US manufacturing from 1900 to 1929 were largely attributable to the rapid technological change accompanying the transition from firm-based electricity generation to reliance on centrally generated electricity.

37. Richard R. Nelson and Gavin Wright (1992) "The Rise and Fall of American Technological Leadership: The Postwar Era in Historical Perspective", *Journal of Economic Literature*, 30(4): 1931–1964, p. 1945.

38. As noted by Nelson and Wright (1992), *op. cit.*, pp. 1944–1945, "The automobile industry was the most spectacular American success story of the interwar period, a striking blend of mass production methods, cheap materials, and fuels. Despite barriers to trade and weak world demand, U.S. cars dominated world trade during the 1920s, and motor vehicles dominated American manufacturing exports."

39. See Meinig (2004), *op. cit.*, pp. 87–96.

40. Nelson and Wright (1992), op. cit., p. 1946.

41. Both trends are noted by Vaclav Smil (2006) *Transforming the Twentieth Century: Technical Innovations and Their Consequences.* Oxford: Oxford University Press, p. 7 and pp. 87–88: "Intensifying traffic necessitated large-scale construction of paved roads, and this was the main reason for hugely increased extraction of sand, rock, and limestone whose mass now dominates the world's mineral production and accounts for a large share of freight transport… Rapid growth of aggregate material consumption would not have been possible without abundant available energy in general, and without cheaper electricity in particular. In turn, affordable materials of higher quality opened up new opportunities for energy industries thanks to advances ranging from fully mechanized coal-mining machines and massive off-shore oil drilling rigs to improved efficiencies of energy converters. These gains were made possible not only by better alloys but also by new plastics, ceramics, and composite materials."

42. Lorie A. Wagner (2002) *Materials in the Economy – Material Flows, Scarcity, and the Environment.* US Geological Survey Circular 1221, US Department of the Interior, US Geological Survey, Denver, CO, pp. 6–7 and figure 5. Wagner defines "non-renewable organic materials" as all products derived from feedstocks of

petroleum and natural gas and coal for non-fuel applications, including resins used in the production of plastics, synthetic fibers and synthetic rubber; feedstocks used in the production of solvents and other petro-chemicals; lubricants and waxes; and asphalt and road oil.

43. Nelson and Wright (1992), *op. cit.*, p. 1934.

44. Wright (1990), *op. cit.*, p. 665. Note that these changing world economic conditions also spelled the end of US global economic advantages in terms of manufacturing during the post-World War II era: "Growing domestic markets outside the United States, and the opening of the world as a common market in resource commodities as well as consumer and producer goods have virtually eliminated the advantages American firms used to have in mass production. And as the networks of technological development and communication have become more oriented to professional peer-group communities, which have themselves become increasingly international, technology has become more accessible to companies that make the requisite investments in research and development, regardless of their nationality. Increasingly, such investments have been made by firms based in other countries. These developments are associated with the fact that large industrial firms are increasingly transnational." (Nelson and Wright (1992), *op. cit.*, pp. 1933–1934).

45. For example, Findlay and O'Rourke (2007), *op. cit.*, pp. 524–525 draw a parallel between the post-World War II globalization that facilitated cheap access to raw materials and energy that permitted industrialization in a handful of small open economies and the similar expansion in global trade that facilitated the British Industrial Revolution in the late 18th century: "As we argued in Chapter 6, while investment and technological change may have been the keys to the British Industrial Revolution, without the possibility of trade that revolution would have been aborted. First of all, trade allowed Britain to import crucial raw materials, chief among these being raw cotton. Second, without trade output prices would have declined precipitously, as firms were forced to sell into an already saturated home market, and input prices would have soared as firms were forced to source raw materials domestically. The result would have been a collapse in profitability, and thus in investment in new capital goods and technologies. Much the same logic applies to countries such as Korea, Taiwan, or Japan during the late twentieth century, which relied heavily on imports of raw materials or capital goods ... and which exported a high and increasing share of their manufacturing output to the rest of the world."

46. Barbier (2011), *op. cit.*, chapter 9.

47. The methodology for determining the historical land use trends depicted in Figure 2.3 is explained in Ramankutty and Foley (1999), *op. cit.* To reconstruct historical croplands, the authors first compiled an extensive database of historical cropland inventory data, at the national and sub-national level, from a variety of sources. Then they used actual 1992 cropland data within a simple land cover change model, along with the historical inventory data, to reconstruct global 5 min resolution data on permanent cropland areas from 1992 back to 1700. The reconstructed changes in historical croplands are consistent with the history of human settlement and patterns of economic development. By overlaying the historical cropland data set over a newly derived potential vegetation data set, the authors determined the extent to which different natural vegetation types have been converted for agriculture. Similar methods were used to examine the extent to which croplands have been abandoned in different parts of the world.

48. Food and Agricultural Organization (FAO) of the United Nations (2010) *Global Forest Resources Assessment 2010, Main Report*. FAO Forestry Paper 163. Rome: FAO.

49. See, for example, D. B. Bray (2010) "Forest Cover Dynamics and Forest Transitions in Mexico and Central America: Towards a 'Great Restoration'?", in H. Nagendra and J. Southworth (eds), *Reforesting Landscapes: Linking Pattern and Process*. Netherlands: Springer, chapter 5, pp. 85–120; FAO (2010), *op. cit.*; M. C. Hansen, et al. (2013) "High-Resolution Global Maps of 21st-Century Forest Cover Change", *Science*, 342: 850–853; N. Hosonuma, et al. (2012) "An Assessment of Deforestation and Forest Degradation Drivers in Developing Countries", *Environmental Research Letters*, 7: 1–12; and Patrick Meyfroidt and Eric F. Lambin (2011) "Global Forest Transition: Prospect for an End to Deforestation", *Annual Reviews of Environment and Resources*, 36: 343–371.

50. Eric F. Lambin and Patrick Meyfroidt (2011) "Global Land Chance, Economic Globalization and the Looming Land Scarcity", *Proceedings of the National Academy of Sciences*, 108: 3465–3472.

51. As noted previously, Piketty (2014), *op. cit.*, p. 164 provides similar evidence of this trend in major industrialized economies: "Over the long run, the nature of wealth was totally transformed: capital in the form of agricultural land was gradually replaced by industrial and financial capital and urban real estate." See also Thomas Piketty and Gabriel Zucman (2014) "Capital is Back: Wealth-Income Ratios in Rich Countries, 1700–2010", *Quarterly Journal of Economics*, 129(3), pp. 1255–1310 forthcoming and especially appendix table A21: Agricultural land/national wealth 1810–2010 (decennial averages), which shows similar trends for the United Kingdom, United States, Japan, Germany, France, Italy, Canada and Australia from 1810 to 2010, available at: http://piketty.pse.ens.fr/fr/capitalisback

52. Barbier (2011), *op. cit.*, chapter 9.

53. The World Bank provides these statistics in its World Development Indicators, which are available at: http://databank.worldbank.org/data

54. Goldsmith (1985), *op. cit.*, p. 2.

55. For example, O'Brien (1997), *op. cit.*, p. 79 summarizes the importance of the telegraph for international capital flows during the late 19th century: "From mid-century intercontinental cables reduced the time taken to communicate commercial intelligence around the globe to hours compared to the weeks and days needed to send messages by land, sea, and rail. Once in place, links by telegraph reduced the risks of investment in production and inventories for distant markets and permitted metropolitan firms to rationalize transactions around the globe."

56. Maurice Obstfeld and Alan M. Taylor (2004) *Global Capital Markets: Integration, Crisis and Growth*. Cambridge: Cambridge University Press, p. 55.

57. See Barbier (2011), *op. cit.*, especially table 7.6, p. 387.

58. For example, O'Rourke and Williamson (1999), *op. cit.*, p. 229 state: "The most obvious explanation for the size of European capital exports is that the New World investment demand was high due to labor and capital requirements associated with frontier expansion. If New World land was to produce food for European consumers and raw materials for factories, railways had to make it accessible, land had to be improved, and housing had to be provided for the new frontier communities. Since the bulk of UK overseas investment went to land-abundant and resource-abundant locations like the New World, this explanation has considerable appeal. The Americas, Australasia, and Russia took almost 68 percent of British

foreign investment ... These regions also took almost 40 percent of German foreign investment and almost 43 percent of French foreign investment ... The amounts going to Britain's African or Asian colonies, such as West Africa, or the Straits and Malay states, were minimal in comparison." Similarly, Gregg Huff (2007) "Globalization, natural resources, and foreign investment: a view from the resource-rich tropics", *Oxford Economic Papers* 59: i127–i155, p. i127 maintains: "Between 1865 and 1914 three-fifths of British, and two-thirds of trans-European, foreign investment went to regions of recent European settlement, or the New World, with only a tenth of global population; just over a quarter of capital went to Asia and Africa where two-thirds of people lived."

59. Obstfeld and Taylor (2004), *op. cit.* provide an excellent discussion of the "stylized facts" of the global capital market in the 19th and 20th centuries.

60. Obstfeld and Taylor (2004), *op. cit.*, table 2.1, pp. 52–53.

61. Obstfeld and Taylor (2004), *op. cit.*, p. 230.

62. This is eloquently described by Obstfeld and Taylor (2004), *op. cit.*, p. 170: "Domestic financial deregulation, like capital-account decontrol, also accelerated in the 1970s. In part, that development flowed from the trend toward freer international financial trade. After the 1950s, countries increasingly allowed homegrown financial institutions to compete for international business within enclaves separated from domestic markets by a strict cordon sanitaire. As resident capital controls were lifted, however, domestic deregulation became a competitive necessity. Domestic deregulation and the consequent growth of the financial sector, in turn, have made it much harder (technically and politically) to reimpose capital-account restrictions effectively today."

63. Piketty (2014), *op. cit.*, pp. 193–194. For an in-depth historical and economic analysis of global capital integration over the past two centuries, see Obstfeld and Taylor (2004), *op. cit.*

64. As noted in the text, for most countries since 1970, the World Bank now provides an estimate of adjusted net national income, which allows for natural capital depreciation as the sum of valuations of net forest depletion, energy depletion and mineral depletion. These statistics are in the World Development Indicators, which are available http://databank.worldbank.org/data. Specifically, in the World Bank's approach, net forest depletion is the product of unit resource rents and the excess of roundwood harvest over natural growth. In a country where incremental growth exceeds wood extraction, net forest depletion would be zero, no matter the absolute volume or value of wood extracted. Energy depletion is the ratio of the present value of energy resource rents, discounted at 4%, to the exhaustion time of the resource (capped at 25 years). Rent is calculated as the product of unit resource rents and the physical quantities of energy resources extracted. It covers hard and soft coal, crude oil and natural gas. Mineral depletion is the ratio of the present value of mineral resource rents, discounted at 4%, to the exhaustion time of the resource (capped at 25 years). Rent is calculated as the product of unit resource rents and the physical quantities of mineral extracted. It covers tin, gold, lead, zinc, iron, copper, nickel, silver, bauxite and phosphate.

3   Wealth, Structure and Functioning of Modern Economies

1. See Edward B. Barbier (2005) *Natural Resources and Economic Development.* Cambridge and New York: Cambridge University Press, chapter 1 and appendix 1.

2. See the Appendix to Chapter 2, which defines gross domestic product (GDP), national income (NI), net national income (NNI) and adjusted net national income (ANNI). The appendix also explains the various adjustments that are required to derive adjusted net national income (ANNI) from conventional economic indicators such as GDP and NI. Similarly, the appendix to this chapter explains the concept of adjusted net savings, which is net national savings plus education expenditure minus energy depletion, mineral depletion and net forest depletion.

3. In Figure 3.2, GDP is the sum of gross value added by all resident producers in the economy plus any product taxes and minus any subsidies not included in the value of the products. GDP per capita is gross domestic product divided by mid-year population. GDP is calculated without making deductions for depreciation of reproducible capital, net additions to human capital or for depletion and degradation of natural resources or depletion and degradation of natural resources. Data are in constant 2005 US dollars.

4. See also Figure 2.8 in Chapter 2, which shows how the share (%) of natural capital depreciation to adjusted net national income has been rising significantly in developing countries since the late 1990s.

5. "G20 Facts and Figures", available from http://www.tusiad.org/__rsc/shared/file/G20-Facts-and-Figures-sheet.pdf

6. The European Union (EU) is a politico-economic union of 28 member states that are located primarily in Europe, and include the France, Germany, Italy and the United Kingdom. These four countries are G20 members in their own right, whereas the European Union represents the collective interests of all 28 of its country members. At the G20 meetings, the EU is represented by the European Commission and the European Central Bank.

7. See especially the Chapter 2 Appendix for a discussion of the relationship between gross domestic product, national income and adjusted net national income, and especially how the latter is derived from taking into account reproducible and natural capital depreciation.

8. See, for example, Intergovernmental Panel on Climate Change (IPCC) Working Group II (2014) *Climate Change 2014: Impacts, Adaptation, and Vulnerability.* Philadelphia: Saunders. Available at: www.ipcc.ch/report/ar5/wg2/

9. G. McGranahan, D. Balk, D. and B. Anderson (2007) "The Rising Tide: Assessing the Risks of Climate Change and Human Settlements in Low Elevation Coastal Zones", *Environment and Urbanization*, 19(1): 17–37.

10. R. J. Nicholls, et al. (2007) *Ranking of the World's Cities Most Exposed to Coastal Flooding Today and in the Future: Executive Summary.* OECD Environment Working Paper No. 1. Paris: OECD. See also Organization for Economic Cooperation and Development (OECD) (2008) *Costs of Inaction on Key Environmental Challenges.* Paris: OECD; and United Nations Development Programme (UNDP) (2008) *Human Development Report 2007/2008. Fighting Climate Change: Human Solidarity in a Divided World.* New York: UNDP.

11. H. Brecht, et al. (2012) "Sea-Level Rise and Storm Surges: High Stakes for a Small Number of Developing Countries", *The Journal of Environment and Development*, 21: 120–138.

12. Edward B. Barbier (2015) "Climate Change Impacts on Rural Poverty in Low-elevation Coastal Zones", Estuarine, Coastal and Shelf Science, in press, http://dx.doi.org/10.1016/j.ecss.2015.05.035"doi:10.1016/j.ecss.2015.05.035.

13. Edward B. Barbier and Anil Markandya (2012) *The New Blueprint for a Green Economy.* London: Routledge/Taylor & Francis, p. 19.

14. Millennium Ecosystem Assessment, 2005. *Ecosystems and Human Well-being: Synthesis.* Washington, DC: Island Press, table 1.
15. Edward B. Barbier (2010) "Poverty, Development, and Environment", *Environment and Development Economics*, 15: 635–660.
16. United Nations, Department of Economic and Social Affairs, Population Division (2014) *World Urbanization Prospects: The 2014 Revision, Highlights.* New York: United Nations. Available at: http://esa.un.org/unpdt/wup/Highlights/WUP2014-Highlights.pdf
17. IPCC (2014), *op. cit.*

4 The Age of Ecological Scarcity

1. See Edward B. Barbier (2011) *Scarcity and Frontiers: How Economies Have Developed Through Natural Resource Exploitation.* Cambridge and New York: Cambridge University Press.
2. See Gretchen C. Daily et al. (2000) "The Value of Nature and the Nature of Value", *Science*, 289: 395–396; Partha Dasgupta (2008) "Nature in economics", *Environmental and Resource Economics*, 39: 1–7; Edward B. Barbier (2011) *Capitalizing on Nature: Ecosystems as Natural Assets.* Cambridge and New York: Cambridge University Press.
3. This is well-documented in Thomas Piketty (2014) *Capital in the Twenty-First Century.* Harvard Cambridge, MA: University Press: and in the earlier work Raymond W. Goldsmith (1985) *Comparative National Balance Sheets: A Study of Twenty Countries, 1688–1978.* Chicago: University of Chicago Press.
4. The classic reference documenting this trend since the 1970s is Piketty (2014), *op. cit.*
5. For the original definition of *ecological scarcity* see Edward B. Barbier (1989) *Economics, Natural Resource Scarcity and Development: Conventional and Alternative Views.* London: Earthscan Publications, pp. 96–97: "The fundamental scarcity problem ... is that as the environment is increasingly being exploited for one set of uses (e.g., to provide sources of raw material and energy, and to assimilate additional waste), the quality of the environment may deteriorate. The consequence is an increasing *relative scarcity* of essential natural services and ecological functions ... In other words, if 'the environment is regarded as a scarce resource', then the 'deterioration of the environment is also an economic problem'."
6. For some relevant examples of this literature, see Edward B. Barbier (2007) "Valuing Ecosystems as Productive Inputs", *Economic Policy*, 22: 177–229; Barbier (2011), Capitalizing on Nature *op. cit.*; Gretchen C. Daily (ed.) (1997) *Nature's Services: Societal Dependence on Natural Ecosystems.* Washington DC: Island Press; Daily, et al. (2000), *op. cit.*; Environmental Protection Agency (EPA) (2009) *Valuing the Protection of Ecological Systems and Services.* A Report of the EPA Science Advisory Board. Washington DC: EPA; Millennium Ecosystem Assessment (MA) (2005) *Ecosystems and Human Well-being: Synthesis.* Washington, DC: Island Press; National Research Council (NRC) (2005) *Valuing Ecosystem Services: Toward Better Environmental Decision Making.* Washington DC: National Academy Press; Stephen Polasky and Kathleen Segerson (2009) "Integrating Ecology and Economics in the Study of Ecosystem Services: Some Lessons Learned", *Annual Review of Resource Economics*, 1: 409–434; and The Economics of Ecosystems and Biodiversity (TEEB) (2010) *The Economics of Ecosystems and Biodiversity: Mainstreaming the Economics of Nature: A Synthesis of the Approach, Conclusions and Recommendations of TEEB.* Bonn, Germany: TEEB.
7. MA (2005), *op. cit.*

8. Daily et al. (2000), *op. cit.*, p. 395.
9. Barbier (2007), *op. cit.*
10. For example, see EPA (2009), *op. cit.*, p. 12: "...the term 'ecosystem' describes a dynamic complex of plant, animal, and microorganism communities and their non-living environment, interacting as a system. Ecosystems encompass all organisms within a prescribed area, including humans. Ecosystem functions or processes are the characteristic physical, chemical, and biological activities that influence the flows, storage, and transformation of materials and energy within and through ecosystems. These activities include processes that link organisms with their physical environment (e.g., primary productivity and the cycling of nutrients and water) and processes that link organisms with each other, indirectly influencing flows of energy, water, and nutrients (e.g., pollination, predation, and parasitism). These processes in total describe the functioning of ecosystems... Ecosystem services are the direct or indirect contributions that ecosystems make to the well-being of human populations. Ecosystem processes and functions contribute to the provision of ecosystem services, but they are not synonymous with ecosystem services. Ecosystem processes and functions describe biophysical relationships that exist whether or not humans benefit from them. These relationships generate ecosystem services only if they contribute to human well-being, defined broadly to include both physical well-being and psychological gratification. Thus, ecosystem services cannot be defined independently of human values."
11. MA (2005), *op. cit.* Although the Millennium Ecosystem reported that global climate regulation by ecosystems has been enhanced, recent scientific evidence reported by the Intergovernmental Panel on Climate Change (IPCC) suggests that this may no longer be the case. See Intergovernmental Panel on Climate Change (IPCC) Working Group II (2014) *Climate Change 2014: Impacts, Adaptation, and Vulnerability.* Philadelphia: Saunders. Available at: www.ipcc.ch/report/ar5/wg2/
12. A. P. Dixon, et al. (2014) "Distribution Mapping of World Grassland Types", *Journal of Biogeography*, 41: 2003–2019; and J. M. Suttie, S. G. Reynolds and C. Batello (2005) *Grasslands of the World*. Rome: Food and Agricultural Organization of the United Nations (FAO).
13. Eric F. Lambin and Patrick Meyfroidt (2011) "Global Land Use Change, Economic Globalization and the Looming Land Scarcity", *Proceedings of the National Academy of Sciences*, 108: 3465–3472.
14. See, for example, Edward B. Barbier et al. (2011) "The Value of Estuarine and Coastal Ecosystem Services", *Ecological Monographs*, 81(2): 169–183; and S. C. Doney, et al. (2012) "Climate Change Impacts on Marine Ecosystems", *Annual Review of Marine Science*, 4: 11–37.
15. Michael W. Beck, et al. (2011) "Oyster Reefs at Risk and Recommendations for Conservation, Restoration, and Management", *BioScience*, 61: 107–116.
16. See, for example, Benjamin S. Halpern et al. (2008) "A Global Map of Human Impact on Marine Ecosystems", *Science*, 319: 948–952; Heike K. Lotze, et al. (2006) "Depletion, Degradation and Recovery Potential of Estuaries and Coastal Seas", *Science*, 312: 1806–1809; Boris Worm, et al. (2006) "Impacts of Biodiversity Loss on Ocean Ecosystem Services", *Science*, 314: 787–790; and Boris Worm, et al. (2009) "Rebuilding Global Fisheries", *Science*, 325: 578–585.
17. See, for example, Doney et al. (2012), *op. cit.*; and U. R. Sumaila, et al. (2011) "Climate Change Impacts on the Biophysics and Economics of World Fisheries", *Nature Climate Change*, 1: 449–456. There is also evidence that the stresses on fisheries from human exploitation are reducing their capacity to withstand climate

variability and change; see B. Planque, et al. (2010) "How Does Fishing Alter Marine Populations' and Ecosystems' Sensitivity to Climate Change?", *Journal of Marine Systems*, 79: 203–417.

18. Freshwater is defined as having a low salt concentration or other dissolved chemical compounds – usually less than 1%. According to I. Shiklomanov (1993) "World Fresh Water Resources", chapter 2 in P. H. Gleick (ed.) *Water in Crisis: A Guide to the World's Fresh Water Resources*. Oxford: Oxford University Press, pp. 13–24, around 3% of the world's water is fresh, and 99% of this supply is either frozen in glaciers and pack ice or found underground in aquifers. Freshwater ecosystems account for the remaining 1% of the world's freshwater sources. Lakes and rivers, which are the main sources for human consumption of freshwater, contain just 0.26% of total global reserves.

19. N. Johnson, C. Revenga and J. Echeverrria (2001) "Managing Water for People and Nature", *Science*, 292: 1071–1072.

20. World Wildlife Fund (WWF) (2014) *Living Planet Report 2014: Species and Spaces, People and Places*. [R. McLellan, L. Iyengar, B. Jeffries and N. Oerlemans (eds)]. Gland, Switzerland: WWF.

21. This example is based on Edward B. Barbier (2013) "Wealth Accounting, Ecological Capital and Ecosystem Services", *Environment and Development Economics*, 18: 133–161.

22. United Nations University (UNU)-International Human Dimensions Programme (IHDP) on Global Environmental Change and United Nations Environment Programme (UNEP) (2012) *Inclusive Wealth Report 2012. Measuring Progress Toward Sustainability*. Cambridge: Cambridge University Press.

23. United Nations University (UNU)-International Human Dimensions Programme (IHDP) on Global Environmental Change and United Nations Environment Programme (UNEP) (2014) *Inclusive Wealth Report 2014. Measuring Progress Toward Sustainability*. Cambridge: Cambridge University Press.

24. This World Bank-led global partnership initiative is Wealth Accounting and the Valuation of Ecosystem Services (WAVES). See www.wavespartnership.org

25. For more discussion of this approach to accounting for ecological capital, see Edward B. Barbier (2012) "Ecosystem Services and Wealth Accounting", chapter 8 in UNU-IHDP-UNEP (2012) *Inclusive Wealth Report 2012, op.cit.*, pp. 165–194. For a more technical treatment based on the same approach, see Barbier (2013), *op. cit.* In developing these methodologies for ecosystems, I have extended approaches to natural capital and wealth accounting, as suggested by Kenneth J. Arrow, et al. (2012) "Sustainability and the Measurement of Wealth", *Environment and Development Economics*, 17: 317–353; Partha Dasgupta (2009) "The Welfare Economic Theory of Green National Accounts", *Environmental and Resource Economics*, 42: 3–38; Kirk Hamilton and M. Clemens (1999) "Genuine Savings Rates in Developing Countries", *World Bank Economic Review*, 13: 333–356; John M. Hartwick (1992) "Deforestation and National Accounting", *Environmental and Resource Economics*, 2: 513–521; and Karl-Göran Mäler (1991), "National Accounts and Environmental Resources", *Environmental and Resource Economics*, 1: 1–15.

26. Although this approach to accounting for the contributions of and any changes to ecological capital appear straightforward, in practice there are numerous issues and challenges that need to be overcome. For further discussion, see Edward B. Barbier (2014) "Challenges to Ecosystem Service Valuation and Wealth Accounting", chapter 7 in United Nations University (UNU)-International Human Dimensions Programme (IHDP) on Global Environmental Change; and United Nations

Environment Programme (UNEP) (2014) *Inclusive Wealth Report 2014. Measuring Progress Toward Sustainability.* Cambridge Cambridge: University Press, pp. 159–177.

5   Structural Imbalance

1. Recall that the Appendix of Chapter 3 also shows how the conventional economic indicator of *gross national saving* (GNS) could be adjusted for changes in reproducible, natural and human capital to attain *adjusted national saving* (ANS), which is GNS less depreciation of domestic reproducible capital assets (consumption of fixed capital), less depreciation of natural capital (net forest depletion, energy depletion and mineral depletion), plus net additions in human capital (from education, health and training expenditures). One could also adjust ANS further for net changes in the stock of ecological capital, thus having a more accurate measure of "adjusted" net savings of an economy that reflects changes in the economy's entire stock of economic wealth.

2. Human capital may also be important for entrepreneurial success in an economy. See, for example, Jens M. Unger, et al. (2011) "Human Capital and Entrepreneurial Success: A Meta-analytical Review", *Journal of Business Venturing*, 26: 341–358.

3. Much of the available information across countries of human capital investment is related to educational expenditures or levels of educational attainment. Ideally, one should also include health and training-related investments. However, measuring the latter contributions has proven to be fraught with difficulties and thus a challenge. See the Appendix to this chapter and the discussion in Gang Liu and Barbara Fraumeni (2014) "Human Capital Measurement: A Bird's Eye View", chapter 3 in United Nations University (UNU)-International Human Dimensions Programme (IHDP) on Global Environmental Change; and United Nations Environment Programme (UNEP) (2014) *Inclusive Wealth Report 2014. Measuring Progress Toward Sustainability.* Cambridge: Cambridge University Press, pp. 83–108.

4. Robert J. Barro and Jong Wha Lee (2013) "A New Data Set of Educational Attainment in the World, 1950–2010", *Journal of Development Economics*, 104: 184–198.

5. Barro and Lee (2013), *op. cit.*

6. For example, Deardorff's Glossary of International Economics, available at: http://www-personal.umich.edu/~alandear/glossary/f.html, defines a *primary* factor as "an input that exists as a stock providing services that contribute to production. The stock is not used up in production, although it may deteriorate with use, providing a smaller flow of services later. The major primary factors are labor, capital, human capital (or skilled labor), land, and sometimes natural resources."

7. This tradition stems from the Hecksher-Ohlin, or factor proportions, theory of how the comparative advantage of a country's production, and thus its trade, is determined. Early developments of this theory stressed strongly that the primary factors key to determining the factor intensity of production and trade were the immobile endowments of an economy. For example, see Paul A. Samuelson (1948) "International Trade and the Explanation of Factor Prices", *The Economic Journal*, 58: 163–184, p. 164: "The present note attempts to throw light on the matter under the simplifying assumptions most suited to the Ohlin analysis: two regions, say Europe and America, each endowed with different proportions of two perfectly immobile factors of production, say land and labor." Similarly, Harry G. Johnson (1957) "Factor Endowments, International Trade and Factor Prices", *The Manchester School*, 25: 270–283, p. 271 states: "...on the production side, technology and the

supply of factors of production in each country are given (the latter implying that factors are immobile between countries)."

8. Adrian Wood (1994) "Give Hecksher and Ohlin a Chance!", *Weltwirtschaftliches Archiv. (Review of World Economy)*, 130: 20–49, 21–22. Note also that Samuelson (1948), *op. cit.*, in his influential development of the factor proportions (Hecksher-Ohlin) theory of trade considered the "two perfectly immobile factors of production" to be "land and labor" and not capital.

9. See Chapter 2, The global integration of financial markets and its impact on the mobility of capital investments has been documented in Maurice Obstfeld and Alan M. Taylor (2004) *Global Capital Markets: Integration, Crisis and Growth.* Cambridge: Cambridge University Press; on more recent trends see also Thomas Piketty (2014) *Capital in the Twenty-First Century.* Cambridge, MA: Harvard University Press.

10. Of course, there may be some "risk premium" for international lending and borrowing in countries that are less politically stable, have poor-functioning markets and chronic debt, and suffer from weak governance and institutions.

11. For example, according to Jörg Mayer and Adrian Wood (2001) "South Asia's Export Structure in a Comparative Perspective", *Oxford Development Studies*, 29: 5–29, 7: "Both labour and skill are also internationally mobile to some extent. Only a small fraction of the world's labour force is able to move among countries, but for some individual countries such mobility is important (and the remittances of their mobile workers are an important export). There is also a high degree of mobility among some of the world's most skilled workers: those with the experience, know-how and contacts needed to produce and sell goods on world markets, which is what exporting is all about. As with capital, the international mobility of highly skilled workers means that their services can usually be obtained to develop the production of goods in which a country's resources give it a comparative advantage, reinforcing the H-O pattern of trade. However, barriers to harnessing the skills of such workers – poor communications facilities or restrictions on direct foreign investment, for example – may impede the realization of a resource-based comparative advantage in particular countries and particular sectors."

12. The argument for considering human and natural capital, but not reproducible capital, as the key immobile factors of production is neatly summarized by Mayer and Wood (2001), *op. cit.*, pp. 6–7: "The resources whose varying supply among countries causes this variation in export composition are three broad ones: skill (or 'human capital', acquired through education and training), land (meaning natural resources of all sorts), and labour (the number of people in the workforce)... By contrast with most other H-O models, capital (physical or financial) is omitted from this list of resources. The reason is that capital, though of vital importance as an input to production, is now highly mobile among countries, so that it cannot plausibly be regarded as a resource of which a large fixed 'endowment' gives some countries a comparative advantage in the production and export of capital-intensive goods. If a country has a comparative advantage in a good because of the abundance of a resource such as copper ore or educated labour, then it can usually obtain the capital needed to develop this resource, either from domestic savings or from abroad. Moreover, because domestic capital markets are linked to international capital markets, the cost of capital is similar in most countries, so differences in capital intensity among sectors do not cause differences in comparative advantage among countries."

13. For example, suppose that the aggregate output Q of an economy can be expressed by a simple relationship with human capital: $Q = AH^\alpha = A(hL)^\alpha$, where $A > 0$ and $\alpha > 0$ are parameters. It can be seen immediately from this expression that, as h increases, so does aggregate output. Also, if p is the price index associated with aggregate output, and all income is paid out as returns to human capital (wages to labor embodied with a given level of skill h), then $pQ = wH = whL$. Choosing H to maximize this expression, and rearranging, yields $\alpha Q/H = \alpha Q/hL = w/p$. This confirms that the real returns to human capital w/p are determined by its marginal productivity, and that these wages are paid to each skilled worker L embodied with a level of human capital h. Finally, the actual income paid per worker is $pQ/L = wh$. As can be seen from this expression, a relatively skilled worker (with a high h) will receive a higher average income compared to a relatively unskilled worker (with a low h).

14. This is analogous to using the term "ecosystem services" a shorthand expression for both ecosystem goods and services.

15. For example, typical industries in an economy that produce relative resource-intensive goods might be food, agriculture, fisheries and forestry, petrochemicals, mining and power generation, and cement, construction, iron and steel, automobiles and transport, and other industries that use considerable amounts of energy and raw materials. Typical industries that produce relatively skill-intensive goods include financial services, information technology and communications, high-tech consumer and intermediate goods, and other industries that require relatively large amounts of skilled labor in some stage of the production process. Of course, many resource-intensive industries produce the basic raw material and energy inputs – for example, food, wood, electricity, chemicals, concrete, etc. – used by most other industries in the economy, including relatively skill-based producers. Likewise, financial services, communications, information technology, computer goods and other relatively skill-intensive products are also used throughout the economy, including by relatively resource-intensive industries. The important point emphasized in this chapter is that the structure imbalance in economies is less related to the purpose of production – to produce intermediate or final goods and services – than the factor intensity of production – whether it uses relatively more human or natural capital.

16. Suppose that, for any sector in the economy, Q is the amount of goods produced using natural capital N and human capital H. The price of the goods is p, owners of the natural resources are paid a rent r and the relative wage rate of skilled labor is w, which is the return to human capital. Let's further assume that output is a function of human and natural capital in the following manner: $Q = AH^\alpha N^{1-\alpha}$, $0 < \alpha < 1$. If all income is paid out as returns to human and natural capital, then $pQ = wH + rN$. It follows from choosing human and natural capital to maximize the last expression that $\alpha Q/H = w/p$ and $(1-\alpha)Q/N = r/p$. The real rent paid for using an additional unit of natural resources is equal to its marginal productivity; similarly, the real wage paid to an additional skilled worker hired is equal to her marginal productivity. Expressing these two relationships as a ratio, we get $w/r = (\alpha/1-\alpha)N/H$. An increase in the input cost ratio w/r will therefore lead to a rise in the use of natural relative to human capital N/H.

17. This relationship between the relative costs of inputs and the relative prices of goods is often referred to as the Stopler-Samuelson effect, after Wolfgang Stopler and Paul

A. Samuelson (1941) "Protection and Real Wages", *Review of Economic Studies*, 9: 58–73.

18. As most economies actively engage in trade through exporting and importing in international markets, the initial relative price of resource to skill-intensive goods $(P^S/P^R)^0$ is likely to be determined in these markets. That is, exported goods from one economy must be competitive with production from other economies in the world prices established in international markets, and goods produced for any domestic market must be competitive at world prices with imports from other economies.

19. This outcome can be illustrated using the assumptions concerning the production in any economic sector as outlined in note 13 above. Recall that output in any sector is a function of human and natural capital $Q = AH^\alpha N^{1-\alpha}$, and the total revenues earned are distributed to human and natural capital $pQ = wH + rN$. The real rent paid for using an additional unit of natural resources is $(1-\alpha)A(H/N)^\alpha = r/p$, and the real wage paid to an additional skilled worker hired is $\alpha A(N/H)^{1-\alpha} = w/p$. One can see from these two expressions that, if the ratio of natural to human capital N/H rises, then the real returns to using natural capital must fall. In contrast, the real wages, and thus the income, of skilled workers must go up.

20. Recall that output in any sector is a function of human and natural capital $Q = AH^\alpha N^{1-\alpha} = A(hL)^\alpha N^{1-\alpha}$, and the total revenues earned are distributed as $pQ = wH + rN = whL + rN$, where h is the amount of human capital per worker and L is the total number of workers hired. It follows that, for each worker, the real income received will be $(Q-rN/p)/L = wh/p$. As established, if the ratio of natural to human capital N/H rises in production as a result of natural resources being relatively cheaper, then the real returns to using natural capital must fall, and the real wages and income of skilled workers must go up. But note that the real income received per worker is wh/p, which will be higher for a relatively skilled worker (with a high h) compared to a low or unskilled worker (with a low h). Thus the gain in real income for relatively skilled workers will be much higher than for low or unskilled workers. In fact, it is even possible for the real income of low and unskilled labor to fall. As shown in Figure 5.4, the relative price of skill-intensive goods P^S/P^R has risen, so that the real purchasing power of unskilled labor across all goods in the economy could decline.

21. Note that, for these effects to occur, the underpricing of natural capital and the high relative wages for skilled labor must be prevalent throughout the world economy, and not just in one or a few countries. As noted previously, almost all economies trade in world markets and are relatively small with respect to those markets. That is, the resource-intensive goods and skill-intensive goods produced by a single economy compete with exports and imports from other countries. This means that the relative price of these goods P^S/P^R will be determined by international supply and demand, and the production of goods by a single economy cannot affect this world price ratio. The implication is that, in Figure 5.4, if the initial price ratio $(P^S/P^R)^0$ is set by the world market, then it cannot be influenced by a distortion occurring within a single economy. That is, if the wage-rental ratio rises in just one economy, this increase in the relative cost of human capital for that economy would have no effect on the world relative price ratio P^S/P^R. None of the effects discussed here would occur. Instead, the relative price of skill-intensive goods would remain at the world price $(P^S/P^R)^0$, and eventually the wage-rental ratio in the single economy would be forced back down to $(w/r)^0$. However, if the underpricing of natural capital and the higher relative wages for skilled labor are pervasive throughout the world

economy, then all economies would experience a rise in $(w/r)^0$ to $(w/r)^1$, natural resources are relatively cheaper to us everywhere, and as a result, world relative prices would also have to increase to $(P^S/P^R)^1$. The consequences outlined in this chapter would therefore follow.

22. For example, Gavin Wright and Jesse Czelusta (2004) "Why Economies Slow: The Myth of the Resource Curse", *Challenge*, 47(2): 6–38, p. 10 describe the expansion of the minerals endowment of the United States in the late 19th and early 20th centuries in the following manner: "On closer examination, the abundance of American mineral resources should not be seen as merely a fortunate natural endowment. It is more appropriately understood as a form of collective learning, a return on large-scale investments in exploration, transportation, geological knowledge, and the technologies of mineral extraction, refining, and utilization...In direct contrast to the notion of mineral deposits as a nonrenewable 'resource endowment' in fixed supply, new deposits were continually discovered, and production of nearly all major minerals continued to rise well into the twentieth century – for the country as a whole, if not for every mining area considered separately."

23. The importance of international mobility of financial and reproducible capital for expanding the amount of land and natural resource supplies available for use by a primary-product exporting small open economy has been shown in economic models developed by Ronald Findlay (1995) *Factor Proportions, Trade, and Growth.* Cambridge, MA: MIT Press; and Ronald Findlay and Mats Lundahal (1994) "Natural Resources, 'Vent-For-Surplus', and the Staples Theory", in G. Meier (ed.), *From Classical Economics to Development Economics: Essays in Honor of Hla Myint.* New York: St. Martin's Press, pp. 68–93. In these models, the relative natural resource abundant, small and open economy can expand its natural capital by allocating more reproducible capital for this purpose. As the domestic and international capital markets are fully integrated, the rate of return on this capital must equal the world interest rate for financial assets. The implication is that the economy will continue to expand its supplies of natural capital until the point of the additional returns for investing reproducible capital for such expansion just equals the world interest rate. Until that point occurs, the returns to investing financial and reproducible capital in expanding natural capital supplies exceeds the opportunity cost of investment (as represented by the world market rate of interest), and thus it is worthwhile to expand the supply of land and natural capital through such financial and reproducible capital investment. Essentially, these models formalize the process of "frontier" (i.e., land and natural resource) expansion observed by Guido di Tella (1982) "The Economics of the Frontier", in C. P. Kindleberger and G. di Tella (eds) *Economics in the Long View.* London: Macmillan, pp. 210–227. According to di Tella (1982, p. 212), realizing the potential economic gains from frontier expansion requires "a substantial migration of capital and people" to exploit the abundant land and resources, which can only occur if this exploitation results in a substantial "surplus", or "abnormal" economic rent. This observation is the basis of di Tella's *disequilibrium abnormal rents hypothesis*; i.e., since frontier expansion takes time, there must be "disequilibrium" periods in which abnormal rents (profits well in excess of costs) can be exploited to simulate further frontier investments. In other words, since frontier (i.e., natural capital) expansion takes time, there must be "disequilibrium" periods in which abnormal rents can be exploited to stimulate further frontier investments, and as a result, "the greater is the rent at the frontier the more intense will be the efforts to expand it, and the quicker will be the pace of

expansion" (di Tella (1982), p. 217). It is this perspective on the role of investments in expanding natural capital supplies in relatively resource abundant economies that is also put forward here.

24. See, for example, Edward B. Barbier (2011) *Scarcity and Frontiers: How Economies Have Developed Through Natural Resource Exploitation.* Cambridge and New York: Cambridge University Press; Ronald Findlay and Kevin H. O'Rourke (2007) *Power and Plenty: Trade, War, and the World Economy in the Second Millennium.* Princeton, NJ: Princeton University Press; Gregg Huff (2007) "Globalization, Natural Resources, and Foreign Investment: A View from the Resource-rich Tropics." *Oxford Economic Papers,* 59: i127–i155; Eric L. Jones (1988) *Growth Recurring: Economic Change in World History.* Clarendon Press, Oxford. Maurice Obstfeld and Alan M. Taylor (2004) *Global Capital Markets: Integration, Crisis and Growth.* Cambridge: Cambridge University Press; Patrick K. O'Brien (1997) "Intercontinental Trade and the Development of the Third World since the Industrial Revolution", *Journal of World History,* 8(1): 75–133; Kevin H. O'Rourke and Jeffrey G. Williamson (1999) *Globalization and History: The Evolution of a Nineteenth-Century Atlantic Economy.* Cambridge, MA: MIT Press; Lloyd G. Reynolds (1985) *Economic Growth in the Third World, 1850–1980.* New Haven, CT: Yale University Press; John C. Weaver (2003) *The Great Land Rush and the Making of the Modern World, 1650–1900.* Montreal: McGill-Queen's University Press; Jeffrey G. Williamson (2006) *Globalization and the Poor Periphery Before 1950.* Cambridge, MA: MIT Press.

25. See, for example, Richard M. Auty (2001) *Resource Abundance and Economic Development.* Oxford: Clarendon Press; Richard M. Auty (2007) "Natural Resources, Capital Accumulation and the Resource Curse", *Ecological Economics,* 61(4): 600–610; Barbier (2011), *op. cit.,* chapter 9; Edward B. Barbier (2005) *Natural Resources and Economic Development.* Cambridge: Cambridge University Press; Kenneth M. Chomitz, with P. Buys, et al. (2007) *At Loggerheads? Agricultural Expansion, Poverty Reduction, and Environment in the Tropical Forests.* Washington DC: The World Bank; Ian Coxhead and Sisira Jayasuriya (2003) *The Open Economy and the Environment: Development, Trade and Resources in Asia.* Northampton, MA: Edward Elgar; Ronald Findlay and Mats Lundahl (1999) "Resource-Led Growth – A Long-Term Perspective: The Relevance of the 1870–1914. Experience for Today's Developing Economies", UNU/WIDER Working Paper No. 162. Helsinki: World Institute for Development Economics Research; H. K. Gibbs, et al. (2010) "Tropical Forests were the Primary Sources of New Agricultural Lands in the 1980s and 1990s", *Proceedings of the National Academy of Sciences,* 107: 16732–16737; Jonathon Isham, et al. (2005) "The Varieties of Resource Experience: Natural Resource Export Structures and the Political Economy of Economic Growth", *World Bank Economic Review,* 19(2): 141–174; Terry L. Karl (1997) *The Paradox of Plenty: Oil Booms and Petro-States.* Berkeley: University of California Press; Eric F. Lambin and Patrick Meyfroidt (2011) "Global Land Use Change, Economic Globalization, and the Looming Land Scarcity", *Proceedings of the National Academy of Sciences,* 108: 3465–3472; Thomas K. Rudel (2007) "Changing Agents of Deforestation: From State-initiated to Enterprise Driven Process, 1970–2000", *Land Use Policy,* 24: 35–41; and Sven Wunder (2003) *Oil Wealth and the Fate of the Forest: A Comparative Study of Eight Tropical Countries.* London: Routledge.

26. This biased effect on production of an increase in supply in one factor endowment is often referred to as the Rybczynski effect after T. M. Rybczynski (1955) "Factor Endowments and Relative Commodity Prices", *Economica,* 22: 336–341.

27. This is the essence behind endogenous growth theories, which argue that investments in research and development (R&D), technological innovation and education

are endogenous processes in the economy that require private and public investments, and thus lead to human capital formation (i.e., increasing the skill levels of the workforce).

28. This can be seen from Figure 2.7 in Chapter 2. In low and lower middle-income economies, 40% of economic wealth consists of natural capital and 46% of human capital. In upper-middle-income countries 25% of wealth is natural capital and 55% human capital. But in high-income economies, only 12% of economic wealth is natural capital, and 64% human capital.

29. Recall that, if H is the human capital stock in an economy, then we can define $H = hL$, where h represents the amount of human capital per worker and L is the total number of workers. Thus, h approximates the skill level of the workforce, which we have suggested can be increased by higher educational attainment. That is, following Barro and Lee (2013), *op. cit.*, let us assume that the educational attainment of the workforce is approximated by the average years of schooling s of the adult population aged 15 and over. Then we can assume that human capital per person increases with s, i.e., $h = h(s)$, $h' > 0$. As we have argued, this is an important relationship that explains why educational expenditures, and complementary investments in training and health, can expand a country's supply of human capital. Note, however, an increase in s only raised the amount of human capital per person h. It does not necessarily mean that the supply of skilled workers, which is essentially $h(s)L$ has increased substantially. In other words, the number of skilled workers L embodied with $h(S)$ in the workforce may not have increased much; instead, the existing pool of skilled workers is simply better educated. This is an important feature of the expansion of human capital, which we will return to again in Chapter 7.

30. See, for example, T. Aronsson and K.-G. Löfgren (1996) "Social accounting and welfare measurement in a growth model with human capital", *Scandinavian Journal of Economics*, 98: 185–201; Kenneth J. Arrow, et al. (2012) "Sustainability and the Measurement of Wealth", *Environment and Development Economics*, 17: 317–353; Partha S. Dasgupta (2009) "The Welfare Economic Theory of Green National Accounts", *Environmental and Resource Economics*, 42: 3–38; Kirk Hamilton and M. Clemens (1999) "Genuine savings rates in developing countries", *World Bank Economic Review*, 13: 333–356; John M. Hartwick (1990) "Natural resources, national accounting and economic depreciation", *Journal of Public Economics*, 43: 291–304; and United Nations University (UNU)-International Human Dimensions Programme (IHDP) on Global Environmental Change and United Nations Environment Programme (UNEP) (2014) *Inclusive Wealth Report 2014. Measuring Progress Toward Sustainability.* Cambridge: Cambridge University Press.

31. See Liu and Fraumeni (2014), *op. cit.*, pp. 85–86.

32. This perspective on human capital is usually attributed to T. W. Schultz (1961) "Investment in Human Capital", *American Economic Review*, 51: 1–17.

33. This is referred to as the *income-based approach* to measuring human capital. See Liu and Fraumeni (2014), *op. cit.*

34. This approach is taken with respect to educational attainment, for example, by Barro and Lee (2013), *op. cit.*

35. UNU–IHDP–UNEP (2014), *op. cit.*

6   The Underpricing of Nature

1. David W. Pearce and Edward B. Barbier (2000) *Blueprint for a Sustainable Economy.* London: Earthscan, p. 157, also describe this vicious cycle: "Important environmental

values are generally not reflected in markets, and despite much rhetoric to the contrary, are routinely ignored in policy decisions. Institutional failures, such as the lack of property rights, inefficient and corrupt governance, political instability and the absence of public authority or institutions, also compound this problem. The result is economic development that produces excessive environmental degradation and increasing ecological scarcity. As we have demonstrated, the economic and social costs associated with these impacts can be significant."

2. For example, William J. Baumol and Wallace E. Oates (1988) *The Theory of Environmental Policy*, 2nd edn. Cambridge and New York: Cambridge University Press, p. 1 state: "the problem of environmental degradation is one in which economic agents imposed external costs upon society at large in the form of pollution. With no prices to provide the proper incentives for reduction of pollution activities, the inevitable result was excessive demands on the assimilative capacity of the environment. The obvious solution to the problem was to place an appropriate price, in this case a tax, on polluting activities so as to internalize the social costs." The recognition that "external costs", such as the damages caused by pollution and other forms of environmental degradation, are not routinely reflected in the market price of goods and services has a long tradition in economics. See, for example, Arthur C. Pigou (1962) *The Economics of Welfare*, 4th edn. London: MacMillan; and Alfred Marshall (1949) *Principles of Economics: An Introductory Volume*, 8th edn. London: MacMillan. In fact, the use of a tax on polluting activities so as to "internalize the social costs" is often referred to as a Pigouvian tax, in honor of Pigou who introduced this concept in the first edition of his book, published in 1920, when describing what he called the "incidental uncharged disservices" that occur when a private producer builds a factory, such as higher congestion, loss of light, and a loss of health for the neighbors.

3. See, for example, David W. Pearce, Anil Markandya and Edward B. Barbier (1989) *Blueprint for a Green Economy*. London: Earthscan, which over 20 years later, was updated and expanded in Edward B. Barbier and Anil Markandya (2012) *A New Blueprint for a Green Economy*. London: Routledge/Taylor & Francis. See also, Dieter Helm (2015) *Natural Capital: Valuing Our Planet*. New Haven and London: Yale University Press; and Nicholas Stern (2007) *The Economics of Climate Change: The Stern Review*. Cambridge and New York: Cambridge University Press.

4. Ian Parry, Dirk Heine, Eliza Lis and Shanjun Li (2014) *Getting Prices Right: From Principle to Practice*. Washington, DC: International Monetary Fund, p. 1.

5. The $480 billion estimate for global fossil fuel subsidies is from Benedict Clements, David Coady, Stefania Fabrizio, Sanjeev Gupta, Trevor Alleyne and Carlo Sdalevich (eds) (2013) *Energy Subsidy Reform: Lessons and Implications*. Washington, DC: International Monetary Fund (IMF). These IMF estimates are for 172 countries in 2011, and include consumer subsidies for gasoline, diesel and kerosene, consumer natural gas and coal subsidies (for 56 countries) and producer subsidies for coal (for 16 countries). The $550 billion estimate for fossil fuel subsidies is from International Energy Agency (IEA) (2014) *World Energy Outlook 2014*. Paris: IEA. These IEA estimates are for 2013 and include subsidies to fossil fuels that are consumed directly by end-users or consumed as inputs to electricity generation. The share of fossil fuel subsidies in GDP and government revenues is estimated by Clements et al. (2013), *op. cit.*

6. Reported in Shelagh Whitley (2013) *Time to Change the Game: Fossil Fuel Subsidies and Climate*. London: Overseas Development Institute. Estimates are from Elizabeth Bast et al. (2012) *Low Hanging Fruit: Fossil Fuel Subsidies, Climate Finance and Sustainable Development*. Washington, DC: Heinrich Böll Stiftung.

7. Whitley (2013), *op. cit.* Estimates are from Global Subsidies Initiative, *Fossil Fuels – At What Cost?* Available at: http://www.iisd.org/gsi/fossil-fuel-subsidies/fossil-fuels-what-cost

8. Shakuntala Makhijani, Stephen Kretzmann and Elizabeth Bast (2014) *Cashing In on All of the Above: Fossil Fuel Production Subsidies Under Obama*. Washington, DC: Oil Change Institute.

9. Elizabeth Bast et al. (2014) *The Fossil Fuel Bailout: G20 Subsidies for Oil, Gas and Coal Exploration*. London: Overseas Development Institute, and Washington, DC: Oil Change International. The members of the Group of 20 include 19 countries (Argentina, Australia, Brazil, Canada, China, France, Germany, India, Indonesia, Italy, Japan, Mexico, Russia, Saudi Arabia, South Africa, South Korea, Turkey, the UK and the US), plus the European Union.

10. See the Appendix to Chapter 2 for discussion of the methodology for estimating adjusted net national income.

11. See, for example, G. W. Evans and E. Kantrowitz (2002) "Socio-economic Status and Health: The Potential Role of Environmental Risk Exposure", *Annual Review of Public Health*, 23: 303–331; Séverine Deguen and Denis Zmirou-Navier (2010) "Social Inequalities in Health Risk Related to Ambient Air Quality", chapter 1 in World Health Organization (WHO), *Environment and Health Risks: A Review of the Influence and Effects of Social Inequalities*. Copenhagen: WHO Regional Office in Europe; Ethan D. Schoolman and Chunbo Ma (2012) "Migration, Class and Environmental Inequality: Exposure to Pollution in China's Jiangsu Province", *Ecological Economics*, 75: 140–151; Liam Downey, Sumner Dubois, Brian Hawkins and Michelle Walker (2008) "Environmental Inequality in Metropolitan America", *Organization & Environment*, 21: 270–294; Diarmid Campbell-Lendrum and Carlos Covalán (2007) "Climate Change and Developing-Country Cities: Implications for Environmental Health and Equity", *Journal of Urban Health: Bulletin of the New York Academy of Medicine*, 34: i108–i117; and M. R. Montgomery (2009) "Urban Poverty and Health in Developing Countries", *Population Bulletin*, 64(2): 1–16.

12. Evans and Kantrowitz (2002), *op. cit.*; Downey et al. (2008), *op. cit.*; Michelle L. Bell and Keita Ebisa (2012) "Environmental Inequality in Exposures to Airborne Particulate Matter Components in the United States", *Environmental Health Perspectives*, 120: 1699–1704; Michelle L. Bell, Antonella Zanobetti and Francesca Dominici (2014) "Who is More Affected by Ozone Pollution? A Systematic Review and Meta-Analysis", *American Journal of Epidemiology*, 180: 15–28.

13. Schoolman and Ma (2012), *op. cit.*; Chunbo Ma (2010) 'Who Bears the Environmental Burden in China? An Analysis of the Distribution of Industrial Pollution Sources?", *Ecological Economics*, 69: 1859–1875; Siqi Zheng and Matthew Kahn (2013) "Understanding China's Urban Pollution Dynamics", *Journal of Economic Literature*, 31(3): 731–772.

14. Deguen and Zmirou-Navier (2010), *op. cit.*

15. M. Ravallion, S. Chen and P. Sangraula (2007) "New Evidence on the Urbanization of Global Poverty", *Population and Development Review*, 33: 667–701.

16. Campbell-Lendrum and Carlos Covalán (2007), *op. cit.*; Montgomery (2009), *op. cit.*

17. Sanit Aksornkoae and Rungrai Tokrisna (2004) "Overview of Shrimp Farming and Mangrove Loss in Thailand", in E. B. Barbier and S. Sathirathai (eds), *Shrimp Farming and Mangrove Loss in Thailand*, Edward Elgar, London and Food and Agricultural Organization of the United Nations (FAO) (2003) Status and Trends in Mangrove Area Extent Worldwide (by M. L. Wilkie and S. Fortuna) Forest Resources Assessment Working Paper, No. 63. Forest Resources Division, FAO, Rome.

18. From 2000 to 2012, Thailand lost another 2.4% of its mangrove area. In 2012, the country still had 1,886 square kilometers of mangroves. These data on mangrove extent and loss in Thailand are from Stuart Hamilton (2014) "Creation of a high spatiotemporal resolution database of continuous measures of global mangrove tree cover for the 21st Century (CGMFC-21): A big-data fusion approach." Available at: https://docs.google.com/spreadsheets/d/1wy6uBL8XVXb7wbQ6bzkbZdxWVy50EM r6vmc5NB3z-5A/edit?pli=1#gid=1342680160.

19. See, for example, E. B. Barbier, S. D. Hacker, C. Kennedy, E. W. Koch, A. C. Stier and B. R. Silliman (2011) "The Value of Estuarine and Coastal Ecosystem Services", *Ecological Monographs*, 81(2): 169–183; S. C. Doney, et al. (2012) "Climate Change Impacts on Marine Ecosystems", *Annual Review of Marine Science*, 4: 11–37; K. L. Erwin (2009) "Wetlands and Global Climate Change: The Role of Wetland Restoration in a Changing World", *Wetlands Ecology and Management*, 17: 71–84; M. E. Spalding, et al. (2014) "The Role of Ecosystems in Coastal Protection: Adapting to Climate Change and Coastal Hazards", *Ocean & Coastal Management*, 90: 50–57; and C. Wilkinson and B. Salvat (2012) "Coastal Resource Degradation in the Tropics: Does the Tragedy of the Commons Apply for Coral Reefs, Mangrove Forests and Seagrass Beds?", *Marine Pollution Bulletin*, 64: 1096–1105.

20. I. Sarntisart and S. Sathirathai (2004) "Mangrove Dependency, Income Distribution and Conservation", chapter 6 in E. B. Barbier and S. Sathirathai (eds), *Shrimp Farming and Mangrove Loss in Thailand*. Cheltenham: Edward Elgar, pp. 96–114.

21. W. M. Bandaranayake (1998) "Traditional and Medicinal Uses of Mangroves", *Mangroves and Salt Marsh*, 2: 133–148; Barbier et al. (2011), *op. cit,*; R. Naylor and M. Drew (1998) "Valuing Mangrove Resources in Kosrae, Micronesia", *Environment and Development Economics*, 3: 471–490; A. Nfotabong, N. Din, S. N. Longonje, N. Koedam and F. Dahdouh-Guebas (2009) "Commercial Activities and Subsistence Utilization of Mangrove Forests Around the Wouri Estuary and the Douala-Edea Reserve (Cameroon)", *Journal of Ethnobiology and Ethnomedicine*, 5: 35–49; P. Rönnbäc, B. Crona and L. Ingwall (2007) "The Return of Ecosystem Goods and Services in Replanted Mangrove Forests – Perspectives from Local Communities in Gazi Bay, Kenya", *Environmental Conservation*, 34: 313–324; United Nations Environment Programme (UNEP) (2014) *The Importance of Mangroves to People: A Call to Action*, J. van Bochove, E. Sullivan, T. Nakamura, (eds). Cambridge: UNEP World Conservation Monitoring Centre; B. B. Walters, et al. (2008) "Ethnobiology, Socio-economics and Management of Mangrove Forests: A Review", *Aquatic Botany*, 89: 220–236; and M. E. Walton, M. Giselle, P. B. Samonte-Tan, J. H. Primavera, G. Edwards-Jones, L. Le Vay (2006) "Are Mangroves Worth Replanting? The Direct Economic Benefits of a Community-Based Reforestation Project", *Environmental Conservation*, 33(4): 335–343.

22. Naylor and Drew (1998), *op. cit.*, p. 488.

23. R. Badola and S. A. Hussain (2005) "Valuing Ecosystems Functions: An Empirical Study on the Storm Protection Function of Bhitarkanika Mangrove Ecosystem, India", *Environmental Conservation*, 32: 85–92; E. B. Barbier (2008) "In the Wake of the Tsunami: Lessons Learned from the Household Decision to Replant Mangroves in Thailand", *Resource and Energy Economics*, 30: 229–249; S. Das and J. R. Vincent (2009) "Mangroves Protected Villages and Reduced Death Toll During Indian Super Cyclone", *Proceedings of the National Academy of Sciences*, 106: 7357–7360; and J. C. Laso Bayas, et al. (2011) "Influence of Coastal Vegetation on the 2004 Tsunami Wave Impact Aceh", *Proceedings of the National Academy of Sciences*, 108: 18612–18617; and

K. McSweeney (2005) "Natural Insurance, Forest Access, and Compound Misfortune: Forest Resources in Smallholder Coping Strategies Before and After Hurricane Mitch in Northeastern Honduras", *World Development*, 33(9): 1453–1471.

24. Badola and Hussain (2005), *op. cit.*; and Das and Vincent (2009), *op. cit.*

25. Das and Vincent (2009), *op. cit.*

26. Badola and Hussain (2005), *op. cit.*

27. McSweeney (2005), *op. cit.*; M. R. Carter, P. D. Little, T. Mogues and W. Negatu (2007) "Poverty Traps and Natural Disasters in Ethiopia and Honduras", *World Development*, 35(5): 835–856; and Edward B. Barbier (2008) "In the Wake of the Tsunami: Lessons Learned from the Household Decision to Replant Mangroves in Thailand", *Resource and Energy Economics*, 30: 229–249.

28. In what follows, the description of institutions and how they reinforce economic processes is influenced by New Institutional Economics (NIE). See, for example, A. Dixit (1996) *The Making of Economic Policy: A Transaction-Cost Politics Perspective.* Cambridge, MA: MIT Press; G. M. Hodgson (1998) "The Approach of Institutional Economics", *Journal of Economic Literature*, 36(1): 166–192; L. McCann, et al. (2005) "Transaction cost measurement for evaluation environmental policies", *Ecological Economics*, 52: 527–542. D. C. North (1990) "A Transaction Cost Theory of Politics", *Journal of Theoretical Politics*, 2(4): 355–367; O. E. Williamson (2000) "The New Institutional Economics: Taking Stock, Looking Ahead", *Journal of Economic Literature*, 38(3): 595–613.

29. The role of such transaction costs in hindering the successful implementation of environmental policies has been well documented; for example, see Lata Gangadharan (2000) "Transaction Costs in Pollution Markets: An Empirical Study", *Land Economics*, 76(4): 601–614; Kerry Krutilla (2002) "Environmental Policy and Transaction Costs", chapter 17 in J .C. J. M. van den Bergh (ed.), *Handbook of Environmental and Resource Economics.* Cheltenham: Edward Elgar; Evy Mettepenningen, Ann Verspecth and Guido Van Huylenbroeck (2009) "Measuring Private Transaction Costs of European Agri-environmental Schemes", *Journal of Environmental Planning and Management*, 52: 649–667; Sandra Rousseau and Stef Proost "Comparing Environmental Policy Instruments in the Presence of Imperfect Compliance – A Case Study", *Environmental and Resource Economics*, 32: 337–365; and Robert N. Stavins (1995) "Transaction Costs and Tradeable Permits", *Journal of Environmental Economics and Management*, 29: 133–148. As noted by Krutilla (2002), *op. cit.*, p. 250, "transactions costs terminology has also been construed more broadly to refer to any costs associated with establishing, administrating, monitoring or enforcing a government policy or regulation", Thus, the transaction costs indicated in area A of Figure 6.3 could be substantially large.

30. See, for example, M. Grubb, T. Chapuis and M. Ha Duong (1995) "The Economics of Changing Course: Implications of Adaptability and Inertia for Optimal Climate Policy", *Energy Policy*, 23: 417–432; A. Micahaelowa and F. Jotzo (2005) "Transaction Costs, Institutional Rigidities and the Size of the Clean Development Mechanism", *Energy Policy*, 33: 511–523; and M. Schwoon and R. S. J. Tol (2006) "Optimal CO_2-abatement with Socio-economic Inertia and Induced Technological Change", *The Energy Journal*, 27(4): 25–59.

31. See, for example, K. W. Easter and S. Archibald (2002) "Water Markets: The Global Perspective", *Water Resources Impact*, 4(1): 23–25; Hellegers, P. J. G. and C. J. Perry (2006) "Can Irrigation Water Use be Guided by Market Forces? Theory and Practice", *Water Resources Development*, 22(1): 79–86; L. McCann and K. W. Easter (2004) "A

Framework for Estimating the Transaction Costs of Alternative Mechanisms for Water Exchange and Allocation", *Water Resources Research*, 40: 1–6; McCann et al. (2005), *op. cit.*

32. Hellegers and Perry (2006), *op. cit.*
33. Easter and Archibald (2002), *op. cit.*; Hellgers and Perry (2006), *op. cit;* McCann and Easter (2004), *op. cit.*; and McCann et al. (2005), *op. cit.*
34. See, for example, Toke Aidt (1998) "Political Internalization of Economic Externalities and Environmental Policy", *Journal of Public Economics*, 69: 1–16; Edward B. Barbier, Richard Damania and Daniel Léonard (2005) "Corruption, Trade and Resource Conversion", *Journal of Environmental Economics and Management*, 50: 276–299; Per Fredriksson (2003) "Political Instability, Corruption and Policy Formation: The Case of Environmental Policy", *Journal of Public Economics*, 87: 1383–1405; R. López and S. Mitra (2000) "Corruption, Pollution, and the Kuznets Environmental Curve", *Journal of Environmental Economics and Management*, 40: 137–150; and J. K. Wilson and R. Damania (2005) "Corruption, Political Competition and Environmental Policy", *Journal of Environmental Economics and Management*, 49: 516–535.
35. Clements et al. (2013), *op. cit.*
36. See, for example, D. Boucher, et al. (2011) *The Root of the Problem: What's Driving Tropical Deforestation Today?* Cambridge, MA: Union of Concerned Scientists; K. Chomitz, et al. (2007) *At Loggerheads? Agricultural Expansion, Poverty Reduction, and Environment in the Tropical Forests.* Washington DC: The World Bank; R. DeFries, et al. (2010) "Deforestation Driven by Urban Population Growth and Agricultural Trade in the Twenty-first Century", *Nature Geoscience*, 3: 178–801; K. Deininger, et al. (2011) *Rising Global Interest in Farmland: Can it Yield Sustainable and Equitable Benefits?* Washington, DC: The World Bank; Food and Agricultural Organization (FAO) of the United Nations (2006) *Global Forest Resources Assessment 2005, Main Report. Progress Towards Sustainable Forest Management.* FAO Forestry Paper 147. Rome: FAO; E. F. Lambin and P. Meyfroidt (2011) "Global Land Use Change, Economic Globalization, and the Looming Land Scarcity", *Proceedings of the National Academy of Sciences*, 108: 3465–3472; and T. Rude (2007) "Changing Agents of Deforestation: From State-initiated to Enterprise Driven Process, 1970–2000", *Land Use Policy*, 24: 35–41.
37. Rudel (2007), *op. cit.*, p. 40. For a detailed economic study of how the self-reinforcing effects of rent-seeking behavior, lobbying and corruption by vested interests contribute to low land productivity and deforestation throughout Latin America, see Erwin H. Bulte, Richard Damania and Ramón López (2007) "On the Gains of Committing to Inefficiency: Corruption, Deforestation and Low Land Productivity in Latin America", *Journal of Environmental Economics and Management*, 54: 277–295.

7   Wealth Inequality

1. This phrase comes from the title of the book by Claudia Goldin and Lawrence F. Katz (2008) *The Race Between Education and Technology.* Cambridge: Harvard University Press, as their work motivates the discussion of the overpricing of human capital in this chapter. In their book, Goldin and Katz provide substantial historical and contemporary evidence that this "race" is the main cause of the rise in the wage premium for skilled workers in the United States, and the subsequent growth in income inequality since 1980. However, it was Jan Tinbergen (1974) "Substitution

of Graduate by other Labour", *Kyklos*, 27: 217–226, who first observed the possibility of this phenomenon occurring, and thus concluded his article by stating (p. 224) that "a reduction in income inequality…depends on the 'race' between demand for third-level manpower due to technological development and supply of it due to increased schooling…" See also his book on this topic, Jan Tinbergen (1975) *Income Distribution: Analysis and Policies*. Amsterdam: North-Holland Publishing.

2. According to Goldin and Katz (2008), *op. cit.*, p. 395: "Skill-biased technological change refers to any introduction of a new technology, change in production methods, or change in the organization of work that increases the demand for more-skilled labor (e.g., college graduates) relative to less-skilled labor (e.g., non-college workers) at fixed relative wages."

3. Goldin and Katz (2008), *op. cit.*

4. Goldin and Katz (2008), *op. cit.* are not the first to make this argument. Since Tinbergen (1974), *op. cit.*, a large literature has emerged that has explored the "race between education and technology"; see Daron Acemoglu and David Autor (2012) "What Does Human Capital Do? A Review of Goldin and Katz's *The Race Between Education and Technology*", *Journal of Economic Literature*, 50: 426–463. However, for a critique of what he calls "the economic textbook model" concerning the race between technology and education, see Anthony B. Atkinson (2008) *The Changing Distribution of Earnings in OECD Countries* (The Rodolfo De Benedetti Lecture Series). New York: Oxford University Press. Although Atkinson acknowledges that the "textbook model" can explain changes in the relative wage of skilled to unskilled workers, he argues that the model's focus on rising demand and the lack of skilled workers is too simplistic to explain changes in income distribution, which is also influenced by different levels of skill and access to the capital market. Instead, Atkinson prefers a behavioral model that focuses on pay norms and superstars as key factors in rising income inequality.

5. Recall that we consider human capital to be the acquired skills and knowledge that distinguish *skilled* from *unskilled* labor in an economy. We also defined the human capital stock in an economy as $H = hL$, where h represents the amount of human capital per worker and L is the total number of workers. Putting these two definitions together, we can distinguish two types of workers, skilled and unskilled, whereby the human capital of skilled workers is represented by $H^S = h^S L^S$ and the human capital of unskilled workers by $H^U = h^U L^U$. By choosing units of human capital so that unskilled human capital is our basic relative unit of measure (i.e., the numeraire), we can denote $H^U = h^U = 1$. It follows that, if human capital H measures the acquired skills and knowledge of skilled relative to unskilled labor, then we have $H = H^S/H^U = h^S L^S/h^U L^U = h^S L^S/L^U$. Thus accumulated human capital H approximately measures the relative number of skilled to unskilled workers in an economy (and *vice versa*).

6. As argued by Goldin and Katz (2008), *op. cit.*, p. 96: "The short-run relative supply of more-skilled workers is assumed to be inelastic, since it is predetermined by factors such as past educational investments, immigration, and fertility." Following this view, the supply curve for human capital (skilled relative to unskilled workers) is a vertical line in Figure 7.1. This perspective also fits with our approach in Chapter 5, in which human capital is treated as a "primary factor" or an "endowment", by which it is meant that the human capital of an economy is largely a factor supply that stays within its country of origin, and though it can be increased in supply through education and other investments, it takes a long time for the skill level of the workforce to rise significantly.

7. Goldin and Katz (2008), *op. cit.*, p. 91.

8. Goldin and Katz (2008), *op. cit.*, p. 90.

9. Goldin and Katz (2008), *op. cit.*, p. 91.

10. David H. Autor and David Dorn (2013) "The Growth of Low-Skill Service Jobs and the Polarization of the US Labor Market", *American Economic Review*, 103: 1553–1597.

11. As explained by Autor and Dorn (2013), *op. cit.*, p. 1590: "We hypothesize that recent computerization has substituted for low-skill workers in performing routine tasks while complementing the abstract, creative, problem-solving, and coordination tasks performed by highly educated workers. As the declining price of computer technology has driven down the wage paid to routine tasks, low-skill workers have reallocated their labor supply to service occupations, which are difficult to automate because they rely heavily on dexterity, flexible interpersonal communication, and direct physical proximity."

12. Organization for Economic Cooperation and Development (OECD) (2011) *An Overview of Growing Income Inequalities in OECD Countries: Main Findings. Divided We Stand: Why Inequality Keeps Rising.* Paris: OECD, p. 31. The OECD member countries that were the focus of the study include: Australia, Austria, Belgium, Canada, Chile, Czech Republic, Denmark, Finland, France, Germany, Greece, Hungary, Ireland, Israel, Italy, Japan, Luxembourg, Mexico, the Netherlands, New Zealand, Norway, Portugal, Spain, Sweden, Turkey, the United Kingdom, and the United States.

13. See, for example, E. Berman and S. Machin (2000) "Skill-biased Technology Transfer Around the World", *Oxford Review of Economic Policy*, 16(3): 12–22; Florence Jaumotte, Subrir Lall and Chris Papageorgiou (2013) "Rising Income Inequality: Technology, or Trade and Financial Globalization?", *IMF Economic Review*, 61(2): 271–309; E. Lee and M. Vivarelli (eds) (2006) *Globalization, Employment, and Income Distribution in Developing Countries.* London: Palgrave Macmillan; E. Meschi and M. Vivarelli (2009) "Trade and Income Inequality in Developing Countries", *World Development*, 37: 287–302. These studies find that, increased forest direct investment from advanced to developing economies (especially middle-income economies) leads to reproducible capital accumulation and rapid adaptation of skill-biased technologies of the advanced economies. The resulting increase for demand for relatively skilled labor in developing economies may then lead to the increase in the skill premium in wages between skilled and unskilled workers, and thus widening income inequality.

14. See the studies cited in the previous note, which suggest that this effect is increasingly occurring in middle-income economies.

15. The link between overpricing of human capital, skill-biased technological change and rising wealth and income inequality is again indicated by evidence from the United States. For example, Steven N. Kaplan and Joshua Rauh (2013) "It's the Market: The Broad-Based Rise in the Return to the Top Talent", *Journal of Economic Perspectives*, 27(3): 35–56, conclude (p. 53): "Overall, we believe that our evidence remains more favorable toward the theories that root inequality in economic factors, especially skill-biased technological change, greater scale, and their interaction. Skill-biased technological change predicts that inequality will increase if technological progress raises the productivity of skilled workers relative to unskilled workers and/or raises the price of goods made by skilled workers relative to those made by unskilled workers. For example, computers and advances in information technology may complement skilled labor and substitute for unskilled labor. This seems likely to provide part, or even much, of the explanation for the increase in pay of professional athletes (technology increases their marginal product by allowing them to reach more consumers), Wall Street investors (technology allows

them to acquire information and trade large amounts more easily) and executives, as well as the surge in technology entrepreneurs in the Forbes 400. Globalization may have contributed to greater scale, but globalization cannot drive the increase in inequality at the top levels given the breadth of the phenomenon across the occupations we study."

16. For example, as noted by Goldin and Katz (2008), *op. cit.*, p. 121: "Throughout the twentieth century, as we have just seen, physical capital and more advanced technologies have been the relative complements of human capital< (by which we mean various types of skills including those gained in formal schooling)."

17. Similarly, Thomas Piketty (2014) *Capital in the Twenty-First Century.* Cambridge, MA: Harvard University Press, p. 243 maintains that the mechanisms behind unequal distribution of wealth "include the supply of and demand for different skills, the state of the educational system, and the various rules and institutions that affect the operation of the labor market and the determination of wages."

18. Goldin and Katz (2008), *op. cit.*, p. 124. It is clear from their analysis that the main driver for this technological change was "purchased electricity", which is electricity purchased from large-scale and centrally generated power plants that burned fossil fuels, which could produce electricity in large amounts and distribute it cheaply through the electricity grid system. Thus, as Goldin and Katz (2008), *op. cit.*, pp. 112–113 note, the implications for fostering skill-based technological change, and thus changing the relative demand for skilled as opposed to unskilled labor, were revolutionary: "Electricity and separate motors for each machine (termed 'unit drive') enabled firms to automate conveying and hauling operations, thereby eliminating substantial numbers of common laborers who simply moved items around the job floor. Many industries were prompted to introduce labor-saving methods with the onset of World War I, including iron and steel, brick manufacturing, pottery, portland cement, pulp and paper, rubber tires and tubes, slaughtering and meat packing, lumber manufacture and woodworking, and mining. Ample and cheap electricity rendered feasible the production of various materials, such as aluminum and other electrochemicals, which disproportionately used skilled labor. Cheap electricity also encouraged a more intensive use of machines, thereby increasing demand for the skilled personnel who maintained them. However, purchased electricity may also have been simply associated with newer factories and technological advances built into a newer capital stock."

19. See Edward B. Barbier (2011) *Scarcity and Frontiers: How Economies Have Developed Through Natural Resource Exploitation.* Cambridge and New York: Cambridge University Press, especially chapters 8 and 9.

20. Ramón López (2010) "Global Economic Crises, Environmental-resource Scarcity and Wealth Concentration", *CEPAL Review*, 102: 27–47.

21. López (2010) *op. cit.*, pp. 28 and 44.

22. According to López, the increasing concentration of wealth is critical to this outcome, because it comes at the expense of growing incomes for the middle class, which are the main sources of growing domestic demand in modern economies that are necessary to sustain high rates of business profits and economic growth. Thus, López (2010), *op. cit.*, p. 41 argues: "The dilemma was how to persuade the middle class to expand its consumption sufficiently to keep per capita GDP growing by 2–2.5% per year, when its real income was only growing at 0.3%…In these conditions, the required consumption growth could only occur if credit was plentiful and cheap, and if the middle class could be induced to accept even higher debt levels."

23. López (2010) *op. cit.*, p. 46.

24. See, for example, Facundo Alvaredo, et al. (2013) "The Top 1 Percent in International and Historical Perspective", *Journal of Economic Perspectives*, 27: 3–20, and Markus Stierli, Anthony Shorrocks, Jim Davies, Rodrigo Lluberas and Antonios Koutsoukis (2014) *Global Wealth Report 2014*. Zurich: Credit Suisse Research Institute. The ten countries with long-term wealth inequality data that are the focus of the latter report are Australia, Denmark, Finland, France, the Netherlands, Norway, Sweden, Switzerland, the United Kingdom and the United States. Alvaredo et al. (2013) also analyze long-term trends for Canada and Japan, but not Denmark, Finland, the Netherlands, Norway and Switzerland.

25. Stierli et al. (2014), *op. cit.*, p. 13.

26. Piketty (2014), *op. cit.*, pp. 193–194. See also Robin Greenwood and David Scharfstein (2013) "The Growth of Finance", *Journal of Economic Perspectives*, 27: 3–28 and Thomas Philippon and Ariell Reshef (2013) "An International Look at the Growth of Modern Finance", *Journal of Economic Perspectives*, 27(2): 73–96.

27. Greenwood and Scharfstein (2013), *op. cit.*; Thomas Philippon and Ariell Reshef (2009) "Wages and Human Capital in the U.S. Financial Industry: 1909–2006", NBER Working Paper 14644. Cambridge, MA: National Bureau of Economic Research.

28. Philippon and Reshef (2013), *op. cit.* The countries studied were Austria, Belgium, Canada, Denmark, Finland, France, Germany, Japan, The Netherlands, Sweden, the United Kingdom and the United States.

29. Philippon and Reshef (2013), *op. cit.* Interestingly, the authors find that, whereas higher relative wages in finance as well as relative wages of skilled labor within this sector are associated with information and communication technology, they are not associated with financial deregulation. Thus, there is little evidence to support the view expressed by some that global financial deregulation has been the principal cause of these relative wage rises. Instead, the evidence supports the overpricing of human capital thesis, with the main beneficiary among skilled workers in the economy appearing to be employees in the financial sector.

30. Alvaredo et al. (2013), *op. cit.*; Josh Bivens and Lawrence Mishel (2013) "The Pay of Corporate Executives and Financial Professionals as Evidence of Rents in Top 1 Percent Incomes", *Journal of Economic Perspectives*, 27: 57–78. The other source of income is commonly referred to as "earned income", which is the income received in return to work.

31. Bivens and Mishel (2013), *op. cit.*

32. Alvaredo et al. (2013), *op. cit.*

33. Bivens and Mishel (2013), *op. cit.*

34. Bivens and Mishel (2013), *op. cit.*

35. Bivens and Mishel (2013), *op. cit.*

36. Bivens and Mishel (2013), *op. cit.*, p. 66.

37. Adam Bonica, Nolan McCarty, Keith T. Poole and Howard Rosenthal (2013) "Why Hasn't Democracy Slowed Rising Inequality?", *Journal of Economic Perspectives*, 27(3): 103–124, p. 104. See also Larry Bartels (2008) *Unequal Democracy: The Political Economy of the New Gilded Age*. Princeton, NJ: Princeton University Press; Joseph E. Stiglitz (2013) *The Price of Inequality*. New York and London: W. W. Norton; Tim Echlin (2013) "The Rich Get Richer: Neoliberalism and Soaring Inequality in the United States", *Challenge*, (March–April), pp. 5–30; as well as Greenwood and Scharfstein (2013), *op. cit.*; López (2010), *op. cit.*; Philippon and Reshef (2009) and (2013), *op. cit.*; Piketty (2014), *op. cit.*

38. Bonica et al. (2013), *op. cit.*, p. 104, who also cite Philippon and Reshaf (2009), *op. cit.*

39. Goldin and Katz (2008), *op. cit.*, pp. 350–351.
40. Acemoglu and Autor (2012), *op. cit.*, pp. 458–459. The reference in this quote is to Larry Bartels (2008) *op. cit.* See also Bonica et al. (2013), *op. cit.*; Stiglitz (2013), *op. cit.* and Koechlin (2013), *op. cit.*
41. Bonica et al. (2013), *op. cit.*, p. 104.
42. These costs include tuition, fees, room and board but excludes grants or scholarships, which for four years at Yale would amount, starting the 2015–2016 academic year, to US$254,532. Other well known private institutions from around the United States have similar costs: Oberlin College $262,484, Williams College $259,612, Reed College $255,172, Harvard $249,760, Stanford $246,592, Emory $246,404, Colorado College $243,980 and Princeton $237,092. These cost data are from http://money.cnn.com/tools/collegecost/collegecost.html.
43. "Briefing: America's elite. An hereditary meritocracy", *The Economist*, 28 January 2015. Available at: http://www.economist.com/news/briefing/21640316-children-rich-and-powerful-are-increasingly-well-suited-earning-wealth-and-power.   The article cites a survey by Harvard's student newspaper, *The Crimson*, which finds that 16% of the 2,023 students accepted into Harvard in 2014 had at least one parent among the university's alumni. *The Economist* article also found that US college tuition and fees in 2014 were almost eight times higher than they were in 1982–1984; in contrast, inflation was just over two times higher.
44. Allie Bidwell, "Average Student Loan Debt Approaches $30,000", *US News and World Report*. 13 November 2014. Available at: http://www.usnews.com/news/articles/2014/11/13/average-student-loan-debt-hits-30-000
45. M. A. Fox, B. A. Connolly and T. D. Snyder (2005) "Youth Indicators 2005: Trends in the Well-Being of American Youth", Washington, DC: US Department of Education, National Center for Education Statistics, cited in Koechlin (2013), *op. cit.*, p. 16.
46. Martha J. Bailey and Susan M. Dynarski (2011) "Gains and Gaps: Changing Inequality in US College Entry and Completion", NBER Working Paper 17633, December 2011. Cambridge, MA: National Bureau of Economic Research.
47. Stierli et al. (2014), *op. cit.*, table 1 on p. 25 and p. 27.
48. Tyler Cowen (2013) *Average is Over: Powering America Beyond the Age of the Great Stagnation*. New York: Dutton, p. 233. For example, Cowen predicts that soon the wealthy will comprise 10% and possibly 15% of the population in the United States, which will make them a powerful political influence, which they will use to oppose broad-based health and educational investment policies. Thus, he argues (p. 233): "Imagine that today's millionaires comprised 10 percent of the citizenry; that make for an extraordinarily influential and politically potent group, much more so than the wealth today. Can you imagine that group funding the entire future by raising taxes on itself? I don't see it."
49. Bonica et al. (2013), *op. cit.*, pp. 104–105. Daron Acemoglu and James A. Robinson (2012) "Is This Time Different? Capture and Anti-Capture of US Politics", *The Economists' Voice*, March 2012, pp. 1–7, http://www.degruyter.com/view/j/ev refer to this process as the "inequality multiplier" (p. 4): "The result of this cocktail of changes, greater inequality, greater power for the wealthy at unchanged levels of inequality, and greater political utility of the thing the wealthy had most of – money – created a new form of 'inequality multiplier': as inequality increased the rich were able to push government regulation and policy in their favor, thus creating even more inequality. Just as in the Gilded Age, this trend threatens the inclusive nature of U.S. economic institutions."

50. Cowen (2013), *op. cit.*, pp. 233–234.
51. Stierli et al. (2014), *op. cit.*, p. 34. For some of the commentators who have expressed these concerns, see Bivens and Mishel (2013), *op. cit.*; Stiglitz (2013), *op. cit.*; Greenwood and Scharfstein (2013), *op. cit.*; López (2010), *op. cit.*; Philippon and Reshef (2009) and (2013), *op. cit.*; Piketty (2014), *op. cit.*; and Koechlin (2013), *op. cit.*
52. For example, Greenwood and Scharfstein (2012), *op. cit.*, p. 26, express the view that this process was behind the expansion of mortgage credit, which led to the financial instability that caused the 2008–2009 Great Recession: "While there may be benefits of expanding access to mortgage credit, there are a number of societal costs from such an expansion, including instability from excessive household leverage. Moreover, the shadow banking system that facilitated this expansion made the financial system more fragile. This runs counter to the traditional 'functional' view of finance, which suggests that a primary function of the financial sector is to dampen the effects of risk by reallocating it efficiently to parties that can bear risks the most easily." Similarly, Bivens and Mishel (2013), *op. cit.*, p. 65 maintain: "...we are convinced by arguments that the wider economy has not benefited from this expansion of finance and that it largely represents overpayment for financial intermediation services that more competitive markets could have delivered more efficiently. Moreover, this expansion of finance actually imposed large negative externalities on the wider economy through the increase in systemic risk that has accompanied the rise in large, complex financial institutions."
53. International Monetary Fund (IMF) (2009) *World Economic Outlook April 2009: Crisis and Recovery*. Washington, DC: IMF, p. 34
54. E. B. Barbier (2010) "Green Stimulus, Green Recovery and Global Imbalances", *World Economics*, 11(2): 149–175; R. J. Caballero and A. Krishnamurthy (2009) "Global Imbalances and Financial Fragility", *American Economic Review*, 99(2): 584–588; M. S. Feldstein (2008) "Resolving the Global Imbalance: The Dollar and the U.S. Saving Rate", *Journal of Economic Perspectives*, 22(3): 113–125; Gary Gorton and Andrew Metrick (2012) "Getting Up to Speed on the Financial Crisis: A One-Weekend-Reader's Guide", *Journal of Economic Literature*, 50(1): 128–150; IMF (2009), *op. cit.*; P. R. Lane (2009) "Forum: Global Imbalances and Global Governance", *Intereconomics*, 44(2): 77–81; López (2010), *op. cit.*
55. Thus, a sovereign wealth fund is directly related to the accumulation of surplus trade earnings by an economy, and should not be confused with foreign currency reserve assets held by monetary authorities for the traditional balance of payments or monetary policy purposes, state-owned enterprises in the traditional sense, government-employee pension funds, or assets managed for the benefit of individuals.
56. Piketty (2014), *op. cit.*, chapter 12.
57. Piketty (2014), *op. cit.*, p. 458.
58. Piketty (2014), *op. cit.*, p. 458.
59. Piketty (2014), *op. cit.*, p. 458.
60. This definition is based on J. Jalan and M. Ravallion (2002) "Geographic Poverty Traps? A Micro Model of Consumption Growth in Rural China", *Journal of Applied Econometrics*, 17: 329–346.
61. M. Ravallion, S. Chen and P. Sangraula (2007) "New Evidence on the Urbanization of Global Poverty", *Population and Development Review*, 33: 667–701.
62. Aart Kraay and David McKenzie (2014) "Do Poverty Traps Exist? Assessing the Evidence", *Journal of Economic Perspectives*, 28: 127–148.
63. World Bank (2003) *World Development Report 2003*. Washington, DC: World Bank.

64. Comprehensive Assessment of Water Management in Agriculture (2007) *Water for Food, Water for Life: A Comprehensive Assessment of Water Management in Agriculture.* London: Earthscan and International Water Management Institute, Colombo, Sri Lanka.

65. World Bank (2008) *Word Development Report 2008: Agricultural Development.* Washington, DC: The World Bank.

66. Edward B. Barbier, Ramón E. López and Jacob P. Hochard (2015) "Debt, Poverty and Resource Management in a Rural Smallholder Economy", *Environmental and Resource Economics*, published online 26 February 2015 http://link.springer.com/article/10.1007/s10640-015-9890-4>; Edward B. Barbier and Jacob P. Hochard (2014) "Poverty and the Spatial Distribution of Rural Populations", Policy Research Working Paper No. 7101. Washington, DC: The World Bank, November; and Edward B. Barbier and Jacob P. Hochard, "Land Degradation, Less Favored Lands and the Rural Poor: A Spatial and Economic Analysis", A Report for the Economics of Land Degradation Initiative, Bonn, Germany. Available at: www.eld-initiative.org

67. See, for example, the long-term trends and evidence for the United States in Autor and Dorn (2013), *op. cit.*

68. International Labor Organization (ILO) (2014) *Global Employment Trends 2014.* Geneva: ILO. Available at: http://www.ilo.org/global/research/global-reports/global-employment-trends/2014/lang – en/index.htm

69. Organization for Economic Cooperation and Development (OECD) (2014) *OECD Employment Outlook 2014.* Paris: OECD, p. 12. Available at: http://www.keepeek.com/Digital-Asset-Management/oecd/employment/oecd-employment-outlook-2014_empl_outlook-2014-en#page1. The OECD member countries are: Australia, Austria, Belgium, Canada, Chile, Czech Republic, Denmark, Finland, France, Germany, Greece, Hungary, Ireland, Israel, Italy, Japan, Luxembourg, Mexico, the Netherlands, New Zealand, Norway, Poland, Portugal, Slovakia, South Korea, Spain, Sweden, Switzerland, Turkey, the United Kingdom, and the United States.

70. Gary Burtless (2012) "Long-Term Unemployment: Anatomy of the Scourge", *The Milken Institute Review*, Third Quarter. Washington, DC: The Brookings Institute. Available at: http://www.brookings.edu/research/articles/2012/07/longterm-unemployment-burtless

71. Acemoglu and Robinson (2012), *op. cit.*

8   Redressing the Structural Imbalance

1. See, for example, Jeremy Rifkin (2011) *The Third Industrial Revolution: How Lateral Power is Transforming Energy, the Economy, and the World.* London: Palgrave Macmillan. Rifkin's positive view of innovation is based on what he calls the "five pillars of the Third Industrial Revolution": (1) shifting to renewable energy; (2) transforming the building stock of every continent into micro-power plants to collect renewable energies on-site; (3) deploying hydrogen and other storage technologies in every building and throughout the infrastructure to store intermittent energies; (4) using Internet technology to transform the power grid of every continent into an energy-sharing inter-grid that interacts in a decentralized way just like the internet; and (5) transitioning the transport fleet to electric plug-in and fuel cell vehicles that can buy and sell electricity on a smart, continental, interactive power grid.

2. See, for example, Ryan Avent, "Special report: The world economy. The third great wave", *The Economist*, 4 October, 2014, pp. 1–5.

3. A similar concern was expressed by *The Economist* magazine's special report on likely impacts on the world economy of the "digital revolution" initiated by ICT and computing innovations; for example, according to Avent (2014), *op. cit.*, p. 4: "This special report will argue that the digital revolution is opening up a great divide between a skilled and wealthy few and the rest of society. In the past new technologies have usually raised wages by boosting productivity, with the gains being split between skilled and less-skilled workers, and between owners of capital, workers and consumers. Now technology is empowering talented individuals as never before and opening up yawning gaps between the earnings of the skilled and the unskilled, capital-owners and labour. At the same time it is creating a large pool of underemployed labour that is depressing investment."

4. Robert J. Gordon (2012) "Is U.S. Economic Growth Over? Faltering Innovation Confronts the Six Headwinds." NBER Working Paper 18315. Cambridge, MA: National Bureau of Economic Research.

5. Gordon (2012), *op. cit.*, p. 11.

6. See Gordon (2012), *op. cit.*, figure 4, p. 13.

7. Gordon (2012), *op. cit.*, pp. 12–15.

8. Gordon (2012), *op. cit.*, p. 14.

9. This view has been expressed by the UNEP (2011) *Towards a Green Economy: Pathways to Sustainable Development and Poverty Eradication – A Synthesis for Policymakers.* Nairobi: UNEP. Available at: www.unep.org/greeneconomy: "This recent traction for a green economy concept has no doubt been aided by widespread disillusionment with our prevailing economic paradigm, a sense of fatigue emanating from the many concurrent crises and market failures experienced during the very first decade of the new millennium, including especially the financial and economic crisis of 2008. But at the same time, we have seen increasing evidence of a way forward, a new economic paradigm – one in which material wealth is not delivered perforce at the expense of growing environmental risks, ecological scarcities and social disparities."

10. UNEP (2011), *op. cit.*

11. Organization for Economic Cooperation and Development (OECD) (2011) *Towards Green Growth.* Paris: OECD. See also the various documents and reports available at the Green Growth Knowledge Platform, http://www.greengrowthknowledge.org/

12. See also Edward B. Barbier (2010) *A Global Green New Deal: Rethinking the Economic Recovery.* Cambridge: Cambridge University Press; Nick Robins, Robert Clover and Charanjit Singh (2009) *Taking Stock of the Green Stimulus,* 23 November, New York: HSBC Global Research; and Nick Robins, Robert Clover and D. Saravanan (2010) *Delivering the Green Stimulus,* 9 March. New York: HSBC Global Research.

13. See http://www.bls.gov/ggs/ggsoverview.htm #definition

14. Pew Charitable Trusts (2009) *The Clean Energy Economy: Repowering Jobs, Businesses and Investments Across America.* Washington, DC: Pew Charitable Trusts. In comparison, the Pew report found that the biotechnology sector employed fewer than 200,000 workers, or approximately 0.1% of total US jobs in 2007, and the fossil fuel sector, including utilities, coal mining, and oil and gas extraction, employed 1.27 million workers in 2007, or about 1% of total US jobs.

15. See the Green Goods and Services Survey of the US Bureau of Labor Statistics. http://www.bls.gov/ggs/news.htm Environmental Business International http://ebionline.org/ebj-archives/1944-ebj-v26n07–08

16. Sustainable Prosperity (2012) *Towards a Green Economy for Canada.* Ottawa: Sustainably Prosperity.

17. Environmental Careers Organization (ECO) Canada (2013) *Profile of Canadian Environmental Employment: Labour Market Research Study 2013*. Available at: https://resourcemanagementdmt.files.wordpress.com/2014/02/profile-of-canadian-environmental-employment.pdf

18. Motoko Aizawa and Chaofei Yang (2010) "Green Stimulus, Green Revolution? China's Mobilization of Banks for Environmental Change", *Journal of Environment and Development*, 19(2): 119–144; M. Ho and Z. Wang (2015) "Green Growth for China?" *Resources*, 188: 40–44; and L. Ping, Y. Danui, L. Pengfei, Y. Zhenyu and D. Zhou (2013) "A Study on Industrial Green Transformation in China", *Nota di Lavoro* 27. Milan, Italy: Fondazione Eni Enrico Mattei.

19. Barbier (2010), *op. cit.*

20. W. Cai, C. Wang, J. Chen and S. Wang (2011) "Green Economy and Green Jobs: Myth or Reality? The Case of China's Power Generation Sector", *Energy*, 36(10): 5994–6003.

21. Ho and Wang (2015), *op. cit.*

22. W.-S. Hwang, I. Oh and J.-D. Lee (2014) "The Impact of Korea's Green Growth Policies on the National Economy and Environment", *BEJ, Economic Analysis and Policy*, 14(4): 1585–1614; and Barbier (2010), *op. cit.*

23. Barbier (2010), *op. cit.*

24. Sam Fankhauser, Alex Bowen, et al. (2013) "Who Will Win the Green Race? In Search of Environmental Competitiveness and Innovation", *Global Environmental Change*, 23: 902–913.

25. Fankhauser et al. (2013), *op. cit.*

26. Fankhauser et al. (2013), *op. cit.*

27. For example, a study of the German feed-in-tariff by C. Böhringer, et al. (2014) "The Impacts of Feed-in Tariffs on Innovation: Empirical Evidence from Germany", CESIFO Working Paper No. 4680. Center for Economic Studies and Ifo Institute, Germany, March 2014 found that the subsidy did lead to a massive growth in electricity production from renewables; however, the policy did not reduce greenhouse gas emissions substantially, as renewable expansion led to too little abatement from other mitigation opportunities such as fuel switching, nor was there a significant boost to clean energy innovation.

28. Fankhauser et al. (2013), *op. cit.*, p. 903.

29. Fankhauser et al. (2013), *op. cit.*, p. 906.

30. Fankhauser et al. (2013), *op. cit.*, p. 911. Similarly, the Asian Development Bank (ADB) and Asian Development Bank Institute (ADBI) (2013) *Low-Carbon Green Growth in Asia: Policies and Practices*. Manila: ADB and ADBI, pp. 18–19 identifies "low-carbon green growth" in Asia as "a process of structural change", which envisions patterns of industrial development, specialization and innovation, "thereby defining low-carbon development as the capacity of an economy to generate new dynamic activities". Thus, a major component of this strategy is to ensure the dissemination of low-carbon and energy-saving technologies, the adaption and dissemination of these technologies throughout the economy, support for infant green firms, government procurement policies to achieve mainstream emission reduction targets, and public sector investments to support these industrial developments. In other words, the approach advocated is to enhance economy-wide "green" structural transformation through a combination of "public investment and industrial as well as trade policies, aiming at encouraging in both cases a strong private sector response".

31. See http://beforeitsnews.com/environment/2014/01/top-u-s-green-economy-trends-and-predictions-for-2014-2489240.html

32. Sustainable Prosperity (2012), *op. cit.*

33. Ho and Wang (2015), *op. cit.*

34. C. Lu, Q. Ton and X. Liu (2010) "The Impacts of Carbon Tax and Complementary Policies", *Energy Policy*, 38: 7278–7285.

35. Hwang et al. (2014), *op. cit.*

36. Sirini Withana (2015) "Overcoming Obstacles to Green Fiscal Reform", Paper for the Green Growth Knowledge Platform Third Annual Conference: Fiscal Policies and the Green Economy Transition: Generating Knowledge – Creating Impact. 29–30 January, Venice, Italy: University of Venice. Available at: http://www.greengrowth-knowledge.org/event/conference2015#node_event_full_group_event_program

37. See Edward B. Barbier and Anil Markandya (2012) *A New Blueprint for a Green Economy.* London: Routledge/Taylor Francis, pp. 114–119. The Organization of Economic Cooperation and Development tracks environmentally motivated subsidies for a number of economies at http://www2.oecd.org/ecoinst/queries/#, which is frequently updated.

38. The ten economies indicated in Table 8.2 are all members of the Group of 20 (G20) largest and most populous economies in the world. Unfortunately, there is yet no available information on environmentally motivated subsidies in the other G20 members.

39. See Edward B. Barbier (2014) "Is Green Growth Relevant for Poor Economies?", Keynote Address, 3rd International Conference: Environment and Natural Resources Management in Developing and Transition Economies, CERDI, Clermont-Ferrand, France: Clermont University, 8–10 October.

40. The reasons for this underinvestment is well known in economics: An important impetus for rapid economy-wide innovation is "technology spillovers", which occur when the inventions, designs and technologies resulting from the research and development (R&D) activities by one firm or industry spread relatively cheaply and quickly to other firms and industries. However, such technology spillovers also undermine the incentives for a private firm or industry to invest in R&D activities. The private investor bears the full costs of financing R&D, and may improve its own technologies and products as a result, but the investor receives no returns from the subsequent spread of these innovations throughout the economy. The consequence is that private firms and industries routinely underinvest in R&D, and the result is less economy-wide innovation overall.

41. Lawrence H. Goulder (2004) *Induced Technological Change and Climate Policy.* Arlington: Pew Center on Global Climate Change. See also Daron Acemoglu, Philippe Aghion, Leonardo Bursztyn and David Hemous (2012) "The Environment and Directed Technical Change", *American Economic Review*, 102(1): 131–166.

42. Acemoglu et al. (2012), *op. cit.*; ADB and ADBI (2013), *op.cit.*; Goulder (2004), *op. cit.*; Hwang et al. (2013), *op. cit.*; Lu et al. (2010), *op. cit.*; M. Blesl, T. Kober, D. Bruchof and R. Kuder (2010) "Effects of Climate and Energy Policy Related Measures and Targets on the Future Structure of the European Energy System in 2020 and Beyond", *Energy Policy*, 38: 6278–6292; Carolyn Fischer and Richard Newell (2008) "Environmental and Technology Policies for Climate Mitigation", *Journal of Environmental Economics and Management*, 55: 142–162; David Popp (2010) "Innovation and Climate Policy", NBER Working Paper 15673. Cambridge, MA: National Bureau of Economic Research.

43. Even the role of renewable energy technologies in ending the problem of global energy poverty is not straightforward. According to United Nations Development

Programme (UNDP) (2010) *Energy for a Sustainable Future: The Secretary-General's Advisory Group on Energy and Climate Change, Summary Report and Recommendations.* New York: UNDP, more than 1.5 billion people live without access to electricity, another billion have only unreliable electricity, and nearly half the world's population depends on traditional biomass fuels for cooking and heating. J. Rogelj, D. L. McCollum and K. Riahi (2013) "The UN's 'Sustainable Energy for All' initiative is compatible with a warming limit of 2°C", *Nature Climate Change*, 3: 545–551, examined the compatibility of achieving three global energy objectives by 2030: providing reliable access to electricity or clean fuels for cooking, or both, to three billion poor people currently without such access; doubling the share of renewable energy in final energy, from 15% to 30%; and doubling the rate of energy efficiency in all economies. The analysis found that ensuring universal access to modern energy services was not only attainable with overall climate mitigation strategies for limiting global warming to 2°C but also was fully consistent with the 2030 energy efficiency objective. The only goal not achieved was for renewable energy, which comprised just 28% of final energy by 2030, because energy access for cooking and heating is provided mainly by switching from biomass to low-pollution fossil fuel alternatives rather than renewables. One also has to be careful in assuming that solar and other renewable energy sources are more financially feasible for the rural poor in remote areas. According to C. E. Casillas and D. M. Kammen (2010) "The Energy-Poverty-Climate Nexus", *Science*, 330: 1181–1182, the use of community-level marginal abatement cost curves in rural Nicaragua indicates that the options for replacing off-grid diesel generation of electricity, which is the main method of expanding rural energy services, can vary considerably in cost. For example, solar photovoltaic electricity would cost villagers over $300 per tCO_2/year conserved, whereas energy efficiency measures, such as meter installation, compact fluorescent lights (CFL) and more effective public lighting, actually save households almost $400 per tCO_2/year mitigated.

9   Making the Transition

1. IEA/OPEC/OECD/World Bank (2010) *Analysis of the Scope of Energy Subsidies and the Suggestions for the G-20 Initiative.* Joint Report Prepared for Submission to the G-20 summit Meeting Toronto (Canada), 26–27 June 2010.
2. This means that for every dollar earned in revenues by OECD farms, 18 cents came from some kind of agricultural subsidy. Organization for Economic Cooperation and Development (OECD) (2014) *Agricultural Policy Monitoring and Evaluation 2014 – OECD Countries.* Paris: OECD,. The OECD member countries include: Australia, Austria, Belgium, Canada, Chile, Czech Republic, Denmark, Estonia, Finland, France, Germany, Greece, Hungary, Iceland, Ireland, Israel, Italy, Japan, South Korea, Luxembourg, Mexico, The Netherlands, New Zealand, Norway, Poland, Portugal, Slovak Republic, Slovenia, Spain, Sweden, Switzerland, Turkey, United Kingdom and United States. In fact, the agricultural subsidy rate for some individual countries is extremely high. According to OECD (2014), *op. cit.* in the European Union, producer support is around 20% of gross farm receipts, and the share is even larger for Japan (56%), South Korea (53%), Norway (53%), Switzerland (49%) and Iceland (41%). The European Union (EU) estimate is for the 27 members; i.e., it excludes Croatia, which joined on 1 July 2013. The 27 EU members are: Austria, Belgium, Bulgaria, Cyprus, Czech Republic, Denmark, Estonia, Finland, France, Germany, Greece, Hungary,

Ireland, Italy, Latvia, Lithuania, Luxembourg, Malta, the Netherlands, Poland, Portugal, Romania, Slovakia, Slovenia, Spain, Sweden and United Kingdom.

3. Grant Potter (2014) "Agricultural subsidies remain a staple in the industrial world", *Vital Signs*. The World Watch Institute. 28 February 2014. Available at: http://vitalsigns.worldwatch.org/vs-trend/agricultural-subsidies-remain-staple-industrial-world

4. Potter (2014), *op. cit.* In addition, it is the mainly rich and large emerging market economies in Asia, Europe and North America that account for 94% of global agricultural subsidies, with only 6% spent in the rest of the world. Thus the subsidies are highly inequitable.

5. United Nations Environmental Programme (UNEP) (2011) *Towards a Green Economy: Pathways to Sustainable Development and Poverty Eradication – A Synthesis for Policymakers*. Nairobi: UNEP.

6. Ussif Rashid Sumaila, et al. (2010) "Subsidies to High Seas Bottom Trawl Fleets and the Sustainability of Deep-Sea Demersal Fish Stocks", *Marine Policy*, 34: 495–497. As the authors estimate the profit earned by bottom trawl fleets is normally not more than 10% of landed value, removal of their subsidies will stop the activities of many of these fleets worldwide, thereby reducing the current threat to deep-sea and high seas fish stocks.

7. Edward B. Barbier and Anil Markandya (2012) *A New Blueprint for a Green Economy*. Routledge/Taylor & Francis: London, pp. 113–118.

8. C. Böhringer, et al. (2014) "The Impacts of Feed-in Tariffs on Innovation: Empirical Evidence from Germany", CESIFO Working Paper No. 4680. Center for Economic Studies and Ifo Institute, Germany, March.

9. Barbier and Markandya (2012), *op. cit.*, chapter 6. The Organization of Economic Cooperation and Development tracks a variety of environmental market-based instruments for a number of high-income and emerging market economies at http://www2.oecd.org/ecoinst/queries/#, which is frequently updated.

10. Barbier and Markandya (2012), *op. cit.*, chapter 6.

11. Benedict Clements, et al. (eds) (2013) *Energy Subsidy Reform: Lessons and Implications*. Washington, DC: International Monetary Fund (IMF). For a further comprehensive study of the overall economic, environmental and health benefits of ending the underpricing of fossil fuels globally, see Ian Parry, Dirk Heine, Eliza Lis and Shanjun Li (2014) *Getting Prices Right: From Principle to Practice*. Washington, DC: International Monetary Fund.

12. Ariel Dinar and R. M. Saleth (2005) "Water Institutional Reforms: Theory and Practice", *Water Policy*, 7: 1–19; C. Dosi and K. W. Easter (2003) "Water Scarcity: Market Failure and the Implications for Water Markets and Privatization", *International Journal of Public Administration*, 26(3): 265–290; K. W. Easter, and S. Archibald (2002) "Water Markets: The Global Perspective", *Water Resources Impact*, 4(1): 23–25; K. Schoengold and D. Zilberman (2007) "The Economics of Water, Irrigation, and Development", in Robert Evenson and Prabhu Pingali (eds), *Handbook of Agricultural Economics*, vol. III. Amsterdam: Elsevier, pp. 2933–2977.

13. Richard D. Horan and James S. Shortle (2011) "Economic and Ecological Rules for Water Quality Trading", *Journal of the American Water Resources Association*, 47: 59–69.

14. Organization for Economic Cooperation and Development (OECD) (2010) *Paying for Biodiversity: Enhancing the Cost-Effectiveness of Payments for Ecosystem Services*. Paris: OECD.

15. In effect, the outputs of R&D activities that generate technology spillovers are *non-rival*, meaning that, once they are available to one firm or industry to use, the product is available to all others to use simultaneously.

16. Lawrence H. Goulder (2004) *Induced Technological Change and Climate Policy*. Arlington: Pew Center on Global Climate Change. See also Daron Acemoglu, et al. (2012) "The Environment and Directed Technical Change", *American Economic Review*, 102(1): 131–166.

17. Acemoglu et al. (2012), *op. cit.*; Goulder (2004), *op. cit.*; Asian Development Bank (ADB) and Asian Development Bank Institute (ADBI) (2013) *Low-Carbon Green Growth in Asia: Policies and Practices*. Manila: ADB and ADBI; W.-S. Hwang, I. Oh and J.-D. Lee (2014) "The Impact of Korea's Green Growth Policies on the National Economy and Environment", *BEJ. Economic Analysis and Policy*, 14(4): 1585–1614; C. Lu, Q. Ton and X. Liu (2010) "The Impacts of Carbon Tax and Complementary Policies", *Energy Policy*, 38: 7278–7285; M. Blesl, et al. (2010) "Effects of Climate and Energy Policy Related Measures and Targets on the Future Structure of the European Energy System in 2020 and Beyond", *Energy Policy*, 38: 6278–6292; Carolyn Fischer and Richard Newell (2008) "Environmental and Technology Policies for Climate Mitigation", *Journal of Environmental Economics and Management*, 55: 142–162; David Popp (2010) "Innovation and Climate Policy", NBER Working Paper 15673. Cambridge, MA: National Bureau of Economic Research.

18. Harry Huizinga, Wolf Wagner and Johannes Voget "Lessons from the taxation of cross-border banking for new financial taxes." *VoxEU.org*, 11 July 2011. Available at: http://www.voxeu.org/article/why-banks-are-under-taxed-and-what-do-about-it. See also Harry Huizinga, Johannes Voget, and Wolf Wagner (2014) "International Taxation and Cross-Border Banking", *American Economic Journal: Economic Policy*, 6(2): 94–125.

19. *Innovation With Impact: Financing 21st Century Development*. A Report by Bill Gates to G20 leaders, Cannes summit, November 2011. http://www.thegatesnotes.com/Topics/Development/G20-Report-Innovation-with-Impact

20. P. B. Spahn (2010) "A Double Dividend", *The Broker*, 22(Oct/Nov): 8–14.

21. Thornton Matheson (2011) "Taxing Financial Transactions: Issues and Evidence", IMF Working Paper WP/11/54. Washington, DC: International Monetary Fund, March 2011.

22. See http://ec.europa.eu/taxation_customs/taxation/other_taxes/financial_sector/index_en.htm for further details on the following discussion and estimates of the implementation of the European Commission's proposed financial transaction tax (FTT). The 11 European Union countries that have agreed to implement an FTT by the end of 2016 are: Austria, Belgium, Estonia, France, Germany, Greece, Italy, Portugal, Slovakia, Slovenia and Spain.

23. Matheson (2011), *op. cit.*; John Grahl and Photis Lysandorij (2014) "The European Commission's Proposal for a Financial Transactions Tax: A Critical Assessment", *Journal of Common Market Studies*, 52(2): 234–249; Thornton Matheson (2012) "Security Transaction Taxes: Issues and Evidence", *International Journal of Tax and Public Finance*, 19: 884–912; Richard T. Page (2010) "Foolish Revenge or Shrewd Regulation? Financial-Industry Tax Law Reforms Proposed in the Wake of the Financial Crisis", *Tulane Law Review*, 85: 191–214; Daniel Shaviro (2012) "The Financial Transactions Tax versus (?) The Financial Activities Tax", Law & Economics Research Paper Series Working Paper No. 12–04. New York University School of Law, March 2012.

24. International Monetary Fund (IMF) (2010) *A Fair and Substantial Contribution by the Financial Sector.* Final Report for the G-20, June, Washington DC: IMF.. Available at: http://www.imf.org/external/np/g20/pdf/062710b.pdf

25. For example, the IMF (2010), *op. cit.* estimated that, during the 2008–2009 financial crisis that led to the Great Recession, the fiscal cost of direct support to financial institutions averaged 2.8% of gross domestic (GDP) for the advanced Group of 20 (G20) countries. In those most affected, however, costs were on the order of 4–6% of GDP. Amounts pledged, including guarantees and other contingent liabilities, averaged 25% of GDP during the crisis. In addition, government debt in advanced G20 countries was projected to rise by almost 40 percentage points of GDP during 2008–2015.

26. Thus, the IMF and other proponents of the FAT argue that it is a better and less distortive tax compared to a financial transaction tax (FTT) for raising revenue from the financial sector. According to Matheson (2011), *op. cit.*, p. 75, "...insofar as an FAT taxes net value added rather than the gross value of transactions, it should be less distortionary than an FTT in raising a given amount of revenue. Because an FTT is levied on gross transaction value while the FAT is levied only on the value added by the financial institutions, the FTT rate necessary to raise the same revenue as an FAT would be much lower. However, despite having a higher rate the FAT would be less distortive because it would cause less cascading." The cascading effect of an FTT occurs when the financial asset is traded heavily, thus imposing multiple layers of tax on some transactions. This means that even an apparently low-rate FTT might result in a high tax burden on some activities that trade an asset many times over. See also comparisons between FATs and FTTs by Grahl and Lysandorij (2014), *op. cit.*; IMF (2010), *op. cit.*; Page (2010), *op. cit.*; and Shaviro (2012), *op. cit.*

27. As pointed out by Huizinga et al. (2011), *op. cit.*, a well-designed financial activities tax should be levied at comparable rates internationally, cover all bank-like financial institutions in a country, and apply only to financial-sector income generated domestically, thus exempting foreign-source, financial-sector income from domestic taxation. These recommendations are supported by the authors' recent study on international taxation and cross-border banking, Huizinga et al. (2014), *op. cit.*

28. The imposition of a 5% financial activities tax (FAT) in Table 9.2 is very modest. In most countries, economy-wide value-added taxes (VAT) are much higher, and imposing an FAT equivalent to VAT rates would raise more revenue. For example, in Germany the VAT is 19%. Thiese Büttner and Katharina Erbe (2013) "FAT or VAT? The Financial Activities Tax as a Substitute to Imposing Value Added Tax on Financial Services", Beiträge zur Jahrestagung des Vereins für Socialpolitik 2013: Wettbewerbspolitik und Regulierung in einer globalen Wirtschaftsordnung – Session: Taxation II, No. B06-V3, available at: https://www.econstor.eu/dspace/bitstream/10419/79959/1/VfS_2013_pid_23.pdf, estimate that an FAT of 19% in Germany would raise €7.655 billion, or US$8.28 billion annually.

29. Claudia Goldin and Lawrence F. Katz (2008) *The Race Between Education and Technology.* Cambridge: Harvard University Press.

30. These include loans originated under the Federal Family Education Loan Program and the Direct Loan Program, Perkins loans and private student loans without government guarantees. The estimates are from the Board of Governors of the Federal Reserve System, Consumer Credit – G.10. Available at: http://www.federalreserve.gov/releases/g19/Current/#table3

31. Büttner and Katharina Erbe (2013), *op. cit.*

32. See Edward B. Barbier (2011) *Scarcity and Frontiers: How Economies Have Developed Through Natural Resource Exploitation.* Cambridge: Cambridge University Press.
33. Gavin Wright and Jesse Czelusta (2004) "Why Economies Slow: The Myth of the Resource Curse", *Challenge*, 47(2): 6–38, pp. 34–36.
34. Ronald Findlay and Mats Lundahl (1999) "Resource-Led Growth – A Long-Term Perspective: The Relevance of the 1870–1914 Experience for Today's Developing Economies", UNU/WIDER Working Paper No. 162. Helsinki: WIDER, pp. 31–32.
35. Paul A. David and Gavin Wright (1997) "The Genesis of American Resource Abundance", *Industrial and Corporate Change*, 6: 203–245.
36. Wright and Czelusta (2004), *op. cit.*
37. For further discussion of the long-run natural resource management and development strategies of Botswana, Malaysia and Thailand, see in particular Barbier (2011), *op. cit.*; Edward B. Barbier (2005) *Natural Resources and Economic Development.* Cambridge, UK: Cambridge University Press; Ian Coxhead and Sisira Jayasuriya (2003) *The Open Economy and the Environment: Development, Trade and Resources in Asia.* Northampton, MA: Edward Elgar; Atsushi Iimi (2007) "Escaping from the Resource Curse: Evidence from Botswana and the Rest of the World", *IMF Staff Papers*, 54: 663–699. Glenn-Marie Lange and Matthew Wright (2004) "Sustainable Development and Mineral Economies: The Example of Botswana", *Environment and Development Economics*, 9(4): 485–505; Maria Sarraf and Moortaza Jiwanji (2001) "Beating the Resource Curse: The Case of Botswana", *Environmental Economics Series.* The World Bank Environment Department. Washington DC: The World Bank; and Jeffrey R. Vincent, Razali M. Ali and Associates (1997) *Environment and Development in a Resource-Rich Economy: Malaysia under the New Economic Policy.* Harvard Institute for International Development: Harvard University Press. However, it should also be noted that, in all three economies, important sectors and populations have yet to gain significantly from improving the sustainability of the main primary producing sectors. In Malaysia, there is concern about the continuing destruction of forests, especially in the more remote Sabah and Sarawak Provinces, and the expansion of oil palm plantations. In Thailand, the loss of mangroves, growing pollution problems and the failure to instigate development in upland regions are major issues. Botswana has still to grapple with a stagnant agricultural sector, large numbers of people living in fragile environments and widespread rural poverty. Finding ways to broaden the economy-wide benefits and improve the sustainability of resource-dependent economies is an ongoing challenge for such small open economies.
38. Barbier (2005) and (2011), *op. cit.*; Sarraf and Jiwanji (2001), *op. cit.*; Thorvaldur Gylfason (2001) "Nature, Power, and Growth", *Scottish Journal of Political Economy*, 48(5): 558–588; Frederick van der Ploeg (2011) "Natural Resources: Curse or Blessing?", *Journal of Economic Literature*, 49: 366–420.
39. Sarraf and Jiwanji (2001), *op. cit*, p. 3.
40. Edward B. Barbier (2012) "Natural Capital, Ecological Scarcity and Rural Poverty", Policy Research Working Paper No. 6232. Washington, DC: The World Bank, October.
41. World Bank (2008) *Word Development Report 2008: Agricultural Development.* Washington DC: The World Bank.
42. C. Elbers, T. Fujii, P. Lanjouw, B. Özler and W. Yin (2007) "Poverty Alleviation Through Geographic Targeting: How Much Does Disaggregation Help?", *Journal of Development Economics*, 83: 198–213.

43. D. Coady, M. Grosh and J. Hoddinott (2004) "Targeting Outcomes Redux", *World Bank Research Observer*, 19(1): 61–85.
44. K. Higgins, K. Bird and D. Harris (2010) "Policy Responses to the Spatial Dimensions of Poverty", ODI Working Paper 328. London: Overseas Development Institute, p. 20.
45. Barbier (2005), *op. cit.*; Barbier, E. B. (2010) "Poverty, Development and Environment", *Environment and Development Economics*, 15: 635–660. David Carr (2009) "Population and Deforestation: Why Rural Migration Matters", *Progress in Human Geography*, 33: 355–378. Jill L. Caviglia-Harris and D. Harris (2008) "Integrating Survey and Remote Sensing Data to Analyze Land Use Scale: Insights from Agricultural Households in the Brazilian Amazon", *International Regional Science Review*, 31: 115–137. Ian Coxhead, Gerald E. Shively and X. Shuai (2002) "Development Policies, Resource Constraints, and Agricultural Expansion on the Philippine Land Frontier", *Environment and Development Economics*, 7: 341–364. S. Dercon, et al. (2009) "The Impact of Agricultural Extension and Roads on Poverty and Consumption Growth in Fifteen Ethiopian Villages", *American Journal of Agricultural Economics*, 91: 1007–1021. M. Maertens, M. Zeller and R. Birner (2006) "Sustainable Agricultural Intensification in Forest Frontier Areas", *Agricultural Economics*, 34: 197–206.
46. Coxhead et al. (2002), *op. cit.*; Dercon et al. (2009), *op. cit.*; Maertens et al. (2006), *op. cit.*; M. R. Bellon, et al. (2005) "Targeting Agricultural Research to Benefit Poor Farmers: Relating Poverty Mapping to Maize Environments in Mexico", *Food Policy*, 30: 476–492; A. Dillon, M. Sharma and X. Zhang (2011) "Estimating the Impact of Rural Investments in Nepal", *Food Policy*, 36: 250–258. Erin Sills and Jill L. Caviglia-Harris (2008) "Evolution of the Amazonian Frontier: Land Values in Rondônia, Brazil", *Land Use Policy*, 26: 55–67.
47. World Bank (2008), *op. cit.*; Christopher B. Barrett (2008) "Smallholder Market Participation: Concepts and Evidence from Eastern and Southern Africa", *Food Policy*, 33: 299–317.
48. Bellon et al. (2005), *op. cit.*; Dercon et al. (2009), *op. cit.*; Dillon et al. (2011), *op. cit.*; A. Ansoms and A. McKay (2010) "A Quantitative Analysis of Poverty and Livelihood Profiles: The Case of Rural Rwanda", *Food Policy*, 35: 584–598. B. Cunguara and I. Darnhofer (2011) "Assessing the Impact of Improved Agricultural Technologies on Household Income in Rural Mozambique", *Food Policy*, 36: 378–390. D. Müller and Z. Zeller (2002) "Land Use Dynamics in the Central Highlands of Vietnam: A Spatial Model Combining Village Survey Data with Satellite Imagery Interpretation", *Agricultural Economics*, 27: 333–354. S. K. Pattanayak, et al. (2003) "Taking stock of agroforestry adoption studies", *Agroforestry Systems*, 57: 173–186. T. Yamano and Y. Kijima (2010) "The Association of Soil Fertility and Market Access with Household Income: Evidence from Rural Uganda", *Food Policy*, 35: 51–59.
49. Müller and Zeller (2002), *op. cit.*
50. S. V. Lall, H. Selod and Z. Shalizi (2006) "Rural–Urban Migration in Developing Countries: A Survey of Theoretical Predictions and Empirical Findings", World Bank Policy Research Working Paper 3915, May 2006. Washington DC: The World Bank, p. 48.
51. See, for example, C. L. Gray (2009) "Rural Out-Migration and Smallholder Agriculture in the Southern Ecuadorian Andes", *Population and Environment*, 30: 193–217. C. Greiner and P. Sakdapolrak (2013) "Rural–Urban Migration, Agrarian Change, and the Environment in Kenya: A Critical Review of the Literature", *Population and Environment*, 34: 524–533. M. Mendola (2008) "Migration and

Technological Change in Rural Households: Complements or Substitutes?", *Journal of Development Economics*, 85: 150–175. M. Mendola (2012) "Review Article: Rural Out-Migration and Economic Development at Origin: A Review of the Evidence", *Journal of International Development*, 24: 102–122. L. K. VanWey, G. R. Guedes and A. O. D'Antona (2012) "Out-Migration and Land-Use Change in Agricultural Frontiers: Insights from Altamira Settlement Project", *Population and Environment*, 34: 44–68.

52. World Bank (2008), *op.cit.*, p. 49.

53. For an excellent summary of the US–China bilateral agreement, see David Biello (2014) "Everything You Need to Know about the U.S.–China Climate Change Agreement", *Scientific American*. 12 November. Available at: http://www.scientificamerican.com/article/everything-you-need-to-know-about-the-u-s-china-climate-change-agreement/

54. For example, Biello (2014), *op. cit.* states: "The agreement between the two countries that together emit more than 40% of global CO_2 pollution suggests a strong deal will be signed by the world's nations in Paris in 2015, under the terms of the United Nations Framework Convention on Climate Change."

55. See Edward B. Barbier "A 2x4x20 Climate Change Agreement", *Triple Crisis*, 23 December 2014. Available at: http://triplecrisis.com/a-2-x-4-x-20-climate-change-agreement/. For the economic arguments as to why increasing economic ties between the US and China fosters their mutual interest to negotiate a bilateral deal on reducing greenhouse gas emissions, see J. Gwatipedza and E. B. Barbier (2014) "Environmental Regulation of a Global Pollution Externality in a Bilateral Trade Framework: The Case of Global Warming, China and the US", *Economics: The Open-Access, Open-Assessment E-Journal*, http://dx.doi.org/10.5018/economics-ejournal. ja.2014–30 There are no page numbers for this open access journal; this is the correct citation: Gwatipedza, J. and E.B. Barbier. 2014. "Environmental Regulation of a Global Pollution Externality in a Bilateral Trade Framework: The Case of Global Warming, China and the US." *Economics: The Open-Access, Open-Assessment E-Journal* 8 (2014–30). http://dx.doi.org/10.5018/economics-ejournal.ja.2014–30

56. According to "G20 Facts and Figures", the G20 economies account for around 90% of the global economy, 80% of international trade, and 75% of the world population. See also Chapter 3.

57. David W. Pearce (2007) "Do We Really Care About Biodiversity?" *Environmental and Resource Economics*, 37: 313–333.

58. For further discussion, see Edward B. Barbier (2012) "Can Global Payments for Ecosystem Services Work?", *World Economics*, 13: 157–172.

59. See Barbier (2012), "Can Global Payments", *op. cit.* for further explanation and discussion.

60. Edward B. Barbier (2012) "Tax 'Societal Ills' to Save the Planet", *Nature*, 483: 30, P. 30 is the correct page number (it is a single-page article).

61. United Nations Development Programme (UNDP) (2006) *Human Development Report 2006. Beyond Scarcity: Power, Poverty and the Global Water Crisis.* New York: UNDP.

62. R. E. Just and S. Netanyahu (1998) "International Water Resource Conflicts: Experience and Potential", chapter 1 in R. E. Just and S. Netanyahu (eds), *Conflict and Cooperation on Transboundary Water Resources*, Kluwer Academic Publishers, Boston, pp. 1–26.

63. E. Stephen Draper and James E. Kundell (2007) "Impact of Climate Change on Trans-Boundary Water Sharing", *Journal of Water Resources Planning and Management*, 133(5): 405–415.

64. Meredith A. Giordano and Aaron T. Wolf (2003) "Sharing Waters: Post-Rio International Water Management", *Natural Resources Forum*, 27: 163–171; Aaron T. Wolf (2007) "Shared Waters: Conflict and Cooperation", *Annual Review of Environment and Resources*, 32: 3.1–3.29.
65. Wolf (2007), *op. cit.*
66. UNDP (2006), *op. cit.*
67. Anik Bhaduri and Edward B. Barbier (2008) "International Water Transfer and Sharing: The Case of the Ganges River", *Environment and Development Economics*, 13: 29–51.
68. Edward B. Barbier and Anik Bhaduri (2015) "Transboundary Water Issues", Chapter 18 in Robert Halvorsen and David Layton (eds), *Handbook on the Economics of Natural Resources*. Edward Elgar: Cheltenham, pp. 502–528.

Conclusion

1. Of course, World War I, the Great Depression of the 1930s and World War II disrupted the steady progress in growth and natural resource use in the world economy. However, outside these periods of economic dislocation, the general pattern of long-run productivity growth, skill-biased technological change and increased resource and energy use continued. See, for example, Edward B. Barbier (2011) *Scarcity and Frontiers: How Economies Have Developed Through Natural Resource Exploitation*. Cambridge and New York: Cambridge University Press; and Claudia Goldin and Lawrence F. Katz (2008) *The Race Between Education and Technology*. Cambridge: Harvard University Press.
2. The members of the Group of 20 (G20) include 19 countries (Argentina, Australia, Brazil, Canada, China, France, Germany, India, Indonesia, Italy, Japan, Mexico, Russia, Saudi Arabia, South Africa, South Korea, Turkey, the UK and the US), plus the European Union.
3. According to the mid-range projections of the United Nations, the world population of 7.2 billion in mid-2013 is projected to increase by almost one billion people within the next twelve years, reaching 8.1 billion in 2025, and to further increase to 9.6 billion in 2050 and 10.9 billion by 2100. See United Nations Department of Social and Economic Affairs (UN DESA) (2013) *World Population Prospects: The 2012 Revision. Volume I: Comprehensive Tables*. New York: United Nations. Available at: http://esa.un.org/wpp/Documentation/pdf/WPP2012_Volume-I_Comprehensive-Tables.pdf
4. Tyler Cowen (2013) *Average is Over: Powering America Beyond the Age of the Great Stagnation*. New York: Dutton, pp. 229–230.
5. Stierli et al. (2014), *op. cit.*, p. 13.
6. United Nations Environment Programme (UNEP) (2012) *Renewable Resources and Conflict. Toolkit and Guidance for Preventing and Managing Land and Natural Resources Conflict*. Nairobi: UNEP Available at: http://www.un.org/en/events/environment-conflictday/pdf/GN_Renewable_Consultation.pdf

Index

Acemoglu, Daron, 157
adjusted net national income (ANNI)
    defined, 50, 57, 120
    developing countries, 66–7
    ecological capital, 95–7, 99–100
    human capital, 102, 120–2
    measurement, 56–8, 72, 99–100, 120–2
    natural capital depreciation, 56–8
    resource dependency, 63–4, 68
    subsidies and underpricing of fossil
        fuels, 127–9
adjusted net savings (ANS), 63
    defined, 79
    Group of 20 economies, 75
    measurement, 78–80
    resource dependency, 64–5, 67
Age of Ecological Scarcity, 81, 94
agricultural land
    less favored and remote, 3, 120,
        143, 162–3, 178, 182–3, 196–201,
        210
    share of wealth, 15, 44–8, 55
Agricultural Transition, 13–14
ancient civilizations, 14, 18
Aristophanes, 14
Arthaśāstra, the, 15
Atlantic economy triangular trade, 26–7,
    29
Australia
    distribution of wealth, 153, 155
    environmentally motivated subsidies,
        179
    financial activities tax, 194
    financial expansion, 53–4, 155
    frontier expansion, 36–8, 46
    green stimulus, 173, 177
    greenhouse gas emissions, 68, 70–5
    human capital investment, 104–5
    natural resource use, 37
    rate of natural capital depreciation, 51
    underpricing of fossil fuels, 128
    water markets, 136
Autor, David, 146, 157

Bairoch, Paul, 23
Balanced Wealth Strategy, 3, 8, 166, 169,
    180–3, 184, 208, 211
    four key elements of, 8, 181, 184
Bank levy, 192, 193, 195–6
Barbier, Edward, 20, 25–6, 96, 131, 173,
    197, 205
Barro, Robert, 106
Beijing, China
    air pollution, 1–2
biological diversity (biodiversity)
    decline, 3, 94
Bivens, Josh, 155–6
Bonica, Adam, 157
Brazil
    agricultural subsidies, 186
    distribution of wealth, 153
    emerging market economy, 44, 70
    greenhouse gas emissions, 68, 70–5
    natural resource use, 25, 44
    underpricing of fossil fuels, 128
    water markets, 136

Canada
    distribution of wealth, 153, 155
    environmentally motivated subsidies,
        179
    financial activities tax, 194
    financial expansion, 53–4, 155
    green economy development, 174, 176
    green stimulus, 173, 177
    greenhouse gas emissions, 68–75
    human capital investment, 104–5
    natural resource use, 25
    rate of natural capital depreciation, 51
    underpricing of fossil fuels, 127–8
    water markets, 136, 189
carbon pricing, 180, 183, 191
carbon taxes, 135, 177, 190, 203, 204, 205
carbon-dependent development, 60,
    68–76, 84, 119, 125–6, 134
    global warming, 60, 70–4, 76
    wealth accumulation, 75, 78

China
  agricultural subsidies, 186
  air pollution, 1–2, 126, 129
  climate change agreement with US, 202
  current account surplus, 160
  distribution of wealth, 153
  emerging market economy, 69, 70
  empires, 16, 18–21, 23–4, 32, 37
  green economy development, 174–5,
    176–7
  green stimulus, 173–4, 177, 180
  greenhouse gas emissions, 68, 71–5
  natural resource use, 44, 46
  underpricing of fossil fuels, 127–9, 188
  water markets, 136
climate change, 7, 60, 76, 78, 93–4, 118,
    123, 127–8, 140, 165, 168–9, 180,
    183–4, 188, 201–11
consumption of domestic fixed capital,
    57, 79, 100, 122
Cowen, Tyler, 158, 210
Credit Suisse
  2014 Global Wealth Report, 152, 153,
    158, 159–60
currency transaction tax (CTT), 192, 205
Czeulusta, Jesse, 198

Daily, Gretchen, 86
developing countries (low and middle-
    income economies)
  air pollution, 129
  Balanced Wealth Strategy, 8, 181, 182,
    184, 196–201
  carbon mitigation policies, 136, 203
  climate change, 76
  ecosystem services, 77, 97, 132–3,
    204–5
  freshwater availability, 189
  green growth, 178, 180
  greenhouse gas emissions, 68
  human capital, 103–7
  innovation and technical change, 146, 148
  land use change, 44–7, 93, 115, 118,
    139, 203
  market-based incentives, 188
  natural capital, 79, 98, 113–16
  rate of natural capital depreciation,
    50–1, 57, 103, 113
  resource-dependent, 5, 59, 60–8, 77, 84,
    114, 134, 180, 182, 184

resource-poor, 44
rural poverty, 3, 120, 132, 143, 159,
    162–3, 182, 210
transboundary water resources,
    206
underpricing of fossil fuels, 127
urban growth, 77, 162
urban poverty, 129, 143, 159, 162, 210
division of labor and specialization, 15
Dorn, David, 146

ecological capital, 82–3, 86–7
  accounting for, 95–7, 99–100, *see also*
    Adjusted Net National Income
  decline of, 84–5, 89–94
  defined, 1, 11, 81, 86
  as a factor endowment, 109, 118
  form of wealth, 82–3, 86
  underpricing, 102
  uniqueness compared to other assets, 81
ecological scarcity, 5, 82–6
  defined, 84
  global market failure, 183, 201, 207,
    211
  increasing, 85–6, 89–94, 97–9, 118, 166,
    209
  institutional inertia, 134
  structural imbalance, 5–6, 101, 109,
    118, 134, 151, 168–9
  vicious cycle, 120, 123–5, 140
economic wealth, 11, 82–3
  defined, 11
  structure of production and, 107–9
ecosystem
  as an asset, 85, *see also* ecological
    capital
  defined, 87–8
  structure and functions, 87–9
ecosystem goods and services (ecosystem
    services), 86–9, 98
  defined, 86, 88
  payment for, 183, 186, 188–9, 202, 203,
    204–5
  underpricing of, 98–9, 129–33
education
  attainment, 106–7, 116, 147
  expenditures, 103–5, 110, 117, *see also*
    human capital, accumulation of
  race with technology, *see* race between
    education and technology

energy
  global consumption, 33, 55, 60, 77, 208
  nuclear, 4, 33, 166, 173, 208
  renewable, 4, 33, 165, 166, 170, 172,
    173, 174–6, 187, 208
England, *see* United Kingdom
environmental degradation
  excessive, 3, 101, 124, 140, 168
  vicious cycle of, 123–5
environmentally harmful (damaging)
    subsidies, 125–6, 135, 137, 140, 177,
    181, 185–7, 189, 191
environmentally motivated subsidies,
    178–9, 181, 185, 187, 189
European Union
  climate change agreement, 202
  financial transactions tax, 192
  G20 member, 70
  green stimulus, 173–4
  greenhouse gas emissions, 70–5, 202
  underpricing of fossil fuels, 128

factor endowment, 108–10
Fankhauser, Sam, 175–6
finance
  rise of, 50–5
  skill intensity of, 155–6
financial activities tax (FAT), 192, 193–4,
    196
financial assets (capital)
  defined, 10–11, 82
  excessive returns, 6, 163, 169, 193
  share of wealth, 53–4, 56
financial stability condition, 193
financial transactions tax (FTT), 192–3,
    205
Findlay, Ron, 36
first global capital boom, 52
fossil fuel era, *see also* Industrial
    Revolution
  defined, 4
  dependency of economies, 125–6, 171
  spread of industrialization, 33–4, 39,
    55, 68, 149–50, 166, 171, 208
  transition out of, 181, 185, 209, 211
fossil fuels
  and industrialization, 4–5, 33–4, 39, 55,
    68, 150, 166, 208
  subsidies, 127–8, 186–7, 189
  underpricing, 125, 126–9, 139, 178, 188

use, 4, 31–4, 36–7, 40–4, 48–50, 60, 68,
    77, 81, 84, 101, 118, 125–6, 140,
    150, 171, 208
France
  agricultural land share of wealth, 48
  distribution of wealth, 153, 155
  empires, 24, 25
  environmentally motivated subsidies,
    179
  financial activities tax, 194
  financial expansion, 52–5, 155
  financial transaction tax, 192
  green economy development, 176, 180
  green stimulus, 173
  greenhouse gas emissions, 69–75
  human capital investment, 104–5
  rate of natural capital depreciation, 51
  underpricing of fossil fuels, 128
freshwater
  climate change and, 78, 94
  declining availability, 3, 7, 76, 77, 93–4,
    109, 123, 140, 184, 189, 210
  markets for, 136, 189, 211
  transboundary agreements, 206–7

Gandhi, Mahatma, 208, 211
gap between rich and poor, 3, 142–3
Germany
  agricultural land share of wealth, 48
  distribution of wealth, 153, 155
  environmentally motivated subsidies,
    178–9
  feed-in-tariff, 187
  financial activities tax, 194, 195
  financial expansion, 52–5, 155
  financial transaction tax, 192
  global imbalances, 160
  green economy development, 175–6,
    180
  green stimulus, 173–4
  greenhouse gas emissions, 69–75
  human capital investment, 104–5
  rate of natural capital depreciation, 51
  underpricing of fossil fuels, 128
Global Frontiers
  and the rise of the West, 22–5
global imbalances, *see also* wealth
    inequality, global imbalances and
global markets
  creating, 183, 201–7, 211

Goldin, Claudia, 144–5, 149–50, 156–7, 195
Goldsmith, Raymond, 50, 53
Gordon, Robert, 170–1
Goulder, Larry, 190
Great Britain, *see* United Kingdom
Great Depression, 40, 43, 52, 54
Great Recession (of 2008–2009), 50, 53, 98, 150, 160–1, 176–7, 191
  green stimulus during, 172–5, 177
green economy
  defined, 172
  emerging sectors of, 174, 178, 187
  policies and, 176–7, 187
  transition to, 165, 172, 175, 176, 178, 191
green growth, *see also* green economy, transition to
  additional policies for developing countries, 196–201
  defined, 172
  innovation and, 185–91
  limits to, 172–80, 185
green innovation
  growth and, 185–91, 195
  race in, 175–8, 180
  underinvestment in, 181, 189–91
green research and development (R&D)
  policies to support, 181, 185, 189–91, 195
  underinvestment in, 177, 180
greenhouse gas (GHG)
  abatement, 135–6, 202–3
  climate change, 60, 76, 78
  emissions, 60, 68, 70–1, 74–6, 202
  intensity (of economies), 72–3
gross domestic product (GDP), 56, 63
gross national income (GNI), 56, 78
gross national saving (GNS), 78
Group of 20 (G20), 70, 127, 152, 173–4, 186, 193, 202, 209
  environmentally harmful subsidies, 186
  green stimulus, 173
  greenhouse gas emissions, 70–5
  subsidies and underpricing of fossil fuels, 127–9
  wealth inequality, 152–3

human capital
  accumulation of, 103, 104–6, 116–18, 146–9, 172, 184, 201
  defined, 1, 102, 121
  demand and supply for, 143–6
  expansion, 116–18
  as a factor endowment, 108–10
  inclusive wealth and, 191–6
  relative price to natural capital, 109–13, 143
  returns to, 110, 113, 144, 156, 159, *see also* skilled workers, relative wage of
  scarcity of, 109–10, 113, 119, 143, 156
  trends in, 103–7
  underinvestment in, 101, 141, 142–3, 146–9, 191, 211
hunter-gatherers, 9, 13

India
  distribution of wealth, 152–3
  emerging market economy, 69, 70
  empires, 14–16, 19–21, 23–4, 37
  financial transaction tax, 192
  Ganges River Treaty, 207
  greenhouse gas emissions, 68, 71–5
  natural resource use, 44, 46
  underpricing of fossil fuels, 128–9, 188
  vulnerability to coastal storms, 133
  water markets, 136
Industrial Revolution
  First Phase, 34, 36–9, 149
  redefining wealth, 32–4
  Second Phase, 4, 34, 39–44, 149–50, 166–7
  Third Phase, 8, 170–2, 181, 211, *see also* Third Industrial Revolution
information and communication technology (ICT), 165, 170–2
institutional inertia, 124, 126, 133–6, 139–40, 148–9, 185, 211
institutions, 133
Intergovernmental Panel on Climate Change (IPCC), 92
International Monetary Fund (IMF), 126, 128, 193–4

Italy
 agricultural land share of wealth, 48
 distribution of wealth, 153
 empires, 18
 environmentally motivated subsidies,
  179
 financial activities tax, 194
 financial expansion, 52–3
 financial transaction tax, 192
 global imbalance, 160
 green economy development, 175, 176,
  180
 green stimulus, 173
 greenhouse gas emissions, 69–75
 human capital investment, 104–5
 rate of natural capital depreciation, 51
 underpricing of fossil fuels, 128

Japan
 agricultural land share of wealth, 46, 48
 climate change agreement, 202
 distribution of wealth, 153–4, 155
 empires, 24, 25
 environmentally motivated subsidies,
  178–9
 financial activities tax, 193–4
 financial expansion, 52–5, 155
 financial transaction tax, 192
 global imbalance, 160
 green economy development, 175–6,
  180
 green stimulus, 173–4, 177
 greenhouse gas emissions, 68–75
 human capital investment, 104–5
 natural resource use, 44, 68
 rate of natural capital depreciation, 51
 trade, 22
 underpricing of fossil fuels, 128

Katz, Lawrence, 144–5, 149–50, 156–7, 195
Kaufman, Herbert, 13
Kraay, Aart, 162

Landes, David, 33
land-use change, 44–8, 93, 114
Lee, Jong Wha, 106
López, Ramón, 150–1
low-elevation coastal zones (LECZ), 76,
  210

McKenzie, David, 162
Maddison, Angus, 23
mangroves, 89–90
 capital accounting (Thailand),
  95–7
 global decline, 93
 underpricing, 129–33
material use (non-renewable), 4,
  42–3, 49, 55, 60, 68, 84, 101,
  166, 208
Millennium Ecosystem Assessment, 86,
  92
Mishel, Lawrence, 155–6

national wealth (capital), 10–12, 59,
  82–3
 as defined conventionally, 10
 as defined in this book, 12, 59
natural capital (assets)
 composition of, 31–2
 decline of, 48–50, 55
 defined, 1, 11
 expansion, 113–16
 as a factor endowment, 109–10
 relative price to human capital, 109–13,
  143
 relative use of, 102, 110–11, 116–17,
  118, 143, 164
 returns to (rental rate of), 110, 120, 125,
  162
 share of wealth, 32, 49–50, 84
 source of economic wealth, 29
 underpricing of, 2, 5, 7–8, 109, 111–13,
  119–20, 124, 165, 168
natural capital depreciation
 accounting for, 50, 56–8, *see also*
  Adjusted Net National Income
 rate of, 50–1, 103, 113, 162
natural resources, *see* natural capital
net national income (NNI), 57
net national saving (NNS), 79

Obstfeld, Maurice, 52
Organizing of Economic Cooperation and
  Development (OECD), 47, 61, 67,
  146, 163, 179, 186, 206
O'Rourke, Kevin, 36
overpricing of skilled labor (human
  capital), 7, 142, 143, 156, 163

Piketty, Thomas, 28, 54, 154, 161–2
Plutus (god of wealth), 14
population
    growth, 19, 46, 93, 162, 210
poverty
    low-elevation coastal zones (LECZ), 76, 210
    pockets of, 6–7, 159, 162, 164, 168–9, 178, 180, 184, 209
    remote and less favored lands, 120, 143, 162–3, 178, 182–3, 196–201, 210
    rural, *see* developing countries, rural poverty
    sinks, 3, 143, 162, 164
    traps (geographic), 162, 178, 182, 196
    urban areas, 1, 3, 76, 120, 129, 143, 159, 162, 164, 178
primary factor (input), 107–10, 114, 118
production
    factor-intensity of, 107
    resource-intensive, 108, 110–13, 115–16, 118–19, 147–8
    skill-intensive, 108, 110–13, 116–17, 118–19, 146–8, 155

race between education and technology, 142, 144–6, 195
"real wealth" of a nation, 1, 12
renewable energy, 4, 33, 165–6, 170, 172–5, 187, 208
reproducible capital (assets)
    accumulation of, 4, 29–30, 46
    defined, 1, 11, 83
    depreciation of, 50, 95, 99
resource-dependent development, 5, 7, 56, 59, 60–8, 77, 178
    environmental impacts 84, 101, 134
    natural capital expansion, 114, 116
    structural transformation, 182, 184, 197
    wealth accumulation, 63–6, 78
rural-urban migration, 183, 197
Russia
    agricultural subsidies, 186
    distribution of wealth, 153
    emerging market economy, 44, 70
    empires, 23, 25, 32
    greenhouse gas emissions, 68, 70–5
    natural resource use, 21, 44
    underpricing of fossil fuels, 127–9, 188

second-phase malaise, 4–8, 170, 172, 180–1, 209
Silk Road, 18, 21
skill-biased technological change, 119–20, 142, 144–8, 149–50, 155, 163, 166, 168–9, 170, 172, 180, 182, 191, 209
skilled workers (labor)
    education, training and healthcare investments and, 103, 110, 116–18, 142
    financial sector and, 6, 155–6, 193
    mobility of, 108
    overpricing of, *see* overpricing of skilled labor
    relationship to human capital, 103, 107, 110, 121
    relative use of, 3, 102, 110–11, 116–17, 118, 146, 164, 209
    relative wage of, 6, 101, 110, 113, 119–20, 142–3, 159, 163
    rising demand relative to supply, 7, 119–20, 142, 168, 170, 182, 209
    scarcity of, 5–6, 209
    wage and income gap (with unskilled workers), 7, 102, 113, 119, 142–3, 146, 168, 170, 209
slavery
    and wealth, 25–9
Smil, Vaclav, 33
South Korea (Republic of Korea)
    distribution of wealth, 153
    environmentally motivated subsidies, 179
    financial activities tax, 194
    financial transaction tax, 192
    green economy development, 175, 176–7, 180
    green stimulus (Green New Deal), 173–4
    greenhouse gas emissions, 69–75
    natural resource use, 44
    underpricing of fossil fuels, 128
sovereign wealth funds (SWF), 161–2, 193, 205
structural imbalance
    global implications, 118–19, 169
    in world economy, 3, 101–2, 118–20, 142–3, 164, 165

structure of production
  economic wealth and, 107–9

tangible assets, 10–11, 82–3, 86
  defined, 10
Taylor, Alan, 52
technological innovation
  race with education, *see* race between
      education and technology
  skill-biased, *see* skill-biased
      technological change
technology-push policies, 180, 190, 195
Third Industrial Revolution, 165, 170–2,
      181, 211, *see also* Industrial
      Revolution, Third Phase
top 1% (wealthiest households), 151, 155,
      156, 210
trading networks
  accumulation of wealth,
      17–19
  promotion of slavery, 18–19

underpricing of nature, 60, 98–9, 101,
      118–19, 123–6, 165, 168
  market-based incentives to correct, 178,
      180–1, 185, 188–9, 190
unemployment
  structural, 6–7, 147, 159, 164, 168–9,
      182, 209
  trends in, 143, 159, 163
United Kingdom (England, Great Britain)
  agricultural land share of wealth, 46,
      48
  distribution of wealth, 153, 155
  empires, 24, 25
  environmentally motivated subsidies,
      179
  financial activities tax, 194
  financial expansion, 52–5, 155
  financial transaction tax, 192
  fossil fuel dependency, 36
  global imbalance, 160, 161
  green economy development, 176, 180
  green stimulus, 173
  greenhouse gas emissions, 69–75
  human capital investment, 104–5
  industrialization, 28–9, 34–5
  rate of natural capital depreciation, 51
  underpricing of fossil fuels, 128

United Nations (UN), 49, 56, 202, 204,
      206, 211
United States
  agricultural land share of wealth, 46,
      48
  air pollution, 126, 129
  climate change agreement with US,
      202
  distribution of wealth, 153, 155,
      156–9
  empires, 24, 25
  environmentally motivated subsidies,
      178–9, 187
  financial activities tax, 193–4, 195
  financial expansion, 52–5, 155
  frontier expansion, 28, 36–7
  global imbalance, 160, 161
  green economy development, 174, 176,
      180
  green stimulus, 173–4
  greenhouse gas emissions, 68–75, 1
      80
  human capital investment, 104–5
  industrialization of, 4, 28–9, 39–44,
      149–50, 166, 208
  information and communication
      technology (ICT), 171
  low carbon-energy adoption, 190–1
  natural resource use, 37, 39–44, 166
  race between education and
      technology, 144–6, 148, 195
  rate of natural capital depreciation, 51
  slavery, 27
  underpricing of fossil fuels, 127–8
  water markets, 136, 189
unskilled workers (labor)
  relationship to human capital, 103, 107,
      110, 121
  relative use of, 3, 102, 143
  relative wage of, 6, 101, 110, 113,
      119–20, 163
  wage and income gap (with skilled
      workers), 7, 102, 113, 119, 142–3,
      146, 168, 170, 209
urban growth (urbanization) 1, 14–16, 35,
      46, 55, 77, 149

vested interests, 124, 126, 137–9, 140,
      148–9, 185, 211

wealth creation, 9, 13–16
wealth inequality
  financial risks and, 159–60
  global imbalances and, 6, 143, 159, 160,
    161, 164, 168–9, 182, 191, 209
  global implications of, 159–63
  insufficient human capital
    accumulation and, 146–9
  political economy of, 156–9
  role of finance, 155–6
  role of natural capital, 149–51

  trends in, 151–4
Wood, Adrian, 108
World Bank, 50, 97,
    200–1
World Economic Forum
  Global Risk Report 2013, 3
world economy
  emergence of, 19–22, 29
World War I, 36–7, 39, 43, 48, 51
World War II, 31, 42–3, 126, 150
Wright, Gavin, 42, 44, 198

Printed and bound by CPI Group (UK) Ltd, Croydon, CR0 4YY